Not For Tourists Guide to

BOSTON

Not For Tourists Inc

Skyhorse Publishing

Designed by:
Not For Tourists, Inc
NFT$_{TM}$—Not For Tourists$_{TM}$ Guide to Boston
www.notfortourists.com

Printed in China
Print ISBN: 978-1-5107-4709-8
Ebook ISBN: 978-1-5107-4714-2
ISSN 2163-9043

16th Edition

Every effort has been made to ensure that the information in this book is as up-to-date as possible at press time. However, many details are liable to change—as we have learned.
Not For Tourists cannot accept responsibility for any consequences arising from the use of this book.

Not For Tourists does not solicit individuals, organizations, or businesses for listings inclusion in our guides, nor do we accept payment for inclusion into the editorial portion of our book; the advertising sections, however, are exempt from this policy. We always welcome communications from anyone regarding ANYTHING having to do with our books; please visit us on our website at www.notfortourists.com for appropriate contact information.

www.skyhorsepublishing.com

10 9 8 7 6 5 4 3 2 1

To Our Fellow Non-Tourists,

This book has every detail you need about the little City on the Hill, from how to catch a game of one of our World Champion teams (Bruins! Sox! Pats!) to where you can get the best pizza on the entire east coast (Santarpio's!).

This book is not only a first-rate guidebook but also a love letter to this very unique and small city. The incredible people you see on the facing page have spent their time scouting out places in the nooks and crannies near and far—from breakfast joints hidden in the back rooms of convenience stores to the incredibly new and ritzy restaurants that now circle the Fort Point Channel; from hobnobbing and enjoying a libation at Top of the Hub's no-cover bar seats in the highest-point-in-the-Prudential-Building's Jazz Lounge, to sidling up to talk philosophy at Harvard Square's basement bargain Grendel's Den, where food is half price much of the time with a three-buck beverage buy-in. We know, we know, it's a thankless job roaming around the city, making sure that every bar has fresh beer on tap, but somehow we'll survive.

If our fellow Non-Tourists will allow us, we want to send you to order a garlic and hot pepper pie in East Boston from Santarpio's and to sit at the bar at The Ashmont Grill to chat up the bartenders. We've got an extra ticket for the Sox game and we're going to have to hit up the Baseball Tavern to make sure to celebrate the right way, before catching a concert at Green Monster-abutting Lansdowne Street's House of Blues chapter. We're going to go see the craziness at Jacques's Cabaret and then pop into the Brattle Bookshop (downtown's Theatre District) to stock up for a quiet evening in, or take in a foreign flick at the landmark, art deco Coolidge Corner movie theatre and then browse in independent ink-on-paper icon Booksmith, across the street (Brookline). Put a whole group of crazy writers in your pocket, and you'll always find the best spot for everything.

Central Boston

Waterfront Boston

JP, Fenway & Roxbury

Brookline & Allston/Brighton

Table of Contents

Map 1 • Beacon Hill / West End

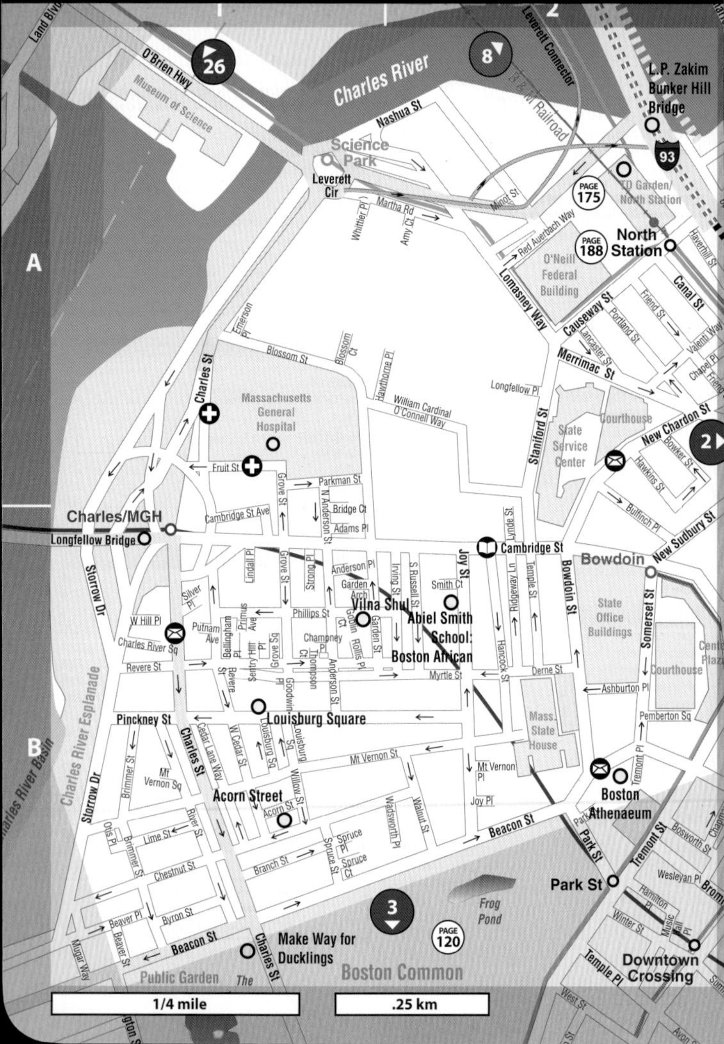

N

Charles River
26
8
2
Land Blvd
O'Brien Hwy
Museum of Science
Leverett Connector
B & M Railroad
L.P. Zakim Bunker Hill Bridge
93
Nashua St
Science Park
Leverett Cir
Martha Rd
Whittier Pl
Amy Ct
Minot St
PAGE 175
TD Garden/ North Station
Red Auerbach Way
PAGE 188
North Station
O'Neill Federal Building
Lomasney Way
Haverhill St
Canal St
Friend St
Portland St
Causeway St
Lancaster St
Valenti Way
Merrimac St
Chapel Pl
Friend St
A
Emerson Pl
Blossom St
Blossom Ct
Hawthorne Pl
Longfellow Pl
Charles St
Massachusetts General Hospital
William Cardinal O'Connell Way
Staniford St
State Service Center
Courthouse
New Chardon St
Bowker St
Hawkins St
Fruit St
Grove St
Parkman St
N Anderson St
Bridge Ct
Adams Pl
Cambridge St Ave
Charles/MGH
Longfellow Bridge
Lynde St
Bulfinch Pl
New Sudbury St
Cambridge St
Bowdoin
Storrow Dr
Lindall Pl
Grove St
Strong Pl
Anderson Pl
Garden Arch
Irving St
S Russell St
Joy St
Smith Ct
Ridgeway Ln
Temple St
Bowdoin St
State Office Buildings
Somerset St
Silver Pl
W Hill Pl
Putnam Ave
Primus Ave
Phillips St
Vilna Shul
Goodwin Ct
Rollins Pl
Garden St
Abiel Smith School: Boston African
Hancock St
Center Plaza
Charles River Sq
Bellingham Pl
Sentry Hill Pl
Grove Sq
Champney Pl
Thompson Ct
Anderson St
Revere St
Revere St
Goodwin Pl
Myrtle St
Derne St
Courthouse
Ashburton Pl
Charles River Esplanade
Louisburg Square
Pinckney St
Mass. State House
Pemberton Sq
B
Charles River Basin
Storrow Dr
Brimmer St
Mt Vernon Sq
Charles St
Cedar Lane Way
W Cedar St
Louisburg Sq
Louisburg Sq
Mt Vernon St
Mt Vernon Pl
Tremont Pl
Acorn Street
Acorn St
Willow St
Wadsworth Pl
Walnut St
Joy Pl
Boston Athenaeum
Otis Pl
Brimmer St
Lime St
River St
Spruce Pl
Spruce St
Beacon St
Park St
Park St
Tremont St
Bosworth St
Chapman Pl
Chestnut St
Branch St
Spruce Ct
Wesleyan Pl
Bromfield St
Frog Pond
3
Park St
Hamilton Pl
Music Hall Pl
Winter St
Beaver Pl
Byron St
Beaver St
Mugar Way
Beacon St
Charles St
Make Way for Ducklings
PAGE 120
Public Garden
The
Boston Common
Temple Pl
Downtown Crossing
West St
Avon St
Summer St

1/4 mile
.25 km

Beacon Hill is still home to some of the most expensive real estate in America. Charming brick row houses reflect a long and storied history; where the State House stands, John Hancock once grazed cows. Full gentrification has yet to reach the West End, where government buildings, hospitals, and tucked-away burrito joints mingle fairly harmoniously.

Landmarks

- **Abiel Smith School** • 46 Joy St [Smith Ct]
  Center of 19th-century African-American Boston.
- **Acorn Street** • b/w West Cedar St & Willow St, running parallel to Chestnut St
  The most photographed street in America.
- **Boston Athenaeum** •
  10 Beacon St [Somerset St]
  617-227-0270
  Old books, including one true crime account bound in the author's skin.
- **Leonard P. Zakim Bunker Hill Memorial Bridge** •
  100 Beverly St [Causeway St]
  World's widest cable-stayed bridge. Boston's newest landmark.
- **Longfellow Bridge** •
  Cambridge St & Charles St
  The "salt and pepper shaker bridge."
- **Louisburg Square** •
  Mt Vernon St & Pinckney St
  Charming square with elegant homes, including John Kerry's.
- **Make Way for Ducklings** •
  Beacon St & Charles St
  Inspired by the Robert McCloskey children's book.
- **Massachusetts General Hospital** •
  55 Fruit St [N Grove St]
  617-726-2000
  The Ether dome, site of the first use of ether; contains an antique surgical museum.
- **TD Garden** • 150 Causeway St [Beverly St]
  617-624-1050
  Looking for the FleetCenter? This is it. Used to be historic Boston Garden.
- **Vilna Shul** • 18 Phillips St [Garden St]
  617-523-2324
  Recently revived Beacon Hill synagogue.

Nightlife

- **21st Amendment** •
  150 Bowdoin St [Mt Vernon St]
  617-227-7100
  Favorite of the State House crowd.
- **6B Lounge** • 6 Beacon St [Tremont Pl]
  617-742-0306
  Martinis and snacks for the after-work crowd.
- **Alibi** • 215 Charles St [Fruit St]
  857-241-1144
  How many restaurants/bars are IN the Liberty Hotel? Sweet lord.
- **Beacon Hill Pub** • 149 Charles St [Silver Pl]
  Dive popular with young Hill residents.
  617-523-1895
- **Cheers** • 84 Beacon St [Brimmer St]
  617-227-9605
  If you must.
- **The Four's** • 166 Canal St [Causeway St]
  617-720-4455
  Sports tavern across from the Garden.
- **The Greatest Bar** •
  262 Friend St [Causeway St]
  617-367-0544
  Big deal.
- **The Harp** • 85 Causeway St [Portland St]
  617-742-1010
  Pack in after an evening at the Garden.
- **The Hill Tavern** • 228 Cambridge St [Irving St]
  617-742-6192
  Middling Beacon Hill hangout.
- **The Sevens** • 77 Charles St [Mt Vernon St]
  617-523-9074
  Sturdy Beacon Hill local.
- **Sullivan's Tap** • 168 Canal St [Causeway St]
  617-742-6968
  Dive. Proper before Celtics and Bruins games.

Beacon Hill / West End

Restaurants

- **75 Chestnut** • 75 Chestnut St [River St]
617-227-2175 • $$$$
Featuring a Sunday jazz brunch.
- **Artu** • 89 Charles St [Pinckney St]
617-227-9023 • $$$
Affordable Italian. Fresh ingredients. Take-out panini.
- **Beacon Hill Bistro** •
25 Charles St [Chestnut St]
800-640-3935 • $$$$
Elegant cooking in a cozy space.
- **Beacon Hill Chocolates** •
91 Charles St [Pinckney St]
617-725-1900 • $$$
Adorable chocolates and truffles in seasonal shapes.
- **Figs** • 42 Charles St [Chestnut St]
617-742-3447 • $$$
Beacon Hill branch of upscale pizza chain.
- **Grotto** • 37 Bowdoin St [Cambridge St]
617-227-3434 • $$$
Good value Italian in a Beacon Hill basement.
- **Harvard Gardens** •
316 Cambridge St [Grove St]
617-523-2727 • $$
More for meeting and drinking than eating.
- **The Hungry I** • 71 Charles St [Mt Vernon St]
617-227-3524 • $$$$
French. Cozy spot for intimate meals.
- **King & I** • 145 Charles St [Silver Pl]
617-227-3320 • $$
No-brainer for decent, inexpensive Thai.
- **Lala Rokh** • 97 Mt Vernon St [W Cedar St]
617-720-5511 • $$$
Alluring Persian in a pleasant Beacon Hill townhouse.
- **Panificio** • 144 Charles St [Silver Pl]
617-227-4340 • $
Paninis, pastries. Try the formaggio.
- **The Paramount** • 44 Charles St [Chestnut St]
617-720-1152 • $$
Popular local spot for all three meals. Fantastic brunch.
- **Ristorante Toscano** •
47 Charles St [Chestnut St]
617-723-4090 • $$$
Northern Italian; change of pace from North End.
- **Scampo** • 215 Charles St [Fruit St]
617-536-2100 • $$$
Inventive Italian dished up for a toffee-nosed crowd.
- **The Upper Crust** • 20 Charles St [Branch St]
617-723-9600 • $$
Fancy schmancy, crisp-crust pizza.

Locals praise the community feel of the square mile that constitutes Beacon Hill. Pubs like **The Sevens** and **The Four's** cater to sports fans, and the crispy pizza at **Upper Crust** causes mini sidewalk traffic jams. The Public Garden and Boston Common function as the neighborhood's backyard.

Shopping

- **Black Ink** • 101 Charles St [Pinckney St]
  617-723-3883
  Amusing tchotchkes, quirky gifts, purty paper.
- **Eugene Galleries** •
  76 Charles St [Mt Vernon St]
  617-227-3062
  A treasure chest of old maps, prints, books.
- **The Flat of the Hill** •
  60 Charles St [Mt Vernon St]
  617-619-9977
  Quirky gifts. Lots of pink.
- **Good** • 98 Charles Street
  617-982-6777
  Lovely gifts.
- **Moxie** • 51 Charles St [Mt Vernon St]
  617-557-9991
  Shoes, bags, accessories.
- **The Red Wagon** • 69 Charles St [Mt Vernon St]
  617-523-9402
  Pricey kids' clothes and toys.
- **Savenor's Market** •
  160 Charles St [Cambridge St]
  617-723-6328
  For a variety of gourmet goodies.

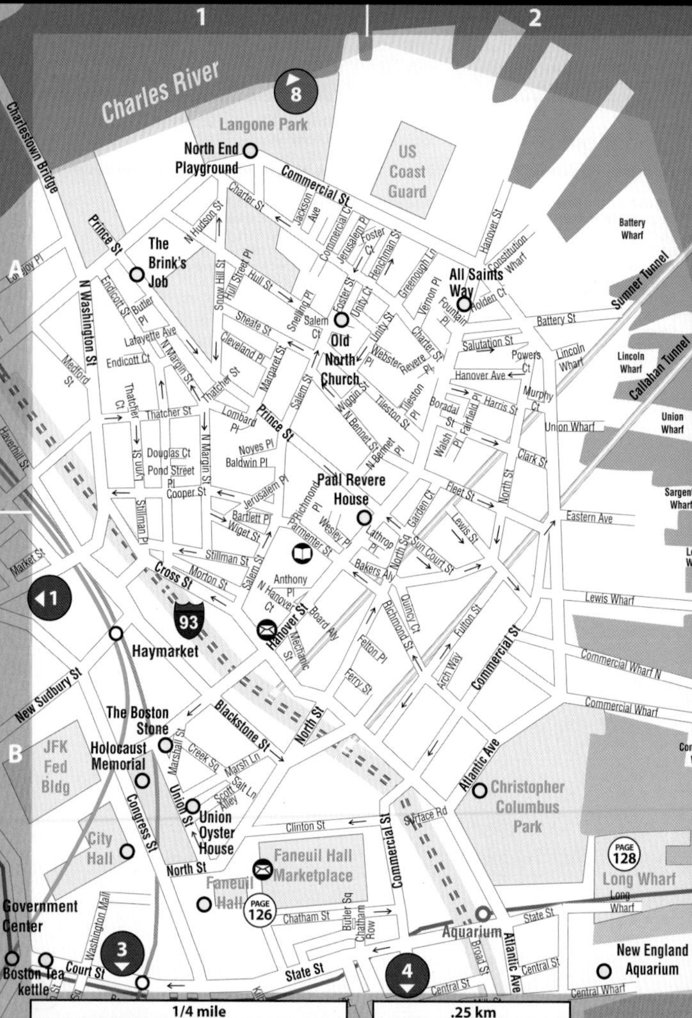

1
2
A
B
Charles River
8
Langone Park
North End Playground
US Coast Guard
Charlestown Bridge
Commercial St
Prince St
The Brink's Job
All Saints Way
Battery Wharf
Sumner Tunnel
Lincoln Wharf
Callahan Tunnel
Union Wharf
Sargents Wharf
Old North Church
Paul Revere House
Haymarket
93
1
New Sudbury St
The Boston Stone
Holocaust Memorial
JFK Fed Bldg
City Hall
Union Oyster House
Faneuil Hall Marketplace
Faneuil Hall
PAGE 126
Christopher Columbus Park
PAGE 128
Long Wharf
Government Center
Boston Tea kettle
3
4
Aquarium
New England Aquarium
State St
Atlantic Ave
Commercial Wharf
Lewis Wharf
1/4 mile
.25 km

Boston's version of Little Italy, the North End is a maze of narrow streets and brick buildings with a decidedly European air. With the Rose Kennedy Greenway fully finished, the connection from the North End is once again green, only this time it's grass instead of steel.

Landmarks

- **All Saints Way** • Hanover St & Battery St
  Peter Baldassari's folksy, handcrafted devotional alley.
- **The Boston Stone** • Marshall St [Hanover St]
  Centre of ye olde city.
- **Boston Tea Kettle** •
  63 Court St [Cambridge St]
  Long before Starbucks, this gigantic 1873 copper kettle was steaming.
- **The Brink's Job** • 165 Prince St [Causeway St]
  Where Brink's Gang robbery occurred in 1950; now used for TD Banknorth Center parking.
- **Christopher Columbus Park** •
  Atlantic Ave & Richmond St
  Destruction of the Artery gives this park new breath.
- **City Hall** • 1 City Hall Plaza [Cambridge St]
  617-635-4000
  The box Faneuil Hall came in.
- **Faneuil Hall** • Congress St & North St
  617-523-1779
  Faneuil Hall (that is, the building) dates from 1742.
- **Holocaust Memorial** • Congress St & Union St
  617-457-8755
  Six glass towers, with victims' numbers representing six camps.
- **Leonard P. Zakim Bunker Hill Memorial Bridge** •
  100 Beverly St [Causeway St]
  World's widest cable-stayed bridge. Boston's newest landmark.
- **New England Aquarium** •
  Central Wharf [Central St]
  617-973-5200
  Check out penguin snack-time.
- **North End Playground** •
  Commercial St & Foster St
  Site of the famous Great Molasses Flood.
- **Old North Church** • 193 Salem St [Hull St]
  617-523-6676
  One if by land, two if by sea.
- **Paul Revere House** • 19 N Sq [Garden Ct St]
  617-523-2338
  Where Paul was born and raised.
- **Union Oyster House** •
  41 Union St [Marshall St]
  617-227-2750
  Oldest restaurant in America, saddle up to oyster bar.

Nightlife

- **Bell in Hand Tavern** •
  45 Union St [Marshall St]
  617-227-2098
  Welcoming thirsty travelers since the 18th century.
- **The Black Rose** • 160 State St [India St]
  617-742-2286
  Tourist-crowded, unremarkable. Try somewhere else first.
- **Boston Beer Works** •
  112 Canal St [Valenti Way]
  617-896-2337
  Cavernous suds shop near the Garden.
- **Boston Sail Loft** •
  80 Atlantic Ave [Commercial Wharf]
  617-227-7280
  Big outside deck on the water, good crowds.
- **Green Dragon** • 11 Marshall St [Hanover St]
  617-367-0055
  Pretend you're Sam Adams while having the same.
- **The Hong Kong** •
  65 Chatham St [Chatham Row]
  617-227-2226
  Scorpion bowl anyone?
- **Paddy O's** • 33 Union St [Marshall St]
  617-263-7771
  The name tells you it's Oirish, you know.
- **Tia's** • 200 Atlantic Ave [State St]
  617-227-0828
  Warm-weather party house.

Restaurants

- **Al's State Street Café** • 112 State St [Broad St]
617-720-5555 • $
Good sandwiches on the cheap, but order fast. You have been warned!
- **Antico Forno** • 93 Salem St [Wiget St]
617-723-6733 • $$$
A home-style North End stand-out. Great pizza.
- **Artu** • 6 Prince St [Hanover St]
617-742-4336 • $$$
Excellent Italian with a modern twist.
- **Billy Tse** • 240 Commercial St [Atlantic Ave]
617-227-9990 • $$$
Pan-Asian near the waterfront.
- **Boston Sail Loft** •
80 Atlantic Ave [Commercial Wharf]
617-227-7280 • $$
Good seafood with a great view.
- **Bova's Bakery** • 134 Salem St [Prince St]
617-523-5601 • $
Baked goods available 24/7!
- **Bricco** • 241 Hanover St [Cross St]
617-248-6800 • $$$$
Boutique Italian cuisine. Rather popular.
- **Caffè Paradiso** •
255 Hanover St [Richmond St]
617-742-1768 • $$
Coffee and cannoli. Local landmark.
- **The Daily Catch** • 323 Hanover St [Prince St]
617-523-8567 • $$$
For those who can stand the heat in the kitchen.
- **Ducali Pizzeria & Bar** •
289 Causeway St [Prince St]
617-742-4144 • $$
Combines North End cuisine with the rowdiness of Faneuil nightlife.
- **Durgin-Park** •
340 Faneuil Hall Marketplace [Congress St]
617-227-2038 • $$$$
Steak & New England comfort food since 1827.
- **Ernesto's** • 69 Salem St [Morton St]
617-523-1373 • $
One of the best slices in town.
- **Galleria Umberto** •
289 Hanover St [Richmond St]
617-227-5709 • $
Tasty, dirt cheap, greasy Italian lunch.
- **Green Dragon** • 11 Marshall St [Hanover St]
617-367-0055 • $$
Pretend you're Sam Adams while having the same.
- **Haymarket Pizza** •
106 Blackstone St [Hanover St]
617-723-8585 • $
Enjoy a great slice in the company of pigeons.
- **L'Osteria** • 104 Salem St [Bartlett Pl]
617-723-7847 • $$$
Family-style red sauce joint.
- **La Famiglia Giorgio** •
112 Salem St [Cooper St]
617-367-6711 • $$
Cheap family style Italian without any fancy pants.
- **La Summa** •
30 Fleet St [William F McClellan Hwy]
617-523-9503 • $$$
More low-key than most North End places, and it will leave your belly satisfied.
- **Lucca** • 226 Hanover St [Cross St]
617-742-9200 • $$$$
Stylish Northern Italian.
- **Mamma Maria** • 3 N Sq [Garden Ct St]
617-523-0077 • $$$$
High-end Italian in a charming townhouse.
- **Massimino's Cucina Italiana** •
207 Endicott St [Lafayette Ave]
617-523-5959 • $$
Out-of-the-way Italian, largely tourist-free.

While Boston is slowly becoming much more respected in culinary circles, the North End has been always been legit. Good luck finding a bad meal. By night, young professionals reemerge from Faneuil Hall and hit the clubs—hard. Night owls stop by **Modern Pastry** for the best cannoli in the city.

- **McCormick & Schmick's** • 1 Faneuil Hall Marketplace [S Market St] 617-720-5522 • $$$$
  Enormous fresh seafood selection in steakhouse atmosphere.
- **Nebo** • 520 Atlantic Ave [Medford St] 617-723-6326 • $$
  Decent North Endish spot. Perfect for a pizza and a carafe of vino.
- **Neptune Oyster** • 63 Salem St [Morton St] 617-742-3474 • $$$$
  Great oysters, of course, and the most amazing lobster roll —worth every penny.
- **Prezza** • 24 Fleet St [Garden Ct St] 617-227-1577 • $$$$$
  High-end Italian. Don't forget to try the Key Lime Martini.
- **Regina Pizzeria** • 11 Thacher St [N Margin St] 617-227-0765 • $$
  If God made pizza, it would almost taste as good as this.
- **Taranta** • 210 Hanover St [Cross St] 617-720-0052 • $$$$
  Delicious Italian food with a Peruvian twist.
- **Theo's Cozy Corner** • 162 Salem St [Tileston St] 617-241-0202 • $
  Cozy diner. Killer hash browns.
- **Trattoria Il Panino** • 11 Parmenter St [Hanover St] 617-720-1336 • $$
  In a sea of Italian restaurants Il Panino is a pearl!
- **Union Oyster House** • 41 Union St [Marshall St] 617-227-2750 • $$$
  Authentic New England experience since 1826.
- **Wagamama Faneuil Hall** • Merchants Row [N Market St] 617-742-9242 • $
  London noodle pros retrace journey of Plymouth forebears.

Shopping

- **Bova's Bakery** • 134 Salem St [Prince St] 617-523-5601
  Pastries, also deli and pizza. Open 24 hours.
- **Brooks Brothers** • 75 State St [Kilby St] 617-261-9990
  Branch of venerable Back Bay clothier.
- **Green Cross Pharmacy** • 393 Hanover St [Clark St] 617-227-3728
  Old-world pharmacy. Also sells Italian sundries.
- **Maria's Pastry Shop** • 46 Cross St [Morton St] 617-523-1196
  Sweet tooth heaven.
- **Mike's Pastry** • 300 Hanover St [Prince St] 617-742-3050
  The most famous of the North End Italian bakeries.
- **Modern Pastry** • 257 Hanover St [Richmond St] 617-523-3783
  Boston's best cannoli? You decide.
- **Monica's Salumeria** • 130 Salem St [Prince St] 617-742-4101
  Homemade takeout and Italian groceries.
- **Newbury Comics** • 1 Faneuil Hall Sq [Court St] 617-248-9992
  Downtown location of successful music/ novelties chain.
- **Salumeria Italiana** • 151 Richmond St [North St] 617-523-8743
  Well-regarded Italian specialties store.
- **Stanza dei Sigari** • 292 Hanover St [Prince St] 617-227-0295
  17-year-olds take note: hookahs available.

Map 3 · Downtown Crossing / Park Square / Bay Village

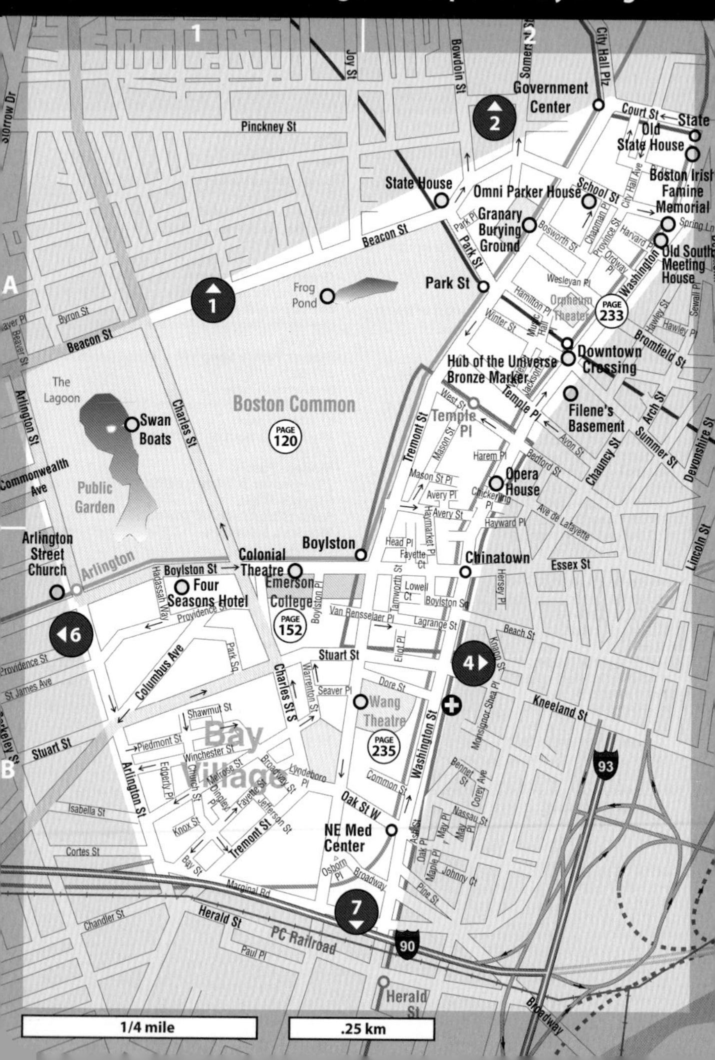

Downtown Crossing is abuzz with pedestrians from all walks of life. You'll find a lively mixture of financial types, shoppers, New England Medical Center doctors, and the down-and-out. The giant hole in the ground from stalled development projects is still here, but maybe someday we'll have that high rise we were promised.

O Landmarks

- **Arlington Street Church** • 351 Boylston St [Arlington St]
  617-536-7050
  Congregation dates from 1729, building from 1861.
- **Boston Common Frog Pond** • Boston Common
  617-635-2120
  Cool statues. Ribbit.
- **Boston Irish Famine Memorial** • Washington St & School St
  Statue commemorating the Great Hunger of the 1840s.
- **Boston Opera House** • 539 Washington St [Ave de Lafayette]
  617-259-3400
  Beaux-Arts landmark open again after many years.
- **Citi Emerson Colonial Theatre** • 106 Boylston St [Tremont St]
  617-482-9393
  Boston's oldest continuously operating theater, since 1900.
- **Four Seasons Hotel** • 200 Boylston St [Charles St]
  617-338-4400
  The preferred local home of the Rolling Stones.
- **Granary Burying Ground** • Tremont St & Park St
  617-635-4505
  Featuring John Hancock, Mother Goose, many others.
- **Hub of the Universe Bronze Marker** • Washington St & Summer St
  Um, located in the floor of a fruit and vegetable stand.
- **John Hancock's Phallic Gravestone** • Tremont & Park St
  Size matters.
- **Old South Meeting House** • 310 Washington St [Milk St]
  617-482-6439
  Where Sam Adams gave the order for the Boston Tea Party.
- **Old State House** • 206 Washington St [Court St]
  617-720-1713
  Oldest surviving public building in Boston.
- **Omni Parker House** • 60 School St [Chapman Pl]
  617-227-8600
  One-time employees include Ho Chi Minh and Malcolm X.
- **Ritz-Carlton Boston Common** • 10 Avery St [Washington St]
  617-574-7100
  Still classy.
- **State House** • Beacon St & Park St
  617-727-3679
  Finished in 1797. Gold dome added later.
- **Wang Theatre** • 270 Tremont St [Hollis St]
  617-482-9393
  Eye-popping, opulent interior. A must see.

Nightlife

- **Jacque's Cabaret** • 79 Broadway [Winchester St]
  617-426-8902
  Drag, but all welcome. Nightly cabaret.
- **Limelight Stage + Studios** • 204 Tremont St [Lagrange St]
  617-423-0785
  Karaoke on a grand scale; private studios available.
- **MJ O'Connor's** • 27 Columbus Ave [Park Sq]
  617-482-2255
  Large Irish pub. Outdoor seating when warm.
- **Parker's Bar** • 60 School St [Chapman Pl]
  617-227-8600
  Elegant. Try the Boston Creme martini.
- **Scholars** • 25 School St [Province St]
  617-248-0025
  Popular for the after-work crowd. Giant boozey punch bowls.
- **Sidebar** • 14 Bromfield St [Washington St]
  617-357-1899
  Don a jersey and knock back some shots.
- **The Tam** • 222 Tremont St [Stuart St]
  617-482-9182
  Local dive.
- **Venu** • 100 Warrenton St [Stuart St]
  617-338-8061
  Always changing; check before you go.

Restaurants

- **49 Social** • 49 Temple Pl [Washington St]
  617-338-9600 • $$$$
  Seasonal plus fresh seafood.
- **Dumpling Cafe** •
  695 Washington St [Kneeland St]
  617-338-8858 • $
  Learn how to eat the soup dumplings. You're welcome.
- **Empire Garden** •
  690 Washington St [Lagrange St]
  617-482-8898 • $$$
  Dim sum for the masses.
- **Erbaluce** • 69 Church St [Shawmut St]
  617-426-6969 • $$$$
  Italian food, Italian wine, Italian camaraderie. Worth the price.
- **Herrera's Mexican Grille** •
  11 Temple Pl [Tremont St]
  617-426-2350 • $
  Good and cheap Cali-Mex.
- **Intermission Tavern** •
  228 Tremont St [Stuart St]
  617-451-5997 • $$
  Drinks and burgers until 1 am.
- **Jacob Wirth** • 31 Stuart St [Dartmouth St]
  617-338-8586 • $$
  German-y. Local institution since 1868 with barroom sing-a-long on Friday nights.
- **Legal Sea Foods** • 558 Washington St [Arlington St]
  617-426-4444 • $$$
  Fresh fish, famous chowder. Legal's sleekest space.
- **Marliave** • 10 Bosworth St [Chapman Pl]
  617-422-0004 • $$
  Cozy, old-time dead end street eats.
- **Mike and Patty's** • 12 Church St [Fayette St]
  617-423-3447 • $
  Eponymous owners whip up the sammies.
- **New Saigon Sandwich** •
  696 Washington St [Kneeland St]
  617-542-6296 • $
  Cheap sandwiches, boxed lunches. Delicious!
- **New York Pizza** •
  224 Tremont St [Lagrange St]
  617-482-3459 • $$
  Perfect for late night noshing.
- **No. 9 Park** • 9 Park St [Beacon St]
  617-742-9991 • $$$$$
  Consistently rated among Boston's best.
- **Penang** • 685 Washington St [Lagrange St]
  617-451-6373 • $$$
  Well-established Malaysian out of NYC.
- **Ruth's Chris Steak House** •
  45 School St [City Hall Ave]
  617-742-8401 • $$$$$
  Ubiquitous chain serving gargantuan portions in Old City Hall.
- **Sam La Grassa's** •
  44 Province St [Bosworth St]
  617-357-6861 • $$
  Monster sandwiches. Try the pastrami.
- **Silvertone Bar & Grill** •
  69 Bromfield St [Tremont St]
  617-338-7887 • $$
  Great after-work lounge with tasty home cooking.
- **Smith & Wollensky** •
  294 Congress St
  617-778-2200 • $$$$$
  The castle has been taken.
- **Sweet Cupcakes** •
  11 School St [Washington St]
  617-227-2253 • $
  Give in to your Sweet tooth.
- **Teatro** • 177 Tremont St [Head Pl]
  617-778-6841 • $$$
  Sleek Italian next to Loews Cinema.
- **Via Matta** • 79 Park Plaza [Hadassah Wy]
  617-422-0008 • $$$$
  Stylish Italian, stylish crowd.
- **Viga** • 291 Devonshire St [Arlington St]
  617-482-1113 • $
  Cheap and tasty take out.
- **Yvonne's** • 2 Winter Pl [Winter St]
  617-267-0047 • $$$
  Eclectic, out-there, and challenging menus in supper club atmosphere.

Locals still mourn the loss of Jordan Marsh. It's hard to get excited about **TJ Maxx** and **Marshall's**. The best way to finish a weekday shopping excursion here is with a scrumptious sandwich from the amazing **Mike & Patty's**. For a top-end meal, try **No. 9 Park** across the Common.

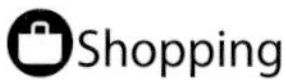

Shopping

- **Beacon Hill Skate Shop** • 135 Charles St S [Fayette St]
  617-482-7400
  Rentals available. Also has hockey gear.
- **Bromfield Camera Co.** • 10 Bromfield St [Washington St]
  617-426-5230
  Decent selection of new and used cameras.
- **CD Spins** • 58 Winter St [Tremont St]
  617-357-0525
  A great place to sell back your old CDs.
- **DSW** • 385 Washington St [Bromfield St]
  617-556-0052
  Oodles and oodles of sho[odl]es.
- **L.J. Peretti** • 2 Park Plaza [Charles St S]
  617-482-0218
  Oldest family-run tobacconist in the country.
- **Lambert's Marketplace** • 140 Tremont St [Temple Pl]
  617-338-6500
  Fruit and veggie stand in the heart of Downtown Crossing.
- **Macy's** • 450 Washington St [Temple Pl]
  617-357-3000
  Once Jordan Marsh. Big outdoor "holiday" tree in December.
- **Marshalls** • 350 Washington St [Franklin St]
  617-338-6205
  Discount clothing and other stuff.
- **Roche Bobois** • 2 Avery St [Washington St]
  617-742-9611
  Très trendy interior design and furnishings.
- **Sweet Cupcakes** • 11 School St [Washington St]
  617-227-2253
  Give in to your Sweet tooth.
- **TJ Maxx** • 350 Washington St [Franklin St]
  617-695-2424
  Put on your bargain-hunting hat. Off-price apparel and housewares.
- **Walgreens** • 24 School St [Washington St]
  617-372-8156
  Huge, upscale, schmancy version of the chain drugstore.

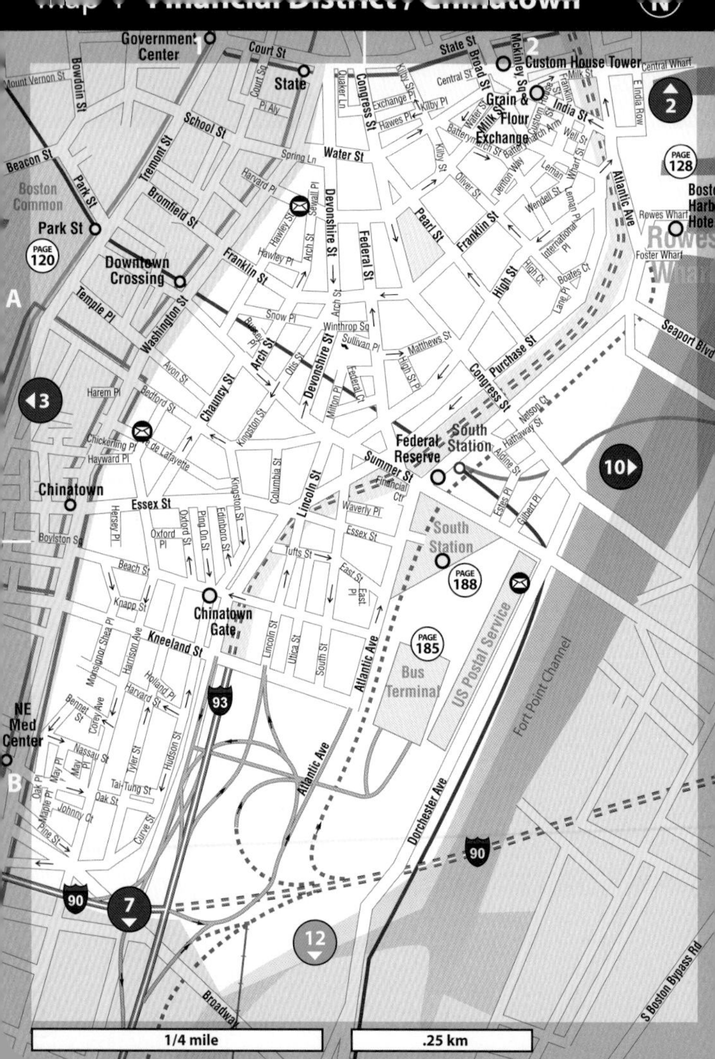

Government Center
Court St
State
State St
Broad St
Mckinley Sq
Custom House Tower
Central Wharf
Milk St
E India Row
Bowdoin St
Mount Vernon St
Court Sq
Pl Aly
Quaker Ln
Congress St
Kilby St
Central St
Exchange Pl
Kilby Pl
Hawes Pl
Grain & Flour Exchange
India St
Water St
Milk St
Batterymarch St
Custom House St
Franklin St
Well St
School St
Tremont St
Beacon St
Park St
Boston Common
Spring Ln
Water St
Harvard Pl
Bromfield St
Sewall Pl
Hawley St
Devonshire St
Federal St
Pearl St
Oliver St
Jenton Way
Leman Pl
Wendell St
Wharf St
Atlantic Ave
Rowes Wharf
Foster Wharf
International Pl
High St
High Ct
Boates Ct
Lane Pl
Park St
PAGE 120
Downtown Crossing
Hawley Pl
Arch St
Franklin St
Temple Pl
Washington St
Snow Pl
Winthrop Sq
Sullivan Pl
Matthews St
High St Pl
Purchase St
Congress St
Seaport Blvd
Bussey Pl
Arch St
Otis St
Devonshire St
Federal Ct
Milton Pl
Avon St
Harem Pl
Bedford St
Chauncy St
Kingston St
Nelson Ct
Hathaway St
Federal Reserve
South Station
Aldine St
Chickering Pl
Hayward Pl
Summer St
Financial Ctr
Chinatown
Essex St
Kingston St
Columbia St
Lincoln St
Waverly Pl
Estes Pl
Gilbert Pl
Hersey Pl
Oxford Pl
Oxford St
Ping On St
Edinboro St
Essex St
South Station
Boylston Sq
Tufts St
Beach St
East St
East St Pl
PAGE 188
Knapp St
Chinatown Gate
Lincoln St
Utica St
South St
Atlantic Ave
PAGE 185
Bus Terminal
US Postal Service
Fort Point Channel
Monsignor Shea Pl
Harrison Ave
Kneeland St
Holland Pl
Harvard St
93
NE Med Center
Bennet St
Corey Ave
Nassau St
May Pl
Tyler St
Hudson St
Atlantic Ave
Oak Pl
Maple Pl
Tai-Tung St
Oak St
Johnny Ct
Pine St
Curve St
Dorchester Ave
90
7
12
Broadway
S Boston Bypass Rd
1/4 mile
.25 km

The center of the Financial District has changed from The Big Dig to the Rose Kennedy Greenway, and as it's getting very little use, it's just as controversial as its predecessor. Sit on the very pristine grass and then hit up the always bustling Chinatown. For an introduction, stroll and windowshop along Beach Street and its cross-streets.

Landmarks

- **Boston Harbor Hotel** • 70 Rowes Wharf [High St] 617-439-7000 The "building with a hole in the middle."
- **Chinatown Gate** • Beach St & Hudson St Everything under the sky is for the people.
- **Custom House Tower** • 3 McKinley Sq [Central St] Boston's first "skyscraper," completed in 1915.
- **Federal Reserve Bank of Boston** • 600 Atlantic Ave [Summer St] 617-973-3463 Easy-to-spot concrete monolith, built in 1983.
- **Grain & Flour Exchange** • 177 Milk St [India St] Gorgeous 1893 building from Shepley, Rutan, and Goolidge.
- **South Station** • Summer St & Atlantic Ave Busier train station, with the new Silver Line and bus terminal.

Nightlife

- **An Tain** • 31 India St [Milk St] 617-426-1870 For after work; DJs on Thursday, Friday.
- **Biddy Early's** • 141 Pearl St [Purchase St] 617-654-9944 Dive bar that tries a little too hard.
- **Bond** • 250 Franklin St [Oliver St] 617-956-8765 Prepare yourself for the line.
- **Elephant & Castle** • 161 Devonshire St [Milk St] 617-350-9977 Large pub handy for groups. Skip the food.
- **Good Life** • 28 Kingston St [Bedford St] 617-451-2622 Martinis and jazz.
- **Howl at the Moon** • 184 High St [Batterymarch St] 617-292-4695 Bros, bachelorettes, buckets of booze. Oh, and dueling pianos.
- **J.J. Foley's** • 21 Kingston St [Summer St] 617-695-2529 Attracts a big after-work crowd.
- **Les Zygomates** • 129 South St [Tufts St] 617-542-5108 Comprehensive wine list, pleasant bar.
- **Mr. Dooley's** • 77 Broad St [Custom House St] 617-338-5656 Irish. Popular after-work drinking spot.
- **Rowes Wharf Bar** • 70 Rowes Wharf [High St] 617-856-7744 Relax with scotch and an armchair.

Restaurants

- **Chacarero** • 101 Arch St [Winter St]
  617-542-0392 • $
  Unique Chilean sandwiches.
- **China Pearl** • 9 Tyler St [Beach St]
  617-426-4338 • $$
  Dim sum for beginners and experts.
- **Gene's Chinese Flatbread Cafe** •
  86 Bedford St [Kingston St]
  617-482-1888 • $
  Xi'an-style hand-pulled noodles and flatbread sandwiches.
- **Gourmet Dumpling House** •
  52 Beach St [Oxford St]
  617-338-6223 • $
  Destination dumplings with a wait to match.
- **Hei La Moon** • 88 Beach St [Lincoln St]
  617-338-8813 • $
  Best Dim Sum in Boston!
- **Hing Shing Pastry** • 67 Beach St [Hudson St]
  617-451-1162 • $
  Best buns in Chinatown.
- **The Hong Kong Eatery** •
  79 Harrison Ave [Knapp St]
  617-423-0838 • $
  Mountains of pork and rice for just a few bucks.
- **Les Zygomates** • 129 South St [Tufts St]
  617-542-5108 • $$$
  French bistro. Comprehensive wine list, pleasant bar.
- **Mei Sum** • 40 Beach St [Harrison Ave]
  617-357-4050 • $
  Another tasty option for bánh mì and baked goods in the heart of Chinatown.
- **Meritage** • 70 Rowes Wharf [High St]
  617-439-3995 • $$$$$
  Serious about pairing food with wine.
- **Milk Street Cafe** • 50 Milk St [Devonshire St]
  617-542-3663 • $
  Dependable lunch option.
- **New Shanghai** • 21 Hudson St [Kneeland St]
  617-338-6688 • $$
  Critically acclaimed Shanghainese.
- **Peach Farm** • 4 Tyler St [Beach St]
  617-482-1116 • $$
  Family-style Cantonese. Cool seafood tanks.
- **Mii Pho** • 17 Beach St [Monsignor Shea Rd]
  617-423-3934 • $
  Phat pho.
- **Sakurabana** • 57 Broad St [Broad St]
  617-542-4311 • $$$
  Good bet for low-key sushi.
- **Shabu-Zen** • 16 Tyler St [Beach St]
  617-292-8828 • $$
  Pay to cook your own food in a delicious broth? Yeah, it is worth it!
- **Shojo** • 9 Tyler St [Beach St]
  617-423-7888 • $$$
  Smart cocktails and sake among ever-changing, fun, Asian-themed bar menu.
- **South Street Diner** •
  178 Kneeland St [South St]
  617-350-0028 • $
  Night shift dining excellence with a liquor license.
- **Taiwan Café** • 34 Oxford St [Oxford Pl]
  617-426-8181 • $$
  Step-ahead, challenging Chinese food.

Chinatown = **Hei La Moon** for dim sum, **Taiwan Café** for the real deal or **Gourmet Dumpling House** for real soup dumplings. For late-night bites, remember that the **South Street Diner** serves well into the night. Some of Boston's top restaurants, including **Radius** and **Meritage**, call the Financial District home.

Shopping

• **BRIX Wine Shop** • 105 Broad St [Well St]
617-542-2749
Upscale wine shop.

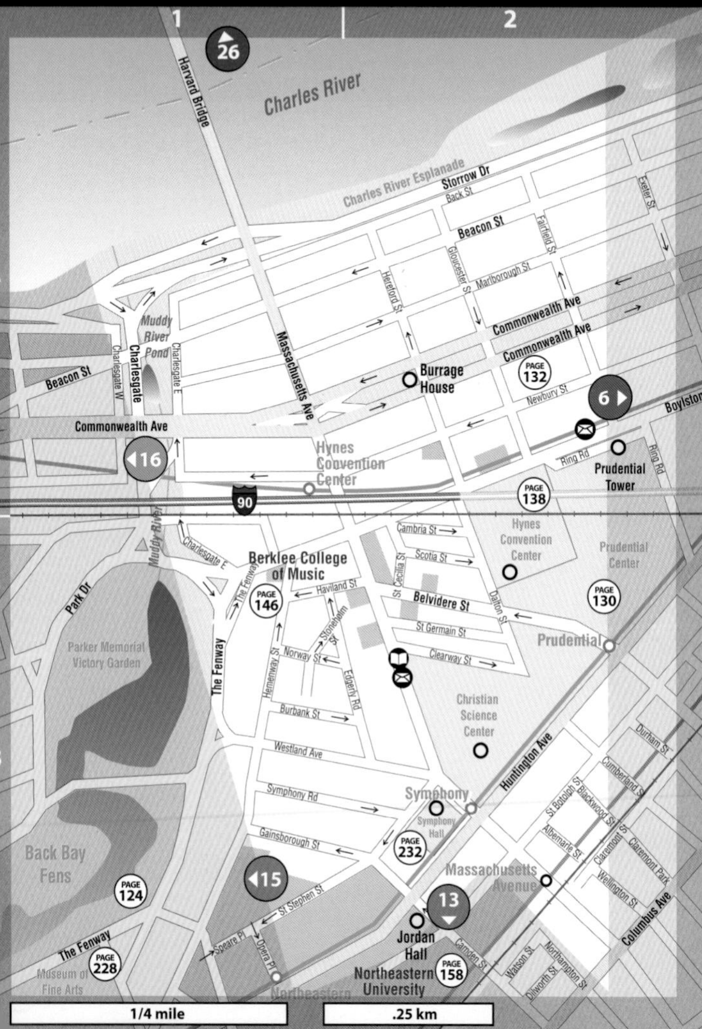

1
2
26
Charles River
Harvard Bridge
Charles River Esplanade
Storrow Dr
Back St
Exeter St
Beacon St
Fairfield St
Gloucester St
Marlborough St
Hereford St
Massachusetts Ave
Commonwealth Ave
Commonwealth Ave
Muddy River Pond
Charlesgate W
Charlesgate
Charlesgate E
Beacon St
Burrage House
PAGE 132
Newbury St
6
Boylston
Commonwealth Ave
16
Hynes Convention Center
Ring Rd
Prudential Tower
Ring Rd
PAGE 138
90
Muddy River
Charlesgate E
Cambria St
Scotia St
Cecilia St
Hynes Convention Center
Prudential Center
Berklee College of Music
The Fenway
PAGE 146
Haviland St
Belvidere St
Dalton St
PAGE 130
Park Dr
St Germain St
Parker Memorial Victory Garden
Stoneholm St
Norway St
Clearway St
Prudential
The Fenway
Hemenway St
Edgerly Rd
Burbank St
Christian Science Center
Westland Ave
Durham St
Huntington Ave
Cumberland St
Symphony Rd
Symphony
Symphony Hall
St Botolph St
Blackwood St
Gainsborough St
PAGE 232
Albemarle St
Claremont St
Claremont Park
Back Bay Fens
15
Massachusetts Avenue
Wellington St
PAGE 124
St Stephen St
13
Columbus Ave
Jordan Hall
The Fenway
Speare Pl
Opera Pl
Camden St
Watson St
Northampton St
PAGE 228
Museum of Fine Arts
PAGE 158
Dilworth St
Northeastern University
Northeastern
1/4 mile
.25 km

Traffic on Mass Ave! MassPIRG on Newbury Street! Berklee students between classes! This area is always insane, and always active. The striking group of buildings that comprises the **Christian Science Center**, together with **the Pru** and 111 Huntington (the "Daily Planet"), looks great at night.

Landmarks

- **Burrage House •**
  314 Commonwealth Ave [Hereford St]
  Nineteenth-century French-Renaissance mansion. Private.
- **Christian Science Center •**
  275 Massachusetts Ave [Westland Ave]
  617-450-3790
  Mother Church, Mapparium, reflecting pool. Quite nice.
- **Hynes Convention Center •**
  900 Boylston St [Gloucester St]
  617-954-2000
  Still a convention center, for now.
- **Jordan Hall •**
  30 Gainsborough St [Huntington Ave]
  617-585-1260
  Hundred-year-old theater seats over 1,000 and has remarkable acoustics.
- **Prudential Tower •**
  800 Boylston St [Fairfield St]
  617-236-3100
  The other tall building. Equally loved and reviled.
- **Symphony Hall •**
  301 Massachusetts Ave [Huntington Ave]
  617-266-1492
  Home of the Boston Symphony Orchestra.

Nightlife

- **Bukowski Tavern** • 50 Dalton St [Scotia St]
  617-437-9999
  100+ beers served with loud, eclectic music.
- **The Corner Tavern •**
  421 Marlborough St [Massachusetts Ave]
  617-262-5555
  Locals only.
- **Dillon's** • 955 Boylston St [Hereford St]
  617-421-1818
  Revisiting the Roaring '20s.
- **King's Dining & Entertainment** • 50 Dalton St [Scotia St]
  617-266-2695
  Bowling, pool, TV sports. Goofy but fun.
- **Lir** • 903 Boylston St [Fenway]
  617-778-0089
  Upscale Irish. Large, handy for sports watchers.
- **McGreevey's** • 911 Boylston St [Hereford St]
  617-262-0911
  They remade the Foggy Goggle? Oh it's still an overpriced meat market. Eh.
- **Pour House** • 907 Boylston St [Gloucester St]
  617-236-1767
  Wide beer selection, cool bartenders.
- **Sonsie** • 327 Newbury St [Hereford St]
  617-351-2500
  People-watching mainstay. Nice French-doors street exposure.
- **Top of the Hub** • 800 Boylston St [Fairfield St]
  617-536-1775
  Great view from the top of the Pru.
- **Towne** • 900 Boylston St [Gloucester St]
  617-247-0400
  Stylish crowd can be a bit snobby.
- **Wally's Café •**
  427 Massachusetts Ave [Columbus Ave]
  617-424-1408
  Cramped jazz landmark. For everyone at least once.

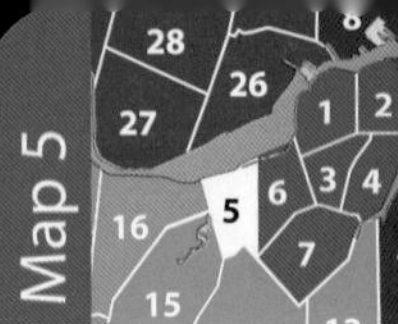

Back Bay (West) / Fenway (East)

Restaurants

- **5 Napkin Burger** • 105 Huntington Ave [Belvidere St] 617-375-2277 • $$
Burgers so good you'll slap your momma.
- **Asta** • 47 Massachusetts Ave [Marlborough St] 617-585-9575 • $$$$
Ur crossword clue and challenging tasting menus.
- **Back Bay Social Club** • 867 Boylston St [Gloucester St] 617-247-3200 • $$
One of the few brunch options in Back Bay.
- **Bukowski Tavern** • 50 Dalton St [Scotia St] 617-437-9999 • $$
Watering hole also has great chili, p.b.j. sandwiches, late hours.
- **Café Jaffa** • 48 Gloucester St [Boylston St] 617-536-0230 • $
Affordable, delicious Middle Eastern.
- **The Capital Grille** • 900 Boylston St [Gloucester St] 617-262-8900 • $$$$$
Arise, Sir Loin!
- **Casa Romero** • 30 Gloucester St [Newbury St] 617-536-4341 • $$$
Mexican. Decent food, good atmosphere.
- **Chilli Duck** • 829 Boylston St [Fairfield St] 617-236-5208 • $$
Thai eatery with modern decor, slightly-elevated prices, and expectedly-tangy sauces.
- **Jasper White's Summer Shack** • 50 Dalton St [Scotia St] 617-867-9955 • $$
Chummy spot to share oysters with pals. Slightly overpriced.
- **Kashmir** • 279 Newbury St [Gloucester St] 617-536-1695 • $$
Excellent *murg saagwala*.
- **Pour House** • 907 Boylston St [Gloucester St] 617-236-1767 • $
Wonderful, cheap bar food. Opens at 8 am.
- **Select Oyster Bar** • 50 Gloucester St [Boylston St] 857-239-8064 • $$$$
Fresh seafood done up elegantly.
- **Sonsie** • 327 Newbury St [Hereford St] 617-351-2500 • $$$$
People-watching mainstay. Nice French-doors street exposure.
- **Top of the Hub** • 800 Boylston St [Fairfield St] 617-536-1775 • $$$$
Almost worth the price for the amazing view atop the Pru.
- **Trident Booksellers & Café** • 338 Newbury St [Hereford St] 617-267-8688 • $
All-day breakfast in a cool bookstore.

Trident Booksellers and Café is a terrific spot for brunching and browsing. Beer drinkers who can handle Tunnel-level stereo volume and a touch of attitude should try **Bukowski's**. Berklee students often sit in at **Wally's**, joining more established musicians to play live jazz most nights of the week.

Shopping

- **DeLuca's Market** • 239 Newbury St [Fairfield St] 617-262-5990 Good deli, pricey fruit, wine, and beer downstairs.
- **Economy True Value Hardware** • 219 Massachusetts Ave [Clearway St] 617-536-4280 Hardware, household needs, cheap furniture. Very popular.
- **Emack & Bolio's** • 290 Newbury St [Gloucester St] 617-536-7127 Innovative ice cream flavors.
- **Forever 21** • 343 Newbury St [Massachusetts Ave] 617-488-3054 Enormous—getting lost is a real concern.
- **John Fluevog** • 2135-1 S Market St 617-266-1079 Indulge the hipster in you with these funky shoes.
- **Johnny Cupcakes** • 279 Newbury St [Gloucester St] 617-375-0100 Trendy T-shirts. Not cupcakes.
- **Johnson Paint Co.** • 355 Newbury St [Massachusetts Ave] 617-536-4244 Tony. Also a selection of stationery.
- **Newbury Comics** • 332 Newbury St [Hereford St] 617-236-4930 Now featuring a large DVD section.
- **Orpheus Performing Arts** • 362 Commonwealth Ave [Massachusetts Ave] 617-247-7200 Focusing on classical music.
- **Sephora** • 800 Boylston St [Fairfield St] 617-262-4200 A makeup wonderland—play before you buy.
- **Sweet Cupcakes** • 49 Massachusetts Ave [Marlborough St] 617-247-2253 Give in to your Sweet tooth.
- **Sweet-N-Nasty** • 90 Massachusetts Ave [Commonwealth Ave] 617-266-7171 Saucy cakes for all [adult] occasions.
- **Trident Booksellers & Café** • 338 Newbury St [Hereford St] 617-267-8688 Busy, independent bookstore/cafe with tons of magazines.
- **Urban Outfitters** • 361 Newbury St [Massachusetts Ave] 617-236-0088 Funky clothes, apartment stuff and novelties.
- **Utrecht Art Supply Center** • 333 Massachusetts Ave [St Botolph St] 617-262-4948 Serious art store near Symphony Hall.

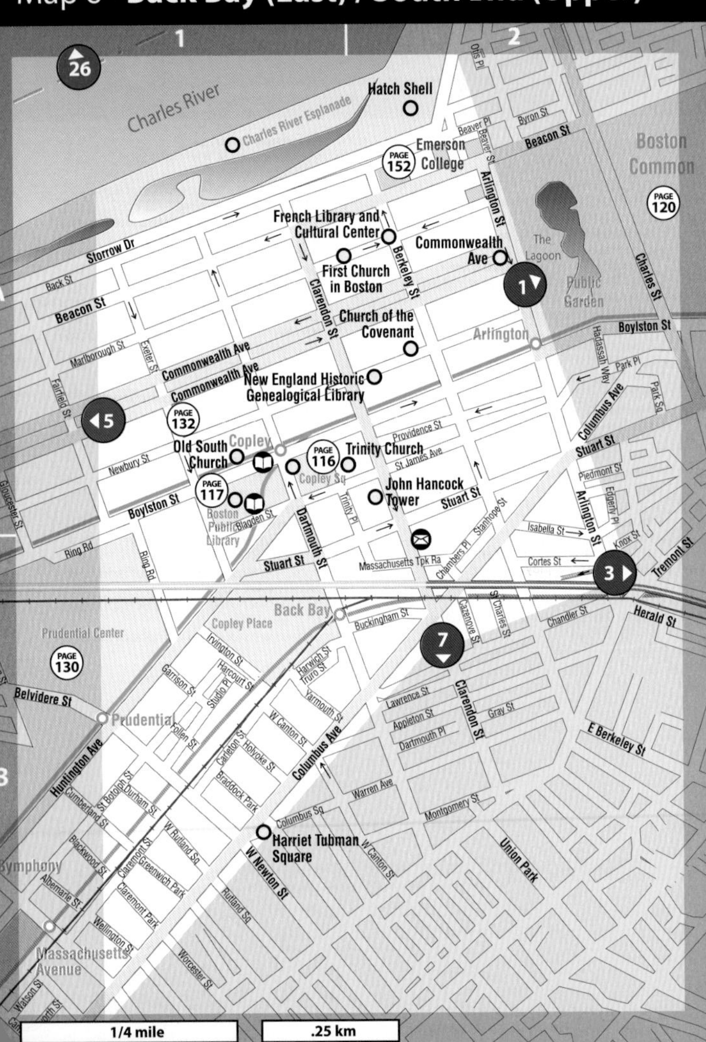

1
2
26
Charles River
Charles River Esplanade
Hatch Shell
Otis Pl
Beaver Pl
Beaver St
Byron St
Beacon St
Boston Common
PAGE 152
Emerson College
PAGE 120
Arlington St
The Lagoon
Public Garden
French Library and Cultural Center
Commonwealth Ave
First Church in Boston
Berkeley St
Storrow Dr
Back St
Beacon St
Charles St
1
Clarendon St
Church of the Covenant
Boylston St
Arlington
Hadassah Way
Park Pl
Park Sq
Marlborough St
Exeter St
Commonwealth Ave
Commonwealth Ave
New England Historic Genealogical Library
Fairfield St
5
PAGE 132
Columbus Ave
Providence St
Stuart St
Old South Church
Copley
PAGE 116
Trinity Church
St James Ave
Piedmont St
Newbury St
Copley Sq
John Hancock Tower
Stuart St
Edgerly Pl
PAGE 117
Trinity Pl
Stanhope St
Gloucester St
Boylston St
Boston Public Library
Blagden St
Dartmouth St
Isabella St
Knox St
Tremont St
Ring Rd
Ring Rd
Stuart St
Massachusetts Tpk Ra
Chambers Pl
Cortes St
3
Back Bay
Buckingham St
Cazenove St
St Charles St
Chandler St
Herald St
Prudential Center
Copley Place
7
PAGE 130
Irvington St
Garrison St
Harcourt St
Harwich St
Truro St
Belvidere St
Studio Pl
Yarmouth St
Lawrence St
Clarendon St
Gray St
Prudential
Appleton St
Follen St
W Canton St
Dartmouth Pl
E Berkeley St
Carleton St
Holyoke St
Columbus Ave
Huntington Ave
St Botolph St
Braddock Park
Warren Ave
Cumberland St
Durham St
Montgomery St
Columbus Sq
Union Park
Harriet Tubman Square
W Canton St
W Rutland Sq
Blackwood St
Claremont St
W Newton St
Symphony
Greenwich Park
Albemarle St
Claremont Park
Rutland Sq
Wellington St
Massachusetts Avenue
Worcester St
Watson St
1/4 mile
.25 km

The eastern end of Back Bay features the "top" of Newbury Street, with its mix of locals, tourists, and international students keeping its mainly highbrow merchants busy. The upper regions of the South End—especially Columbus Avenue—are now home to excellent restaurant upon excellent restaurant, with a culturally correct number of galleries thrown in as well.

Landmarks

- **Boston Public Library—Central •**
  700 Boylston St [Exeter St]
  617-536-5400
- **Charles River Esplanade •** Storrow Drive
  Great place to run or read a book.
- **Church of the Covenant •**
  67 Newbury St [Berkeley St]
  617-266-7480
  Gothic revival church called "absolutely perfect" by Oliver Wendell Holmes.
- **Commonwealth Ave •**
  Commonwealth Ave & Mass Ave
  Boston's most distinguished promenade with oddest collection of statues.
- **Copley Square •** Boylston St & Dartmouth St
  Back Bay's living room.
- **First Church in Boston •**
  66 Marlborough St [Clarendon St]
  617-267-6730
  Founded 375 years ago.
- **French Library and Cultural Center •**
  53 Marlborough St [Berkeley St]
  617-912-0417
  Classes, food, and movies, tous en francais.
- **Hatch Shell •** Esplanade [Congress St]
  Where the Pops play each July 4th.
- **John Hancock Tower •**
  200 Clarendon St [St James Ave]
  New England's tallest building, designed by I.M. Pei.
- **New England Historic Genealogical Library •**
  101 Newbury St [Clarendon St]
  617-536-5740
  Trace your roots back to the Mayflower.
- **Old South Church •**
  645 Boylston St [Dartmouth St]
  617-536-1970
  Northern Italian Gothic, finished in 1875.
- **Trinity Church •**
  206 Clarendon St [St James Ave]
  617-536-0944
  Romanesque, with massive open interior. Completed in 1877.

Nightlife

- **Anchovies •**
  433 Columbus Ave [Braddock Park]
  617-266-5088
  Easy-going neighborhood joint.
- **Champions •**
  110 Huntington Ave [Harcourt St]
  617-927-5304
  Sports. Food wins no trophies.
- **City Bar •** 65 Exeter St [Boylston St]
  617-933-4800
  At the Lenox Hotel.
- **Clery's •** 113 Dartmouth St [Columbus Ave]
  617-262-9874
  Bar with food. Location is its best attribute.
- **Club Café •** 209 Columbus Ave [Berkeley St]
  617-536-0966
  Gay: restaurant in front, scoping in back.
- **Lolita Cocina & Tequila Bar •**
  271 Dartmouth St [Newbury St]
  617-369-5609
  Tacos and margaritas. Vampy with a tinge of goth.
- **Storyville •** 90 Exeter St [Huntington Ave]
  617-236-1134
  A pinch of New Orleans nightlife in Beantown.

Restaurants

- **Abe & Louie's** • 793 Boylston St [Fairfield St]
617-536-6300 • $$$$
Popular local steakhouse.
- **b.good** • 131 Dartmouth St [Columbus Ave]
617-424-5252 • $
Healthy, quick lunches.
- **Brasserie Jo** •
120 Huntington Ave [W Newton St]
617-425-3240 • $$$$
French brasserie near Symphony Hall. Usually very busy.
- **Davio's** • 75 Arlington St [Stuart St]
617-357-4810 • $$$$
Good food, but it's about the river view.
- **Flour Bakery + Café** •
131 Clarendon St [Stanhope St]
617-437-7700 • $
Beyond exceptional bakery. Also serves dinners for take-away.
- **Georgetown Cupcake** •
83 Newbury St [Clarendon St]
617-927-2250 • $
Best cupcakes hands down, flat out.
- **Grill 23 & Bar** • 161 Berkeley St [Stuart St]
617-542-2255 • $$$$$
Classic steakhouse. Ideal for business dinners.
- **House of Siam** •
542 Columbus Ave [Worcester St]
617-267-1755 • $$
If you are off to the symphony, this is a good bet.
- **Lolita Cocina & Tequila Bar** •
271 Dartmouth St [Newbury St]
617-369-5609 • $$
Tacos and margaritas. Vampy with a tinge of goth.
- **Mistral** • 223 Columbus Ave [Cahners Pl]
617-867-9300 • $$$$
Superb. Great bar, too. Look sharp.
- **Oak Long Bar + Kitchen** •
138 St James Ave [Trinity Pl]
617-585-7222 • $$$
Go for the old school Boston vibe, not the overpriced menu and mediocre martinis.
- **Parish Café** • 361 Boylston St [Arlington St]
617-247-4777 • $$
Inventive sandwiches. Full bar too.
- **Red Lantern** • 39 Stanhope St [Clarendon St]
617-262-3900 • $$$$
Asian fusion in old Hard Rock Building; industry hot spot.
- **The Salty Pig** •
130 Darthmouth St [Columbus Ave]
617-536-6200 • $$
Meat is king: Fantastic charcuterie plates and excellent smoked meats.
- **Tico** • 222 Berkeley St [St. James Ave]
617-351-0400 • $$$
Legit tapas joint that is always full and rocking.

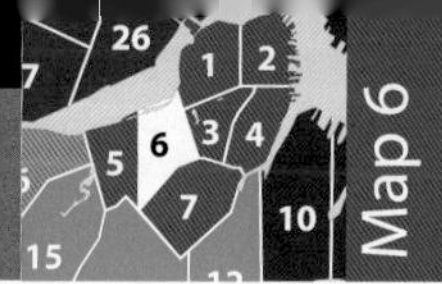

Grab a great sandwich at **Parish Café**, some tapas at **Tico**, or, if you're operating on an expense account, a steak at **Grill 23**. If you're just thirsty, you can always hit the roof-deck at **Rattlesnake**.

Shopping

- **Anthropologie** • 203 Newbury St [Fairfield St]
  617-262-0545
  Clothes, accessories and colorful *objets d'home*.
- **Apple Store** • 815 Boylston St [Fairfield St]
  617-385-9400
  Mac Mecca.
- **Barneys New York** •
  100 Huntington Ave [Harcourt St]
  617-385-3300
  For those of you with lots of disposable income.
- **Brooks Brothers** •
  46 Newbury St [Berkeley St]
  617-267-2600
  Flagship store of company operating since 1818.
- **Crate & Barrel** • 777 Boylston St [Fairfield St]
  617-262-8700
  Back Bay location of Chicago behemoth.
- **H&M** • 100 Newbury St [Clarendon St]
  855-466-7467
  Disposable chic from Swedish mega-merchant.
- **The Hempest** • 301 Newbury St [Exeter St]
  617-421-9944
  Don't ask if they sell screens.
- **International Poster Gallery** •
  460C Harrison Ave [Exeter St]
  617-375-0076
  Prints and posters from around the world.
- **Lindt Master Chocolatier** •
  704 Boylston St [Exeter St]
  617-236-0571
  Nifty gifts for your Swiss miss.
- **Lord & Taylor** • 760 Boylston St [Fairfield St]
  617-262-6000
  Featuring new façade.
- **Lush** • 144 Newbury St [Dartmouth St]
  617-262-0354
  British cosmetics merchant.
- **Marathon Sports** • 671 Boylston St [Exeter St]
  617-267-4774
  Run! Run! Run!
- **Neiman Marcus** • 5 Copley Pl [Dartmouth St]
  617-536-3660
  Needless Markup?
- **Paper Source** • 338 Boylston St [Arlington St]
  617-536-3444
  DIY paper crafts and quirky gifts.
- **Saks Fifth Avenue** •
  800 Boylston St [Gloucester St]
  617-262-8500
  A posh shopping experience.
- **Shreve, Crump & Low** •
  39 Newbury St [Berkeley St]
  617-267-9100
  Boston jewelers since 1796.
- **The Tannery** • 711 Boylston St [Berkeley St]
  617-267-5500
  Known for huge selection. Hit-or-miss service.
- **Teuscher Chocolates** •
  230 Newbury St [Fairfield St]
  617-536-1922
  For the Swiss chocoholic in you.
- **Urban Grape** •
  303 Columbus Ave [Dartmouth St]
  857-250-2509
  Wine rookies are welcomed in this friendly, well-stocked shop.

1
2
A
B
Arlington
Boylston
Chinatown
Commonwealth Ave
Copley
Clarendon St
Arlington St
Columbus Ave
Stuart St
Kneeland St
Charles St S
Berkeley St
Dartmouth St
Boylston St
Stuart St
Ring Rd
Oak St W
NE Med Ctr
Tremont St
90
Massachusetts Tpk Ra
Corning St
93
Pine St
Framingham Worcester Line
Buckingham St
Back Bay
Chandler St
Herald St
Paul Pl
3
Herald St
William E Mullins Way
Broadway
Prudential
Huntington St
Needham Line
Lawrence St
Appleton St
Dartmouth Pl
Warren Ave
Gray St
Village Ct
Castle Ct
Emerald Ct
Waterford St
Traveler St
4
6
E Berkeley St
E Berkeley St
Dwight St
Fort Point Channel
Columbus Sq
Canton St
Montgomery St
W Brookline St
Pembroke St
W Newton St
Union Park
Hanson St
Milford St
Taylor St
Groton St
Fay St
Paul Sullivan Way
Thayer St
W 4th St
SoWa Building
Albany St
Randolph St
Union Park St
Rutland Sq
Concord Sq
Concord Pl
Tremont St
Claremont Park
Wellington St
Massachusetts Avenue
Cathedral of the Holy Cross
Monsignor Reynolds Way
Malden St
Wareham St
Plympton St
13
Shawmut Ave
Washington St
Mystic St
Worcester St
W Springfield St
Massachusetts Ave
Camden St
Newton St
E Canton St
E Dedham St
Andrews St
E Brookline St
Sharon St
12
Northampton St
Worcester Sq
Mass. Ave
E Newton St
Stoughton St
Thorn St
Harrison Ave
E Concord St
Boston University Medical Center
Albany St
Widett Cir
Food Mart Rd
Gen Pulaski Skwy
S Bay Ave
Lenox St
Melnea Cass
Harrison Ave
Melnea Cass Blvd
Southampton St
Washington St
1/4 mile
.25 km

The South End is America's largest Victorian neighborhood, has the city's largest gay population, and, after years of gentrification, is now a "destination" spot. All this hipness, of course, makes the South End more expensive than it was a decade ago. Ultra-trendy boutiques rub shoulders with family-friendly brasseries (especially on happening Tremont Street).

Landmarks

- **Cathedral of the Holy Cross •**
  1400 Washington St [Union Park St]
  617-542-5682
  Mother church of the Archdiocese of Boston.
- **SoWa Artists Guild •**
  450 Harrison Ave [Thayer St]
  A converted warehouse, now home to several galleries.

Nightlife

- **The Beehive •** 541 Tremont St [Milford St]
  617-423-0069
  There's an old-timey, speakeasy feel to the place.
- **The Boston Eagle •**
  520 Tremont St [Dwight St]
  617-542-4494
  Casual gay local, mostly denim and leather.
- **Delux Café •** 100 Chandler St [Clarendon St]
  617-338-5258
  Small, hip spot with good eats, music.
- **Franklin Café •** 278 Shawmut Ave [Hanson St]
  617-350-0010
  Mainly a restaurant, but a good bar choice too.
- **J.J. Foley's •** 117 E Berkeley St [Fay St]
  617-728-9101
  One of the oldest family-run bars in the city.

Restaurants

- **Addis Red Sea** • 544 Tremont St [Waltham St]
617-426-8727 • $$
Ethiopian. Get jiggy with some injera.
- **Appleton Café** •
123 Appleton St [Appleton St]
617-859-8222 • $
Melt-in-your-mouth muffins meet sandwiches with a twist.
- **Aquitaine** • 569 Tremont St [Union Park St]
617-424-8577 • $$$$
A solid French bistro.
- **B&G Oysters** • 550 Tremont St [Waltham St]
617-423-0550 • $$$$
Stylish oyster shop. Good wine list. Best lobster rolls in town!
- **Banyan Bar + Refuge** •
553 Tremont St [Montgomery St]
617-556-4211 • $$$
Fun Asian-inflected small plates; great to share.
- **Da Vinci Ristorante** •
162 Columbus Ave [Isabella St]
617-350-0007 • $$$
South End's answer to the North End hegemony on Italian food.
- **Delux Café** • 100 Chandler St [Clarendon St]
617-338-5258 • $$
Small, hip spot with good eats, music.
- **El Triunfo** • 147 E Berkeley St [Harrison Ave]
617-542-8499 • $
Cheap tacos. Good tongue!
- **Flour Bakery + Café** •
1595 Washington St [Rutland St]
617-267-4300 • $
Beyond exceptional bakery. Also serves dinners for take-away.
- **Franklin Café** • 278 Shawmut Ave [Hanson St]
617-350-0010 • $$$
Delicious late-night option.
- **Gaslight Brasserie** •
560 Harrison Ave [Waltham St]
617-422-0224 • $$
Good French food. Stainless steel bar is a nice touch.
- **L'Espalier** • 774 Boylston St [Newbury St]
617-262-3023 • $$$$$
One of Boston's best. If you want the experience and have the cash , spend it here.
- **Masa** • 439 Tremont St [Appleton St]
617-338-8884 • $$$$
Tiniest $1 tapas specials we've ever seen.
- **Mela** • 578 Tremont St [Upton St]
617-859-4805 • $$
Two words: lunch buffet.
- **Metropolis Café** • 584 Tremont St [Upton St]
617-247-2931 • $$$
Try the cranberry pancakes for brunch.
- **Mike's City Diner** •
1714 Washington St [W Springfield St]
617-267-9393 • $
A trusty not-too-greasy spoon.
- **Myers + Chang** •
1145 Washington St [E Berkeley St]
617-542-5200 • $$
Fun Asian fusion.

Start your night at **Delux**, a beloved neighborhood bar complete with Elvis shrine. Pick up some steaks for dinner at **The Butcher Shop**. When darkness falls, hit up **The Beehive** for a great nightlife scene. The morning after, treat your stomach to **Mike's City Diner** or the pajama brunch at **Tremont 647**. If you're still alive after all that, call us. Bring pictures…and mimosas.

- **Oishii Boston** •
  1166 Washington St [E Berkeley St]
  617-482-8868 • $$$$$
  The only place with better sushi is their other location.
- **Orinoco** • 477 Shawmut Ave [W Concord St]
  617-369-7075 • $$$
  The South End puts a twist on Venezuelan food and it's delicious!
- **Picco** • 513 Tremont St [E Berkeley St]
  617-927-0066 • $$
  The gated community of ice cream. Serves pizza, too.
- **South End Pita** • 473 Albany St [Union Park St]
  617-556-2600 • $
  South End shawarma that will hook you for life.
- **Stella** • 1525 Washington St [E Brookline St]
  617-247-7747 • $$$
  Too Stylish, whitish spot. Mostly Italian menu.
- **Teranga** •
  1746 Washington St [Massachusetts Ave]
  617-266-0003 • $$
  Senegalese—a welcome addition to the worldly South End.
- **Toro** • 1704 Washington St [Springfield St]
  617-536-4300 • $$$
  Fun, fresh take on tapas.
- **The Upper Crust** •
  683 Tremont St [W Newton St]
  617-927-0090 • $$
  Fancy schmancy, crisp-crust pizza.

Shopping

- **Blackbird Doughnuts** •
  492 Tremont St [Berkeley St]
  617-482-9000
  Crazy, fun, transporting doughnuts.
- **Bobby from Boston** •
  19 Thayer St [Harrison Ave]
  617-423-9299
  Vintage clothing with a particularly awesome men's section.
- **BRIX Wine Shop** •
  1284 Washington St [Savoy St]
  617-542-2749
  Upscale wine shop.
- **The Butcher Shop** •
  552 Tremont St [Waltham St]
  617-423-4800
  Neighborhood meat shop. Also a wine bar serving specialties.
- **Holbrow Flowers** •
  540 Albany St [E Dedham St]
  800-273-8057
  Flowers!
- **Ilex** • 73 Berkeley St [Chandler St]
  617-422-0300
  Florist.
- **Lekker** • 1313 Washington St [Rollins St]
  617-542-6464
  Unique, modern home furnishings.
- **Picco** • 513 Tremont St [E Berkeley St]
  617-927-0066
  Ice cream handy to the BCA.
- **South End Buttery** •
  314 Shawmut Ave [Union Park St]
  617-482-1015
  Churning out the treats.
- **South End Formaggio** •
  268 Shawmut Ave [Milford St]
  617-350-6996
  Cheese, cured meats, dry goods, and wine.

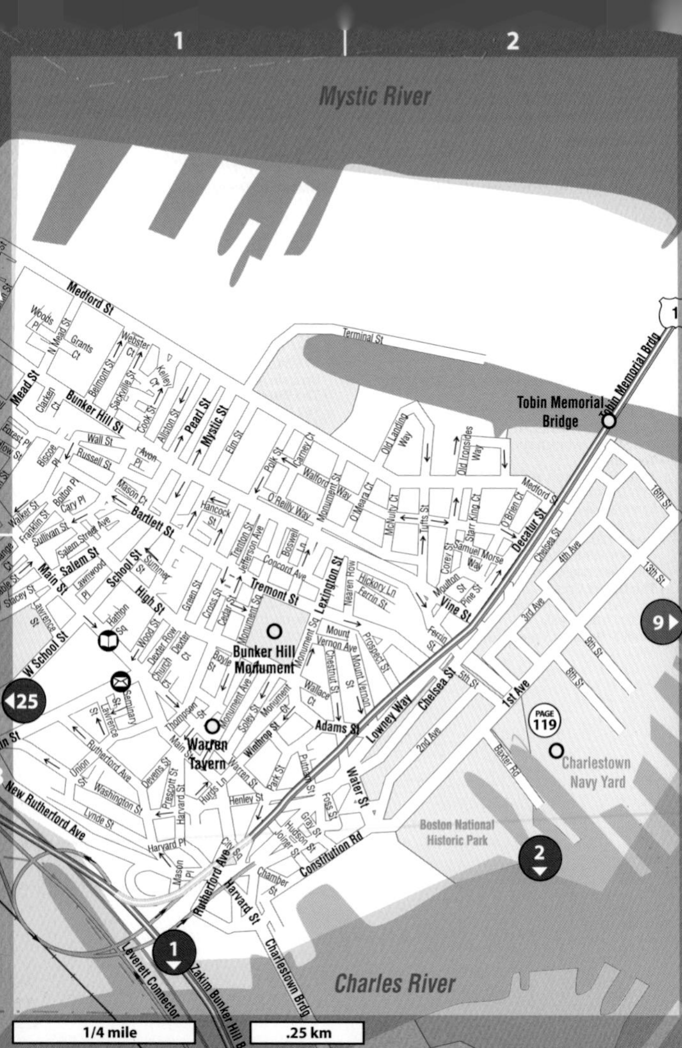

1
2
A
B
Mystic River
Charles River
Tobin Memorial Bridge
Bunker Hill Monument
Warren Tavern
Charlestown Navy Yard
Boston National Historic Park
PAGE 119
25
9
2
1
Medford St
Bunker Hill St
Main St
Tremont St
Chelsea St
1st Ave
Constitution Rd
Rutherford Ave
New Rutherford Ave
Leverett Connector
Zakim Bunker Hill Brdg
Charlestown Brdg
Tobin Memorial Brdg
Terminal St
1/4 mile
.25 km

Yes, Charlestown really is the same neighborhood depicted in Ben Affleck's *The Town*—from Irish gangsters to the most bank robbers and car thieves per capita. But despite the public housing blocks that still sit along the edge of town, Charlestown is now an upscale, quaint community. Still, if you see someone in a nun mask? Look away.

Landmarks

- **Bunker Hill Monument •**
  Monument Ave [High St]
  617-242-5641
  Battle actually took place on nearby Breed's Hill.
- **Charlestown Navy Yard •**
  Warren St & Constitution Rd
  617-242-5601
  Home of the *USS Constitution* ("Old Ironsides").
- **Tobin Memorial Bridge** • US-1
  Lovingly photographed in *Mystic River*.
- **The Warren Tavern** • 2 Pleasant St [Main St]
  617-241-8142
  One of Paul Revere's favorite watering holes.

Nightlife

- **Sullivan's Pub** • 85 Main St [Harvard St]
  617-242-9515
  Relaxed pub off of Thompson Square.
- **The Warren Tavern** • 2 Pleasant St [Main St]
  617-241-8142
  One of Paul Revere's favorite watering holes.

Restaurants

- **Brewer's Fork** • 7 Moulton St [Vine St]
  617-337-5703 • $$
  Oysters, wood-fired pizza, and most of all, beer.
- **Figs** • 67 Main St [Monument Ave]
  617-242-2229 • $$$
  Charlestown branch of upscale pizza chain.
- **Ironside Grill** • 25 Park St [Warren St]
  617-242-1384 • $$
  Formerly managed by Raymond Burr.
- **Jenny's Pizza** • 320 Medford St [Allston St]
  617-242-9474 • $
  Subs too. Nice view of the, erm, Autoport.
- **Navy Yard Bistro & Wine Bar •**
  1 6th St [1st Ave]
  617-242-0036 • $$
  Mid-priced bistro fare near the ships.
- **Ninety Nine** • 29 Austin St [Lawrence St]
  617-242-8999 • $$
  Take your step-kids.
- **Sorelle** • 100 City Sq [Park St]
  617-242-5980 • $
  Tasty sandwiches, baked goods, alcohol too.
- **Sorelle** • 1 Monument Ave [Main St]
  617-242-2125 • $
  Tasty sandwiches, baked goods, alcohol too.
- **Tangierino** • 83 Main St [Monument Ave]
  617-242-6009 • $$$
  Rockin' Moroccan.
- **The Warren Tavern** • 2 Pleasant St [Main St]
  617-241-8142 • $$
  One of Paul Revere's favorite watering holes.

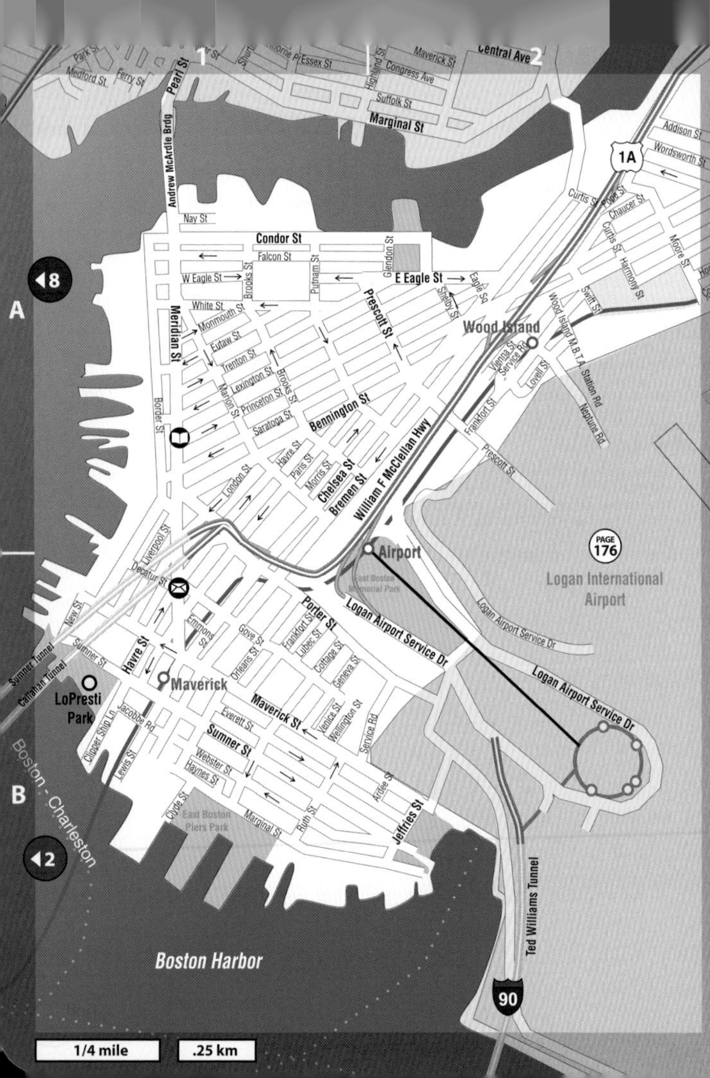

Central Ave
Maverick St
Congress Ave
Essex St
Suffolk St
Marginal St
Park St
Medford St
Ferry St
Pearl St
Andrew McArdle Brdg
1A
Addison St
Wordsworth St
Curtis St
Pope St
Chaucer St
Harmony St
Moore St
Swift St
Nay St
Condor St
Falcon St
Glendon St
W Eagle St
Brooks St
Putnam St
E Eagle St
Eagle Sq
Shelby St
White St
Monmouth St
Meridian St
Prescott St
Wood Island
Eutaw St
Trenton St
Lexington St
Princeton St
Marion St
Border St
Saratoga St
Bennington St
Vienna St
Service Rd
Lovell St
Wood Island M.B.T.A. Station Rd
Neptune Rd
Frankfort St
Havre St
Paris St
Morris St
London St
Chelsea St
Bremen St
William F McClellan Hwy
Airport
East Boston Memorial Park
PAGE 176
Logan International Airport
Liverpool St
Decatur St
New St
Emmons St
Gove St
Porter St
Lubec St
Cottage St
Geneva St
Orleans St
Logan Airport Service Dr
Sumner Tunnel
Callahan Tunnel
Sumner St
LoPresti Park
Maverick
Maverick St
Everett St
Venice St
Wellington St
Service Rd
Clipper Ship Ln
Jacobbe Rd
Lewis St
Webster St
Haynes St
Ardee St
Jeffries St
Clyde St
East Boston Piers Park
Marginal St
Ruth St
Boston - Charleston
Ted Williams Tunnel
90
Boston Harbor
A
B
8
2
1/4 mile
.25 km

One of the last predominantly ethnic neighborhoods in Boston, and isolated from the city by water, Eastie's tree-lined streets and classic triple-deckers are home to a Latin American community that's just starting to see the gentrification from Southie move in. Maverick Square is busy, but you'll want to make the walk up to Day Square to get a better sense of the turf.

Landmarks

- **LoPresti Park** • Summer St
  Best view of the Boston skyline and harbor for landlubbers.

Nightlife

- **Kelley's Square Pub** •
  84 Bennington St [Marion St]
  617-567-4627
  Neighborhood local, try the ribs.

Restaurants

- **Angela's Cafe** • 131 Lexington St [Brooks St]
  617-567-4972 • $$
  By far the best Mexican food in town prepared by someone else's Grandma…
- **Jeveli's** • 387 Chelsea St [Bennington St]
  617-567-9539 • $
  Italian. Has a bar.
- **KO Pies at the Shipyard** •
  256 Marginal St [Jeffries St]
  617-418-5234 • $$
  Australian food and market, including savory meat and vegetarian pies.
- **La Terraza** • 19 Bennington St [Porter St]
  617-561-5200 • $$
  Straight-forward Colombian cooking. Try the flan.
- **Pollos A La Brasa El Chalan** •
  405 Chelsea St [Saratoga St]
  617-567-9452 • $
  Finest pollo in Eastie.
- **Rincon Limeno** • 409 Chelsea St [Shelby St]
  617-569-4942 • $
  Specializing in Peruvian rotisserie chicken.
- **Santarpio's Pizza** • 111 Chelsea St [Porter St]
  617-567-9871 • $
  Thin and crispy. Get a side of lamb and homemade sausage from the grill.
- **Taco Mex** • 65 Maverick Sq [Sumner St]
  617-569-2838 • $
  Tongue taco, a sign of real Mexican.
- **Taqueria Cancun** •
  192 Sumner St [Maverick Sq]
  617-567-4449 • $
  Don't count on tequila slammers.
- **Topacio** • 120 Meridian St [London St]
  617-567-9523 • $$
  Pupusas! Specifically, the best ones of all time.

Shopping

- **Brazilian Soccer House** •
  110 Meridian St [London St]
  617-569-1164
  The place to get your soccer kit.
- **Emack & Bolio's** • 23 White St [Marion St]
  617-492-1907
  Innovative ice cream flavors.
- **Globos y Fiestas** •
  268 Bennington St [Chelsea St]
  617-569-4908
  Order your piñatas here.
- **Lolly's Bakery** • 158 Bennington St [Brooks St]
  617-567-9461
  Quality panadería.

N
South Station
Chinatown
Courthouse
Institute of Contemporary Art
PAGE 227
Children's Museum
Fort Point Channel
Seaport World Trade Center
World Trade Center
Silver Line Way
BCEC
Boston Convention & Exhibition Center
PAGE 136
Broadway
Andrew
Thomas Park
South Boston Liquor Mart
Columbia Rd
Carson Beach
Columbus Park
Old Harbor
E Broadway
W Broadway
Summer St
Congress St
Congress St Bridge
Northern Ave
Fan Pier
Fish Pier
Essex St
Kneeland St
Atlantic Ave
Dorchester Ave
Washington St
Albany St
S Boston Bypass Rd
Old Colony Ave
Dorchester St
William J Day
Preble St
Crowley Rogers Way
W 4th St
W 2nd St
W 1st St
Dresser St
Gillette Park
Foundary St
Traveler St
Food Mart Rd
Access Rd
Milheroer Pl
Alger St
Humboldt Pl
Dexter St
Telegraph St
Dixfield St
Story St
Colebrook St
Emerson St
Henderson Ave
Power House St
Purchase St
Sleeper St
Farnsworth St
Thomson Pl
Stillings St
Boston Wharf Rd
E Service Rd
B St
WTC Ave
Necco St
Necco Ct
Melcher St
Binford St
Wormwood St
Mt Washington Ave
Granite St
Midway St
Richards St
Baldwin St
D St
Butler St
Inman St
Fargo St
93
90
◀4
11▶
◀12
A
B
1/4 mile
.25 km

Southie seems to be in its renaissance. The formerly locals-only neighborhood has attracted yuppies, artists, and college students with a flurry of new condos, restaurants, and a short commute downtown. For proof of this, take a look at the Fan Pier by the ICA, which is Boston's hippest address, currently exploding with restaurants and new buildings.

Landmarks

- **Boston Children's Museum •**
  308 Congress St [Sleeper St]
  617-426-6500
  Featuring the giant Hood milk bottle.
- **Boston Convention & Exhibition Center •**
  415 Summer St [D St]
  617-954-2100
  The Southie Starship.
- **Boston Sailing Center •**
  Lewis Wharf [Atlantic Ave]
  617-227-4198
  Ahoy, matey! Learn to sail the high seas.
- **Boston Tea Party Ship & Museum •**
  306 Congress St [Sleeper St]
  617-338-1773
  Site of not-so-civil disobedience.
- **Institute of Contemporary Art •**
  100 Northern Ave [Boston Wharf Rd]
  617-478-3100
  Stunning new building. Oh, and the art's pretty good too.
- **South Boston Liquor Mart •**
  295 Old Colony Ave [Jenkins St]
  617-269-3600
  Whitey Bulger's HQ.

Nightlife

- **Drink •** 348 Congress St [Farnsworth St]
  617-695-1806
  Craft cocktail specialists; sit by the ice block.
- **The Junction •** 110 Dorchester St [Silver St]
  617-268-6429
  Low-key neighborhood spot.
- **Lincoln Tavern & Restaurant •**
  425 W Broadway St [F St]
  617-765-8636
  Fancy for Southie. Crazy crowded.
- **Lucky's Lounge •** 355 Congress St [A St]
  617-357-5825
  Well-liked retro cocktail lounge. Music most nights.
- **Shenannigans •** 332 W Broadway [D St]
  617-269-9509
  Popular watering hole.
- **Stats •** 77 Dorchester St [W Broadway St]
  617-268-9300
  Sports bar by day, meat market by night.
- **Whitey's •** 268 W Broadway St [D St]
  617-606-5971
  Bare bones bar with a patronage of tough guys.

Restaurants

- **Amrheins** • 80 W Broadway [A St]
617-268-6189 • $$
Has been here since Southie was mostly German.
- **Barking Crab** • 88 Sleeper St [Northern Ave]
617-426-2722 • $$
Make a mess while viewing the harbor skyline.
- **The Daily Catch** • 2 Northern Ave [Sleeper St]
617-772-4400 • $$$
Italian seafood specialists' Moakley Courthouse spot.
- **Flour Bakery + Café** •
12 Farnsworth St [Congress St]
617-338-4333 • $
Beyond exceptional bakery. Also serves dinners for take-away.
- **Legal Harborside** • 270 Northern Ave [D St]
617-477-2900 • $$$$
Three floors of ever-increasing cost; Seaport's crown jewel doing gangbuster business.
- **Lucky's Lounge** • 355 Congress St [A St]
617-357-5825 • $$
Well-liked retro cocktail lounge. Music most nights.
- **Menton** • 354 Congress St [Thomson Pl]
617-737-0099 • $$$$
Barbara Lynch's French-inflected fine dining destination.
- **Mul's Diner** • 75 W Broadway [A St]
(617) 268-5748 • $
Three words. Grilled blueberry muffins.
- **Row 34** • 383 Congress St [Boston Wharf Rd]
617-553-5900 • $$$$
Sea-to-table seafood, emphasis on oysters.
- **Sportello** • 348 Congress St [A St]
617-737-1234 • $$$
Excellent modern Italian. Nice alternative to the North End.
- **Teriyaki House** • 32 W Broadway [Dorchester Ave]
617-269-2000 • $
The best Japanese delivery in an Irish 'hood.

South Boston (West) / Fort Point

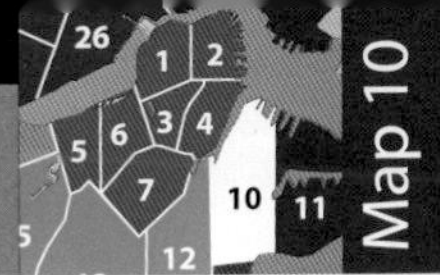

For after-work drinks in the summer, nothing beats **Barking Crab**. Drinkin' establishments are great here—especially **Lucky's** and **Shenannigans**. Finish your new pad with retro pieces from **Front**. Foodies go crazy for **Sportello**—their inventive cuisine is fantastic. Try the Bolognese.

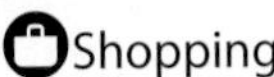

Shopping

• **Machine Age** • 121 Boston St [Fargo St]
617-464-0099
Modern furniture in a huge space.

• **Scooters Go Green** •
220 Old Colony Ave [Gustin St]
617-269-0050
Want to save the earth and don't mind looking like a dork? Buy a scooter!

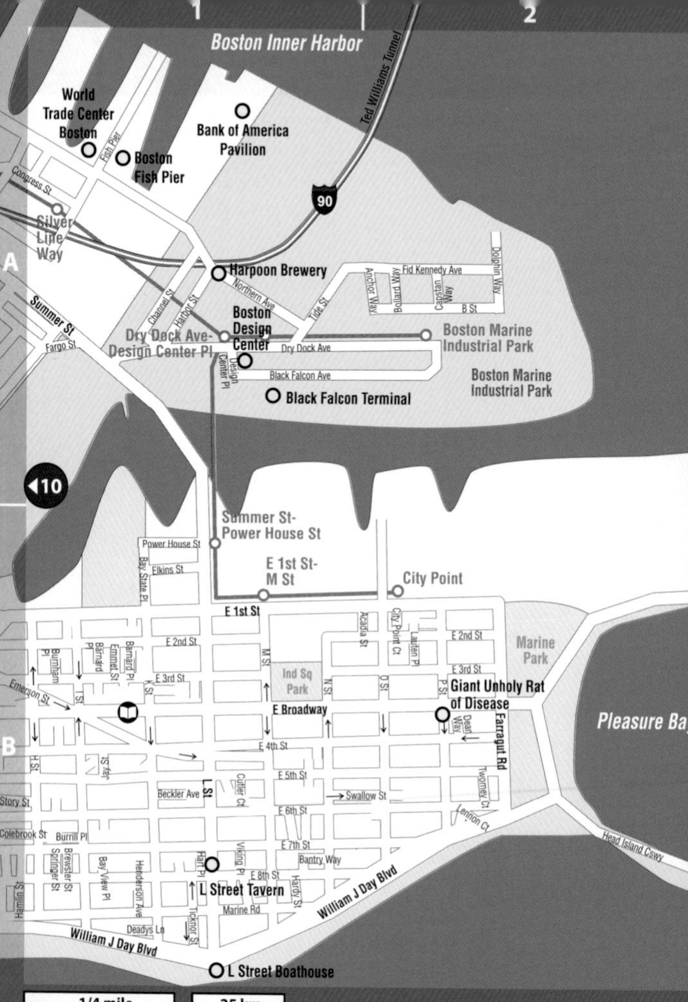

1
2
Boston Inner Harbor
Ted Williams Tunnel
World Trade Center Boston
Boston Fish Pier
Fish Pier
Bank of America Pavilion
Congress St
Silver Line Way
90
A
Harpoon Brewery
Northern Ave
Fid Kennedy Ave
Dolphin Way
Anchor Way
Bollard Way
Capstan Way
B St
Tide St
Channel St
Harbor St
Summer St
Fargo St
Dry Dock Ave-Design Center Pl
Boston Design Center
Design Center Pl
Dry Dock Ave
Black Falcon Ave
Boston Marine Industrial Park
Boston Marine Industrial Park
Black Falcon Terminal
10
Summer St-Power House St
Power House St
Elkins St
Bay State Pl
E 1st St-M St
City Point
E 1st St
Acadia St
City Point Ct
Lawfen Pl
E 2nd St
E 2nd St
E 3rd St
E 3rd St
Marine Park
Burnham Pl
Barnard Pl
Emmet St
K St
M St
Ind Sq Park
N St
O St
P St
Giant Unholy Rat of Disease
Emerson St
I St
E Broadway
Dean Way
Farragut Rd
Pleasure Bay
B
E 4th St
H St
E 5th St
L St
Cutler Ct
Beckler Ave
Swallow St
Twomey Ct
Story St
E 6th St
Lennon Ct
Colebrook St
Burrill Pl
E 7th St
Bantry Way
Head Island Cswy
Springer St
Brewster St
Bay View Pl
Henderson Ave
Hart Pl
Viking Pl
E 8th St
L Street Tavern
Hardy St
William J Day Blvd
Hamlin St
Marine Rd
Tickner St
Deadys Ln
William J Day Blvd
L Street Boathouse
1/4 mile
.25 km

Known as a working class Irish 'hood in a very Irish city, Southie's ethnic and socioeconomic makeup is slowly changing. Many young professionals, swayed by Southie's charm and priced out of other neighborhoods, are renovating triple-deckers.

Landmarks

- **Bank of America Pavilion** •
  290 Northern Ave [Massachusetts Tpke]
  617-728-1690
  Music venue.
- **Black Falcon Terminal** •
  1 Black Falcon Ave [Design Center Pl]
  617-330-1500
  Heavily trafficked cruise boat terminal.
- **Boston Design Center** •
  1 Design Center Pl [Black Falcon Ave]
  617-338-6610
  For interior design junkies; several dozen showrooms.
- **Boston Fish Pier** • 212 Northern Ave [D St]
  Opened in 1914, the oldest working fish port.
- **Giant Unholy Rat of Disease** • P St
  OMG! Kill it. It's dead? KILL IT AGAIN!
- **Harpoon Brewery** •
  306 Northern Ave [Harbor St]
  617-574-9551
  Brewery tours, seasonal special events.
- **L Street Bathhouse** • William J Day Blvd & L St
  Old-timey bathhouse, home of the L Street Brownies.
- **L Street Tavern** • 658 E 8th St [L St]
  617-268-4335
  Infinitely better than "Cheers," Damon's pub in that movie.
- **World Trade Center Boston** •
  200 Seaport Blvd [World Trade Center Ave]
  617-385-5000
  Event space that's part of "The Seaport Experience."

Nightlife

- **L Street Tavern** • 658 E 8th St [L St]
  617-268-4335
  No nonsense local. Appeared in *Good Will Hunting*.
- **Murphy's Law** • 837 Summer St [E 1st St]
  617-269-6667
  Occasional live acoustic acts.
- **The Punk and Poet** • 658 E Broadway [K St]
  617-269-2537
  For socializing and television watching.

Restaurants

- **Aura** • 1 Seaport Ln [Northern Ave]
  617-385-4300 • $$$$
  Seafood for doing deals over.
- **Cafe Mamtaz** • 87 L St [Emerson St]
  617-464-4800 • $$
  Finally, ethnic food comes to Southie. For real this time.
- **Café Porto Bello** • 672 E Broadway [K St]
  617-269-7680 • $$
  Straight-forward, honest Italian.
- **Galley Diner** • 11 P St [E 2nd St]
  617-464-1024 • $
  Of *No Reservations* fame.
- **L Street Diner & Pizzeria** • 108 L St [E 5th St]
  617-268-1155 • $
  Southie standby.
- **Local 149** • 149 P St [E 6th St]
  617-269-0900 • $$
  Replacing a beloved local isn't easy, but the best beer selection in Boston helps.
- **LTK** • 225 Northern Ave [D St]
  617-330-7430 • $$$
  Hip cousin to Legal chain has attentive service, iPod docks.
- **No Name Restaurant** •
  15 Fish Pier St E [Northern Ave]
  617-423-2705 • $$
  Attracts tourists and waterfront workers alike.
- **The Punk and Poet** • 658 E Broadway [K St]
  617-269-2537 • $$
  For socializing and television watching.

During the summer, sea-bathers gather at the beaches along Dorchester Bay, or "The Irish Riviera." Good beer spots abound—take a tour of **Harpoon Brewery** for the samples of the freshest possible ale. Take your pick from several great restaurants along the waterfront or hit up **No Name Restaurant** for reliable seafood.

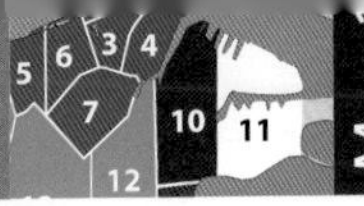

Shopping

- **K and 8th Street Market** • 362 K St [8th St]
  617-269-9810
  Old school neighborhood market, fantastic meats.
- **Ku De Ta** • 663 E Broadway [K St]
  617-269-0008
  A slice of Newbury St prices, in Southie.
- **Miller's Market** • 336 K St [E 7th St]
  857-696-0225
  Apparently, the coldest beer in town.
- **Stapleton Floral** •
  635 E Broadway [Emerson St]
  617-269-7271
  Florist.
- **Stapleton Floral** • 200 Seaport Blvd [D St]
  617-399-9960
  Strategically designed horticultural fauna to please the eye…? Florist.

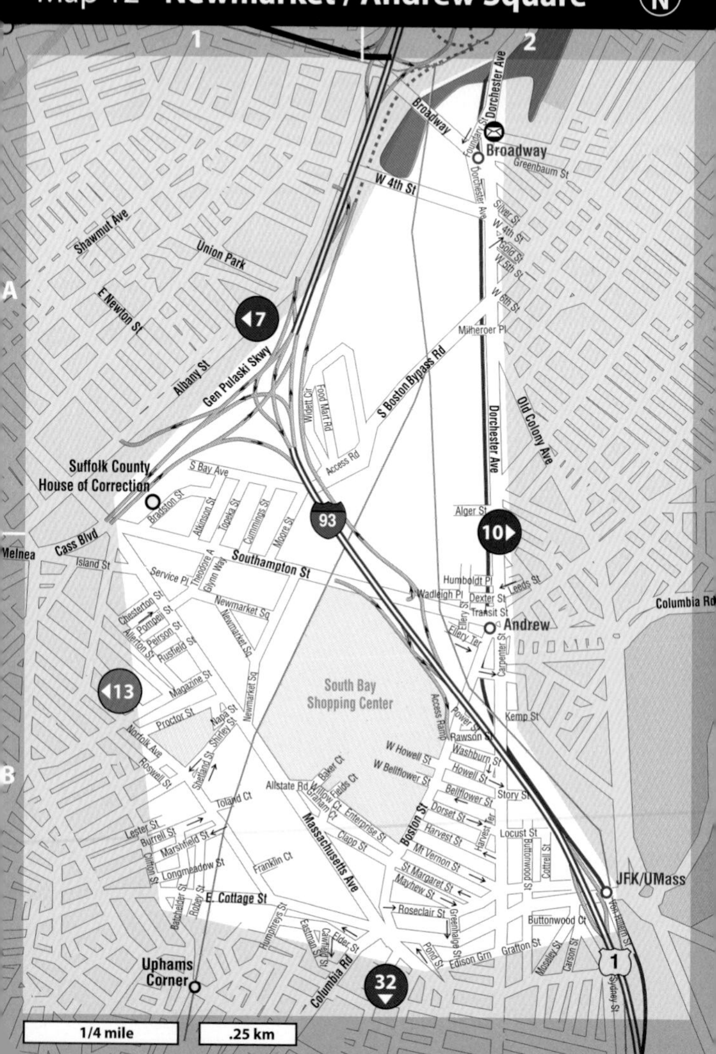

Map 12 • Newmarket / Andrew Square
N
1
2
A
B
Broadway
Dorchester Ave
Foundary St
Broadway
Greenbaum St
W 4th St
Silver St
W 4th St
Gold St
W 5th St
W 6th St
Milheroer Pl
Shawmut Ave
Union Park
E Newton St
7
Albany St
Gen Pulaski Skwy
Widett Cir
Food Mart Rd
S Boston Bypass Rd
Dorchester Ave
Old Colony Ave
Access Rd
Suffolk County
House of Correction
S Bay Ave
Bradston St
Atkinson St
Topeka St
Cummings St
Moore St
93
Alger St
10
Melnea
Cass Blvd
Island St
Theodore A Glynn Way
Southampton St
Service Pl
Humboldt Pl
Wadleigh Pl
Dexter St
Leeds St
Transit St
Columbia Rd
Ellery St
Ellery Ter
Andrew
Carpenter St
Newmarket Sq
Chesterton St
Pompeii St
Allerton St
Peirson St
Rusfield St
Newmarket Sq
Newmarket Sq
Magazine St
13
South Bay
Shopping Center
Access Ramp
Power St
Rawson St
Kemp St
Proctor St
Napa St
Shirley St
Norfolk Ave
Roswell St
Shetland St
W Howell St
W Bellflower St
Washburn St
Howell St
Bellflower St
Story St
Baker Ct
Allstate Rd
Willow Ct
Fields Ct
Graham Ct
Enterprise St
Toland Ct
Boston St
Dorset St
Harvest St
Harvest Ter
Locust St
Lester St
Burrell St
Marshfield St
Massachusetts Ave
Clapp St
Mt Vernon St
Buttonwood St
Cottrell St
Clifton St
Longmeadow St
Franklin Ct
St Margaret St
Mayhew St
JFK/UMass
Batchelder St
Robey St
E. Cottage St
Roseclair St
Greenhalge St
Buttonwood Ct
Von Hillern St
Humphreys St
Eastman St
Cawfield St
Elder St
Pond St
Edison Grn
Grafton St
Moseley St
Carson St
1
Sydney St
Uphams
Corner
Columbia Rd
32
1/4 mile
.25 km

Food distributors, u-store warehouses, and the big box chains at South Bay Shopping Center are the heart of this commercial and industrial area. Unless you've got a trip to Target, Home Depot, or are visiting family at the Suffolk County House of Correction, you'll find only the fraying edges of Southie, Dorchester, and Roxbury worth a deeper look.

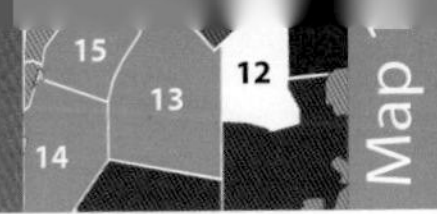

Landmarks

- **Suffolk County House of Correction •** 20 Bradston St [Southampton St]
  617-635-1000
  Just so you know.

Nightlife

- **Dot Tavern •** 840 Dorchester Ave [Harvest St]
  617-288-6288
  Neighborhood local.
- **Sports Connection Bar & Grill •** 560 Dorchester Ave [Leeds St]
  617-268-4119
  Featuring "a big screen TV."

Restaurants

- **224 Boston Street •** 224 Boston St [St Margaret St]
  617-265-1217 • $$$
  Big Portions, Good Prices! Oh crap!
- **Andrew Square House of Pizza •** 395 Dorchester St [Dorchester Ave]
  617-268-1940 • $
  No frills Greek-style pizza.
- **The Avenue Grille •** 856 Dorchester Ave [Mt Vernon St]
  617-288-8000 • $$
  Always something tasty here. A good choice.
- **Baltic Deli & Café •** 632 Dorchester Ave [Father Songin Way]
  617-268-2435 • $
  Foods from the old country.
- **Café Polonia •** 611 Dorchester Ave [Boston St]
  617-269-0110 • $
  Polish. Small, inviting, authentic. Have a Zywiec.
- **The Hen House Wings 'n Waffles •** 1033 Massachusetts Ave [Proctor St]
  617-442-9464 • $
  Chicken, waffles, cholesterol.
- **Liberty Diner •** 1003 Massachusetts Ave [Magazine St]
  617-442-9262 • $
  Who doesn't love a good egg sandwich?
- **Restaurant Laura •** 688 Columbia Rd [Elder St]
  617-825-9004 • $$
  Scary outside, lovely Cabo Verde inside. Live music.
- **Singh's Roti Shop •** 692 Columbia Rd [Elder St]
  617-282-7977 • $
  Huge roti. Also try the channa doubles.
- **Taqueria Casa Real •** 860 Dorchester Ave [Mt Vernon St]
  617-282-3135 • $
  Mexican; good hot sauce options.
- **Victoria's Diner •** 1024 Massachusetts Ave [Proctor St]
  617-442-5965 • $
  Great diner chow, loads of sausage, and open 24 hours on weekends!

Shopping

- **Home Depot •** 5 Allstate Rd [Massachusetts Ave]
  617-442-6110
  Got wood?
- **Marshalls •** 8 Allstate Rd [Massachusetts Ave]
  617-442-5050
  Discount clothing and other stuff.

Map 13 • Roxbury

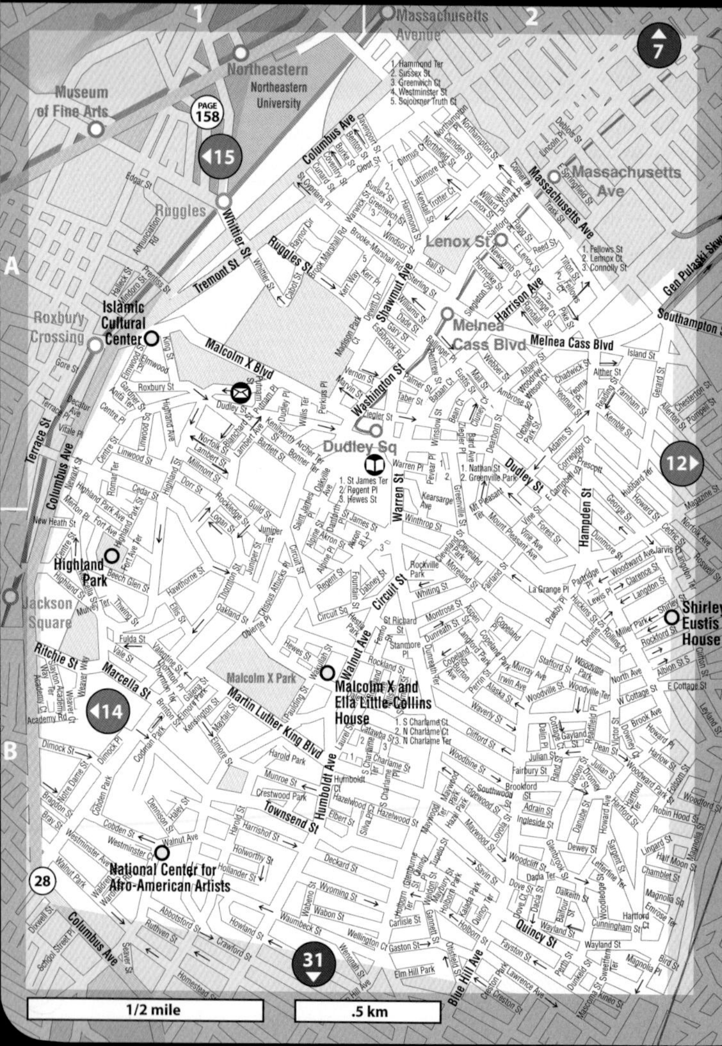
1
2
A
B
Massachusetts Avenue
7
Northeastern
Northeastern University
Museum of Fine Arts
PAGE 158
15
Ruggles
Whittier St
Tremont St
Ruggles St
Columbus Ave
1. Hammond Ter
2. Sussex St
3. Greenwich Ct
4. Westminster St
5. Sojourner Truth Ct
Massachusetts Ave
Lenox St
Shawmut Ave
Harrison Ave
1. Fellows St
2. Lenox Ct
3. Connolly St
Gen Pulaski Skwy
Southampton St
Islamic Cultural Center
Roxbury Crossing
Malcolm X Blvd
Melnea Cass Blvd
Washington St
Dudley Sq
Warren St
Dudley St
12
1. St James Ter
2. Regent Pl
3. Hewes St
1. Nathan St
2. Greenville Park
Terrace St
Highland Park
Jackson Square
Circuit St
Walnut Ave
Hampden St
Shirley Eustis House
Ritchie St
Marcella St
14
Malcolm X Park
Malcolm X and Ella Little-Collins House
Martin Luther King Blvd
1. S Charlame Ct
2. N Charlame Ct
3. N Charlame Ter
Humboldt Ave
Townsend St
National Center for Afro-American Artists
28
Columbus Ave
31
Blue Hill Ave
Quincy St
1/2 mile
.5 km

There's a beauty to Roxbury, despite its roughness. Dudley Square is Roxbury's commercial center, but businesses are also finding opportunity closer to the busy Orange Line and along Blue Hill Avenue. Highlights include **The National Center of Afro-American Artists**, the largest mosque in New England, and the view from Fort Hill.

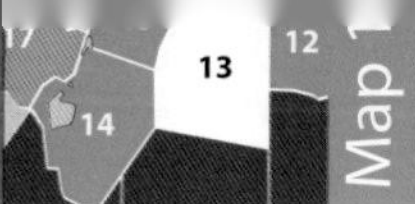

Landmarks

- **Highland Park** • Fort Ave & Beech Glen St
  Little visited Fort Hill monument with great views
- **Islamic Cultural Center** •
  100 Malcolm X Blvd [Elmwood St]
  617-427-2636
  Largest mosque in the Northeast.
- **Malcolm X Ella Little Collins House** •
  72 Dale St [Wakullah St]
  Malcolm X lived here with his sister during formative years.
- **National Center for Afro-American Artists** •
  300 Walnut Ave [Cobden St]
  617-442-8614
  Puddingstone mansion holds Nubian tomb model, afternoon hours.
- **Shirley-Eustis House** •
  33 Shirley St [Clifton St]
  617-442-2275
  Tour this 18th-century royal governor's country estate.

Nightlife

- **C&S Tavern** • 380 Warren St [Maywood St]
  617-442-7023
  Neighborhood local.
- **Slade's** • 958 Tremont St [Davenport St]
  617-442-4600
  Dancing, mostly R&B and hip-hop.

Restaurants

- **Ali's Roti Restaurant** •
  1035 Tremont St [Coventry St]
  617-427-1079 • $
  Indian food lovers will take naturally to this Trinidadian gem.
- **Dayib Cafe** • 722 Shawmut Ave [Williams St]
  617-427-0099 • $
  Authentic Middle Eastern. The tea is an absolute must.
- **Haley House Bakery Café** •
  12 Dade St [Washington St]
  617-445-0900 • $
  The best jerk chicken. Ever.
- **Ideal Sub Shop** • 522 Dudley St [Burrell St]
  617-442-1560 • $
  The freshest, largest, best-deal-ever subs.
- **M & M Ribs** •
  155 Southampton St [Theodore Glynn Way]
  617-306-0788 • $
  Saucy ribs, tangy baked beans, gooey mac 'n' cheese.
- **Merengue** • 156 Blue Hill Ave [Julian St]
  617-445-5403 • $$
  Dominican. Tropical vibe. Gets props from the Sox.
- **Peking House** • 160 Dudley St [Warren St]
  617-442-9215 • $$
  Solid chicken dishes and fried rice.
- **Silver Slipper Restaurant** •
  2387 Washington St [Dudley St]
  617-442-4853 • $
  Breakfast in all its greasy glory; great grits.
- **Ugi's Subs** • 68 Warren St [Dudley St]
  617-427-7032 • $
  Old school sandwich shop with a mean steak and cheese.

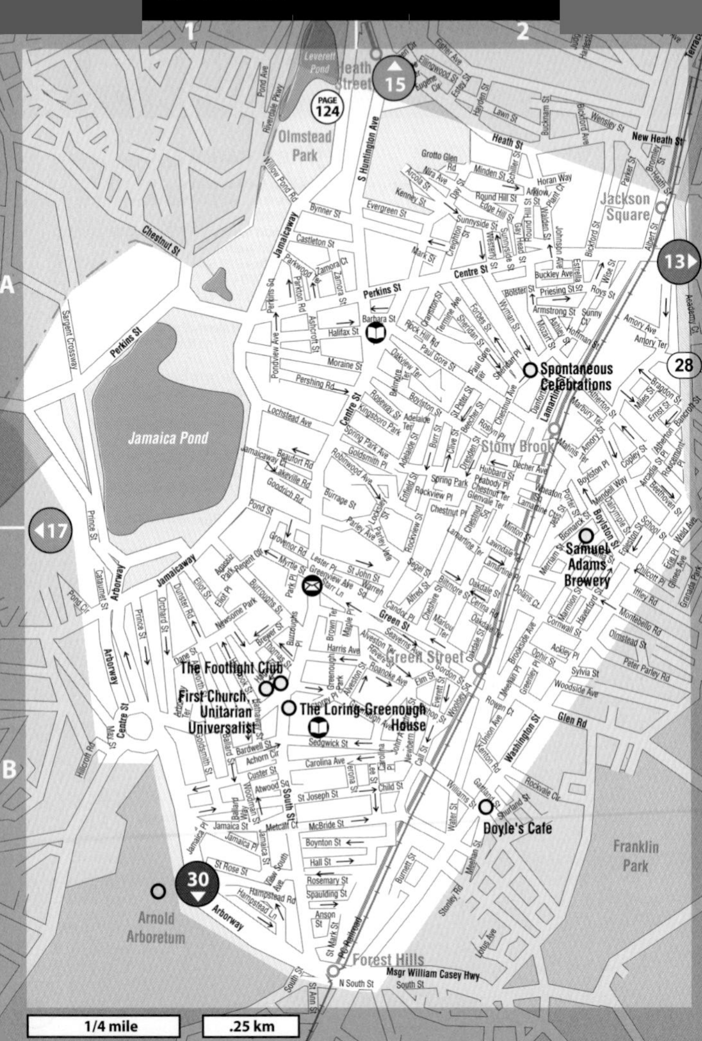
1
2
A
B
Leverett Pond
Heath Street
15
PAGE 124
Olmstead Park
Jackson Square
13
28
17
30
Jamaica Pond
Stony Brook
Green Street
Forest Hills
Arnold Arboretum
Franklin Park
Spontaneous Celebrations
Samuel Adams Brewery
The Footlight Club
First Church, Unitarian Universalist
The Loring-Greenough House
Doyle's Cafe
S Huntington Ave
Jamaicaway
Riverdale Pkwy
Pond Ave
Willow Pond Rd
Chestnut St
Perkins St
Sargent Crossway
Prince St
Arborway
Centre St
Heath St
New Heath St
Lamartine St
Washington St
South St
Boylston St
Green St
Glen Rd
Msgr William Casey Hwy
N South St
Amory Ave
Amory Ter
Lochstead Ave
Pershing Rd
Moraine St
Halifax St
Castleton St
Bynner St
Evergreen St
Minden St
Round Hill St
Lawn St
Wensley St
Mark St
Sunnyside St
Dunster Rd
Orchard St
Eliot St
Pond St
Sedgwick St
Carolina Ave
St Joseph St
McBride St
Boynton St
Hall St
Rosemary St
Spaulding St
Hampstead Rd
St Rose St
Jamaica Pl
Williams St
Brookside Ave
Olmstead St
Peter Parley Rd
Montebello Rd
Rockvale Cir
Stonley Rd
Lotus Ave
South St
St Ann St
Pc Railroad
1/4 mile
.25 km

Heavy gentrification in Jamaica Plain means that the population of new parents pushing strollers is at an all-time high. Other residents include artists, hipsters, young professionals, eco-friendly folk, and lesbians. Perhaps the neighborhood with the most access to green areas, Jamaica Pond and the Arnold Arboretum provide ample space for joggers to sprint and bikers to ride. The addition of a **Whole Foods**, joining the **Harvest Co-op Market**, has solidified the community's reputation as being pro-organic and locally farmed foods.

Landmarks

- **Arnold Arboretum** • 125 Arborway [Centre St]
  617-524-1718
  The most famous collection of trees in America, an oasis.
- **Doyle's Café** •
  3484 Washington St [Williams St]
  617-524-2345
  A century's worth of pols have slapped backs here.
- **First Church in Jamaica Plain** •
  6 Eliot St [Centre St]
  617-524-1634
  The first church in Jamaica Plain, ca. 1853. Impressive stone facade, creepy graveyard.
- **The Footlight Club** • 7 Eliot St [Centre St]
  617-524-3200
  Oldest running theatre in the US.
- **The Loring-Greenough House** •
  12 South St [Centre St]
  617-524-3158
  Built as a country estate in 1760. Open for tours.
- **Samuel Adams Brewery** •
  30 Germania St [Brookside Ave]
  617-368-5080
  Love the product, but not much of an experience.
- **Spontaneous Celebrations** •
  45 Danforth St [Boylston St]
  617-524-6373
  JP community arts organization.

Nightlife

- **Bella Luna Restaurant and Milky Way Lounge** •
  284 Amory St [Minton St]
  617-524-6060
  Dance club-Chuck E. Cheese's hybrid.
- **Brendan Behan Pub** •
  378 Centre St [Sheridan St]
  617-522-5386
  Well-liked Irish local. Relaxed atmosphere.
- **Canary Square** •
  435 S Huntington Ave [Moraine St]
  617-524-2500
  Swanky haven for craft beer fanatics.
- **Costello's Tavern** • 723 Centre St [Harris Ave]
  617-522-9263
  Friendly JP tavern; decent food and darts.
- **Doyle's Café** •
  3484 Washington St [Williams St]
  617-524-2345
  Trusty Irish landmark. Good grub and a mean Bloody Mary.
- **Jeanie Johnston Pub** • 144 South St [Hall St]
  617-983-9432
  Darts, karaoke, live music, local flavor.
- **Midway Cafe** •
  3496 Washington St [Williams St]
  617-524-9038
  Local watering hole featuring a variety of live bands.
- **Samuel Adams Brewery** •
  30 Germania St [Brookside Ave]
  617-368-5080
  Tours and samples.

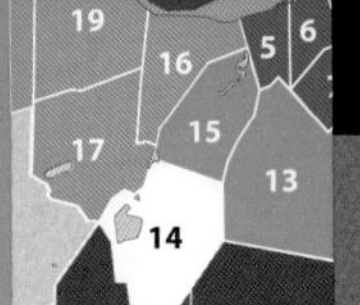

Jamaica Plain

Restaurants

- **Alex's Chimis** • 358 Centre St [Forbes St]
  617-522-5201 • $
  How can you complain about a giant plate full of chicken and chicharrones?
- **The Blue Nile** • 389 Centre St [Day St]
  617-522-6453 • $$
  Ethiopian. Heaping servings for small prices.
- **Bukhara** • 701 Centre St [Burroughs St]
  617-522-2195 • $$
  Well-liked Indian bistro. Level of tastiness is like a mystery wheel.
- **Cafe Beirut** • 654 Centre St [Green St]
  617-522-7264 • $
  Scrumptious Middle Eastern street food on the cheap.
- **Captain Nemo's** • 367 Centre St [Creighton St]
  617-971-0100 • $
  Run by sweet as pie siblings.
- **The Dogwood Café** •
  3712 Washington St [Arborway]
  617-522-7997 • $$
  Enjoy your wood-fired pizzas while listening to an actual human playing an actual piano.
- **Doyle's Café** •
  3484 Washington St [Williams St]
  617-524-2345 • $$
  The history and great atmosphere make up for the mediocre food.
- **El Oriental de Cuba** •
  416 Centre St [Paul Gore St]
  617-524-6464 • $$
  Always packed. So, be ready to wait for your cubano.
- **FoMu** • 617 Centre St [St John St]
  617-553-2299 • $
  Damn good vegan ice cream. (It's vegan?!)
- **Galway House** • 710 Centre St [Burroughs St]
  617-524-9677 • $
  Resisting the onion rings is futile.
- **The Haven** • 2 Perkins St [Centre St]
  617-524-2836 • $$
  Fortifying Scottish fare. Heart attack alert: deep fried Mars bars.
- **JP Seafood Café** • 730 Centre St [Harris Ave]
  617-983-5177 • $$
  Some like it. Some don't. I don't.
- **Miami Restaurant** •
  381 Centre St [Sheridan St]
  617-522-4644 • $
  Go for the cubano…don't leave without a beef patty.
- **Monumental Cupcakes** •
  36 South St [Sedgwick St]
  617-522-1729 • $
  Epic desserts (obviously) and rotating vegetarian/vegan lunch specials.
- **The Real Deal** • 736 Centre St [Harris Ave]
  617-522-1181 • $
  Sandwiches and wraps named after gangsters.
- **Ruggerio's** • 3345 Washingston St [Green St]
  617-522-7184 • $
  Everything sold can be delivered. Yes, even cigarettes and booze.
- **Sorella's** • 388 Centre St [Sheridan St]
  617-524-2016 • $
  Worth waiting for famous, diner-style breakfasts.
- **Ten Tables** • 597 Centre St [Pond St]
  617-524-8810 • $$$
  Short, precise, inspired menu. Delicious.
- **Tostado Sandwich Bar** •
  300 Centre St [Estrella St]
  617-477-8691 • $
  New spins on standard Cubans. Freshest fruit smoothies around.
- **Tres Gatos** • 470 Centre St [Boylston St]
  617-477-4851 • $$
  Record store, tapas bar and bookstore ingeniously fused.
- **Vee Vee** • 763 Centre St [Elliot St]
  617-522-0145 • $$
  Not only cares about your eating experience but also where the food comes from.
- **Wonder Spice Café** •
  697 Centre St [Burroughs St]
  617-522-0200 • $$
  Tasty Cambodian/Thai. Well named. Get their Crispy Fish!
- **Yely's Coffee Shop** •
  284 Centre St [Chestnut Ave]
  617-524-2204 • $
  Coffee? The counter is stacked full of pork, chicken, sausages, and plantains.

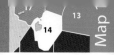

Centre Street functions as the main artery in JP, lined with restaurants, boutiques, and vintage/consignment shops. **The Blue Nile** dishes out heaping sharing-sized platters of Ethiopian delicacies on the cheap. If Middle Eastern's your bag, it doesn't get much better than the shawarma at **Café Beirut**. Grab a Guinness and a shot of Fernet at the **Brendan Behan Pub**. Jackson Square and Washington Street offer the flavors of its Puerto Rican, Dominican, and Cape Verdean communities.

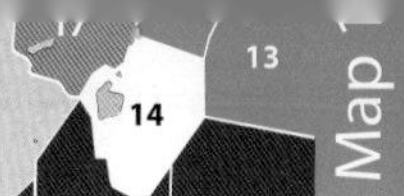

Shopping

- **40 South Street** • 40 South St [Sedgwick St]
  617-522-5066
  Retro duds, mostly from the '80s.
- **Blue Frog Bakery** • 3 Green St [Centre St]
  617-983-3765
  Bread pudding muffins, whoopie pies, coffee and espresso.
- **Boing! JP's Toy Shop** •
  667 Centre St [Harris Ave]
  617-522-7800
  Friendly toy shop.
- **Boomerangs** • 716 Centre St [Burroughs St]
  617-524-5120
  Used clothing and housewares.
- **City Feed and Supply** •
  66 Boylston St [Chestnut Ave]
  617-524-1657
  Popular neighborhood grocery, meeting spot.
- **Eye Q Optical** • 615 Centre St [Pond St]
  617-983-3937
  Designer eyeglasses.
- **Fat Ram's Pumpkin Tattoo** •
  374 Centre St [Sheridan St]
  617-522-6444
  Skilled ink artists with degrees in fine art.
- **Fire Opal** • 683 Centre St [Seaverns Ave]
  617-524-0262
  Upscale craft gallery.
- **Hatched** • 668 Centre St [Seaverns Ave]
  617-524-5402
  Small boutique specializing in organic clothing for little ones.
- **J.P. Licks** • 659 Centre St [Starr Ln]
  617-524-6740
  Popular ice cream shop.
- **JP Knit and Stitch** • 461 Centre St [Moraine St]
  617-942-2118
  Yarn store + knitting classes.
- **Kitchenwitch** • 671 Centre St [Seaverns Ave]
  617-524-6800
  Adorable cooking gadgets galore.
- **Salmagundi** • 765 Centre St [Eliot St]
  617-522-5047
  Check out the coolest selection in the city.
- **Tres Gatos** • 470 Centre St [Boylston St]
  617-477-4851
  Record store, tapas bar and bookstore ingeniously fused.
- **When Pigs Fly** • 613 Centre St [Pond St]
  617-522-4948
  Old-world style, handcrafted, artisanal breads.

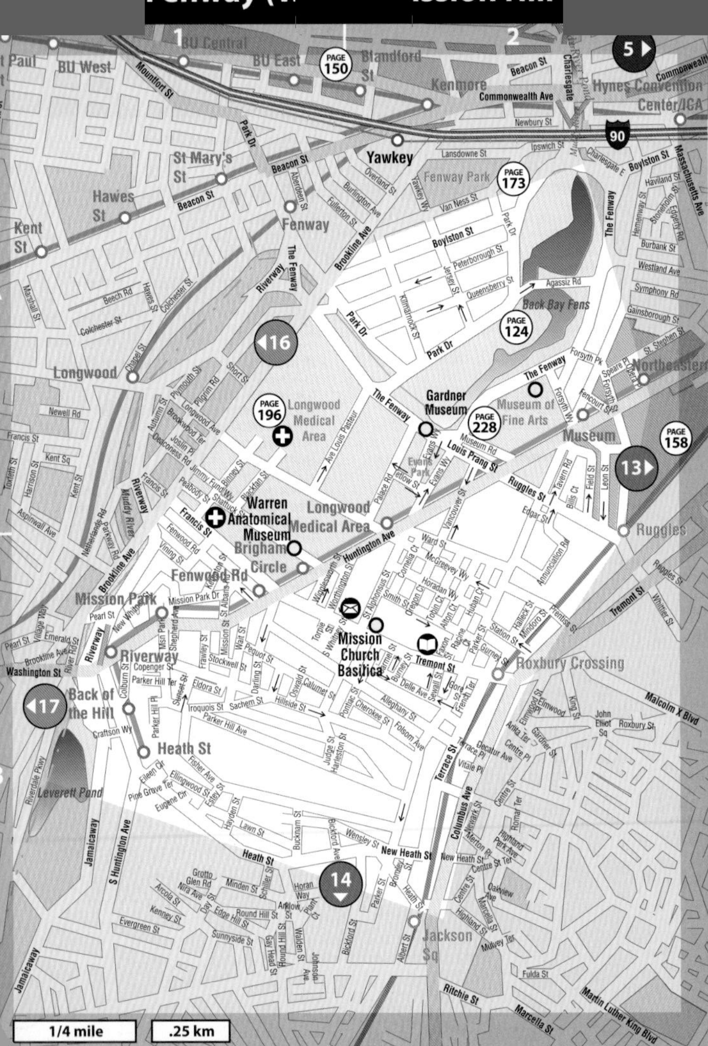
Fenway (W
ission Hill
1
2
BU Central
BU West
BU East
St Paul
PAGE 150
Blandford St
Kenmore
Beacon St
Charlesgate
Commonwealth Ave
Hynes Convention Center/ICA
5
Newbury St
90
Mountfort St
Park Dr
Yawkey
Lansdowne St
Ipswich St
Boylston St
Massachusetts Ave
St Mary's St
Beacon St
Overland St
Fenway Park
PAGE 173
Hawes St
Aberdeen St
Burlington Ave
Yawkey Wy
Van Ness St
Kent St
Fenway
Fullerton St
Brookline Ave
The Fenway
Boylston St
Peterborough St
Haviland St
Hemenway St
Burbank St
Westland Ave
Symphony Rd
Gainsborough St
St. Stephen St
Riverway
Jersey St
Queensberry St
Agassiz Rd
Back Bay Fens
Marshall St
Beech Rd
Hawes St
Colchester St
Colchester St
Park Dr
Kilmarnock St
PAGE 124
Park Dr
16
Longwood
Chapel St
Short St
Plymouth St
Pilgrim Rd
Forsyth Pk
Speare Pl
Northeastern
The Fenway
Newell Rd
Autumn St
Longwood Ave
Brookwood Ter
Joslin Pl
Deaconess Rd
PAGE 196
Longwood Medical Area
Ave Louis Pasteur
The Fenway
Gardner Museum
Museum of Fine Arts
PAGE 228
Forsyth Wy
Fencourt St
Museum
PAGE 158
Francis St
Kent Sq
Toxteth St
Harrison St
Kent St
Jimmy Fund Wy
Binney St
Museum Rd
Louis Prang St
13
Evans Way Park
Evans Wy
Palace Rd
Tetlow St
Vancouver St
Ruggles St
Tavern Rd
Field St
Leon St
Riverway
Muddy River
Francis St
Peabody St
Shattuck St
Blackfan St
Aspinwall Ave
Netherlands Rd
Parkway Rd
Warren Anatomical Museum
Longwood Medical Area
Francis St
Fenwood Rd
Vining St
Brigham Circle
Huntington Ave
Ward St
McGreevey Wy
Edgar St
Bills Ct
Ruggles
Annunciation Rd
Ruggles St
Brookline Ave
Fenwood Rd
Mission Park
Mission Park Dr
St Albans
Wigglesworth St
Worthington St
Cornelia Ct
St Alphonsus St
Smith St
Oregon Ct
Horadan Wy
Tobin Ct
Alton Ct
Huban Ct
Halleck St
Mindoro St
Prentiss St
Tremont St
Whittier St
Pearl St
Village Way
Emerald St
New Whitney St
Msn Park
Shepherd Ave
Fawley St
Mission St
Wait St
Pequot St
Torpie St
S Whitney St
Mission Church Basilica
Tremont St
Racine Ct
Parker St
Station St
Gurney St
Roxbury Crossing
Pearl St
Riverway
Brookline Ave
River Rd
Riverway
Copenger St
Stockwell St
Darling St
Oswald St
Calumet St
Carmel St
Burney St
Washington St
Parker Hill Ter
Sunset St
Eldora St
Delle Ave
Sewall St
Gore St
French Ter
Malcolm X Blvd
17
Back of the Hill
Colburn St
Iroquois St
Sachem St
Hillside St
Pontiac St
Cherokee St
Alleghany St
Elmwood St
King St
John Eliot Sq
Roxbury St
Parker Hill Pl
Parker Hill Ave
Folsom Ave
Anita Ter
Gardner St
Craftson Wy
Heath St
Judge St
Harleston St
Terrace St
Terrace Pl
Decatur Ave
Centre Pl
Vitale Pl
Fisher Ave
Riverdale Pkwy
Leverett Pond
Eileen Cir
Pine Grove Ter
Ellingwood St
Estey St
Eugene Cir
Hayden St
Columbus Ave
Newark St
Centre St
Romar Ter
Lawn St
Bucknam St
Bickford Ave
Wensley St
Merton Pl
Highland Park Ave
Jamaicaway
S Huntington Ave
Heath St
New Heath St
New Heath St
Centre St Ter
Grotto Glen Rd
Minden St
Schiller St
14
Horan Way
Oakview Ave
Arcola St
Nira Ave
Day St
Edge Hill St
Round Hill St
Parker St
Bromley St
Heath St
Highland St
Marcella St
Kenney St
Evergreen St
Sunnyside St
Gay Head St
Hill St
Walden St
Johnson Ave
Bickford St
Albert St
Jackson Sq
Mulvey Ter
Fulda St
Jamaicaway
Ritchie St
Marcella St
Martin Luther King Blvd
1/4 mile
.25 km

Ah, Mission Thrill. The place where culture, education, and sports meet, you can wander among fine art museums, green parks, eclectic colleges, top medical centers, and historic Fenway Park. While high-rise condos are changing the face of Fenway, Mission Hill remains a funky mix of students, families, and young professionals.

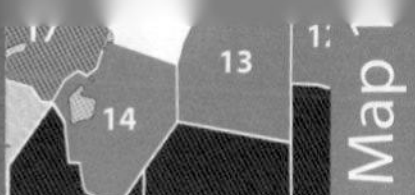

Landmarks

- **Isabella Stewart Gardner Museum •**
  25 Evans Way [Palace Rd]
  617-566-1401
  Eccentric collection highlighting the Renaissance and the pleasures of having money. A gem.
- **Mission Church of Boston •**
  1545 Tremont St [Pontiac St]
  617-445-2600
  Mission Hill landmark. Recently renovated.
- **Museum of Fine Arts •**
  465 Huntington Ave [Museum Rd]
  617-267-9300
  Arguably one of the top museums in the country. Go for the Copleys.
- **Warren Anatomical Museum •**
  10 Shattuck St [Binney St]
  617-432-6196
  Phineas Gage's skull and other medical oddities.

Nightlife

- **The Baseball Tavern •**
  1270 Boylston St [Yawkey Way]
  617-867-6526
  Sports tavern with a focus on Fenway.
- **Flann O'Brien's •**
  1619 Tremont St [Wigglesworth St]
  617-566-7744
  Spirited Brigham Circle local.
- **Jerry Remy's •** 1265 Boylston St [Yawkey Way]
  617-236-7369
  Staggering amount of TVs and boisterous Sox fans.
- **Machine •** 1254 Boylston St [Ipswich St]
  617-536-1950
  Large gay club.
- **Punter's Pub •** 450 Huntington Ave [Parker St]
  617-427-2005
  Student dive.
- **Ramrod •** 1254 Boylston St [Yawkey Wy]
  617-266-2986
  Gay denim-and-leather crowd; various theme nights.
- **Sweet Caroline's •**
  1260 Boylston St [Ipswich St]
  617-424-1260
  Bar food has never been so good (so good! so good!).

Fenway (West) / Mission Hill

Restaurants

- **Bravo** • 465 Huntington Ave [Museum Rd]
  617-369-3474 • $$$$
  At the MFA. Stick with the art.
- **Brigham Circle Chinese Food** •
  728 Huntington Ave [Fenwood Rd]
  617-278-2000 • $
  Two words: Wonton soup. Or is that three? Won ton soup? Eh. Get it.
- **Chacho's** • 1502 Tremont St [Burney St]
  617-445-6738 • $
  Pizza and subs.
- **Chicken Lou's** • 50 Forsyth St [Greenleaf St]
  617-859-7017 • $
  "Sex on a bagel" and spicy fries. Slobber.
- **Citizen Public House and Oyster Bar** •
  1310 Boylston St [Kilmarnock St]
  617-450-9000 • $$
  Whole suckling pig roasts. You read that right.
- **Crispy Dough Pizzeria** •
  1514 Tremont St [Burney St]
  617-445-7799 • $
  Specialty thin crust pies and slices.
- **Halal Indian Cuisine** •
  736 Huntington Ave [Fenwood Rd]
  617-232-5000 • $
  Decent and different for this part of town.
- **J.P. Licks** • 1618 Tremont St [Huntington Ave]
  617-566-6676 • $
  Homemade ice cream plus cafe.
- **Longwood Grille & Bar** •
  342 Longwood Ave [Brookline Ave]
  617-232-9770 • $$$
  Hotel restaurant serving medical community designed like a chain restaurant.
- **Mama's Place** • 764 Huntington Ave [Wait St]
  617-566-1300 • $
  Greek goodness. Gyros and baklava.

Fenway (West) / Mission Hill

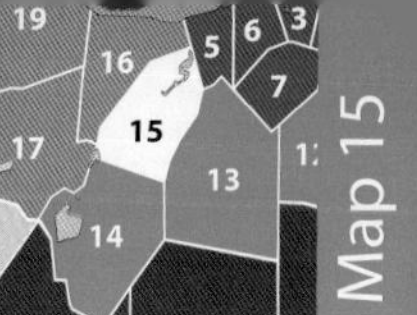

Foodies began flocking to the booming Fenway side of Boylston Street after places like **Tasty Burger** and **Citizen's Public House** set up shop. In Mission Hill, **Penguin Cafe** makes delicious pizzas with creative toppings, and the best pints flow at **Flann O'Brien's**. **Chicken Lou's** has been a Northeastern breakfast institution for years.

- **The Mission •**
  724 Huntington Ave [Tremont St]
  617-566-1244 • $$
  Convenient, full-service bar & grill.
- **Montecristo Mexican Grill •**
  748 Huntington Ave [Fenwood Rd]
  617-232-2228 • $$
  Nachos piled high with everything except the kitchen sink.
- **Penguin Pizza •**
  735 Huntington Ave [Francis St]
  617-277-9200 • $
  Recommended, and not just for the name.
- **The Squealing Pig •**
  134 Smith St [Washington St]
  617-566-6651 • $
  Toasties served by indifferent staff.
- **Sushi Station •**
  1562 Tremont St [St Alphonsus St]
  617-738-0888 • $
  Quality maki; wallet-friendly.
- **Sweet Caroline's •**
  1260 Boylston St [Ipswich St]
  617-424-1260 • $$
  Bar food has never been so good (so good! so good!).
- **Sweet Cheeks •**
  1381 Boylston St [Kilmarnock St]
  617-266-1300 • $$
  Sloppy and smoky BBQ. Can be ordered by the pound.
- **Thaitation •** 129 Jersey St [Park Dr]
  617-585-9909 • $$
  Head and shoulders above Brown Sugar. Go for lunch.
- **Tiger Mama •**
  1363 Boylston St [Kilmarnock St]
  617-425-6262 • $$$
  Fanboy Southeast Asian cuisine enthusiastically delivered.

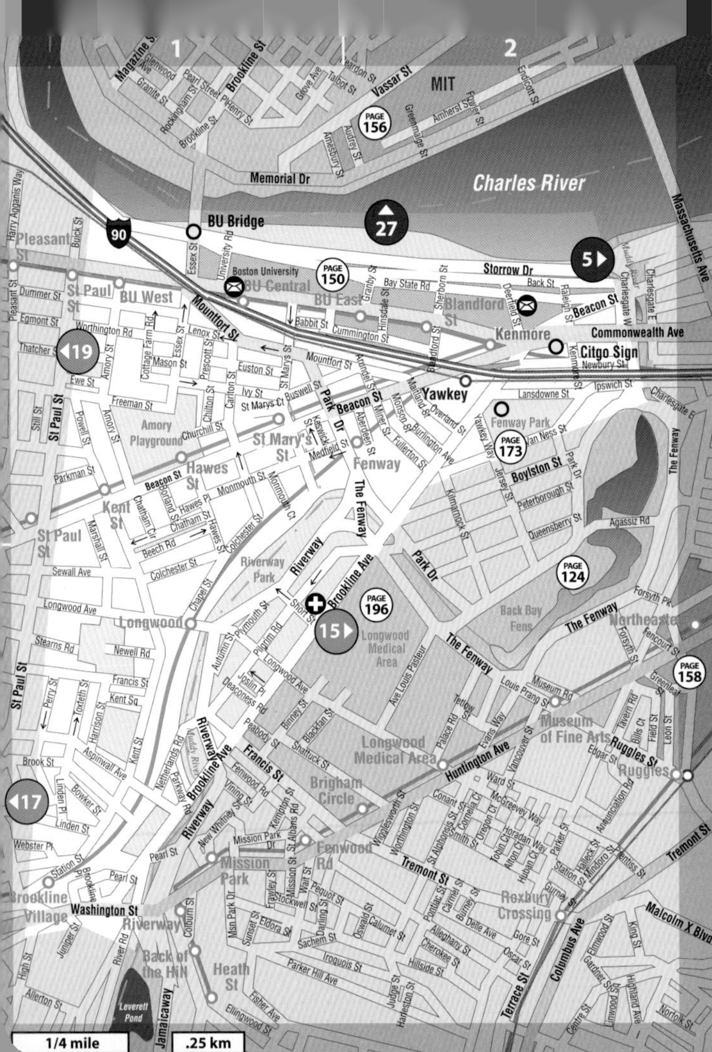
1
2
Magazine St
Glenwood Ave
Granite St
Pearl Street Pl
Henry St
Rockingham St
Brookline St
Grove Ave
Reardon St
Talbot St
Vassar St
MIT
Endicott St
Amherst St
Fowler St
Greenmalge St
PAGE 156
Audrey St
Amesbury St
Memorial Dr
Charles River
Massachusetts Ave
BU Bridge
27
90
Essex St
University Rd
Boston University
BU Central
PAGE 150
Granby St
Bay State Rd
Sherborn St
Storrow Dr
Back St
5
Deerfield St
Raleigh St
Beacon St
Charlesgate W
Charlesgate E
Harry Agganis Way
Pleasant St
Buick St
St Paul St
BU West
BU East
Hinsdale St
Blandford St
Dummer St
Egmont St
Mountfort St
Babbit St
Cummington St
Kenmore
Commonwealth Ave
Worthington Rd
Lenox St
Bradford St
Citgo Sign
Thatcher St
19
Cottage Farm Rd
Mason St
Prescott St
Euston St
St Marys St
Mountfort St
Kenmore St
Newbury St
Amory St
Ewe St
Ivy St
Arundel St
Yawkey
Ipswich St
Lansdowne St
Freeman St
Chilton St
Carlton St
St Marys Ct
Buswell St
Park Dr
Beacon St
Miner St
Maitland St
Overland St
Still St
St Paul St
Powell St
Amory Playground
Churchill St
St Mary's St
Keswick St
Aberdeen St
Monson St
Burlington Ave
Fullerton St
Yawkey Way
Fenway Park
PAGE 173
Van Ness St
The Fenway
Medfield St
Fenway
Hawes St
Parkman St
Beacon St
Borland St
Monmouth St
Monmouth Ct
Boylston St
Park Dr
Jersey St
Peterborough St
Kent St
Chatham Cir
Hawes Pl
Chatham St
Colchester St
Kilmarnock St
Queensberry St
Agassiz Rd
Marshall St
Beech Rd
The Fenway
Sewall Ave
Colchester St
Riverway Park
Riverway
Brookline Ave
Park Dr
PAGE 124
Chapel St
Longwood Ave
Plymouth St
Short St
PAGE 196
Back Bay Fens
Forsyth Pk
Longwood
15
Longwood Medical Area
The Fenway
Northeastern
Stearns Rd
Newell Rd
Autumn St
Pilgrim Rd
Fencourt St
Forsyth St
PAGE 158
Francis St
Kent Sq
Longwood Ave
Ave Louis Pasteur
Greenleaf St
Perry St
Toxteth St
Joslin Pl
Deaconess Rd
Louis Prang St
Museum Rd
Tetlow St
Harrison St
Kent St
Binney St
Blackfan St
Palace Rd
Evans Way
Vancouver St
Museum of Fine Arts
Tavern Rd
Bills Ct
Field St
Leon St
Brook St
Aspinwall Ave
Netherlands Rd
Riverway
Muddy River
Peabody St
Shattuck St
Longwood Medical Area
Huntington Ave
Edgar St
Ruggles St
Ruggles
Linden Pl
Bowker St
Brookline Ave
Parkway Rd
Fenwood Rd
Francis St
Brigham Circle
Ward St
Conant St
Cornelia Ct
McGreevey Way
Annunciation Rd
17
Linden St
Riverway
Vining St
New Whitney St
Kempton St
St Albans Rd
Wigglesworth St
Worthington St
St Alphonsus St
Smith St
Oregon Ct
Horadan Way
Parker St
Webster Pl
Pearl St
Mission Park Dr
Fenwood Rd
Tobin Ct
Alton Ct
Huban Ct
Halleck St
Mindoro St
Prentiss St
Tremont St
Station St
Mission Park
Mission St
Tremont St
Station St
Pearl St
Wait St
Pequot St
Brookline Village
Washington St
Frawley St
Stockwell St
Pontiac St
Carmel St
Burney St
Roxbury Crossing
Gurney St
Malcolm X Blvd
Riverway
Colburn St
Msn Park Dr
Eldora St
Darling St
Oswald St
Calumet St
Delle Ave
Gore St
Columbus Ave
Juniper St
Sunset St
Sachem St
Allegheny St
Oscar St
Elmwood St
King St
Back of the Hill
Heath St
Iroquois St
Cherokee St
High St
River Rd
Parker Hill Ave
Hillside St
Gardner St
Terrace St
Linwood St
Highland Ave
Allerton St
Leverett Pond
Jamaicaway
Fisher Ave
Ellingwood St
Judge St
Haleston St
Centre St
Norfolk St
1/4 mile
.25 km

Under the watchful triangular eye of the **Citgo Sign**, the Kenmore Square area is notable for sprawling Boston University, the nightclub scene on Lansdowne Street, and, of course, **Fenway Park**. Beyond Fenway and the core of Kenmore Square, urban bustle gives way to the more serene residential neighborhoods of affluent Brookline.

Landmarks

- **BU Bridge** • Essex St & Mountfort St
  Arguably Boston's best river/skyline view.
- **Citgo Sign** • Commonwealth Ave & Beacon St
  Beloved Kenmore Square landmark.
- **Fenway Park** • 4 Yawkey Way [Brookline Ave]
  617-267-9440
  Home to the Sox since 1912.

Nightlife

- **Bleacher Bar** •
  82 Lansdowne St [Brookline Ave]
  617-262-2424
  Just your average looks-into-Fenway-Park sports bar.
- **Cask 'N Flagon** •
  62 Brookline Ave [Lansdowne St]
  617-536-4840
  Just behind the Green Monster. Nothing special.
- **The Dugout** •
  722 Commonwealth Ave [St Marys St]
  617-247-8656
  Babe Ruth's basement dive bar of choice.
- **Game On!** • 82 Lansdowne St [Brookline Ave]
  617-351-7001
  Yet another sports bar near Fenway.
- **House of Blues** • 15 Lansdowne St [Ipswich St]
  888-693-2583
  Huge new Landsdowne Street spot for all things musical.
- **Lansdowne Pub** • 9 Lansdowne St [Ipswich St]
  617-247-1222
  Bawdy, brawly and lowbrow.
- **The Lower Depths** •
  476 Commonwealth Ave [Kenmore St]
  617-266-6662
  Gourmet tater tot platters and craft beer.
- **Lucky Strike Lanes** •
  145 Ipswich St [Lansdowne St]
  617-437-0300
  Uber gaming and lounge establishment.
- **Yard House** •
  126 Brookline Ave [Burlington Ave]
  617-236-4083
  Drinking a yard of beer is actually kinda awkward.

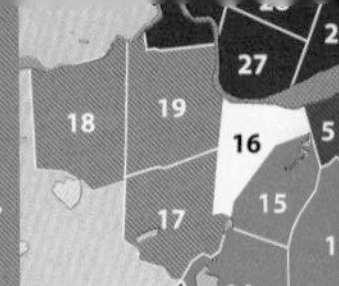

Kenmore Square / Brookline (East)

Restaurants

- **Boston Beer Works** •
  61 Brookline Ave [Lansdowne St]
  617-536-2337 • $$
  Cavernous suds shop across from Fenway Park.
- **Cornwall's** •
  654 Beacon St [Commonwealth Ave]
  617-262-3749 • $$
  Eat only to soak up pints.
- **Eastern Standard** •
  528 Commonwealth Ave [Kenmore St]
  617-532-9100 • $$$
  At the Hotel Commonwealth with lip-smackingly good drinks.
- **Emack and Bolio's** •
  140 Brookline Ave [Fullerton St]
  617-262-1569 • $
  Fruity Pebbles-encrusted cones. Need I say more?
- **India Quality** •
  484 Commonwealth Ave [Kenmore St]
  617-267-4499 • $$
  Quality Indian. The name says it all.
- **Mei Mei** •
  506 Park Drive [Buswell St]
  857-250-4959 • $$$
  Farm-to-table Chinese-American cuisine by way of food truck.
- **Noodle Street** •
  627 Commonwealth Ave [Sherborn St]
  617-536-3100 • $
  Unexpected spices transcend everyday Asian fare.
- **Nud Pob** •
  738 Commonwealth Ave [St Marys St]
  617-232-9992 • $
  Yes, you can call it "nude pub." We do.
- **O'Leary's Pub** • 1010 Beacon St [St Marys St]
  617-734-0049 • $$
  Try the Guinness stew.
- **Taberna de Haro** • 999 Beacon St [St Marys St]
  617-277-8272 • $$$
  Solid tapas spot with a great sherry menu.
- **Uburger** • 636 Beacon St [Raleigh St]
  617-536-0448 • $
  Burgers and frappes right by BU.

With the addition of the gigantic **House of Blues**, some of the former club options have lessened in quantity, but not in quality. For non-clubbers, **Elephant Walk** or **Taberna de Haro** are both excellent dining options. For those lucky enough to score tickets, the best entertainment in the world is at **Fenway Park**.

Shopping

- **Bed Bath & Beyond** • 401 Park Dr [Brookline Ave] 617-536-1090 For when holes are growing in your towels.
- **Blick Art Materials** • 401 Park Dr [Brookline Ave] 617-247-3322 Art-supply megashop plus custom framing.
- **Economy True Value Hardware** • 1012 Beacon St [St Marys St] 617-277-8811 Hardware, household needs, cheap furniture. Very popular.
- **Guitar Center** • 1255 Boylston St [Ipswich St] 617-247-1389 Also has drums, keys, etc.
- **Hunt's Photo and Video** • 514 Commonwealth Ave [Kenmore St] 617-778-2222 Good selection of used cameras.
- **Japonaise Bakery** • 1020 Beacon St [Carlton St] 617-566-7730 Mmmm…curry donut.
- **Nuggets** • 486 Commonwealth Ave [Kenmore St] 617-536-0679 Sells only used recordings. Quite fun to browse.
- **REI** • 401 Park Dr [Brookline Ave] 617-236-0746 Seattle co-op for the gearhead.

1
2
A
B
Winchester St
Beacon St
Coolidge Corner
St Paul St
Kent St
Washington St
Summit Ave
Fairbanks St
Washington Sq
Brandon Hall
Tappan St
Dean Rd
Beaconsfield
Harvard St
Washington St
Aspinwall Ave
School St
Brookline Village
Brookline Hills
Washington
Boylston St
Cypress St
Brookline Reservoir
Frederick Law Olmsted National Historic Site
Lee St
Warren St
Cottage St
Chestnut St
Perkins St
Jamaicaway
High St
Jamaica Pond
19
16
15
14
1/4 mile
.25 km

This neighborhood is a vibrant mix of old and new, urban and suburban, old-fashioned and eclectic. Long-time residents in stately Victorian homes share quiet neighborhood parks, diverse restaurants and shops, and a buzzing nightlife with transient college students and well-paid young professionals.

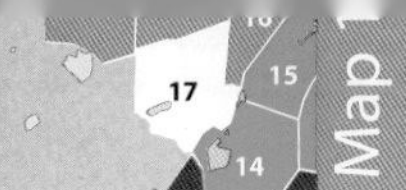

O Landmarks

- **Frederick Law Olmsted National Historic Site •** 99 Warren St [Welch Rd]
  617-566-1689
  Genius of American landscapes, the ultimate home office.

Nightlife

- **Matt Murphy's Pub •**
  14 Harvard St [Webster Pl]
  617-232-0188
  Popular Irish pub. Good food and music.
- **The Publick House •**
  1648 Beacon St [Washington St]
  617-277-2880
  Focus here is on the beers.
- **The Washington Square Tavern •**
  714 Washington St [Beacon St]
  617-232-8989
  Pub/restaurant with slightly overpriced food.

Restaurants

- **The Abbey** • 1657 Beacon St [Winthrop Rd]
  617-730-8040 • $$
  Homey neighborhood joint with an impressive beer list.
- **Boca Grande** • 3 Harvard St
  617-739-3900 • $
  Lots of good taqueria fare. Consider ordering carnitas.
- **Brookline Family Restaurant** •
  305 Washington St [Holden St]
  617-277-4466 • $$
  Top notch Turkish food.
- **Chef Chow's House** •
  230 Harvard St [Webster St]
  617-739-2469 • $$
  Decent Chinese food outside of Chinatown.
- **Curry House** • 1335 Beacon St [Harvard St]
  617-734-3971 • $
  Fast food Indian.
- **Dok Bua** • 411 Harvard St [Fuller St]
  617-232-2955 • $
  Tastiest Thai around! Their best dishes are not the noodle dishes.
- **Fugakyu** • 1280 Beacon St [Pleasant St]
  617-738-1268 • $$$
  Sushi, very popular. Be prepared to wait.
- **Hops N Scotch** • 1306 Beacon St [Pleasant St]
  617-232-8808 • $$
  Order scotch or beer, but avoid the signature drink.
- **La Morra** • 48 Boylston St [High St]
  617-739-0007 • $$$$
  Popular Northern Italian.
- **Martin's Coffee Shop** •
  35 Harvard St [Pierce St]
  617-566-0005 • $
  Brookline Village's own greasy spoon features breakfast, heavenly home fries.
- **Matt Murphy's Pub** •
  14 Harvard St [Webster Pl]
  617-232-0188 • $$
  Stylish Irish pub with good food and occasional live music.
- **Michael's Deli** •
  256 Harvard St [Longwood Ave]
  617-738-3354 • $
  Deli authenticity in Coolidge Corner.
- **Orinoco** • 22 Harvard St [Pierce St]
  617-232-9505 • $$$
  Make sure to make a reservation for their Saturday tasting table.
- **Pho Lemongrass** •
  239 Harvard St [Webster St]
  617-731-8600 • $$
  Pho, Brookline-style.
- **Pomodoro** • 24 Harvard St [Webster Pl]
  617-566-4455 • $$
  That means tomato in Italian.
- **Rani Indian Bistro** •
  1353 Beacon St [Webster St]
  617-734-0400 • $$
  Serving all your Indian favorites alongside some Hyderabadi specialties.
- **The Regal Beagle** •
  308 Harvard Ave [Babcock St]
  617-739-5151 • $$
  The moonshine cocktail is one of the best in Boston.
- **Rod Dee** • 1424 Beacon St [Summit Ave]
  617-738-4977 • $
  So tasty that we wish it was more than just a small take-out joint.
- **Shawarma King** • 1383 Beacon St [Park St]
  617-731-6035 • $
  Excellent Middle Eastern; informative service, fresh fruit beverages, traditional desserts.
- **Super Fusion Cuisine** •
  690 Washington St [Beacon St]
  617-277-8221 • $$
  Sushi purists will appreciate the lack of sauces and toppings.
- **Virginia's Fine Foods** •
  8 Cypress St [Washington St]
  617-566-7775 • $
  Slightly pricey shop with multiple breads for sandwiches, including veggie-friendly fare.
- **The Washington Square Tavern** •
  714 Washington St [Beacon St]
  617-232-8989 • $$$
  Good American food, but not as cheap as the name might suggest.

Brookline is a place where specialty shops mingle with chain stores, and an ethnic array of food spans from the inexpensive **Rani Indian Bistro** and **Boca Grande** to the upscale **Fireplace** and **Fugakyu**. The popular Art Deco **Coolidge Corner Theater** shows first-run, repertory, midnight movies, and occasional burlesque.

Shopping

- **Athan's European Bakery** • 1621 Beacon St [Washington St] 617-734-7028 To Exquisite baked goods, chocolates, gelato, and espresso.
- **EC Florist** • 224 Washington St [Davis Ct] 617-232-3693 Florist.
- **Eureka Puzzles** • 1349 Beacon St [Centre St] 617-738-7352 Old-timey gamers' heaven.
- **Madras Masala** • 191 Harvard St [Marion St] 617-566-9943 Indian Grocery store with a good selection of chutneys and prepared food
- **Marathon Sports** • 1638 Beacon St [University Rd] 617-735-9373 Run! Run! Run!
- **Mint Julep** • 1302 Beacon St [Harvard St] 617-232-3600 Boutique for the ladies or for the men looking for a gift for the ladies.
- **New England Comics** • 316 Harvard St [Babcock St] 617-566-0115 Study break reading material, some independent comics.
- **Paper Source** • 1361 Beacon St [Webster St] 617-264-2800 DIY paper crafts and quirky gifts.
- **Party Favors** • 1356 Beacon St [Webster St] 617-566-3330 Satisfies your sweet tooth and your inner party animal.
- **Wild Goose Chase** • 1355 Beacon St [Webster St] 617-738-8020 Crafts, gifts. A flea market, Brookline-style.

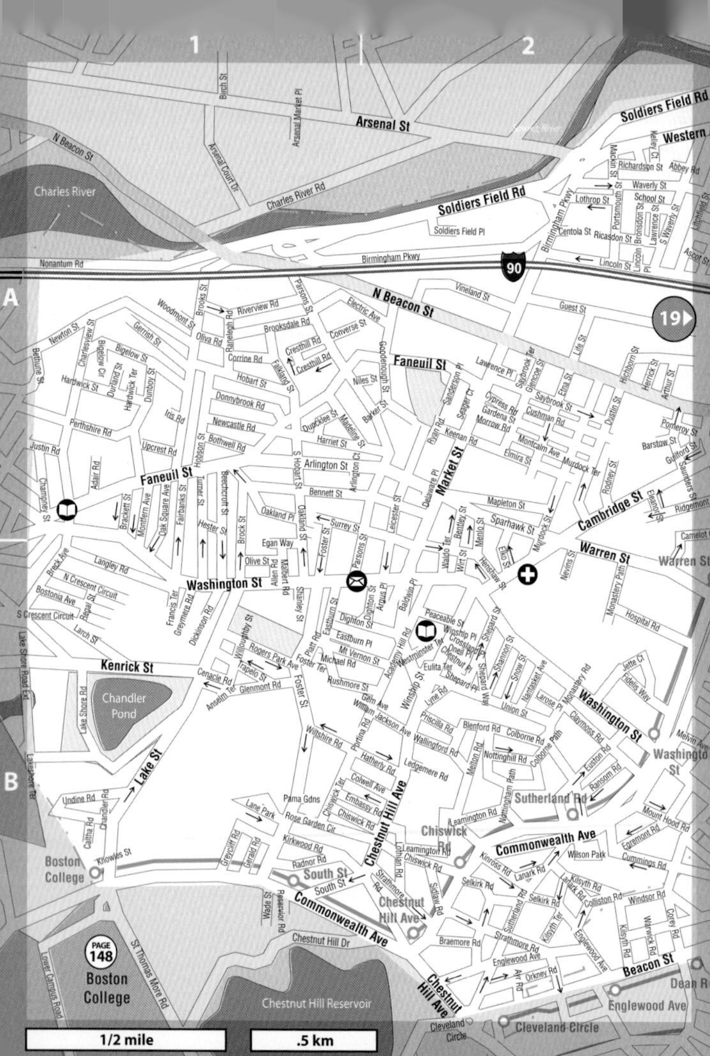

1
2
A
B
Arsenal St
Soldiers Field Rd
Western
Charles River
Charles River Rd
N Beacon St
Soldiers Field Pl
Birmingham Pkwy
Nonantum Rd
90
19
Faneuil St
Market St
Washington St
Cambridge St
Warren St
Kenrick St
Chandler Pond
Lake St
Chestnut Hill Ave
Commonwealth Ave
Sutherland Rd
Chiswick Rd
South St
Beacon St
Boston College
Chestnut Hill Reservoir
Cleveland Circle
Englewood Ave
Washington St
PAGE 148
Boston College
1/2 mile
.5 km

Brighton is the more sedate half of the Allston-Brighton duo but, like its rowdier neighbor, it attracts plenty of college students and young folk. Narrow, tangled, residential streets surround the cluster of shops and restaurants on Washington Street in Brighton Center.

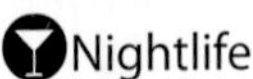

Nightlife

- **Cityside** • 1960 Beacon St [Sutherland Rd]
  617-566-1002
  Hit the patio if it's nice outside.
- **The Green Briar** • 304 Washington St [Wirt St]
  617-789-4100
  Pub with frequent live rock.
- **Irish Village** • 224 Market St [Saybrook St]
  617-787-5427
  Popular, relaxed local.
- **Mary Ann's** • 1937 Beacon St [Ayr Rd]
  617-566-3253
  BC student dump.

Restaurants

- **Bamboo** •
  1616 Commonwealth Ave [Washington St]
  617-734-8192 • $$
  Very good Thai at Washington Street.
- **Cityside** • 1960 Beacon St [Sutherland Rd]
  617-566-1002 • $$
  More for watching television than dining.
- **Corrib Pub** • 396 Market St [Surrey St]
  617-787-0882 • $$
  Irish breakfast of champions.
- **Devlin's** • 332 Washington St [Waldo Terrace]
  617-779-8822 • $$$
  A little bit of downtown in Brighton.
- **Eagle's Deli** • 1918 Beacon St [Ayr Rd]
  617-731-3232 • $
  BC meatheads eating meat.
- **The Green Briar** • 304 Washington St [Wirt St]
  617-789-4100 • $$
  Generic pub food. Stick with beer.
- **IHOP** • 1850 Soldiers Field Rd [N Beacon St]
  617-787-0533 • $
  Pancakes anytime.
- **Moogy's** • 154 Chestnut Hill Ave [Colwell Ave]
  617-254-8114 • $
  Enjoy a cheese omelette while playing Connect Four.
- **Roggie's** •
  356 Chestnut Hill Ave [Englewood Ave]
  617-566-1880 • $$
  Hang out with BC kids, drink beer, and eat greasy food.
- **Tasca** •
  1612 Commonwealth Ave [Washington St]
  617-730-8002 • $$
  Good (but not great) tapas for all budgets!

Shopping

- **Amanda's Flowers** •
  12 Tremont St
  617-782-0686
  Ever watch *Bed of Roses*? Hand delivered with a smile.
- **New Balance Factory Store** •
  173 Market Street
  617-779-7429
  Running gear for cheap runners.
- **Staples** •
  1660 Soldiers Field Rd [Soldiers Field Pl]
  617-254-4822
  Printer ink and other more reasonably priced supplies.

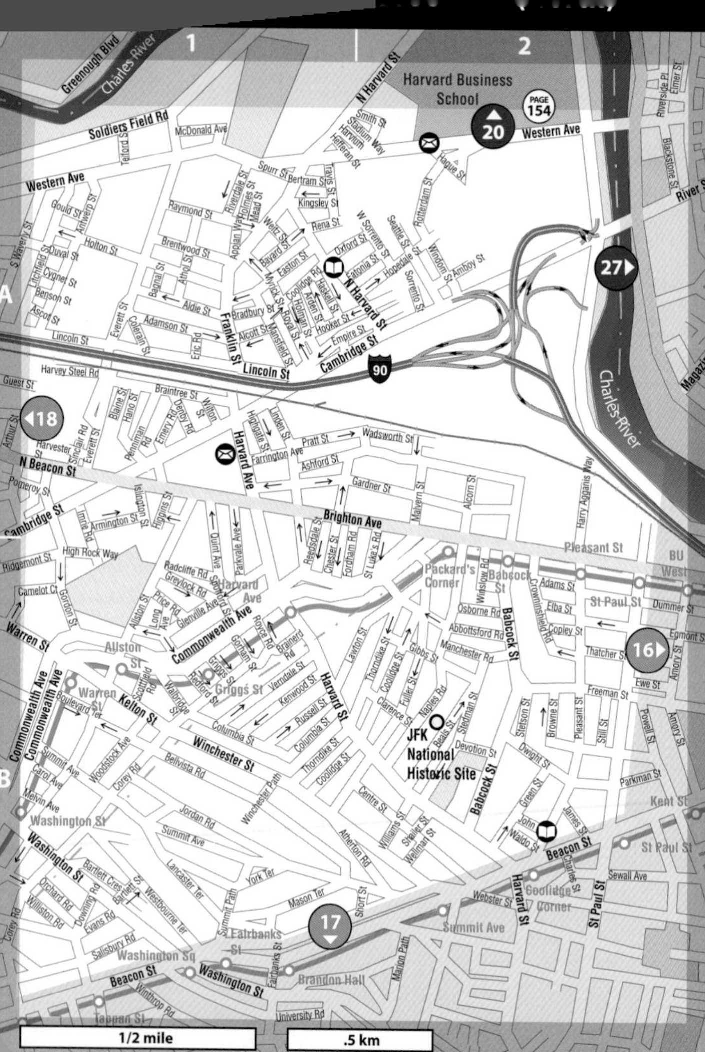

1
2
A
B
Harvard Business School
PAGE 154
20
27
18
16
17
Charles River
Greenough Blvd
Soldiers Field Rd
Western Ave
N Harvard St
Cambridge St
Lincoln St
Franklin St
90
N Beacon St
Harvard Ave
Brighton Ave
Commonwealth Ave
Packard's Corner
Harvard Ave
Allston St
Griggs St
Warren St
Babcock St
Pleasant St
BU West
St Paul St
JFK National Historic Site
Winchester St
Kelton St
Washington St
Beacon St
Coolidge Corner
Summit Ave
Fairbanks St
Brandon Hall
Washington Sq
Tappan St
Kent St
Harry Agganis Way
1/2 mile
.5 km

For most Bostonians, crowded living and rowdy students define Allston. There's no place in the city where so many cheap eats, dive bars, and used goods are crammed into so few blocks. It's a dirty mashup and the city is better for it.

Landmarks

- **JFK National Historic Site •**
  83 Beals St [Harvard St]
  617-566-7937
  Understated residential home, open only in summer.

Nightlife

- **The Avenue •**
  1249 Commonwealth Ave [Royce Rd]
  617-903-3110
  Cheap drafts and college kids.
- **Brighton Music Hall •**
  158 Brighton Ave [Harvard Ave]
  617-562-8800
  See some great bands up close. Real close.
- **Common Ground •**
  85 Harvard Ave [Gardner St]
  617-783-2071
  Defending Allston.
- **Deep Ellum •**
  477 Cambridge St [Brighton Ave]
  617-787-2337
  Chic enough to make you forget you're in Allston.
- **The Draft •** 34 Harvard Ave [Cambridge St]
  617-783-9400
  Hipsters and jocks make nice.
- **Great Scott •**
  1222 Commonwealth Ave [Harvard Ave]
  617-566-9014
  Loud, live music in a small, dark place.
- **Harry's Bar & Grill •**
  1430 Commonwealth Ave [Kelton St]
  617-738-9990
  Casual and roomy, with a mostly neighborhood crowd.
- **Model Café •** 7 N Beacon St [Cambridge St]
  617-254-9365
  Allston staple, with all the usual suspects.
- **Myung Dong 1st Ave •**
  90 Harvard Ave [Brighton Ave]
  617-206-3229
  Korean equivalent of *Saved by the Bell*'s The Max. Win.
- **O'Brien's •** 3 Harvard Ave [Cambridge St]
  617-782-6245
  Live rock, mostly local acts.
- **Paradise Rock Club •**
  967 Commonwealth Ave [Harry Agganis Wy]
  617-562-8800
  Major rock acts. Tasty food and smaller bands in lounge.
- **Scullers Jazz Club •**
  400 Soldiers Field Rd [Cambridge St]
  617-562-4111
  Live jazz most nights. In the Doubletree.
- **Silhouette Lounge •**
  200 Brighton Ave [Allston St]
  617-206-4565
  A room full of darts and drunks.
- **Tavern in the Square •**
  161 Brighton Ave [Harvard Ave]
  617-782-8100
  All you can eat brunch buffet. All you can watch sports.
- **White Horse Tavern •**
  116 Brighton Ave [Linden St]
  617-254-6633
  Always hopping, great for sports.
- **Wonder Bar •** 186 Harvard Ave [Glenville Ter]
  617-351-2665
  Wannabe Soho, patronized by wannabe yups.

Restaurants

- **@Union** • 174 Harvard Ave [Glenville Terrace]
617-779-0077 • $$
The perfect place to nurse a hangover.
- **Allston Diner** • 431 Cambridge St [Denby Rd]
617-208-8741 • $$
Soul food, Allston-style.
- **Anna's Taqueria** •
446 Harvard St [Thorndike St]
617-277-7111 • $
It doesn't mean much, but they roll up one of the best burritos in town.
- **BonChon** • 123 Brighton Ave [Linden St]
617-254-8888 • $$
The other KFC: Korean fried chicken. Better than the Colonel's.
- **Bottega Fiorentina** •
313 Harvard St [Babcock St]
617-232-2661 • $
Tuscan sandwiches to go.
- **The Breakfast Club** •
270 Western Ave [McDonald Ave]
617-783-1212 • $$
The shiniest diner found outside New Jersey.
- **Buk Kyung II** • 151 Brighton Ave [Harvard Ave]
617-254-2775 • $
Top-notch Korean food. Good luck finding a parking space on weekends.
- **Charlie's Pizza & Café** •
177 Allston St [Kelton St]
617-277-3737 • $
You would never guess by the name, but they also have Middle Eastern food.
- **Coolidge Corner Clubhouse** •
307 Harvard St [Babcock St]
617-566-4948 • $$
Home of the Big Papi Burger.
- **Dorado** • 401 Harvard St [Naples Street]
617-566-2100 • $
Never had a cemita? Best sandwich ever.
- **Garlic 'n Lemons** •
133 Harvard Ave [Brighton Ave]
617-783-8100 • $
Get your shawarma fix.
- **Grasshopper** • 1 N Beacon St [Cambridge St]
617-254-8883 • $$
Hip Asian vegan.
- **Habanero Mexican Grill** •
166 Brighton Ave [Park Vale Ave]
617-254-0299 • $
El Salvadoran chow. Hell yes to the fried plantains.
- **La Mamma** • 190 Brighton Ave [Quint Ave]
617-783-1661 • $
Stick with the empanadas and Chilean specialties.
- **Lone Star Taco Bar** •
479 Cambridge St [Brighton Ave]
617-782-8226 • $$
Tacos and tequila—what could go wrong?

Allston (South) / Brookline (North)

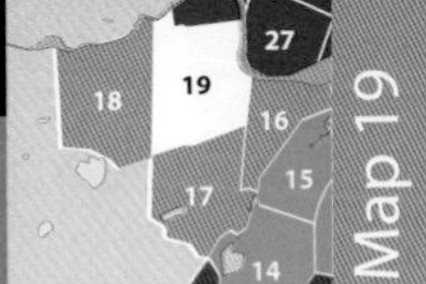

Allston Rock City! Clubs drive the scene here, with live music and DJs every night of the week. Check **Paradise**, **Great Scott**, and even the velvet rope at **Wonder Bar**. Taps dominate **Sunset Grill** and **Big City**. As for food, we've been known to fantasize about kebabs at **Saray** and bánh mì at **Super 88**.

- **Padaria Brasil** • 125 Harvard Ave [Brighton Ave] 617-202-6783 • $ One pão de queijo, please.
- **Paradise Rock Club** • 967 Commonwealth Ave [Harry Agganis Wy] 617-562-8800 • $$ Major rock acts. Tasty food and smaller bands in Lounge.
- **Pho Viet** • 1095 Commonwealth Ave [Brighton Ave] 617-562-8828 • $ Best Vietnamese subs (bánh mì) in town for just a few bucks.
- **Roast Beast** • 1080 Commonwealth Ave [Naples Rd] 617-877-8690 • $ Stuffed deli sandwiches with your choice of a bazillion sauces.
- **Shanghai Gate** • 204 Harvard Ave [Brainerd Rd] 617-566-7344 • $$ Challenging/rewarding Chinese dishes in welcoming setting.
- **Spike's Junkyard Dogs** • 108 Brighton Ave [Linden St] 617-254-7700 • $ Quick sausage fix.
- **Steve's Kitchen** • 120 Harvard Ave [Brighton Ave] 617-254-9457 • $ The best diner in Allston even though Lisa no longer works there.
- **Super 88 Food Court** • 1 Brighton Ave [Malvern St] 617-787-2288 • $ Boston's largest Asian food court.
- **Tavern in the Square** • 161 Brighton Ave [Harvard Ave] 617-782-8100 • $ All-you-can-eat brunch buffet. All-you-can-watch sports.
- **The Upper Crust** • 286 Harvard St [Green St] 617-734-4900 • $ Fancy schmancy pizza with Wi-Fi.
- **Victoria Seafood** • 1029 Commonwealth Ave [Winslow Rd] 617-783-5111 • $ Good food and dirt cheap prices! Great Chinese seafood options.
- **YoMa** • 5 N Beacon St [Cambridge St] 617-783-1372 • $ Fantastic Burmese food finally arrives to Boston!
- **Zaftigs Delicatessen** • 335 Harvard St [Shailer St] 617-975-0075 • $$ Comfort food for breeders who brunch.

Shopping

- **Berezka International Food Store** • 1215 Commonwealth Ave [Linden St] 617-787-2837 Russian goods for the slavophile.
- **Brookline Booksmith** • 279 Harvard St [Green St] 617-566-6660 Indie + used, with book clubs and readings monthly.
- **Brookline News and Gifts** • 313 Harvard St [Babcock St] 617-566-9634 Since 1963, chances are they have what you're looking for.
- **Catering by Andrew** • 402 Harvard St [Naples Rd] 617-731-6585 Shabbot bakery, Thursdays and Fridays only.
- **Clear Flour Bread** • 178 Thorndike St [Lawton St] 617-739-0060 Lines out the door for Boston's honest bread.
- **Fire Opal** • 320 Harvard St [Babcock St] 617-739-9066 Upscale craft gallery.
- **Herb Chambers Vespa Boston** • 22 Brighton Ave [St Lukes Rd] 617-254-4000 Imagine you are in Italy with its better drivers.
- **In Your Ear** • 957 Commonwealth Ave [Harry Agganis Wy] 617-787-9755 Good selection of independent, experimental music.
- **Israel Book Shop** • 410 Harvard St [Fuller St] 617-566-7113 Books in Hebrew.

Allston (South) / Brookline (North)

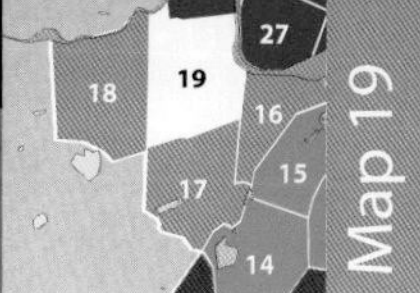

The sporty and outdoorsy converge on **City Sports** and **Eastern Mountain Sports**. Boston's also a biking town, and riders can get tune-ups, gear, and honest advice at **International Bicycle Center**. You can always find some good stuff at spots like **TJ Maxx** and **Urban Outfitters**, both of which come in handy more often than not. Oh, and we love the ice cream at **J.P. Licks**.

- **J.P. Licks** • 311 Harvard St [Babcock St]
  617-738-8252
  Popular Boston ice cream institution.
- **Kolbo Fine Judaica Gallery** •
  437 Harvard St [Coolidge St]
  617-731-8743
  Good place for Jewish gifts.
- **Kupel's Bakery** • 421 Harvard St [Fuller St]
  617-566-9528
  Old school bagel joint.
- **Orchard Skate Shop** •
  156 Harvard Ave [Brighton Ave]
  617-782-7777
  For hipsters who travel by skateboard instead of bicycle.
- **Regeneration Tattoo** •
  155 Harvard Ave [Glenville Ave]
  617-782-1313
  Good addition to the Allston punk scene.
- **Stingray Body Art** •
  1 Harvard Ave [Cambridge St]
  617-254-0666
  Huge tattoo parlor with sassy boutique.
- **TJ Maxx** • 525 Harvard St [Verndale St]
  617-232-5420
  Off-price apparel and housewares.
- **Urban Outfitters** •
  226 Harvard Ave [Brainerd Rd]
  617-232-0321
  Hipster funky outfits for the urbanites.
- **Urban Renewals** •
  122 Brighton Ave [Linden St]
  617-783-8387
  Top thrift shop with clothes, gifts, and kitsch.
- **Zipper Hospital** • 318 Harvard St [Babcock St]
  617-277-0039
  The place to go for fixing zippers and tailoring.

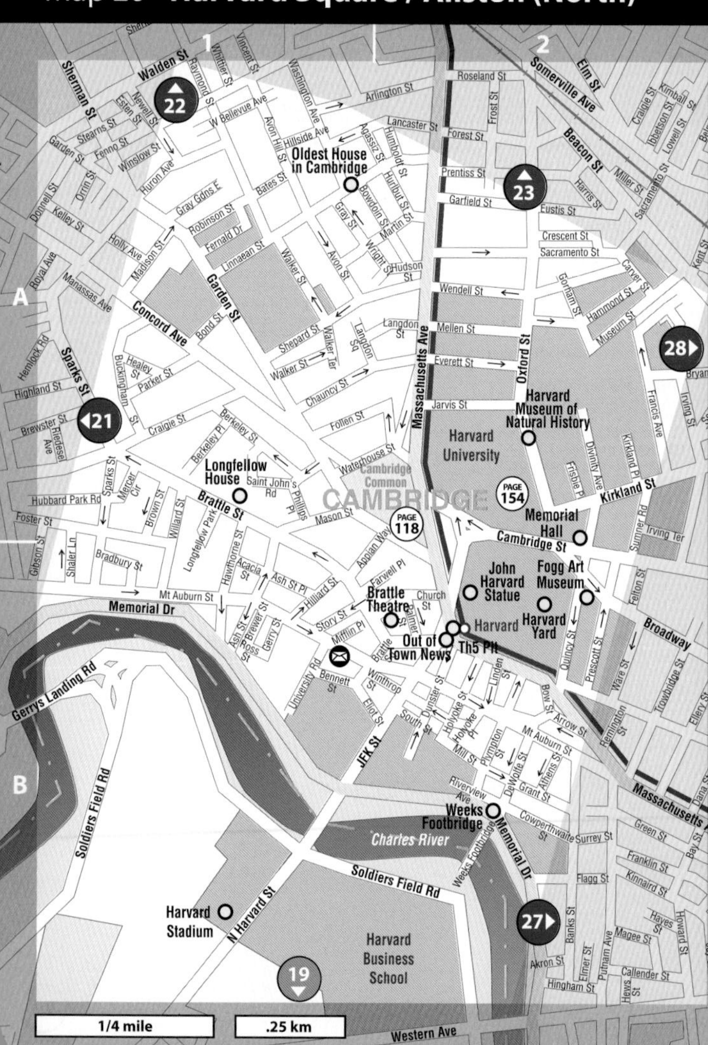

1
2
A
B
22
23
21
28
27
19
Oldest House in Cambridge
Longfellow House
Harvard Museum of Natural History
Harvard University
Cambridge Common
CAMBRIDGE
PAGE 154
PAGE 118
Memorial Hall
John Harvard Statue
Fogg Art Museum
Harvard Yard
Harvard
Brattle Theatre
Out of Town News
Th5 Plt
Weeks Footbridge
Charles River
Harvard Stadium
Harvard Business School
Walden St
Sherman St
Raymond St
Whittier St
Vincent St
Washington Ave
Arlington St
Roseland St
Somerville Ave
Elm St
Kimball St
Craigie St
Ibbetson St
Lowell St
Beacon St
Frost St
Forest St
Lancaster St
Agassiz St
Humboldt St
Hurlbut St
Prentiss St
Garfield St
Eustis St
Miller St
Harris St
Sacramento St
Crescent St
Kent St
Carver St
Gorham St
Hammond St
Museum St
Newell St
Esten St
Stearns St
Fenno St
Garden St
Winslow St
Huron Ave
W Bellevue Ave
Avon Hill St
Hillside Ave
Bates St
Bowdoin St
Gray St
Martin St
Wright St
Hudson St
Orrin St
Donnell St
Kelley St
Gray Gdns E
Robinson St
Fernald Dr
Linnaean St
Walker St
Avon St
Holly Ave
Madison St
Royal Ave
Manassas Ave
Concord Ave
Bond St
Shepard St
Walker Ter
Langdon Sq
Langdon St
Wendell St
Mellen St
Everett St
Jarvis St
Oxford St
Massachusetts Ave
Hemlock Rd
Sparks St
Highland St
Healey St
Buckingham St
Parker St
Chauncy St
Follen St
Brewster St
Riedesel Ave
Craigie St
Berkeley St
Berkeley Pl
Waterhouse St
Saint John's Rd
Phillips Pl
Hubbard Park Rd
Mercer Cir
Brown St
Willard St
Brattle St
Mason St
Appian Way
Foster St
Gibson St
Shaler Ln
Bradbury St
Longfellow Park
Hawthorne St
Acacia St
Ash St Pl
Farwell Pl
Mt Auburn St
Hilliard St
Church St
Memorial Dr
Ash St
Brewer St
Gerry St
Ross St
Story St
Mifflin Pl
Palmer St
Gerrys Landing Rd
University Rd
Bennett St
Winthrop St
Eliot St
JFK St
South St
Dunster St
Holyoke St
Holyoke Pl
Mill St
Plympton St
Linden St
DeWolfe St
Athens St
Grant St
Riverview Ave
Bow St
Arrow St
Cowperthwaite St
Surrey St
Francis Ave
Irving St
Divinity Ave
Kirkland Pl
Frisbie Pl
Kirkland St
Sumner Rd
Irving Ter
Cambridge St
Felton St
Broadway
Quincy St
Prescott St
Ware St
Trowbridge St
Ellery St
Remington St
Dana St
Green St
Franklin St
Bay St
Kinnaird St
Flagg St
Hayes St
Howard St
Magee St
Banks St
Putnam Ave
Elmer St
Akron St
Callender St
Hingham St
Hews St
Soldiers Field Rd
N Harvard St
Weeks Footbridge
Western Ave
Bryant
1/4 mile
.25 km

After nearly 400 years of existence, Harvard Square remains more than just a destination for students. It is, in fact, a beautiful intersection between old and new, where historic buildings and austere colonial brick mingle with trendy chains and hip indie boutiques. The neighborhood shines in spring and fall, but is also a surprisingly charming spot during the holiday season—especially if you need to get some shopping done.

Landmarks

- **Brattle Theatre** • 40 Brattle St [Church St]
  617-876-6837
  Oldest repertory cinema in Boston, since 1953 and still projecting.
- **Fogg Art Museum** • 32 Quincy St [Broadway]
  617-495-9400
  Fine collection, more humane scale than the MFA.
- **Harvard Museum of Natural History** •
  26 Oxford St [Kirkland St]
  617-495-3045
  The public face of the botanical, zoological, and geological museums.
- **Harvard Stadium** •
  N Harvard St & Soldiers Field Rd
  The nation's oldest stadium.
- **Harvard Yard** • Kirkland Street, b/w Broadway, Quincy St, Peabody St, & Massachusetts Ave
  The core of the campus, full of historical landmarks.
- **John Harvard Statue** •
  Massachusetts Ave [Quincy St]
  The "statue of the three lies."
- **Longfellow House** •
  105 Brattle St [Longfellow Park]
  617-876-4491
  Home of Henry W. Longfellow, as well as Washington's HQ.
- **Memorial Hall** • 45 Quincy St [Cambridge St]
  617-496-4595
  Gorgeous architecture and interior. Try to see a show there.
- **Oldest House in Cambridge** •
  21 Linnaean St [Bowdoin St]
  Built in 1681. Tours available by appointment in the summer.
- **Out of Town News** •
  Harvard Sq [John F Kennedy St]
  617-354-1441
  The sensible Harvard Square rendezvous spot.
- **The Pit** • Harvard Sq [John F Kennedy St]
  Favorite hang-out for the counter-culture kids.
- **Weeks Footbridge** •
  Memorial Dr & DeWolfe St
  Most beautiful bridge on the Charles, hosts full moon tangos.

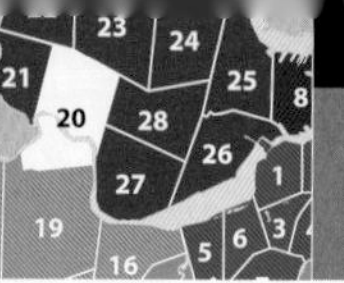

Nightlife

- **Cambridge Common** • 1667 Massachusetts Ave [Hudson St] 617-547-1228 Dark, comfy, familiar, yummy food.
- **Charlie's Kitchen** • 10 Eliot St [Winthrop St] 617-492-9646 Old School by the old school. Great jukebox.
- **Club Passim** • 47 Palmer St [Church St] 617-492-7679 Folk singer-songwriter landmark and vegetarian restaurant.
- **Grendel's Den** • 89 Winthrop St [JFK St] 617-491-1160 Harvard Square mainstay.
- **Hong Kong** • 1238 Massachusetts Ave [Plympton St] 617-864-5311 The scorpion bowls are a Harvard Square tradition.
- **John Harvard's Brewery** • 33 Dunster St [Mt Auburn St] 617-868-3585 Large and loud, good for crowds.
- **Lizard Lounge** • 1667 Massachusetts Ave [Hudson St] 617-547-0759 Great spot to kick back to live music.
- **Noir Bar** • 1 Bennett St [Eliot St] 617-661-8010 More pretentious than sophisticated.
- **Nubar** • 16 Garden St [Waterhouse St] 617-234-1365 Classy comfort in the Sheraton Commander.
- **Regattabar** • 1 Bennett St [Eliot St] 617-661-5000 Serious jazz club.
- **Russell House Tavern** • 14 JFK St [Brattle St] 617-500-3055 Soak up the history AND the booze!
- **Shay's Pub & Wine Bar** • 58 JFK St [South St] 617-864-9161 Lo-fi wine bar and pub with outdoor seating.
- **Temple Bar** • 1688 Massachusetts Ave [Sacramento St] 617-547-5055 Popular and impressed with itself.
- **Whitney's Cafe** • 37 JFK St [Mt Auburn St] 617-354-8172 One of the last dives in Harvard Square.

Harvard Square / Allston (North)

Without skipping a beat, a new crop of cocktail lounges, rustic taverns, and international eateries has found its way into Harvard Square's heart. Visit **Russell House Tavern** and **First Printer** for rustic fare with a dash of history. For street grub, visit **Zinneken's** or **Otto**. Old standbys remain, showing no signs of stopping: **Charlie's Kitchen** for juicy burgers, **Shay's** for people watching, and **Cardullo's** for aisles of drool-inducing goodies.

Restaurants

- **Alden & Harlow** • 40 Brattle St [Story St]
  617-864-2100 • $$$
  Elegantly prepared repurposed farm-to-table ingredients.
- **BerryLine** •
  1668 Massachusetts Ave [Hudson St]
  617-492-3555 • $
  Fro-yo a go-go.
- **BonChon** • 57 JFK St [Winthrop St]
  617-868-0981 • $$
  Korean fried chicken comes to Cambridge.
- **Border Café** • 32 Church St [Palmer St]
  617-864-6100 • $$
  Feeding students sub-par Tex-Mex for years.
- **Café Pamplona** • 12 Bow St [Arrow St]
  617-492-0352 • $
  Mellow Cuban hangout with outdoor patio.
- **Cambridge, 1** • 27 Church St [Palmer St]
  617-576-1111 • $$
  Tasty innovative pizzas and salads. Relaxed, stripped-down space.
- **Charlie's Kitchen** • 10 Eliot St [Winthrop St]
  617-492-9646 • $
  Old School at the old school. Best jukebox around!
- **Clover Harvard Square** •
  7 Holyoke St [Massachusetts Ave]
  617-640-1884 • $
  Locavores 'n herbivores. Based on the popular foodtruck.
- **Darwin's Ltd.** • 148 Mt Auburn St [Brewer St]
  617-354-5233 • $
  Hidden Harvard Square refuge.
- **Falafel Corner** • 8 Eliot St [Mt Auburn St]
  617-441-8888 • $
  Late-night Greek on the quick and cheap.
- **Felipe's Taqueria** •
  21 Brattle Street
  617-354-9944 • $
  Late night burritos in The Garage. Mind the drunks.
- **Flat Patties** • 33 Brattle St [Brattle Sq]
  617-871-6871 • $
  Try their shredded pork sandwich and an order of fries.
- **Giulia** • 1682 Massachusetts Ave [Hudson St]
  617-441-2800 • $$$
  Market fresh Italian with artisanal flair.
- **Grafton Street** •
  1230 Massachusetts Ave [Bow St]
  617-497-0400 • $$$
  High-volume, high-end Irish restaurant offering an ecclectic menu.
- **Grendel's Den** • 89 Winthrop St [JFK St]
  617-491-1160 • $
  For the laid-back academic. Reasonable prices. Excellent after work specials.
- **Harvest** • 44 Brattle St [Story St]
  617-868-2255 • $$$$
  Excellent. Nice garden terrace.
- **John Harvard's Brewery** •
  33 Dunster St [Mt Auburn St]
  617-868-3585 • $$
  Large and loud, good for crowds.
- **Le's** • 36 Dunster St [Mt Auburn St]
  617-960-0239 • $$
  Reliable Vietnamese. You can't go wrong here.
- **Legal Sea Foods** •
  20 University Rd [Bennett St]
  617-491-9400 • $$$
  Charles Square outpost of the popular chain.
- **Maharaja** • 57 JFK St [Winthrop St]
  617-547-2757 • $$
  Ornate Northern Indian.
- **Mr. Bartley's** •
  1246 Massachusetts Ave [Plympton St]
  617-354-6559 • $
  Classic burger joint across from the Yard.
- **Nubar** • 16 Garden St [Waterhouse St]
  617-234-1365 • $$$
  Classy comfort in the Sheraton Commander.

Harvard Square / Allston (North)

- **Otto** • 1432 Massachusetts Ave [Church Ave]
  617-873-0888 • $
  Eclectic slices by way of Portland, Maine.
- **Park** • 59 JFK St [Eliot St]
  617-491-9851 • $$
  Choose-your-own-adventure gastropub.
- **The Red House** • 98 Winthrop St [JFK St]
  617-576-0605 • $$$
  Seasonal menus served in an old red house.
- **Russell House Tavern** • 14 JFK St [Brattle St]
  617-500-3055 • $$
  Modern tavern, heavy on the meat.
- **Shepard** • 1 Shepard St [Massachusetts Ave]
  617-714-5295 • $$$$
  Seasonal, French-inflected cuisine with good vegetable options.
- **Sweet Cupcakes** • 0 Brattle St [Palmer St]
  617-547-2253 • $
  Give in to your Sweet tooth.
- **Takemura Japanese Restaurant** •
  18 Eliot St [Brattle St]
  617-492-6700 • $$
  Creative sushi on a budget.
- **Tasty Burger** • 40 JFK St [Mt Auburn St]
  617-425-4444 • $
  Reads more like a fast food joint than the Fenway outpost.
- **Zinneken's** •
  1154 Massachusetts Ave [Arrow St]
  617-876-0836 • $
  Belgian waffle emporium. 'Nuff said.

Shopping

- **Abodeon** •
  1731 Massachusetts Ave [Prentiss St]
  617-497-0137
  Retro housewares.
- **Anthropologie** • 48 Brattle St [Story St]
  617-354-3031
  For the wealthy hipster.
- **Black Ink** • 5 Brattle St [Brattle Sq]
  866-497-1221
  A blend of quirky and handy gifts.
- **Bob Slate Stationer** • 30 Brattle St [Eliot St]
  617-547-1230
  Fancy paper and some art supplies.
- **Brattle Square Florist** • 31 Brattle St [Eliot St]
  617-876-9839
  Delphinium paradise.
- **Cardullo's Gourmet Shoppe** •
  6 Brattle St [Brattle Sq]
  617-491-8888
  Craving Swedish ginger cookies? International, gourmet goodies.
- **Eye Q Optical** • 12 Eliot St [Bennett St]
  617-354-3303
  Designer eyeglasses.
- **The Games People Play** •
  1100 Massachusetts Ave [Remington St]
  617-492-0711
  Games, puzzles, and other items humans are wont to play.
- **Harvard Book Store** •
  1256 Massachusetts Ave [Plympton St]
  617-661-1515
  An independent bookstore selling new, used, and remainders.

Harvard Square / Allston (North)

You can spend a solid afternoon shopping around Harvard Square. **Newbury Comics**, **Black Ink**, and **Leavitt & Peirce** are great for gift shopping (for yourself or anyone else). The **Urban Outfitters** bargain basement has savings that will melt your face off. Recharge at **Tealuxe**, and flip through a book at the **Co-op** or **Harvard Bookstore**.

- **Harvard Co-op** • 1400 Massachusetts Ave [Dunster St] 617-499-2000 Good for books, maps, and school stuff.
- **In Your Ear** • 72 Mt Auburn St [Holyoke Pl] 617-491-5035 Good selection of independent, experimental music.
- **J.P. Licks** • 1312 Massachusetts Ave [Holyoke St] 617-492-1001 Bostonian ice cream institution. Try the Peanut Butter Sauce.
- **L.A. Burdick Homemade Chocolates** • 52 Brattle St [Story St] 617-491-4340 Sublime confections and some killer hot chocolate.
- **Leavitt & Peirce** • 1316 Massachusetts Ave [Holyoke St] 617-547-0576 Best tobacconist in Cambridge. Chess sets too.
- **Lizzy's Ice Cream** • 29 Church St [Palmer St] 617-354-2911 Homemade.
- **Lush** • 30 JFK St [Winthrop St] 617-497-5874 British cosmetics merchant.
- **Marathon Sports** • 1654 Massachusetts Ave [Shepard St] 617-354-4161 Run! Run! Run!
- **Mint Julep** • 6 Church St [Palmer St] 617-576-6468 Boutique for the ladies or for the men looking for a gift for the ladies.
- **Newbury Comics** • 36 JFK St [Mt Auburn St] 617-491-0337 A zoo on weekends.
- **Nomad** • 1771 Massachusetts Ave [Prentiss St] 617-497-6677 An eclectic mix with a Mexican bent.
- **Oona's** • 1210 Massachusetts Ave [Bow St] 617-491-2654 Nifty little vintage shop.
- **Out of Town News** • Harvard Sq [John F Kennedy St] 617-354-1441 The sensible Harvard Square rendezvous spot.
- **Planet Records** • 144 Mt Auburn St [Brewer St] 617-492-0693 CDs, some vinyl. Grab a $1 "mystery bag."
- **Raspberry Beret** • 2302 Massachusetts Ave [Martin St] 617-354-3700 Vintage and consignment threads and jewelry.
- **Staples** • 57 JFK St [Winthrop St] 617-491-1166 Printer ink and other more reasonably priced supplies.
- **Stereo Jack's Records** • 1686 Massachusetts Ave [Sacramento St] 617-497-9447 Specializing in jazz, blues, and the like.
- **Sweet Cupcakes** • 0 Brattle St [Palmer St] 617-547-2253 Give in to your Sweet tooth.
- **Tealuxe** • 0 Brattle St [Hague St] 617-441-0077 Good spot to hide from Harvard Square crowds.
- **Tess and Carlos** • 20 Brattle St [Church St] 617-864-8377 Well-chosen selection of pricey designer clothing and accessories.
- **Urban Outfitters** • 11 JFK St [Brattle Sq] 617-864-0070 Funky clothes and apartment stuff. Great bargain basement.

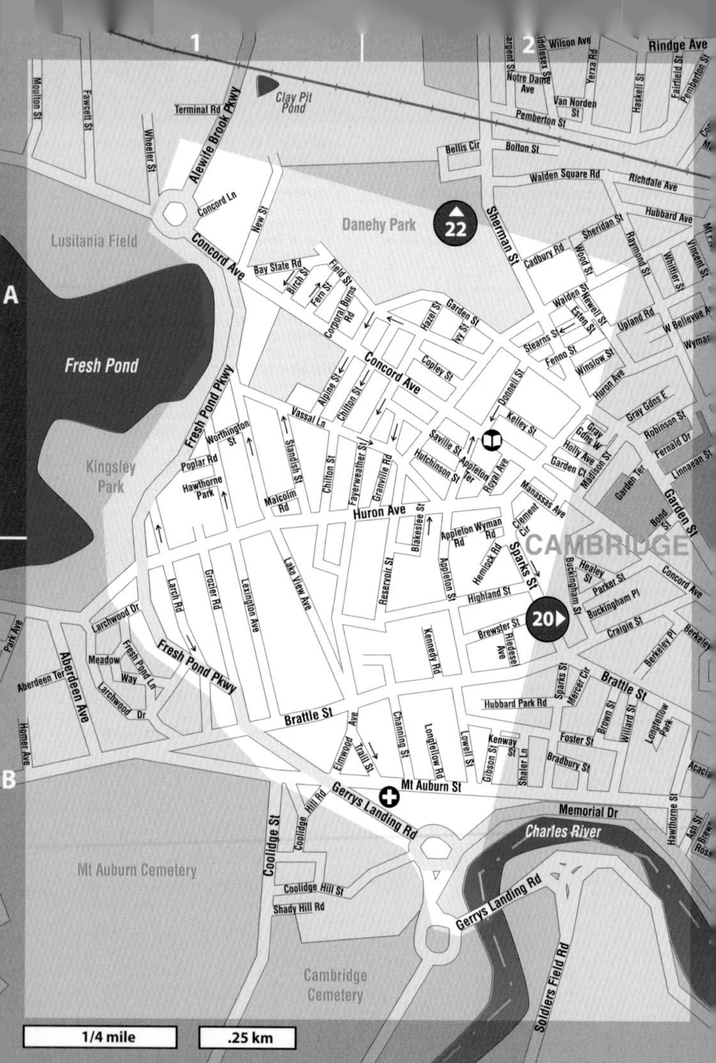

1
2
A
B
Clay Pit Pond
Danehy Park
Lusitania Field
Fresh Pond
Kingsley Park
CAMBRIDGE
Mt Auburn Cemetery
Cambridge Cemetery
Charles River
22
20
Concord Ave
Fresh Pond Pkwy
Alewife Brook Pkwy
Huron Ave
Brattle St
Mt Auburn St
Gerrys Landing Rd
Memorial Dr
Sherman St
Garden St
Ridge Ave
Sparks St
Soldiers Field Rd
Coolidge St
1/4 mile
.25 km

Tucked behind bustling Harvard Square, this hushed suburban community is nice for a pleasant, house-viewing stroll, but little else. Beautiful **Mt. Auburn Cemetery** is certainly a neighborhood highlight. Stop by and pay your respects to such long-ago dignitaries as Winslow Homer and Henry Cabot Lodge.

Restaurants

- **Armando's** • 163 Huron Ave [Concord Ave]
  617-354-8275 • $
  Cheap and delicious pizza.
- **Full Moon** • 344 Huron Ave [Chilton St]
  617-354-6699 • $$
  For a night out with the children.
- **Genki Ya** •
  231 Alewife Brook Pkwy [Concord Ave]
  617-661-8200 • $$
  Impressive, organic strip-mall sushi.
- **Hi-Rise Bread Company** •
  208 Concord Ave [Huron Ave]
  617-876-8766 • $
  Every neighborhood should have a place this good.
- **Ma Magoo's Pizza & Sub Shop** •
  6 Concord Ln [Alewife Brook Pkwy]
  617-354-9139 • $
  The chicken finger sub is a local favorite.
- **Trattoria Pulcinella** •
  147 Huron Ave [Concord Ave]
  617-491-6336 • $$$$
  For those not going to the North End.

Shopping

- **Circle Furniture** •
  199 Alewife Brook Pkwy [Concord Ave]
  617-876-3988
  Tons of cool, unique home furnishings.
- **Formaggio Kitchen** •
  244 Huron Ave [Appleton St]
  617-354-4750
  Cheese and other gourmet imports.
- **Henry Bear's Park** •
  Porter Square Shopping Center
  [Massachusetts Ave]
  617-547-8424
  Chi-chi toy store.

Map 22 • North Cambridge / West Somerville

Once upon a time, this neighborhood was dominated by slaughterhouses and a slightly less refined clientele. Today it's a bit different, blending NPR culture with town-center appeal. (Peter Sagal used to hang out here!) Vegan vittles, farmers markets, hip taverns, and young families abound—quite an advance over the slaughterhouses.

Landmarks

- **Somerville Theatre •**
  55 Davis Sq [Highland Ave]
  617-625-5700
  Movies, concerts, and more.

Nightlife

- **The Burren •** 247 Elm St [Chester St]
  617-776-6896
  Well-known Irish; live music.
- **Five Horses Tavern •**
  400 Highland Ave [Grove St]
  617-764-1655
  All hail the Beer Star!
- **Foundry on Elm •** 255 Elm St [Chester St]
  617-628-9999
  Decent draft list, excellent cocktails.
- **The Painted Burro •** 219 Elm St [Summer St]
  617-776-0005
  Flights of tequila, trips to the floor.
- **PJ Ryan's •** 239 Holland St [Broadway]
  617-625-8200
  Brick and beer bar.
- **Redbones •** 55 Chester St [Herbert St]
  617-628-2200
  Don't dig on swine? Then come spin the beer wheel.
- **Saloon •** 255 Elm St [Chester St]
  617-628-4444
  Brown liquors and local brews a la speakeasy.
- **Sligo Pub •** 237 Elm St [Bowers Ave]
  617-625-4477
  A landmark of sorts.
- **Somerville Theatre •**
  55 Davis Sq [Highland Ave]
  617-625-5700
  Occasional live music.
- **Spoke •** 89 Holland St [Simpson Ave]
  617-718-9463
  Less wine bar than journey; all booze is thoughtfully curated.

Restaurants

- **Amsterdam Falafel Shop** • 248 Elm St [Chester St] 617-764-3334 • $ Pros: mouthwatering pita and huge toppings bar. Con: sparse seating.
- **Anna's Taqueria** • 236 Elm St [Chester St] 617-666-3900 • $ Fastest burritos in town.
- **Blue Shirt Cafe** • 424 Highland Ave [Elm St] 617-629-7641 • $ Feel the force of vitamin B12.
- **Café Barada** • 2269 Massachusetts Ave [Dover St] 617-354-2112 • $ Relaxed Middle Eastern.
- **Dave's Fresh Pasta** • 81 Holland St [Irving St] 617-623-0867 • $ Homemade pasta and sauces.
- **Diesel Café** • 257 Elm St [Chester St] 617-629-8717 • $ Coffee and sandwich shop with an attitude.
- **Diva Indian Bistro** • 246 Elm St [Chester St] 617-629-4963 • $$ Flashy and tasty, but pricey.
- **Five Horses Tavern** • 400 Highland Ave [Grove St] 617-764-1655 • $$ Coat your stomach before the booze kicks in.
- **Foundry on Elm** • 255 Elm St [Chester St] 617-628-9999 • $$ Popular (read: crowded) brasserie-tavern hybrid.
- **Greek Corner** • 2366 Massachusetts Ave [Dudley St] 617-661-5655 • $$ Small corner, huge portions.
- **House of Tibet** • 235 Holland St [Broadway] 617-629-7567 • $$ Delicious. But where's the yak butter?
- **Istanbul'lu** • 237 Holland St [Broadway] 617-440-7387 • $$ Delightful Turkish.
- **iYo Cafe** • 234 Elm St [Grove St] 617-764-5295 • $ Make your own froyo…or waffle.
- **Jasper White's Summer Shack** • 149 Alewife Brook Pkwy [Rindge Ave] 617-520-9500 • $$$ Seafood. More a hangar than a shack.
- **Jose's** • 131 Sherman St [Bellis Cir] 617-354-0335 • $$ It's all about the margaritas.
- **Joshua Tree** • 256 Elm St [Chester St] 617-623-9910 • $$ Achtung, baby.
- **Martsa on Elm** • 233 Elm St [Grove St] 617-666-0660 • $$ Your meal is best accompanied by a Tibetan tea.
- **Orleans** • 65 Holland St [Buena Vista Rd] 617-591-2100 • $$$ People-watching, food. Don't look so expectant.
- **Out of the Blue** • 215 Elm St [Grove St] 617-776-5020 • $$$ Good value for seafood, Italian. Colorful room.
- **The Painted Burro** • 219 Elm St [Summer St] 617-776-0005 • $$ Hip, high-end hacienda.
- **Posto** • 187 Elm St [Windom St] 617-625-0600 • $$ Rustic, wood-fired pizza and the like.
- **Qingdao Garden** • 2382 Massachusetts Ave [Alberta Ter] 617-492-7540 • $ Casual, delicious. Sells dumplings-to-go in bulk.

In this 'hood, there's no shortage of variety with food and entertainment. **Redbones** still delivers with colossal 'cue and beer. **Dave's Fresh Pasta** keeps slingin' awesome sammies and perfecto pasta. Newer editions like **Five Horses, Saloon**, and **True Bistro** have found their niche as welcome neighborhood scenes. **Sacco's Bowl Haven** has joined forces with Flatbread Company to create fantastic 'za, cocktails, and candlepin bowling—don't even think about skipping out.

- **Redbones** • 55 Chester St [Herbert St]
617-628-2200 • $$
Don't dig on swine? Then come spin the beer wheel.
- **Renee's Cafe** • 198 Holland St [Claremon St]
617-623-2727 • $
No-cash, early-closing pancake heaven. Try the specials.
- **Rudy's Café** • 248 Holland St [Newbury St]
617-623-9201 • $$
Serving up generous Tex-Mex portions with a loco selection of tequila.
- **Sabur** • 212 Holland St [Moore St]
617-776-7890 • $$$
Food from Greece, North Africa, and the Balkans in a casbah-like atmosphere.
- **True Bistro** • 1153 Broadway [Holland St]
617-627-9000 • $$
Vegan date spot.

Shopping

- **Buffalo Exchange** • 238 Elm St [Grove St]
617-629-5383
Trendy recycled duds.
- **Caning Shoppe** • 99 Albion St [Lowell St]
617-776-0100
Hand-crafted chairs, vintage pieces, and other home furnishings.
- **Capone Foods** •
14 Bow St. [Union Sq]
617-629-2296
Pasta, sauces, and other specialties from The Boot.
- **China Fair Inc.** •
2100 Massachusetts Ave [Walden St]
617-864-3050
Inexpensive kitchen gear and housewares.
- **Dave's Fresh Pasta** • 81 Holland St [Irving St]
617-623-0867
Homemade pasta, sammies, produce, beer, & wine: heaven in Davis.
- **Davis Squared** •
409 Highland Ave [College Ave]
617-666-6700
Somerville-centric gift shop. Not that there's anything wrong with that.
- **Magpie** • 416 Highland Ave [Grove St]
617-623-3330
Featuring over 350 indie crafters and artists.
- **McKinnon's Meat Market** •
239 Elm St [Grove St]
617-666-0888
Smart choice before a barbecue.
- **Modern Homebrew Emporium** •
2304 Massachusetts Ave [Rice St]
617-498-0400
Everything for your home-brewing needs.
- **Nellie's Wildflowers** •
72 Holland St [Buena Vista Rd]
617-625-9453
Ask for assistance from Joyce, the friendly owner.
- **Pemberton Farms** •
2225 Massachusetts Ave [Rindge Ave]
617-491-2244
Local and organic groceries, sammies, and plants.
- **Staples** •
186 Alewife Brook Pkwy [Terminal Rd]
617-547-3948
Printer ink and other more reasonably priced supplies.
- **Sunshine Lucy's** •
93 Holland St [Simpson Ave]
617-776-2011
Awesome vintage pieces.

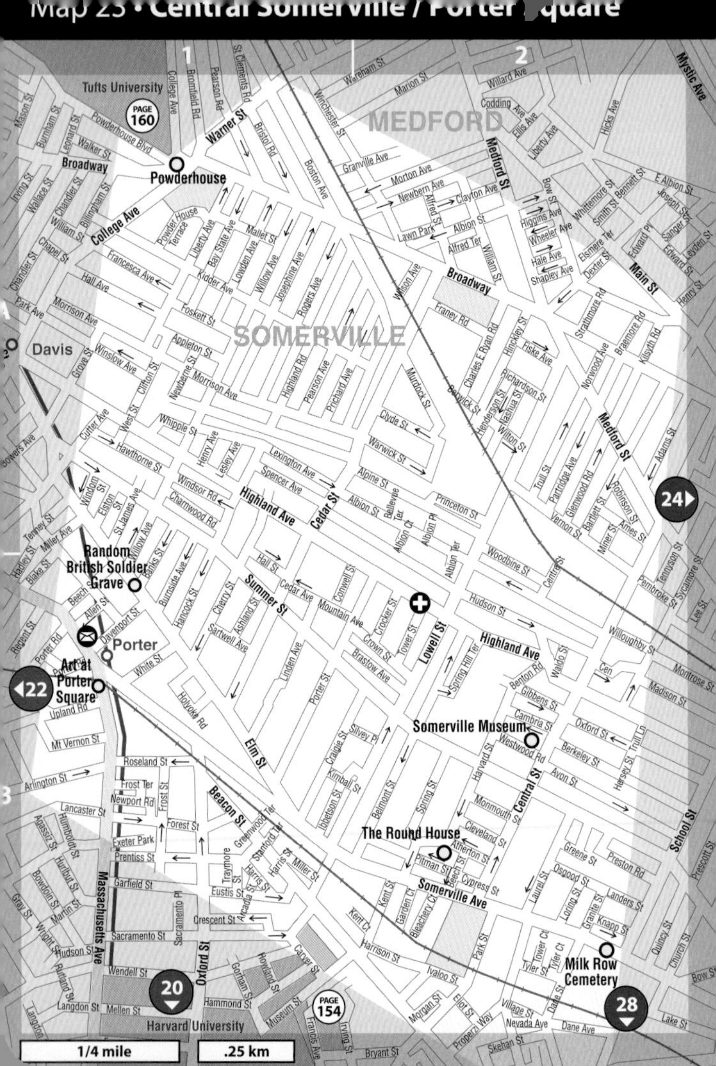

1
2
Tufts University
PAGE 160
MEDFORD
SOMERVILLE
Powderhouse
Davis
Porter
Random British Soldier Grave
Art at Porter Square
Somerville Museum
The Round House
Milk Row Cemetery
Harvard University
PAGE 154
24
22
20
28
Broadway
College Ave
Powderhouse Blvd
Warner St
Medford St
Main St
Mystic Ave
Highland Ave
Cedar St
Summer St
Elm St
Beacon St
Lowell St
Central St
School St
Somerville Ave
Massachusetts Ave
Oxford St
Willard Ave
Wareham St
Marion St
Winchester St
Boston Ave
Granville Ave
Morton Ave
Newbern Ave
Clayton Ave
Albion St
Alfred Ter
Lawn Park
William St
Codding Ave
Ellis Ave
Liberty Ave
Hicks Ave
Bow St
Higgins Ave
Wheeler Ave
Hale Ave
Shapley Ave
Whittemore St
Smith St
Bennett St
E Albion St
Joseph St
Sanger St
Edward Pl
Edward St
Leyden St
Henry St
Elsmere Ter
Dexter St
Franey Rd
Wilson Ave
Charles E Ryan Rd
Hinckley St
Fiske Ave
Strathmore Rd
Braemore Rd
Kilsyth Rd
Norwood Ave
Richardson St
Nashua St
Henderson St
Wilton St
Berwick St
Murdock St
Clyde St
Warwick St
Alpine St
Albion St
Bellevue Ter
Albion Ct
Albion Pl
Albion Ter
Princeton St
Trull St
Partridge Ave
Glenwood Rd
Bartlett St
Robinson St
Ames St
Miner St
Vernon St
Adams St
Woodbine St
Centre St
Tennyson St
Sycamore St
Lee St
Pembroke St
Hudson St
Willoughby St
Montrose St
Madison St
Waldo St
Benton Rd
Gibbens St
Cambria St
Westwood Rd
Oxford St
Berkeley St
Avon St
Hersey St
Trull Ln
Harvard St
Monmouth St
Cleveland St
Atherton St
Pitman St
Beech St
Cypress St
Greene St
Preston Rd
Osgood St
Loring St
Laurel St
Granite St
Landers St
Knapp St
Quincy St
Church St
Prescott St
Bow St
Lake St
Dane Ave
Dane St
Tower Ct
Tyler Ct
Tyler St
Park St
Nevada Ave
Village St
Skehan St
Properzi Way
Eliot St
Ivaloo St
Morgan St
Harrison St
Kent Ct
Kent St
Garden Ct
Bleachery Ct
Spring St
Belmont St
Ibbetson St
Kimball St
Craigie St
Silvey Pl
Porter St
Linden Ave
Crown St
Brastow Ave
Tower St
Crocker St
Conwell St
Mountain Ave
Cedar Ave
Hall St
Spring Hill Ter
Bristol Rd
St Clements Rd
Pearson Rd
Bromfield Rd
College Ave
Mason St
Burnham St
Leonard St
Walker St
Irving St
Wallace St
Chandler St
Billingham St
William St
Chapel St
Francesca Ave
Hall Ave
Park Ave
Morrison Ave
Powder House Terrace
Liberty Ave
Bay State Ave
Mallet St
Lowden Ave
Willow Ave
Josephine Ave
Rogers Ave
Kidder Ave
Foskett St
Appleton St
Newberne St
Morrison Ave
Highland Rd
Pearson Ave
Prichard Ave
Winslow Ave
Grove St
Clifton St
West St
Whipple St
Cutter Ave
Hawthorne St
Henry Ave
Lesley Ave
Lexington Ave
Spencer Ave
Windsor Rd
Charnwood Rd
Windom St
Elston St
St James Ave
Willow Ave
Banks St
Burnside Ave
Hancock St
Cherry St
Ashland St
Sartwell Ave
Tenney St
Miller Ave
Hadley St
Blake St
Beech St
Allen St
Davenport St
White St
Holyoke Rd
Regent St
Porter Rd
Upland Rd
Mt Vernon St
Arlington St
Roseland St
Frost Ter
Newport Rd
Frost St
Lancaster St
Forest St
Exeter Park
Prentiss St
Garfield St
Traymore St
Eustis St
Greenwood Ter
Stanford Ter
Harris St
Miller St
Arcadia St
Crescent St
Sacramento Pl
Sacramento St
Agassiz St
Humboldt St
Hurlbut St
Bowdoin St
Martin St
Gray St
Wright St
Hudson St
Rutland St
Wendell St
Langdon St
Mellen St
Hammond St
Gorham St
Museum St
Howland St
Carver St
Francis Ave
Irving St
Bryant St
1/4 mile
.25 km

Porter Square feels less polished than Harvard and Davis, and living space here and in neighboring Somerville is slightly more affordable. Shops and restaurants are concentrated on Mass Ave, and a mix of young people, families, and townies populates the residential neighborhoods.

Landmarks

- **Art at Porter Square •** Massachusetts Ave & Somerville Ave
  The T's best public art display.
- **Milk Row Cemetery •** 439 Somerville Ave [School St]
  Historic 1804 boneyard. Next to a supermarket.
- **Powder House •** Broadway & College Ave
  Revolutionary War-era gunpowder store, park centerpiece.
- **The Round House •** 36 Atherton St [Beech St]
  Round since 1856. Not open to the public.
- **Somerville Museum •** 1 Westwood Rd [Central St]
  617-666-9810
  Great exhibits of Somerville history.

Nightlife

- **Christopher's •** 1920 Massachusetts Ave [Porter Rd]
  617-876-9180
  Large selection of drafts, friendly staff, warm food.
- **Newtowne Grille •** 1945 Massachusetts Ave [Davenport St]
  617-661-0706
  Divey, but lively.
- **Olde Magoun's Saloon •** 518 Medford St [Lowell St]
  617-776-2600
  Nicer than it looks. Neighborhood favorite with good beer and Sox games.
- **On the Hill Tavern •** 499 Broadway [Medford St]
  617-629-5302
  DJs Thursday through Saturdays.
- **Samba Bar & Grill •** 608 Somerville Ave [Kent St]
  617-718-9177
  Brazilian vibe.
- **Toad •** 1912 Massachusetts Ave [Porter Rd]
  617-497-4950
  Cramped but fun. Live music nightly.

Central Somerville / Porter Square

Restaurants

- **Anna's Taqueria** • 822 Somerville Ave [Acadia Park] 617-661-8500 • $ Fastest burritos in town.
- **Ball Square Cafe** • 708 Broadway St [Willow Ave] 617-623-2233 • $ Belgian waffles loaded with whipped cream. Drool.
- **Café Mami** • 1815 Massachusetts Ave [Roseland St] 617-547-9130 • $ It's amazing what they can do with a little ground beef and an egg.
- **Café Rustica** • 356 Beacon St [Roseland St] 617-491-8300 • $ Friendly neighborhood café.
- **Christopher's** • 1920 Massachusetts Ave [Porter Rd] 617-876-9180 • $$ Good for relaxing on a wet day.
- **Highland Kitchen** • 150 Highland Ave [Central St] 617-625-1131 • $$ Lovely liquids and solids.
- **Kelly's Diner** • 674 Broadway [Boston Ave] 617-623-8102 • $ Old-school greasy spoon known for its "Kiss My Grits!" service.
- **Lyndell's Bakery** • 720 Broadway [Willow Ave] 617-625-1793 • $ Old-fashioned bakery.
- **Passage to India** • 1900 Massachusetts Ave [Porter Rd] 617-497-6113 • $$ Good Indian, served late. Try the curries.
- **Pescatore** • 158 Boston Ave [Broadway] 617-623-0003 • $$ Secret spot for amazing Italian seafood.
- **Petsi Pies** • 285 Beacon St [Sacramento St] 617-661-7437 • $ Name a dinner or dessert pie…any pie…and they probably make it.
- **R.F. O'Sullivan & Son** • 282 Beacon St [Sacramento St] 617-491-9638 • $ Quite possibly the best burgers in Boston.
- **Sound Bites** • 704 Broadway [Willow Ave] 617-623-8338 • $ For filling breakfasts.
- **Sugar & Spice** • 1933 Massachusetts Ave [Davenport St] 617-868-4200 • $$$ Thai food when you're not in the mood for the Japanese.
- **Tu Y Yo** • 858 Broadway [Walker St] 617-623-5411 • $$ Authentic Mexican—no burritos here.
- **Wang's Fast Food** • 509 Broadway [Hinckley St] 617-623-2982 • $ Best Mandarin hole-in-the-wall on this side of the river. Try the dumplings.
- **Yume Wo Katare** • 1923 Massachusetts Ave [Davenport St] 617-714-4008 • $$ All the rage ramen joint. Be prepared to stand in line.

With a less concentrated bar and restaurant scene than Davis or Harvard, Porter often gets overlooked—but that just means fewer crowds for those in the know. Check out **Highland Kitchen** for wicked cocktails and tip-top pub grub, or head to **Toad** where there's live music every night. Get baked at some of the best bakeries in the Boston area: **Petsi Pies**, **When Pigs Fly**, or **Lyndell's Bakery**.

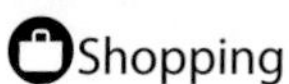

Shopping

- **Big Fish, Little Fish** • 55 Elm St [Cedar St]
  617-666-2444
  Pet store with more than just fish.
- **Cambridge Clogs** •
  1798 Massachusetts Ave [Stone Ct]
  617-497-1516
  Great for sock enthusiasts, too.
- **Joie de Vivre** •
  1792 Massachusetts Ave [Arlington St]
  617-864-8188
  Silly gifts, nostalgic toys, good stocking stuffers.
- **Lyndell's Bakery** • 720 Broadway [Willow Ave]
  617-625-1793
  Tasty pastries.
- **Paper Source** •
  1810 Massachusetts Ave [Arlington St]
  617-497-1077
  DIY paper crafts and quirky gifts.
- **Porter Square Books** •
  25 White St [Somerville Ave]
  617-491-2220
  Fiercely independent!
- **WardMaps** •
  1735 Massachusetts Ave [Prentiss St]
  617-497-0737
  Antique maps and other local images for sale. Worth visiting.
- **When Pigs Fly** •
  241 Elm St
  617-776-0021
  All-natural sourdough breads.
- **Yesterday Service, Inc.** •
  191 Highland Ave [Benton Rd]
  617-547-8263
  Sells instruments and hard-to-find sheet music.

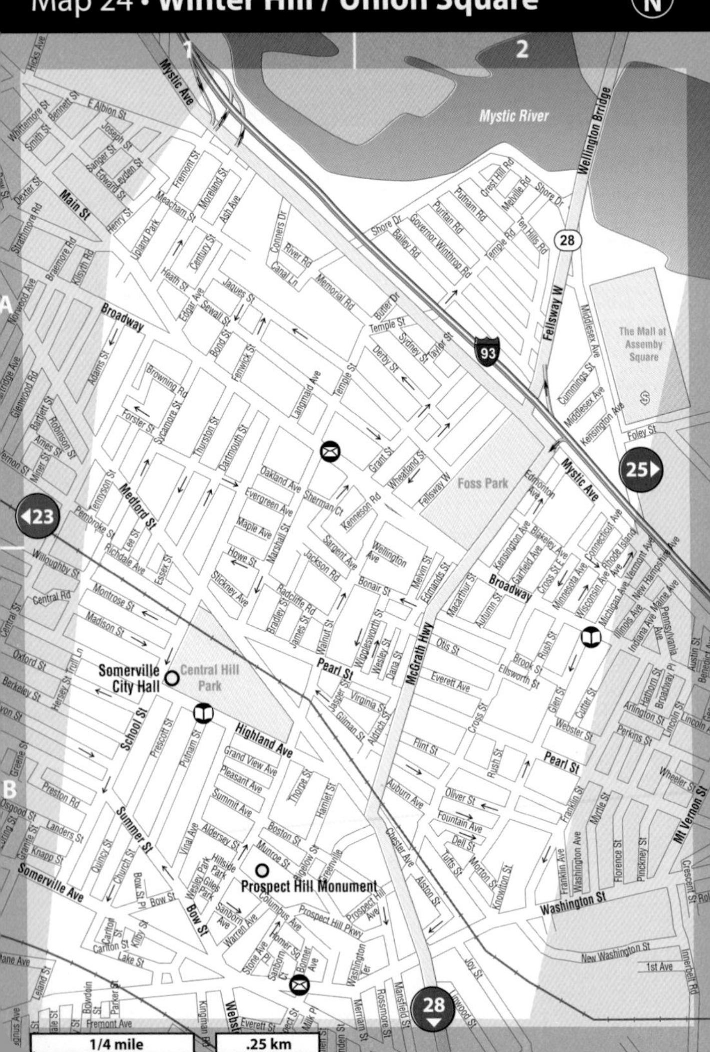
Mystic River
Wellington Bridge
Mystic Ave
Main St
Broadway
Medford St
Foss Park
McGrath Hwy
Pearl St
Highland Ave
Somerville City Hall
Central Hill Park
Prospect Hill Monument
Summer St
Somerville Ave
Washington St
The Mall at Assemby Square
Fellsway W
School St
Bow St
1/4 mile
.25 km

Here you'll find remnants of Somerville's working-class neighborhoods, **City Hall**, the charming Italian Renaissance Revival central library donated by Andrew Carnegie, and **Prospect Hill**, where America's first flag was raised in 1776. Still, lively and diverse Union Square continues to grow into an extension of Davis Square, with farm-to-table restaurants, hip boutiques, and outdoor film series.

Landmarks

- **Prospect Hill Monument** • Munroe St b/w Prospect Hill Ave & Walnut St
  Excellent view of Boston from Somerville.
- **Somerville City Hall** • 93 Highland Ave [School St]
  617-625-6600
  A classic New England municipal building.

Nightlife

- **Backbar** • 9 Sandborn Ct [Union Sq]
  617-718-0249
  Unique, locally sourced beers and old-timey cocktails.
- **The Independent** • 75 Union Sq [Stone Ave]
  617-440-6022
  Irish pub on one side, upscale bar on the other.
- **P.A.'s Lounge** • 345 Somerville Ave [Hawkins St]
  617-776-1557
  Cool spot for live, modern rock.
- **Sally O'Brien's** • 335 Somerville Ave [Hawkins St]
  617-666-3589
  Local bands, local sports, decent pub food.

Restaurants

- **Bronwyn** • 255 Washington St [Bonner Ave]
  617-776-9900 • $$$
  Farm-fresh bierhall food.
- **Cantina La Mexicana** • 247 Washington St [Bonner Ave]
  617-776-5232 • $
  The real deal. Terrific flautas.
- **Casa B** • 253 Washington St [Bonner Ave]
  617-764-2180 • $$$
  Tasty tapas in a button-cute setting.
- **Ebi Sushi** • 290 Somerville Ave [Union Sq]
  617-764-5556 • $$
  Decent sushi finally comes to Union.
- **Fasika Ethiopian Restaurant** • 145 Broadway [Rush St]
  617-628-9300 • $$
  Best Ethiopian in town in the oddest setting.
- **J & J Restaurant & Takeout** • 157 Washington St [McGrath Hwy]
  617-625-3978 • $
  Cheap, generously-portioned Portuguese with attached grocery store!
- **La Brasa** • 124 Broadway [Glen St]
  617-764-1412 • $$$
  Wood-fired locally sourced grub with international sensibility.
- **Leone's** • 292 Broadway [Marshall St]
  617-776-2511 • $
  Meatball subs that are To-Die-For.
- **Machu Picchu** • 307 Somerville Avenue
  617-628-7070 • $
  Peruvian. Definitely worth trying.
- **Neighborhood Restaurant & Bakery** • 25 Bow St [Walnut St]
  617-623-9710 • $
  Big, good breakfasts + patio = summer morning bliss.
- **Sarma** • 249 Pearl St [Marshall St]
  617-764-4464 • $$$
  Meze dishes with universal Mediterranean influences; great beverage program.
- **Sweet Ginger** • 22 Bow St [Walnut St]
  617-625-5015 • $$
  Typical, tasty Thai.

Shopping

- **Bombay Market** • 359 Somerville Ave [Kilby St]
  617-623-6614
  Good Indian grocery, Bollywood movies.
- **Bostonian Florist** • 92 Highland Ave [School St]
  617-629-9300
  Florist.
- **Christmas Tree Shops** • 177 Middlesex Ave [Cummings St]
  617-623-3428
  Everything including the kitchen sink.
- **Mudflat Studio** • 81 Broadway [Wisconsin Ave]
  617-628-0589
  Pottery classes and studios.
- **Reliable Market** • 45 Union Sq [Warren Ave]
  617-623-9620
  Overflowing East Asian grocer.
- **Ricky's Flower Market** • 238 Washington St [Union Sq]
  617-628-7569
  Great outdoor market. Mind the traffic, though.
- **Somerville Grooves** • 26 Union Sq [Somerville Ave]
  617-666-1749
  Post-punk vinyl, t-shirts, books, and the like.

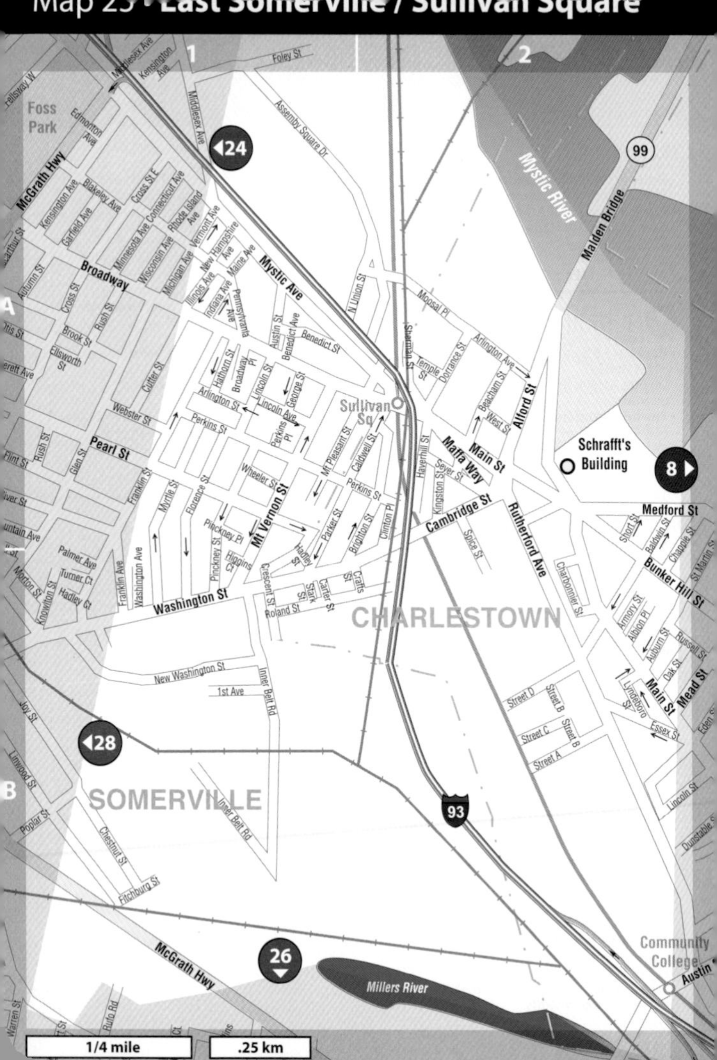
1
2
A
B
Foss Park
Middlesex Ave
Kensington Ave
Foley St
Edmonton Ave
Middlesex Ave
24
Assemby Square Dr
99
Mystic River
Malden Bridge
McGrath Hwy
Kensington Ave
Blakeley Ave
Cross St E
Connecticut Ave
Rhode Island Ave
Garfield Ave
Minnesota Ave
Wisconsin Ave
Vermont Ave
New Hampshire Ave
Michigan Ave
Maine Ave
Mystic Ave
Broadway
Autumn St
Cross St
Illinois Ave
Indiana Ave
Pennsylvania Ave
N Union St
Moosal Pl
Rush St
Brook St
Ellsworth St
Austin St
Benedict Ave
Benedict St
Sherman St
Arlington Ave
Temple St
Dorrance St
Hathorn St
Broadway Pl
Lincoln St
George St
Beacham St
Alford St
Cutter St
Arlington St
Lincoln Ave
Sullivan Sq
West St
Webster St
Perkins St
Perkins Pl
Caldwell St
Main St
Schrafft's Building
8
Pearl St
Mt Pleasant St
Haverhill St
Maffa Way
Flint St
Rush St
Glen St
Wheeler St
Seyer St
Franklin St
Myrtle St
Florence St
Perkins St
Kingston St
Medford St
Cambridge St
Rutherford Ave
Short St
Baldwin St
Chappie St
Mt Vernon St
Pinckney Pl
Parker St
Brighton St
Clinton Pl
Spice St
Palmer Ave
Turner Ct
Hadley Ct
Morton St
Knowlton St
Franklin Ave
Washington Ave
Pinckney St
Higgins Ct
Hadley St
Crafts St
Charbonnier St
Bunker Hill St
St Martin St
Washington St
Crescent St
Stark St
Carter St
Roland St
CHARLESTOWN
Armory St
Albion Pl
Auburn St
Russell St
New Washington St
1st Ave
Inner Belt Rd
Street D
Street B
Oak St
Lyndeboro St
Main St
Mead St
Street C
Street B
Street A
Essex St
Joy St
28
Linwood St
SOMERVILLE
Inner Belt Rd
93
Lincoln St
Poplar St
Chestnut St
Fitchburg St
McGrath Hwy
26
Millers River
Community College
Austin
Warren St
Rufo Rd
1/4 mile
.25 km

People go to Sullivan Square for the Orange Line or if they have a package at UPS. The historic **Schrafft's Building**, formerly the country's largest candy factory, looms over this throughway of a neighborhood from Cambridge/Somerville to Charlestown, Everett, and Malden.

Landmarks

- **Schrafft's Building** •
  529 Main St [Mishawum St]
  Once the country's largest candy factory.

Nightlife

- **Tavern at the End of the World** •
  108 Cambridge St [Parker St]
  617-241-4999
  Not as far as it sounds, but worth the trip.

Restaurants

- **Mount Vernon** • 14 Broadway [Mt Pleasant St]
  617-666-3830 • $$
  Sleepy spot with occasional lobster specials.
- **Vinny's** • 76 Broadway [Hathorn St]
  617-628-1921 • $$$
  Quality home-style Italian tucked behind a deli.

Shopping

- **Home Depot** • 75 Mystic Ave [N Union St]
  617-623-0001
  Got wood?
- **Vinny's** • 76 Broadway [Hathorn St]
  617-628-1921
  Damn good Italian cold-cuts.

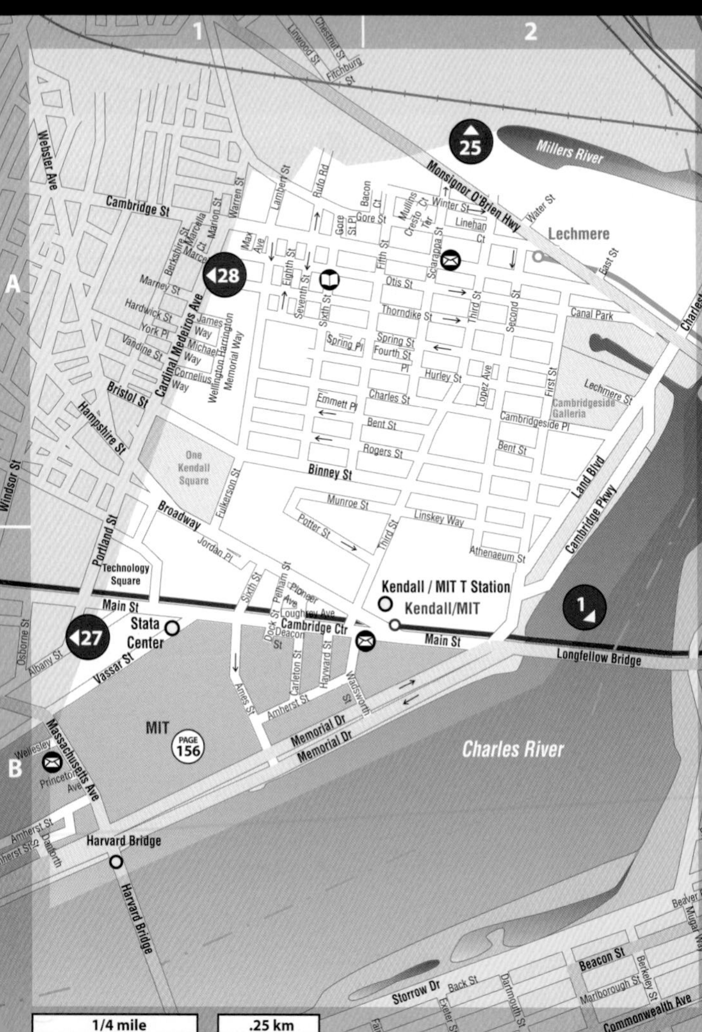

1
2
A
B
Millers River
Monsignor O'Brien Hwy
Lechmere
Cambridge St
Webster Ave
Windsor St
Cardinal Medeiros Ave
Hampshire St
Bristol St
Broadway
Binney St
One Kendall Square
Technology Square
Portland St
Main St
Stata Center
Kendall / MIT T Station
Kendall/MIT
Cambridge Ctr
Longfellow Bridge
Land Blvd
Cambridge Pkwy
Cambridgeside Galleria
Canal Park
Charles River
Memorial Dr
Vassar St
Massachusetts Ave
MIT
PAGE 156
Harvard Bridge
Storrow Dr
Beacon St
Commonwealth Ave
Marlborough St
Back St
Dartmouth St
Exeter St
Berkeley St
1/4 mile
.25 km

Once dominated by countless factories producing candy and candles, East Cambridge is now dominated by MIT and countless labs and tech companies. The factory buildings still stand, but have been repurposed as post-industrial offices, condos, and trendy bars and restaurants. There are some newer, sleeker architectural specimens 'round these parts, the most striking example being the **Stata Center**.

Landmarks

- **Harvard Bridge •**
  Massachusetts Ave [Memorial Dr]
  364 smoots and an ear, the Harvard Bridge leads to MIT.
- **Kendall / MIT T Station •** Main St [Broadway]
  Every T-Stop should have musical instruments by MIT students.
- **MIT Stata Center •** 32 Vassar St [Main St]
  Frank Gehry's curvy and colorful MIT building.

Nightlife

- **Cambridge Brewing Company •**
  1 Kendall Sq [Hampshire St]
  617-494-1994
  Decent microbrews. Some outdoor seating.
- **Champions Sports Bar •**
  50 Broadway
  617-252-4444
  Ultra-modern setting, hotel bar clientele.
- **Flat Top Johnny's •**
  1 Kendall Sq [Hampshire St]
  617-494-9565
  Cambridge's best large pool hall.
- **Meadhall •** 4 Cambridge Ctr [Ames St]
  617-714-4372
  Mead, of course, but over 100 draft beers, too.

Restaurants

- **Abigail's** • 291 3rd St [Binney St]
  617-945-9086 • $$
  Satisfactory New American with lots of libations.
- **Aceituna Cafe** •
  605 W Kendall St [Athenaeum St]
  617-252-0707 • $$
  Mediterranean for lunch at the Genzyme building.
- **Bambara** • 25 Land Blvd [Cambridgeside Pl]
  617-868-4444 • $$$
  Hit-or-miss at Hotel Marlowe.
- **Black Sheep** • 350 Main St [Dock St]
  617-577-1300 • $$
  In the Kendall Hotel. Go for breakfast.
- **Catalyst** • 300 Technology Sq [Albany St]
  617-576-3000 • $$$
  Mostly New England fare, with a farm-to-table twist.
- **Courthouse Seafood** •
  498 Cambridge St [6th St]
  617-491-1213 • $$
  One step removed from bobbing for fish.
- **Desfina** • 202 3rd St [Charles St]
  617-868-9098 • $$
  Old-school Greek for new school geeks.
- **Fuji at Kendall** • 300 3rd St [Binney St]
  617-252-0088 • $$
  Runs the Japanese gamut, with delicious smoothies to boot.
- **Helmand Restaurant** • 143 1st St [Bent St]
  617-492-4646 • $$$
  Delightful, authentic. Family ties with Afghanistan's president.
- **Legal Sea Foods** •
  5 Cambridge Center [Dock St]
  617-864-3400 • $$$
  Another Legal Seafoods for your fishy pleasure.
- **Loyal Nine** • 660 Cambridge St [Max Ave]
  617-945-2576 • $$$
  Sea-and-farm-to-table rustic modern New England.
- **Second Street Café** • 89 2nd St [Spring St]
  617-661-1311 • $$
  Plenty of fresh, inexpensive choices.
- **West Bridge** • 1 Kendall Sq [Binney St]
  617-945-0221 • $$$
  Modern industrial French-fusion fare.

Just a few years ago, this neck of the woods was Deadsville after 5 p.m. Today it's home to a growing contingent of taverns, lounges, and eateries, giving it a new life after the whistle blows. Grab some grub at **Fuji**, libations at **Cambridge Brewing Company** or **Meadhall**, and a flick at **Kendall Square Cinema**.

Shopping

- **Apple Store** •
  100 Cambridgeside Pl [Land Blvd]
  617-528-7970
  Mac heaven in the Galleria.
- **Best Buy** • 100 Cambridgeside Pl [Land Blvd]
  617-577-8866
  Awful, annoying electronics retailer.
- **Cambridge Antique Market** •
  201 Monsignor O'Brien Hwy [Water St]
  617-868-9655
  Five floors to keep you busy.
- **David's Famous Name Shoes** •
  75 First St [Spring St]
  617-354-3730
  Sans mall shoe shop!
- **H&M** •
  100 Cambridgeside Pl [Commercial Ave]
  855-466-7467
  Disposable chic from Swedish mega-merchant.
- **Marshalls** • 22 McGrath Hwy [Gore St]
  617-776-0674
  Discount clothing and other stuff.
- **Mayflower Poultry Company** •
  621 Cambridge St [8th St]
  617-547-9191
  Live poultry, fresh killed.
- **New Deal Fish Market** •
  622 Cambridge St [Fulkerson St]
  617-876-8227
  Relief, reform, and recovery in fish form.

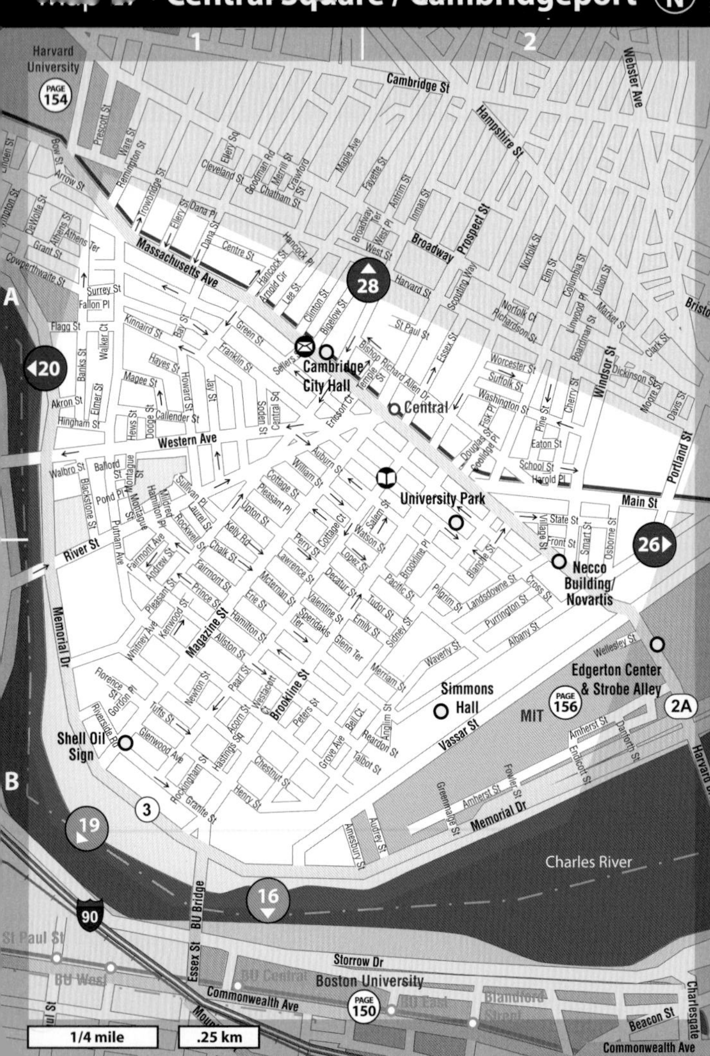

1
2
A
B
Harvard University
PAGE 154
Cambridge St
Webster Ave
Hampshire St
Prescott St
Ware St
Remington St
Bow St
Arrow St
DeWolfe St
Athens St
Athens Ter
Grant St
Cowperthwaite St
Trowbridge St
Ellery St
Ellery Sq
Cleveland St
Goodman Rd
Merrill St
Crawford St
Chatham St
Maple Ave
Fayette St
Antrim St
Inman St
Dana Pl
Dana St
Centre St
Hancock Pl
Hancock St
Arnold Cir
Lee St
Massachusetts Ave
Broadway Ter
West Pl
West St
Broadway
Prospect St
Norfolk St
Elm St
Columbia St
Union St
Bristol
28
Harvard St
Scouting Way
Norfolk Ct
Richardson St
Linwood Pl
Boardman St
Market St
Clark St
Surrey St
Fallon Pl
Flagg St
Kinnaird St
Bay St
Green St
Clinton St
Bigelow St
St Paul St
Essex St
Worcester St
Suffolk St
Washington St
Windsor St
Dickinson St
Moore St
Davis St
20
Banks St
Walker Ct
Franklin St
Hayes St
Magee St
Howard St
Jay St
Sellers St
Cambridge City Hall
Bishop Richard Allen Dr
Temple St
Central
Fisk Pl
Pine St
Cherry St
Akron St
Elmer St
Hingham St
Hews St
Dodge St
Callender St
Soden St
Central Sq
Ericsson Ct
Eaton St
Western Ave
Douglas St
Coolidge Pl
School St
Harold Pl
Portland St
Walbro St
Balford St
Blackstone St
Pond Pl
Montague St
Montague St
Mildred Hamilton Pl
Sullivan Pl
Auburn St
William St
Cottage St
Pleasant Pl
University Park
Main St
Laurel St
Rockwell St
Upton St
Cottage Ct
Salem St
State St
Village St
Front St
Smart St
Osborne St
26
River St
Putnam Ave
Fairmont Ave
Andrew St
Kelly Rd
Chalk St
Perry St
Watson St
Lopez St
Brookline Pl
Blanche St
Necco Building/ Novartis
Memorial Dr
Fairmont St
Pleasant St
Prince St
Lawrence St
Decatur St
Pacific St
Pilgrim St
Landsdowne St
Cross St
Kenwood St
Magazine St
Mcternan St
Erie St
Hamilton St
Valentine St
Speridakis Ter
Tudor St
Emily St
Sidney St
Purrington St
Albany St
Whitney Ave
Allston St
Glenn Ter
Waverly St
Wellesley St
Edgerton Center & Strobe Alley
Florence St
Gordon Pl
Riverside Rd
Newton St
Pearl St
Westacott Ct
Brookline St
Peters St
Merriam St
Simmons Hall
PAGE 156
MIT
2A
Tufts St
Acorn St
Bell Ct
Anglim St
Amherst St
Danforth St
Shell Oil Sign
Glenwood Ave
Hastings Sq
Grove Ave
Reardon St
Talbot St
Vassar St
Endicott St
Harvard Br
Rockingham St
Chestnut St
Henry St
Granite St
3
19
Greenough St
Fowler St
Amherst St
Memorial Dr
Amesbury St
Audrey St
Charles River
16
90
BU Bridge
Essex St
St Paul St
Storrow Dr
BU West
BU Central
Boston University
Commonwealth Ave
PAGE 150
BU East
Blandford Street
Beacon St
Charlesgate
Commonwealth Ave
1/4 mile
.25 km

Central Square is a mix of MIT residences, biotech companies, and rock clubs—a place where hipsters, scientists, and vagrants live in harmony. And somehow there are so surprisingly nice apartments in Cambridgeport. Sadly, the old **Necco Candy Factory** is now a research facility. However, the gorgeous **Cambridge City** Hall has not been converted to a biotech lab…yet. Satisfy your grocery needs (and tasty organic food supplies) at **Harvest Co-op**.

Landmarks

- **Cambridge City Hall** •
795 Massachusetts Ave [Bigelow St]
617-349-4000
Recently got a needed facelift.
- **Former Necco Building** •
250 Massachusetts Ave [Landsdowne St]
Yet another candy company leaves Cambridge.
- **MIT Edgerton Center** •
77 Massachusetts Ave [Vassar St]
617-253-4629
4th floor of Building 4 displays of slow-mo destructive photography and tech.
- **Shell Oil Sign** • 187 Magazine St [Granite St]
Can't miss it. Logo designed by Raymond Loewy.
- **Simmons Hall** • 229 Vassar St [Concord Ave]
617-253-5107
Agressively modernist MIT dorm by Stephen Holl.
- **University Park** •
Massachusetts Ave & Sidney St
Complex of cool structural and landscape architecture.

Nightlife

- **Cantab Lounge** •
738 Massachusetts Ave [Pleasant St]
617-354-2685
Legendary quasi-dive. Little Joe Cook still plays.
- **The Field** • 20 Prospect St [Massachusetts Ave]
617-354-7345
Dark and gritty Irish pub.
- **The Middle East** •
472 Massachusetts Ave [Douglas St]
617-864-3278
Venerable venue that gets high-profile music bookings.
- **Middlesex Lounge** •
315 Massachusetts Ave [State St]
617-868-6739
Rotating DJ line-up, fun modular seating.
- **Miracle of Science** •
321 Massachusetts Ave [State St]
617-868-2866
Energetic mainstay, always playing cool music.
- **The People's Republik** •
876 Massachusetts Ave [Lee St]
617-491-6969
Toast 'til 2:00.
- **Phoenix Landing** •
512 Massachusetts Ave [Brookline St]
617-576-6260
Irish pub with club music every night.
- **The Plough & Stars** •
912 Massachusetts Ave [Hancock St]
617-576-0032
Well-loved local. Frequent live music.

Restaurants

- **Area Four** • 500 Technology Sq [Main St]
617-758-4444 • $$
Techster coffee in Cambridge's Area IV.
- **The Asgard** •
350 Massachusetts Ave [Blanche St]
617-577-9100 • $$
Enormous "Celtic" gastropub.
- **Asmara** • 739 Massachusetts Ave [Pleasant St]
617-864-7447 • $$
Once was the only Ethiopian restaurant in Cambridge.
- **Baraka Café** • 80 Pearl St [William St]
617-868-3951 • $$
A tiny restaurant serving up some good Morrocan cuisine.
- **Beantown Taqueria** •
245 Massachusetts Ave [Lansdowne St]
617-441-8689 • $
There's always room for late-night tacos.
- **Brookline Lunch** •
9 Brookline St [Massachusetts Ave]
617-354-2983 • $
Popular diner. For food, not service.
- **Cafe Sushi** •
1105 Massachusetts Ave [Remington St]
617-492-0434 • $$
Revelatory sushi doing best to destabilize yellowtail-maguro-industrial complex.
- **Central Kitchen** •
567 Massachusetts Ave [Pearl St]
617-491-5599 • $$$
Simple Mediterranean menu featuring incredibly flavorful dishes with great wines to match.
- **Coast Cafe** • 233 River St [Rockwell St]
617-354-7644 • $
Breadcumb-laden fried chicken, mac 'n cheese 'n collard greens.
- **Craigie on Main** •
853 Main St [Massachusetts Ave]
617-497-5511 • $$$$$$
Expensive and slow but wonderful French-American bistro on Main St.
- **Cuchi Cuchi** • 795 Main St [Cherry St]
617-864-2929 • $$$
You either love this place or hate it. Find out for yourself!
- **Dolphin Seafood** •
1105 Massachusetts Ave [Remington St]
617-661-2937 • $$
Unpretentious fish house.
- **Falafel Palace** • 25 Central Sq [Pleasant St]
617-864-0827 • $
Located in what was once a White Castle.
- **Flour Bakery + Café** •
190 Massachusetts Ave [Albany St]
617-225-2525 • $
Beyond exceptional bakery. Also serves dinners for take-away.
- **Four Burgers** •
704 Massachusetts Ave [Prospect St]
617-441-5444 • $
Truth in advertising. The menu? Four Burgers.
- **Green Street Grill** •
280 Green St [Magazine St]
617-876-1655 • $$$
New American, seasonal, local-based menu.
- **India Pavilion** • 17 Central Sq [Pleasant St]
617-547-7463 • $$
Reliable Indian that's been a part of Central Square forever. A decent value.

It may not being the prettiest girl at the ball, but Central sure knows how to have fun. Seeing a rock show at **The Middle East** earns you instant cred. Sophisticated hipsters frequent **Central Kitchen**, **Falafel Palace**, **Cantab**, and **Miracle of Science**. The sweet-toothed love **Flour + Bakery**, but to forgo a scoop from **Toscanini's** is a downright sin.

- **Life Alive** • 765 Massachusetts Ave [Inman St]
  617-354-5433 • $$
  Colorful vegetarian cuisine served in a cheerful locale.
- **Mary Chung** •
  464 Massachusetts Ave [Douglas St]
  617-864-1991 • $$
  This Central Square institution is still going strong.
- **The Middle East** •
  472 Massachusetts Ave [Douglas St]
  617-864-3278 • $$
  Cheap and tasty food before going to see a show.
- **Miracle of Science** •
  321 Massachusetts Ave [State St]
  617-868-2866 • $$
  Energetic neighborhood mainstay. Great burgers, quesadillas.
- **Moksa** • 450 Massachusetts Ave [Brookline St]
  617-661-4900 • $$
  Asian tapas, some on a stick.
- **Rangzen Tibetan Restaurant** •
  24 Pearl St [Green St]
  617-354-8881 • $$
  For a feast fit for a monk try the Gyakor Tibetan Hot Pot.
- **Thelonious Monkfish** •
  524 Massachusetts Ave [Norfolk St]
  617-441-2116 • $$
  Sushi and jazz, together at last!
- **Zoe's** •
  1105 Massachusetts Ave [Remington St]
  617-495-0055 • $
  Retro-ish diner food, breakfast all day.
- **ZuZuBar** •
  474 Massachusetts Ave [Douglas St]
  617-864-3278 • $$$
  Funky, colorful. Make a meal of maza.

Shopping

- **Cheapo Records** •
  538 Massachusetts Ave [Norfolk St]
  617-354-4455
  A treasure trove of older tunes.
- **Economy True Value Hardware** •
  438 Massachusetts Ave [Main St]
  617-500-1595
  Hardware, household needs, cheap furniture. Very popular.
- **Great Eastern Trading Company** •
  49 River St [Auburn St]
  617-354-5279
  Like the Garment District's little sister on crack.
- **Hubba Hubba** •
  534 Massachusetts Ave [Norfolk St]
  617-492-9082
  Focusing on the naughty bits.
- **Micro Center** • 730 Memorial Dr [Riverside Rd]
  617-234-6400
  Computer have-it-all. Avoid going on Saturdays.
- **Pandemonium Books** •
  4 Pleasant St [Massachusetts Ave]
  617-547-3721
  Books, Role-Playing Supplies, and tables for all your D&D needs.
- **Shalimar India Food and Spices** •
  571 Massachusetts Ave [Pearl St]
  617-868-8311
  Huge selection of spices.
- **Ten Thousand Villages** •
  694 Massachusetts Ave [Western Ave]
  617-876-2414
  Free-trade, handmade crafts from around the world.
- **Toscanini's** • 899 Main St [Columbia St]
  617-491-5877
  In our opinion, Boston's best ice cream.
- **University Stationery** •
  311 Massachusetts Ave [State St]
  617-547-6650
  A friendly little shop near MIT.

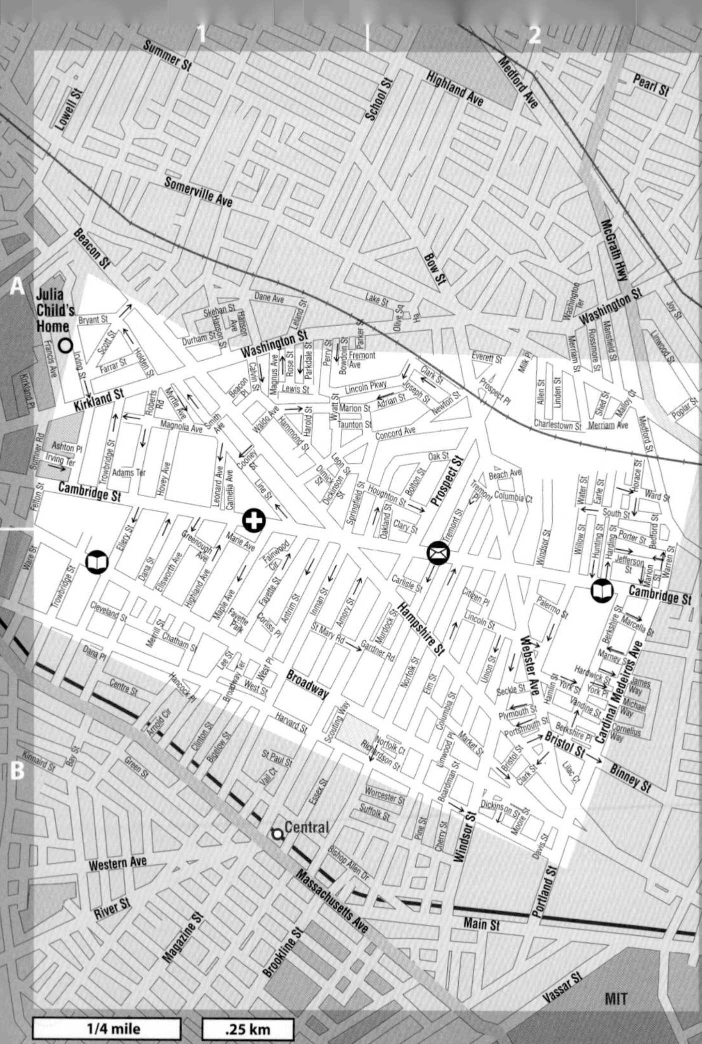

1
2
A
B
Summer St
Lowell St
School St
Highland Ave
Medford Ave
Pearl St
Somerville Ave
Beacon St
Bow St
McGrath Hwy
Julia Child's Home
Bryant St
Francis Ave
Kirkland Pl
Irving St
Scott St
Farrar St
Holden St
Kirkland St
Skehan St
Hanson St
Hanson Ave
Durham St
Dane Ave
Leland St
Lake St
Olive Sq
Washington St
Calvin St
Magnus Ave
Rose St
Parkdale St
Perry St
Bowdoin St
Parker St
Fremont Ave
Lewis St
Beacon Pl
Lincoln Pkwy
Clark St
Joseph St
Adrian St
Newton St
Everett St
Prospect Pl
Milk Pl
Washington Ter
Washington St
Merriam St
Rossmore St
Mansfield St
Linwood St
Joy St
Allen St
Linden St
Shed St
Malloy Ct
Poplar St
Charlestown St
Merriam Ave
Medford St
Roberts Rd
Myrtle Ave
Smith Ave
Magnolia Ave
Waldo Ave
Hammond St
Harold St
Watt St
Marion St
Taunton St
Concord Ave
Sumner Rd
Ashton Pl
Irving Ter
Trowbridge St
Adams Ter
Hovey Ave
Leonard Ave
Camelia Ave
Cooney St
Line St
Dimick St
Leon St
Dickinson St
Springfield St
Houghton St
Belton St
Oak St
Prospect St
Beach Ave
Tremont Pl
Columbia Ct
Water St
Earle St
Horace St
Ward St
South St
Felton St
Cambridge St
Ellery St
Greenough Ave
Marie Ave
Fairwood Cir
Oakland St
Clary St
Tremont St
Windsor St
Willow St
Hunting St
Harding St
Porter St
Bedford St
Jefferson St
Marion St
Warren St
Ware St
Trowbridge St
Dana St
Ellsworth Ave
Highland Ave
Maple Ave
Fayette St
Antrim St
Inman St
Amory St
Carlisle St
Citizen Pl
Palermo St
Cambridge St
Cleveland St
Fayette Park
Corliss Pl
St Mary Rd
Gardner Rd
Murdock St
Hampshire St
Lincoln St
Berkshire St
Marcella St
Merrill St
Chatham St
Dana Pl
Lee St
Broadway Ter
West Pl
Broadway
Norfolk St
Elm St
Union St
Webster Ave
Marney St
Cardinal Medeiros Ave
Hardwick St
York St
York Pl
James Way
Centre St
Hancock Pl
West St
Seckle St
Hamlin St
Vandine St
Michael Way
Arnold Cir
Harvard St
Scouting Way
Columbia St
Plymouth St
Portsmouth St
Berkshire Pl
Cornelius Way
Clinton St
Bigelow St
Norfolk Ct
Richardson St
Linwood Pl
Market St
Bristol St
Bristol St
Clark St
Lilac Ct
Binney St
Kinnaird St
Bay St
Green St
St Paul St
Vail Ct
Essex St
Worcester St
Suffolk St
Boardman St
Dickinson St
Moore St
Central
Pine St
Cherry St
Windsor St
Davis St
Western Ave
Bishop Allen Dr
Portland St
River St
Massachusetts Ave
Main St
Magazine St
Brookline St
Vassar St
MIT
1/4 mile
.25 km

Inman Square is an almost-hidden treasure at the center of the Cambridge/Somerville vortex. But its older, cozy Cantabrigian apartments are slowly being converted to condos, which means the secret is getting out. Folks from the rest of Boston are increasingly finding their way to Inman, particularly when they're hungry.

Landmarks

- **Julia Child's Home** • 103 Irving St [Bryant St]
  The kitchen was dismantled and moved to the Smithsonian.

Nightlife

- **Atwood's Tavern** •
  877 Cambridge St [Hunting St]
  617-864-2792
  Food 'til late and live local music.
- **Bukowski Tavern** •
  1281 Cambridge St [Oakland St]
  617-497-7077
  100+ beers. More chill than its Boston brother.
- **The Druid** •
  1357 Cambridge St [Springfield St]
  617-497-0965
  Well-liked Irish pub.
- **Lilypad** • 1353 Cambridge St [Hampshire St]
  617-395-1393
  Performance space for experimental and avant-garde artists.
- **Lord Hobo** • 92 Hampshire St [Windsor St]
  617-250-8454
  Good food, good beer, good God, let's cheer!
- **Parlor Sports** • 1 Beacon St [Dickinson St]
  617-576-0231
  Best sports bar in Cambridge.
- **Ryles Jazz Club** • 212 Hampshire St [Inman St]
  617-876-9330
  Two-level club with jazz, world, Latin.
- **Thirsty Scholar Pub** •
  70 Beacon St [Cooney St]
  617-497-2294
  Laid-back neighborhood local. Good food, too.

Restaurants

- **All Star Pizza Bar** • 1238 Cambridge St [Prospect St] 617-547-0836 • $$ Foodie pies. Pricey but creative.
- **All-Star Sandwich Bar** • 1245 Cambridge St [Prospect St] 617-868-3065 • $ Old-fashioned favorites like Mom used to make.
- **Amelia's Trattoria** • 111 Harvard St [Davis St] 617-868-7600 • $$$ The best Italian in this area.
- **Bergamot** • 118 Beacon St [Kirkland St] 617-576-7700 • $$$ Modern fine-dining with simple, local fare. Excellent.
- **BISq** • 1071 Cambridge St [Webster Ave] 617-714-3693 • $$$ Ecumenical bar bites and whole-animal feasts.
- **Bondir** • 279 Broadway [Elm St] 617-661-0009 • $$$ Another farm-to-table joint—not that we're complaining.
- **City Girl Café** • 204 Hampshire St [Inman St] 617-864-2809 • $$ Comfy and cool. Try the lasagna.
- **Dali** • 415 Washington St [Beacon St] 617-661-3254 • $$$ Fun taparia. Worth the wait. Usually worth the price.
- **The Friendly Toast** • 1 Kendall Sq [Hampshire St] 617-621-1200 • $$ Late-night spot for the domestic American hipster.
- **Ginger Exchange** • 1287 Cambridge St [Oakland St] 617-250-8618 • $$ Adequate sushi. Great happy hour roll specials.
- **The Kirkland Tap & Trotter** • 425 Washington St [Beacon St] 857-259-6585 • $$$ Tony Maws' molecular gastropub.
- **Koreana** • 158 Prospect St [Broadway] 617-576-8661 • $$ Cooking tasty bulgogi right at your table.
- **Midwest Grill** • 1124 Cambridge St [Norfolk St] 617-354-7536 • $$$ Brazilian sword-play.
- **Muqueca** • 1008 Cambridge St [Columbia St] 617-354-3296 • $$ Their specialty is a Brazilian-style seafood stew.
- **Olé Mexican Grill** • 11 Springfield St [Cambridge St] 617-492-4495 • $$ Delicious guacamole made right at your table.
- **Oleana** • 134 Hampshire St [Elm St] 617-661-0505 • $$$$ Top-notch Mediterranean. Patio seating in warm weather.
- **Punjabi Dhaba** • 225 Hampshire St [Cambridge St] 617-547-8272 • $ Some of the best Indian food for dirt cheap.
- **Puritan & Company** • 1166 Cambridge St [Tremont St] 617-615-6195 • $$$ Fresh New American with an emphasis on local flavors.
- **S&S Restaurant** • 1334 Cambridge St [Oak St] 617-354-0777 • $$ Serving deli, comfort food for eighty years.
- **Trina's Starlight Lounge** • 3 Beacon St [Dickinson St] 617-576-0006 • $$$ Old school Southern cocktails and vittles.
- **Tupelo** • 1193 Cambridge St [Tremont St] 617-868-0004 • $$ Food for the southerner in y'all.

Eats and treats. Choose from over 100 beers at **Bukowski's**, relax with a classy cocktail at **Trina's Starlight Lounge**, or get the best of both worlds at Lord Hobo. Sample farm-to-table Mediterranean fare at **Oleana** or homestyle Southern cookin' at **Tupelo**. Tour the famous **Taza Chocolate**, sift through threaded treasures at **The Garment District**, then sit in a hot tub at **Inman Oasis** and call it a day.

Shopping

- **Boston Costume Company** •
  200 Broadway [Davis St]
  617-482-1632
  Rentals and sales.
- **Christina's Homemade Ice Cream** •
  1255 Cambridge St [Prospect St]
  617-492-7021
  Clever flavors; good spice shop next door.
- **The Garment District** •
  200 Broadway [Davis St]
  617-876-5230
  Vintage threads, costumes, clothing by-the-pound.
- **Inman Oasis** •
  243 Hampshire St [Cambridge St]
  617-491-0176
  Get hydrated in the community hot tubs.
- **Royal Pastry Shop** •
  738 Cambridge St [Marion St]
  617-547-2053
  Caters to a devoted clientele.
- **Target** • 180 Somerville Ave [Mansfield St]
  617-776-4036
  Oh, you know.
- **Taza Chocolate** • 561 Windsor St [South St]
  617-284-2232
  Local, stone-ground chocolate.
- **Wine & Cheese Cask** •
  407 Washington St [Beacon St]
  617-623-8656
  Wine, cheese, specialties.

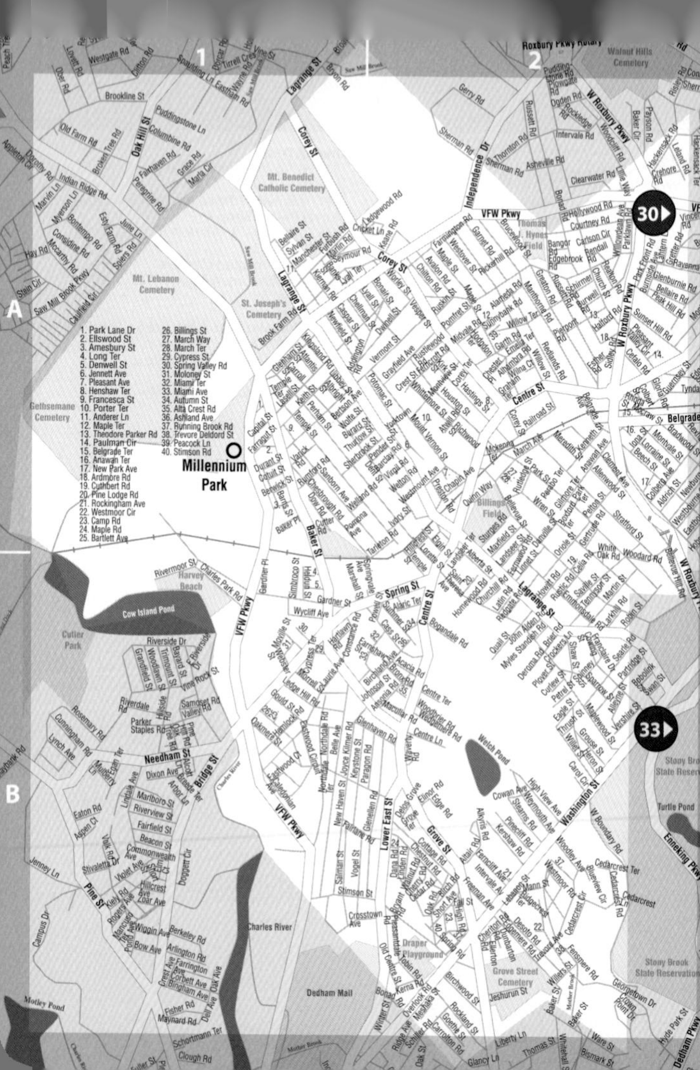

1
2
A
B
30
33
Millennium Park
1. Park Lane Dr
2. Ellswood St
3. Amesbury St
4. Long Ter
5. Denwell St
6. Jennett Ave
7. Pleasant Ave
8. Henshaw Ter
9. Francesca St
10. Porter Ter
11. Anderer Ln
12. Maple Ter
13. Theodore Parker Rd
14. Paulman Cir
15. Belgrade Ter
16. Anawan Ter
17. New Park Ave
18. Ardmore Rd
19. Cuthbert Rd
20. Pine Lodge Rd
21. Rockingham Ave
22. Westmoor Cir
23. Camp Rd
24. Maple Rd
25. Bartlett Ave
26. Billings St
27. March Way
28. March Ter
29. Cypress St
30. Spring Valley Rd
31. Moloney St
32. Miami Ter
33. Miami Ave
34. Autumn St
35. Alta Crest Rd
36. Ashland Ave
37. Running Brook Rd
38. Trevore Deldord St
39. Peacock Ln
40. Stimson Rd
Roxbury Pkwy Rotary
Walnut Hills Cemetery
Mt. Benedict Catholic Cemetery
Mt. Lebanon Cemetery
St. Joseph's Cemetery
Gethsemane Cemetery
Thomas J. Hynes Field
Billings Field
Harvey Beach
Cow Island Pond
Cutler Park
Welch Pond
Stony Brook State Reservation
Turtle Pond
Charles River
Draper Playground
Grove Street Cemetery
Dedham Mall
Motley Pond
VFW Pkwy
W Roxbury Pkwy
Centre St
Lagrange St
Corey St
Spring St
Baker St
Washington St
Independence Dr
Belgrade Ave
Needham St
Bridge St
Pine St
Lower East St
Grove St
Enneking Pkwy
Dedham Pkwy
Oak Hill St
Brookline St
Saw Mill Brook Pkwy

West Roxbury is a suburb-within-the-city community, with selective shopping and some good food. **Millennium Park** has fields, paths, and playgrounds, and a drive along VFW can be nice when the construction isn't bad and the trees are in bloom. The area exists as a middle ground between suburban Newton and city communities like Roslindale. With supermarkets and places to park, West Roxbury is a good place to settle if you want to stay in the city and own an affordable house.

Landmarks

- **Millennium Park** • VFW Pkwy & Gardner St
  Clear your head by flying a kite.

Restaurants

- **Comella's** • 1844 Centre St [Corey St]
  617-327-8600 • $$
  Get a mess of eggplant parm, lasagna, ziti, mozz…
- **Himalayan Bistro** •
  1735 Centre St [Manthorne Rd]
  617-325-3500 • $$$
  Nepali for your inner sherpa.
- **Mary Ann's Breakfast and Lunch** •
  223 Grove St [Washington St]
  617-469-7426 • $
  Solid breakfast shop.
- **Masona Grill** • 4 Corey St [Park St]
  617-323-3331 • $$$$
  Euro-Peruvian eclectic grill, West Roxbury's best
- **Porter Cafe** • 1723 Centre St [Esther Rd]
  617-942-2579 • $$
  Comfort food and heavy beer. You'll need a nap after.
- **Rox Diner** • 1881 Centre St [Corey St]
  617-327-1909 • $$
  Who says diner food can't be refined?
- **Viva Mi Arepa** •
  5197 Washington St [Grove St]
  617-323-7844 • $
  Empanadas and arepas to die for.
- **West on Centre** •
  1732 Centre St [Manthorne Rd]
  617-323-4199 • $$$
  Casual American; plenty of brick and mahogany.

Shopping

- **Bay Sweets Market** •
  120 Spring St [Gardner St]
  617-327-3737
  Middle Eastern grocery.
- **Boomerangs** • 1870 Centre St [Hastings St]
  617-323-0262
  Resale store that supports the AIDS Action Committee. Good karma, great prices.
- **Jack Davis Florist** • 2097 Centre St [Temple St]
  617-323-4237
  Florist.
- **Roche Bros** • 1800 Centre St [Willow St]
  617-469-5747
  Pre-made meat kabobs.

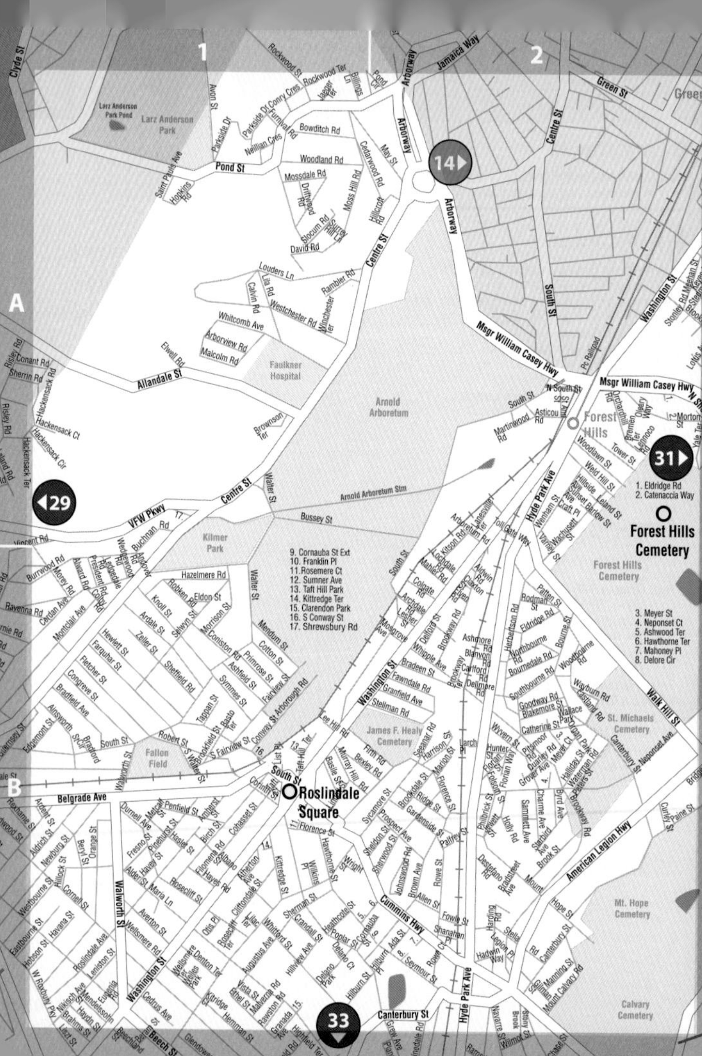
1
2
A
B
14
29
31
33
Larz Anderson Park Pond
Larz Anderson Park
Arnold Arboretum
Faulkner Hospital
Kilmer Park
Fallon Field
James F. Healy Cemetery
Forest Hills
Forest Hills Cemetery
St. Michaels Cemetery
Mt. Hope Cemetery
Calvary Cemetery
Roslindale Square
Green
Clyde St
Avon St
Rockwood St
Rockwood Ter
Billings Ln
Pond Cir
Arborway
Jamaica Way
Green St
Centre St
Parkside Dr
Parkside Dr
Conry Cres
Jaeger Ter
Furnival Rd
Neillian Cres
Bowditch Rd
Woodland Rd
Pond St
Saint Pauls Ave
Hopkins Rd
Mossdale Rd
Driftwood Rd
Moss Hill Rd
Cedarwood Rd
May St
Hillcroft Rd
Slocum Rd
Surrey Hill Ln
David Rd
Louders Ln
Lila Rd
Calvin Rd
Rambler Rd
Westchester Rd
Winchester Ter
Whitcomb Ave
Arborview Rd
Malcolm Rd
Elwell Rd
Allandale St
South St
Washington St
Msgr William Casey Hwy
Pc Railroad
Stonley Rd
Meehan St
Keyes Pl
Brookley
Lotus Ave
N South St
St Ann St
Asticou Rd
Martinwood Rd
Orchardhill Rd
Olgery Way
Bremen Ter
Kenmoco
Morton St
N Shea
Yale Ter
Tower St
Woodlawn St
Weld Hill St
Leland St
Hillside St
Sunset Ave
Craft Pl
Barlow St
Wenham St
Wachusett St
Varney St
Hyde Park Ave
1. Eldridge Rd
2. Catenaccia Way
Risley Rd
Conant Rd
Sherrin Rd
Hackensack Rd
Hackensack Ct
Hackensack Cir
Hackensack Ter
Leland Rd
Brownson Ter
Walter St
Arnold Arboretum Stm
Bussey St
VFW Pkwy
Vincent Rd
Buchnan Rd
Andover Rd
Wedgewood Rd
President Rd
Ledgedale Rd
Colbert Rd
Alward Rd
Morey Rd
Burrwood Rd
Ravenna Rd
Cerdan Ave
Montclair Ave
Hazelmere Rd
Robken Rd
Eldon St
Knoll St
Selwyn St
Morrison St
Ardale St
Hewlett St
Zeller St
Farquhar St
Fletcher St
Coniston Rd
Sheffield Rd
Primrose St
Ashfield St
Cotton St
Mendum St
Fairview St
Arborough Rd
Symmes St
Tappan St
Brookfield St
Basto Ter
Congreve St
Bradfield Ave
Ainsworth St
Edgemont St
Guernsey St
Bradeen
Bradford
Robert St
S Walter St
S Fairview St
Conway St
9. Cornauba St Ext
10. Franklin Pl
11. Rosemere Ct
12. Sumner Ave
13. Taft Hill Park
14. Kittredge Ter
15. Clarendon Park
16. S Conway St
17. Shrewsbury Rd
Arboretum Rd
Kitson Rd
Lochdale
Mahler Rd
Colgate Rd
Archdale Rd
Lanesville Ter
Toll Gate Way
Aldwin Rd
Clayton
Mosgrove Ave
Delford St
Brookway Rd
Whipple Ave
Bradeen St
Fawndale Rd
Granfield Ave
Stellman Rd
Ashmore Rd
Blanvon Rd
Carlford Rd
Dellmore Rd
Herbertson Rd
Rodman St
Patten St
Eldridge Rd
Bourne St
Northbourne Rd
Bournedale Rd
Woodbourne Rd
Southbourne Rd
Goodway Rd
Blakemore St
Wallace Park
Wayburn Rd
Eastland Rd
Walk Hill St
3. Meyer St
4. Neponset Ct
5. Ashwood Ter
6. Hawthorne Ter
7. Mahoney Pl
8. Delore Cir
Wyvern St
Catherine St
Hunter St
Florian St
Florian Way
Pitsmoor Rd
Quarley Rd
Meyer Ct
Grover Ave
Halliday St
Waterman Rd
St Peters St
Canterbury St
Neponset Ave
Bridge St
Lee Hill Rd
Firth Rd
Bexley Rd
Murray Hill Rd
Basile St
Seaman Rd
Harrison St
Marion St
Larch Pl
South St
List Pl
Taft Hill Ter
Corinth St
Belgrade Ave
Penfield St
Amherst St
Durnell Ave
Metcalf St
Birch St
Cohasset St
Florence St
Hawthorne St
Sycamore St
Prospect Ave
Brookdale St
Ridge St
Gardenside St
Florence St
Palfrey St
Philbrick St
Jewett St
Folsom St
Holly Rd
Sammett Ave
Charme Ave
Byrd Ave
Brook St
Starbird Ave
Brookway Rd
American Legion Hwy
Curley St
Paine St
Ardent St
Rexhame St
Aldrich St
Newburg St
Beryl St
Orange St
Fresno St
Pinehurst St
Hasler St
Filomena Rd
Albano St
Hayes Rd
Alder St
Maria Ln
Rosecliff St
Atherton Ave
Kittredge St
Wilkins Pl
Wright St
Sheldon St
Sherwood St
Johnswood Rd
Brown Ave
Rowe St
Allen St
Fowle St
Harding Rd
Destefano Rd
Bradstreet Ave
Mount
Hope St
Stella Rd
Legion Pl
Hadwin Way
Canterbury St
Manning St
Gilman St
Mount Calvary Rd
Hillock St
Cornell St
Westbourne St
Havana St
Eastbourne St
Hobson St
W Roxbury Pky
Roslindale Ave
Leniston St
Eugenia Rd
Walworth St
Averton St
Wellsmere Rd
Clifftondale St
Lilac Ter
Otis Pl
Rosecliff Ter
Whitford St
Sherman St
Crandall St
Heathcote St
Cornauba St
Poplar St
Delano Ct
Hillview Ave
Augustus Ave
Cummins Hwy
Ada St
Hilburn St
Seymour St
Rowe Ct
Shanahan Pl
Wellsmere Park
Denton Ter
Washington St
Vista St
Ethel St
Malverna Rd
Rawston Rd
Granada Ave
Highfield Ter
Delano Park
Hilburn Pl
Nikisch Ave
Mendelssohn St
Haydn St
Brahms St
Liszt St
Cedrus Ave
Kittridge St
Hemman St
Beech St
Glendower Rd
Beechland St
Canterbury St
Grew Ave
Pinedale Rd
Hyde Park Ave
Navarre St
Brook
Stony
Wilmot St
Chase St
Ramsdell

Over the last few decades, **Roslindale Square** (also known as Roslindale Village) has received awards for turning a virtual ghost town into a nice place to live through local shops and some great restaurants. The city subsidies didn't hurt either. Walking through the village area, one gets the sense of a community proud of itself. As a bonus, Roslindale Village is within walking distance of the **Arnold Arboretum**, the best park in Boston and possibly the best urban park in America.

Landmarks

- **Forest Hills Cemetery** •
  95 Forest Hills Ave [Morton St]
  617-524-0128
  This 250-acre beautiful cemetery is not only home to such literary greats as E. E. Cummings but is also a great spot to picnic and bike ride.
- **Roslindale Square** •
  Washington St [Belgrade Ave]
  Or, Roslindale Village.

Nightlife

- **JJ Foley's Fireside Tavern** •
  30 Hyde Park Ave [Weld Hill St]
  617-524-9849
  A great old man bar that is slowly being taken over by the young'uns.

Restaurants

- **Birch Street Bistro** • 14 Birch St [Corinth St]
  617-323-2184 • $$
  Inviting place to kick back for dinner.
- **Delfino** • 754 South St [Taft Ct]
  617-327-8359 • $$$
  Tiny, popular spot serving good-quality Italian.
- **Napper Tandy's** • 4195 Washington St [Basile St]
  617-323-8400 • $$
  Townies abound.
- **Pleasant Cafe** • 4515 Washington St [Cedrus Ave]
  617-323-2111 • $$
  Pizza and other basics. Don't be scared of the sketchy exterior.
- **Redd's in Rozzie** •
  4257 Washington Ave [Corinth St]
  617-325-1000 • $$
  Southern American feel good, stick to your ribs food. Get the hush puppies!
- **Romano's Pizzeria & Taqueria** •
  4249 Washington St [Poplar St]
  617-325-2885 • $
  Two great foods under one roof.
- **Roslindale House of Pizza** •
  4168 Washington St [Bexley Rd]
  617-327-9170 • $
  Pizza. Ya know, pizza.
- **Shanti Taste of India** •
  4197 Washington St [Basile St]
  617-325-3900 • $$
  Authentic Indian with a posh backdrop.
- **Sophia's Grotto** • 22 Birch St [Corinth St]
  617-323-4595 • $$
  Cozy family trattoria. Enjoy the mussels in the courtyard.
- **Village Sushi & Grill** • 14 Corinth St [Birch St]
  617-363-7874 • $$
  Japanese and Korean.
- **Yucatàn Tacos** • 1417 Centre St [Knoll St]
  617-323-7555 • $
  Authentic Mexican food, apparently.

Shopping

- **Atlas Liquors** •
  591 Hyde Park Ave [Cummins Hwy]
  617-323-8202
  Sousing the locals since 1933.
- **Boston Cheese Cellar** • 18 Birch St [Corinth St]
  617-325-2500
  NFT loves cheese. And free samples.
- **Droubi Bakery** • 4198 Washington St [Basile St]
  617-325-1585
  Cheap veggies and fruit along with delicious Middle Eastern baked goods.
- **Exotic Flowers** •
  609 American Legion Hwy [Canterbury St]
  617-942-4803
  Florist.
- **Fornax Bread Company** •
  27 Corinth St [Washington St]
  617-325-8852
  Sandwiches, too.
- **Joanne Rossman** • 6 Birch St [Belgrade Ave]
  617-323-4301
  Curios for the rich. Cool stuff, nice lady.
- **Roslindale Fish Market** •
  38 Poplar St [Washington St]
  617-327-9487
  Come early for fresh fish.
- **Solera** • 16 Birch St [Corinth St]
  617-469-4005
  A shrine to wine.
- **Thrift Shop of Boston** •
  33 Corinth St [Cohasset St]
  617-325-5300
  Packed with tons of potential treasures and friendly staff.

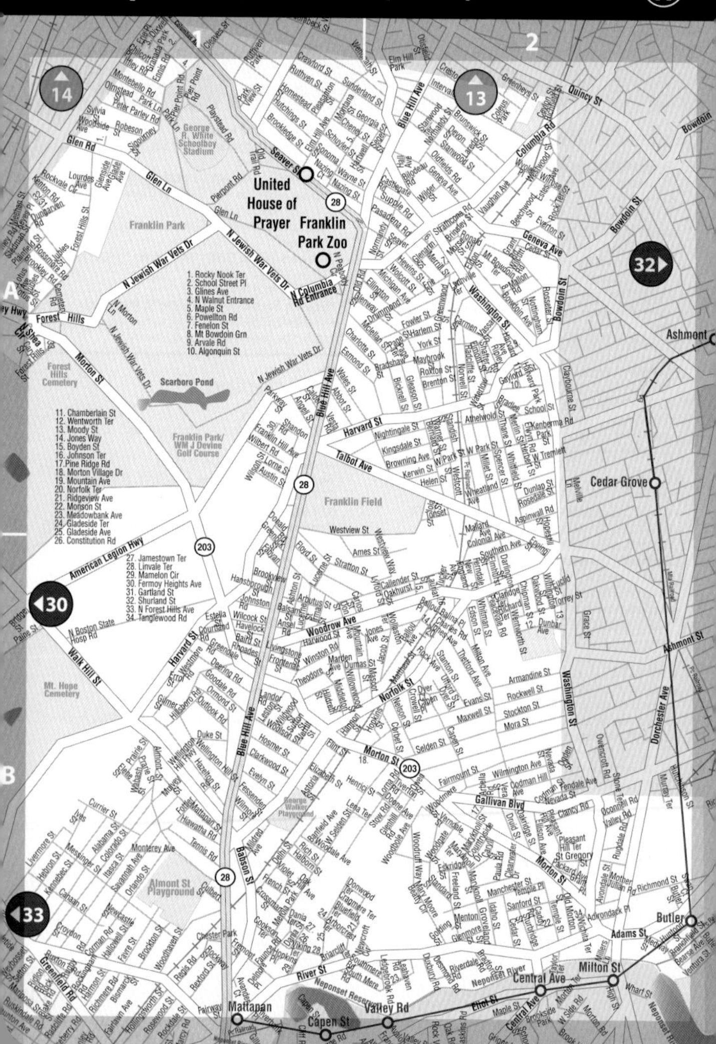

1
2
A
B
14
13
32
30
33
United House of Prayer
Franklin Park Zoo
Franklin Park
Scarboro Pond
George R. White Schoolboy Stadium
Forest Hills Cemetery
Franklin Park/ WM J Devine Golf Course
Franklin Field
Mt. Hope Cemetery
Almont St Playground
George Walker Playground
Elm Hill Park
1. Rocky Nook Ter
2. School Street Pl
3. Glines Ave
4. N Walnut Entrance
5. Maple St
6. Powellton Rd
7. Fenelon St
8. Mt Bowdoin Grn
9. Arvale Rd
10. Algonquin St
11. Chamberlain St
12. Wentworth Ter
13. Moody St
14. Jones Way
15. Boyden St
16. Johnson Ter
17.Pine Ridge Rd
18. Morton Village Dr
19. Mountain Ave
20. Norfolk Ter
21. Ridgeview Ave
22. Monson St
23. Meadowbank Ave
24. Gladeside Ter
25. Gladeside Ave
26. Constitution Rd
27. Jamestown Ter
28. Linvale Ter
29. Mamelon Cir
30. Fermoy Heights Ave
31. Gartland St
32. Shurland St
33. N Forest Hills Ave
34. Tanglewood Rd
28
203
Ashmont
Cedar Grove
Butler
Milton St
Central Ave
Valley Rd
Capen St
Mattapan
Blue Hill Ave
Washington St
Morton St
American Legion Hwy
N Jewish War Vets Dr
Columbia Rd
Harvard St
Talbot Ave
Woodrow Ave
Norfolk St
Gallivan Blvd
River St
Dorchester Ave
Bowdoin St
Geneva Ave
Quincy St
Glen Rd
Glen Ln
Forest Hills
Walk Hill St
Seaver St
Ashmont St
Adams St
Eliot St
Neponset River
Neponset Reservation

Mattapan is mostly residential and home to about 40,000 people. It has a growing Haitian-American community (the largest in Massachusetts), and has smaller communities whose roots are in many of the nations of the Caribbean. This is reflected in the wealth of Caribbean restaurants located on Blue Hill Avenue.

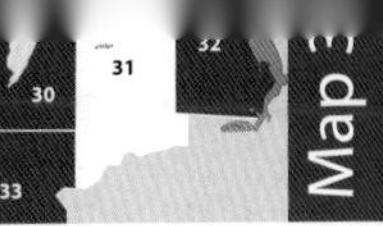

O Landmarks

- **Franklin Park Zoo Bear Cages •**
  1 Franklin Park Rd [Blue Hill Ave]
  The abandoned bear cages outside the zoo's fences make for a creepy outing.
- **United House of Prayer •**
  206 Seaver St [Elm Hill Ave]
  617-445-3246
  Impressive Mishkan Tefila synagogue, now church and soul food kitchen.

Restaurants

- **Ali's Roti** • 1188 Blue Hill Ave [Morton St]
  617-298-9850 • $
  You have not experienced life until you dive into a delicious roti.
- **Bon Appetit •**
  1138 Blue Hill Ave [Livingstone St]
  617-825-5544 • $$
  Haitian food supposedly makes you a better lover.
- **Brothers** • 1638 Blue Hill Ave [Fairway St]
  617-298-5224 • $
  Southern. Huge side portions.
- **Flames** • 469 Blue Hill Ave [Georgia St]
  617-989-0000 • $$
  Unusually stylish for this neighborhood.
- **Genki Ya** • 398 Harvard St [Naples Rd]
  617-277-3100 • $$
  Mr. T says that's how sushi is done foo!
- **Lenny's Tropical Bakery •**
  1195 Blue Hill Ave [Deering Rd]
  617-296-2587 • $
  Double parking for the patties.
- **P&R Ice Cream** • 1284 Blue Hill Ave [Evelyn St]
  617-296-0922 • $
  Nothing beats a beef patty followed by a scoop of Grape Nut ice cream.
- **Pit Stop Bar-B-Q •**
  888 Morton St [Cemetery Rd]
  617-436-0485 • $
  A rib shack, literally. Stick to the ribs.
- **Simco's** • 1509 Blue Hill Ave [Regis Rd]
  617-296-3800 • $
  Boston's best hotdogs since the 1930s.
- **United House of Prayer •**
  206 Seaver St [Elm Hill Ave]
  617-445-3246 • $
  Friendly soul food in basement of Boston's old stadt shul.

Shopping

- **Dark Horse Antiques •**
  1162 Washington St
  617-298-1031
  Antiques. Friendly.
- **Le Foyer Bakery** • 132 Babson St [Fremont St]
  617-298-0535
  Long lines for patties at this Haitian bakery.
- **Taurus Records •**
  1282 Blue Hill Ave [Evelyn St]
  617-298-2655
  Small shop is best source for reggae, tons of singles.

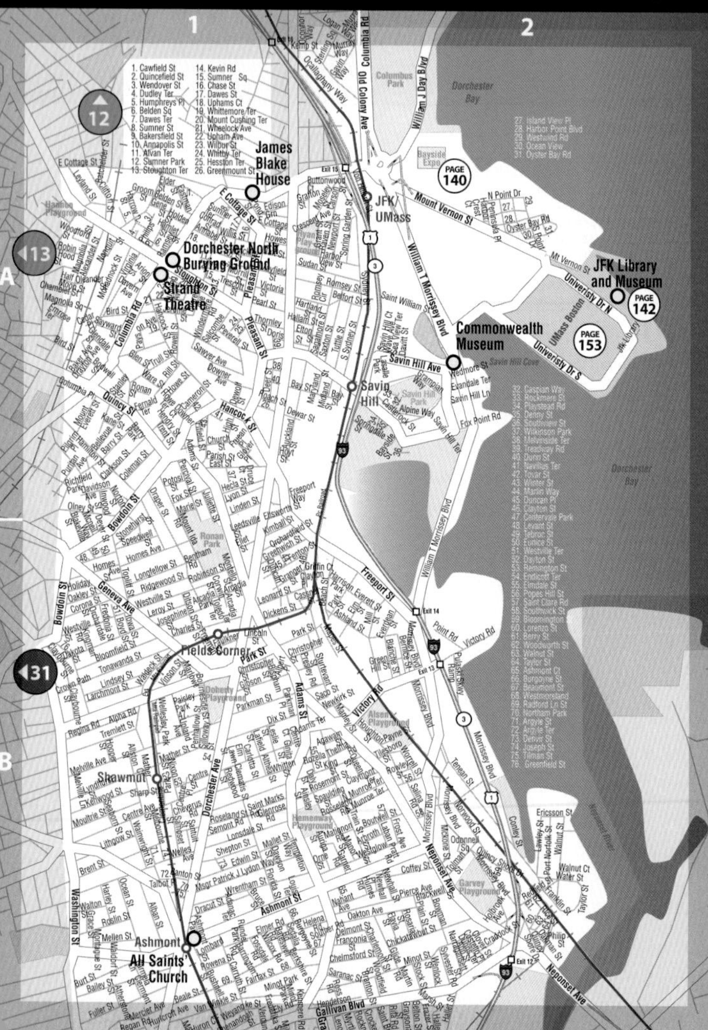
1
2
A
B
12
13
31
1. Cawfield St
2. Quincefield St
3. Wendover St
4. Dudley Ter
5. Humphreys Pl
6. Belden Sq
7. Dawes Ter
8. Sumner St
9. Bakersfield St
10. Annapolis St
11. Alvan Ter
12. Sumner Park
13. Stoughton Ter
14. Kevin Rd
15. Sumner Sq
16. Chase St
17. Dawes St
18. Uphams Ct
19. Whittemore Ter
20. Mount Cushing Ter
21. Wheelock Ave
22. Upham Ave
23. Wilbur St
24. Whitby Ter
25. Hesston Ter
26. Greenmount St
27. Island View Pl
28. Harbor Point Blvd
29. Westwind Rd
30. Ocean View
31. Oyster Bay Rd
32. Caspian Way
33. Rockmere St
34. Playstead Rd
35. Denny St
36. Southview St
37. Wilkinson Park
38. Melvinside Ter
39. Treadway Rd
40. Dunn St
41. Bavillus Ter
42. Tovar St
43. Winter St
44. Marlin Way
45. Duncan Pl
46. Clayton St
47. Centervale Park
48. Levant St
49. Tebroc St
50. Eunice St
51. Westville Ter
52. Dayton St
53. Remington St
54. Endicott Ter
55. Elmdale St
56. Popes Hill St
57. Saint Clare Rd
58. Southwick St
59. Bloomington St
60. Lorenzo St
61. Berry St
62. Woodworth St
63. Walnut St
64. Taylor St
65. Ashmont Ct
66. Burgoyne St
67. Beaumont St
68. Westmoreland
69. Radford Ln St
70. Northam Park
71. Argyle St
72. Argyle Ter
73. Denver St
74. Joseph St
75. Tilman St
76. Greenfield St
James Blake House
Dorchester North Burying Ground
Strand Theatre
JFK/UMass
JFK Library and Museum
Commonwealth Museum
Savin Hill
Fields Corner
Shawmut
Ashmont
All Saints' Church
PAGE 140
PAGE 142
PAGE 153
Columbus Park
Dorchester Bay
Bayside Expo
UMass Boston
Savin Hill Park
Ronan Park
Doherty Playground
Ryan Playground
Hemenway Playground
Garvey Playground
Alsen Playground
Hannon Playground
Neponset River
Exit 12
Exit 13
Exit 14
Exit 15
Columbia Rd
Old Colony Ave
William J Day Blvd
Mount Vernon St
William T Morrissey Blvd
University Dr N
University Dr S
Savin Hill Ave
Dorchester Ave
Adams St
Geneva Ave
Bowdoin St
Washington St
Neponset Ave
Gallivan Blvd
Freeport St
Victory Rd
Hancock St
Pleasant St
Quincy St
Ashmont St
Morrissey Blvd

(In)famous for protecting turf, Dorchester is a collection of distinct neighborhoods and ethnicities. Uphams Corner, Savin Hill, Fields Corner, Ashmont, Codman Square, and Grove Hall are but a few of the areas that comprise Boston's largest district. If all you think about when you hear Dorchester is crime, you're missing out on an amazing section of the city—for eating, and for cheaper rents than some of the more upscale 'hoods.

Landmarks

- **All Saints' Church •**
  209 Ashmont St [Bushnell St]
  617-436-6370
  Founded in 1867. Beautiful stained glass.
- **The Blake House •** 735 Columbia Rd [Pond St]
  Built in 1648, Boston's oldest house.
- **Commonwealth Museum •**
  220 Morrissey Blvd [Dominic J Bianculli Blvd]
  617-727-9268
  Operated by the Massachusetts Historical Society.
- **Dorchester North Burying Ground •**
  Columbia Rd & Stoughton St
  Interesting and eerie gravestones spanning 4 centuries.
- **John F. Kennedy Presidential Library and Museum •** Morrissey Blvd & Columbia Pt
  617-514-1600
  Houses 21 permanent exhibits examining JFK's life and work.
- **Strand Theatre •** 543 Columbia Rd [Dudley St]
  617-635-1403
  Vaudeville, movie house time capsule. Under renovation.

Nightlife

- **Boston Bowl •**
  820 Morrissey Blvd [Freeport St]
  617-825-3800
  Open 24 hours. Family fun all night long.
- **dbar •** 1236 Dorchester Ave [Hoyt St]
  617-265-4490
  Hip, gay bar. Food till 10 pm, then the dancing starts.
- **Eire Pub •** 795 Adams St [Gallivan Blvd]
  617-436-0088
  Politicians and sports fans welcome.
- **Harp & Bard •**
  1099 Dorchester Ave [Savin Hill Ave]
  617-265-2893
  Patio makes this a summertime Irish standout.
- **Tom English Bar •**
  957 Dorchester Ave [Howes St]
  617-288-7748
  A dive, no doubt, but a friendly one.

Restaurants

- **Ashmont Grill •** 555 Talbot Ave [Ashmont St]
  617-825-4300 • $$$
  Bringing flair to Peabody Square.
- **Banh Mi Ba Le •**
  1052 Dorchester Ave [William St]
  617-265-7171 • $
  Wonderful crisp Vietnamese sandwiches.
- **The Blarney Stone •**
  1505 Dorchester Ave [Park St]
  617-436-8223 • $$
  Hodgepodge of good pub-type food.
- **McKenna's Cafe •**
  109 Savin Hill Ave [S Sydney St]
  617-825-8218 • $
  Four words: sweet potato home fries.
- **O Ya •** 9 East St [South St]
  617-654-9900 • $$$$$
  Amazing sushi that is not easy on the wallet.
- **Pho 2000 •** 198 Adams St [Arcadia St]
  617-436-1908 • $$
  Serving a delicious 7 course beef dinner.
- **Restaurante Cesaria •**
  266 Bowdoin St [Draper St]
  617-282-1998 • $$
  Something for everyone—grilled octopus to chicken parmesean.
- **Shanti: Taste of India •**
  1111 Dorchester Ave [Savin Hill Ave]
  617-929-3900 • $$
  Go for the goat.

Shopping

- **Boston Winery •** 26 Ericsson St [Walnut St]
  617-265-9463
  Make your own wine, own your own barrel.
- **Coleen's Flower Shop •**
  912 Dorchester Ave [Grafton St]
  617-282-0468
  Cute florist on Dot Ave.
- **Euromart •** 808 Dorchester Ave [Locust St]
  617-825-1969
  Polish meats, beers, and pirogies.
- **Greenhill's Irish Bakery •**
  780 Adams St [Henderson Rd]
  617-825-8187
  Soda bread, scones and sandwiches with blood pudding.

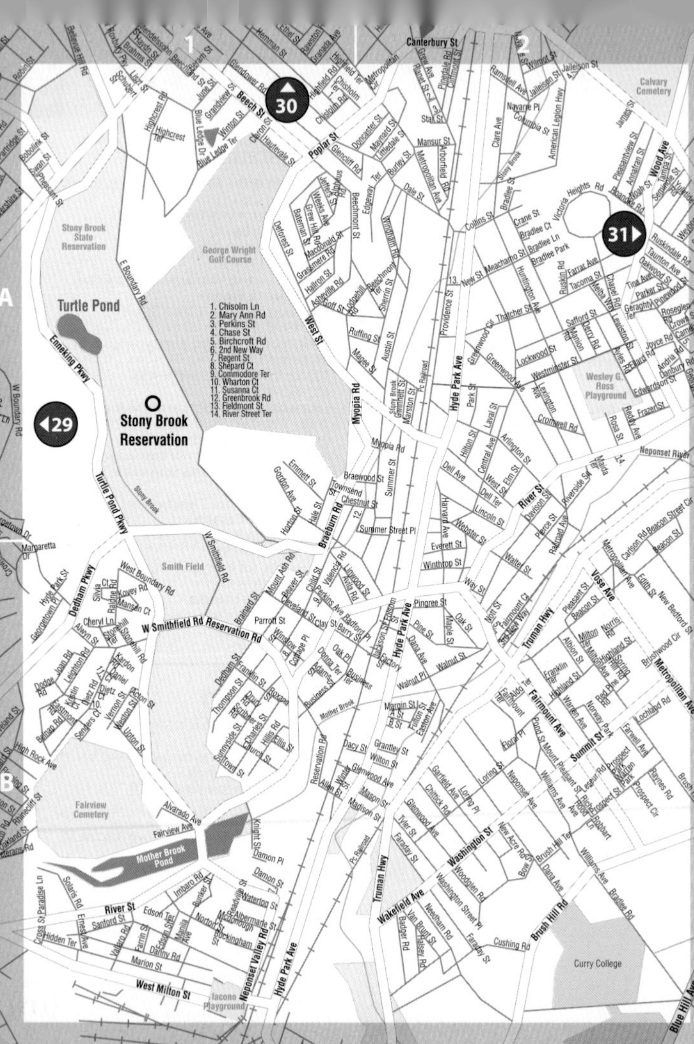

1
2
A
B
30
31
29
Turtle Pond
Stony Brook Reservation
Stony Brook State Reservation
George Wright Golf Course
1. Chisolm Ln
2. Mary Ann Rd
3. Perkins St
4. Chase St
5. Birchcroft Rd
6. 2nd New Way
7. Regent St
8. Shepard Ct
9. Commodore Ter
10. Wharton Ct
11. Susanna Ct
12. Greenbrook Rd
13. Fieldmont St
14. River Street Ter
Calvary Cemetery
Wesley G. Ross Playground
Smith Field
Fairview Cemetery
Mother Brook Pond
Mother Brook
Stony Brook
Neponset River
Curry College
Iacono Playground
Canterbury St
Beech St
Poplar St
West St
Hyde Park Ave
Metropolitan Ave
American Legion Hwy
Wood Ave
Enneking Pkwy
Turtle Pond Pkwy
E Boundary Rd
W Boundary Rd
Dedham Pkwy
W Smithfield Rd
Reservation Rd
Braeburn Rd
Myopia Rd
River St
Truman Hwy
Fairmount Ave
Summit St
Washington St
Wakefield Ave
Brush Hill Rd
Blue Hill Ave
Neponset Valley Rd
West Milton St
River St
Vose Ave
Metropolitan Ave
Cummins Hwy
Greenwood Ave
Cromwell Rd
Sunnyside St
Prospect Park
Pc Railroad

Almost as large as Franklin Park, **Stony Brook Reservation** covers 475 acres and includes low hills, dense woods, rock outcroppings, and marshland. The park's largest feature is Turtle Pond, where you can fish for perch and sunfish. There are also several miles of bicycle paths and the most extensive hiking opportunities within the city limits. Among the park's many recreational facilities is the John F. Thompson Center, New England's first recreational facility designed specifically to accommodate handicapped visitors.

Landmarks

- **Stony Brook Reservation** • Turtle Pond Pkwy
  617-333-7404
  Great option for biking and hiking.

Nightlife

- **Master McGrath** • 1154 River St [Winthrop Rd]
  617-364-3662
  Like a real life Cheers.

Restaurants

- **Rincon Caribeno** • 18 Fairmount Ave [River St]
  617-360-9775 • $
  A new addition to Fairmont that serves predominately Puerto Rican food.

Shopping

- **Capone Foods** • 14 Bow St [Garfield Ave]
  617-629-2296
  All your specialty food shop needs.
- **Ron's Gourmet Ice Cream** •
  1231 Hyde Park Ave [Everett St]
  617-364-5274
  Candlepins too!
- **Tutto Italiano** • 1889 River St [Solaris Rd]
  617-361-4700
  Deli. A mayoral favorite.

Overview

Copley Square is named after Boston-born portrait painter John Singleton Copley (1738–1815), America's first great artist. His portraits of America's founding fathers are on display at the Massachusetts Historical Society, across the street from the square, and at the Museum of Fine Arts. The Boston Marathon, held annually on Patriots' Day (the third Monday in April), ends on Boylston Street. A BosTix outlet, the place to score discounted theater tickets, stands at the corner of Boylston Street and Dartmouth Street. The farmers market fills the square Tuesdays and Fridays from 11 am to 6 pm, late May through November. The Friends of Copley Square sponsors its annual Holiday Tree Lighting the week after Thanksgiving. Summer months bring folk and swing dancing performances to the square on Tuesday evenings, as well as a bevy of sun-seeking loungers.

Architecture & Sculpture

The Boston Public Library is America's oldest public library. The Renaissance-revival style structure holds within it over seven million books, as well as busts of famous writers and prominent Bostonians. Big bonus: It offers wireless Internet access. Across the square you'll find the neo-Romanesque Trinity Church, designed by notable architect H.H. Richardson. The stained glass windows alone are worth a trip inside.

John Hancock Tower

The John Hancock Mutual Life Insurance Company, which already inhabited buildings on Clarendon Street and Berkeley Street, needed more space to house its employees, so it opted to build a 60-story black glass tower. What better place to put it than next to the Public Library and an old church? Designed by architect Henry Cobb, and completed in 1976, the John Hancock Tower became famous for being the tallest building in New England, and simultaneously infamous for falling apart.

Locals were upset when a foundation collapse in the early stages of construction nearly sucked Trinity Church into the ground. They became outraged when, in January 1973, one of the building's 10,000-plus glass windows "popped off" and shattered on the ground below, followed by dozens more 500-pound window panes. All told, 65 panes fell onto the roped-off area below the building before workers changed the solder used to mount the windows. In the meantime, locals had dubbed the Hancock "The Plywood Palace," in reference to the black plywood sheets put in place to substitute for the fallen panes. Not long after, engineers discovered the building was in danger of being sheared in half by the wind, resulting in another expensive fix. Today, the Hancock Tower stands sturdy, tall, and proud, and locals have even grown to love it. (Classic Boston photo op: Trinity Church is reflected in the mirrored side of the Hancock Tower, a clichéd but perfect example of Boston's mix of old and new.)

The observation deck on the 60th floor, originally opened to the public in response to community feedback, was permanently closed for security reasons after the events of September 11, 2001. Height junkies must now head over to the nearby Prudential Center for a what-a-view fix.

How to Get There—Driving

From the south, take I-93 N to Exit 18 (Massachusetts Avenue/Roxbury). Follow signs to Massachusetts Avenue and turn right. Turn right on Huntington Avenue, then left onto Dartmouth Street. From the north, take I-93 S to Exit 26 (Storrow Drive). Follow Storrow Drive west to the Copley Square exit. Turn right onto Beacon Street and, after two blocks, turn left onto Clarendon Street. After five blocks, turn right onto St. James Avenue. This is one of two examples in the city (the other being the Pru) where the "look up, locate the giant building, and drive towards it" method of navigation works well.

How to Get There—Mass Transit

Take the Green Line to the Copley stop. Alternatively, take the Orange Line to the Back Bay stop, exit, and head to your right along Dartmouth Street. Again, if you're not sure which way to go, look for the giant glass building.

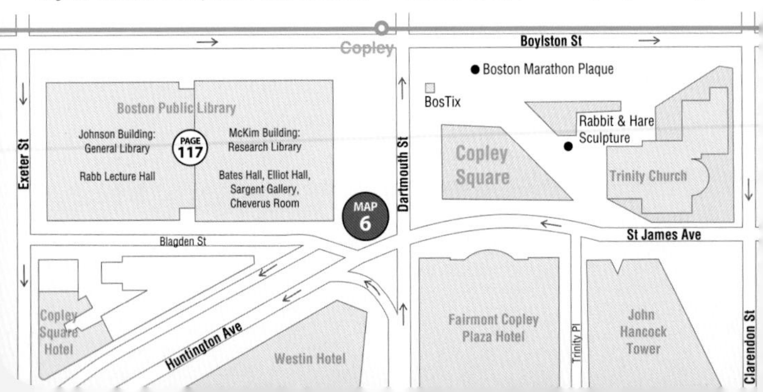

General Information

NFT Map:	6
Address:	700 Boylston St, Boston, MA 02116
Phone:	617-536-5400
Website:	www.bpl.org
Hours:	Mon–Thurs: 9 am–9 pm, Fri–Sat: 9 am–5 pm, Sun: 1 pm–5 pm (Oct–May)

Overview

The Boston Public Library, founded in 1848, was the country's first publicly-supported municipal library. The BPL was also the first public library to lend a book and the first to institute a children's room. All adult Massachusetts residents are entitled to borrowing and research privileges to the 7.5 million books currently house at the BPL. Its circulating collection and the Norman B. Leventhal Map Center (home to a whopping 350,000 maps), Rare Books and Manuscripts Department (M–F 9 am–5 pm), and many other research-oriented nooks and crannies continue to attract scholars and tourists alike. Additionally, the BPL's ever-changing exhibits are always good for a free, rainy day activity, as are the frequent talks by bestselling authors.

The BPL's main branch is the Central Library, composed of two august buildings adjacent to Copley Square that hold a lot more than just books. Facing Dartmouth Street, the McKim Building (the "old wing") was designed by noted 19th-century architect Charles Follen McKim and opened in 1895. The old wing, which houses the Research Library, is built around a delightful Italianate courtyard that offers readers a most un-library-like place to relax with a book. A set of murals painted by John Singer Sargent hangs inside. Sargent, better known for his portraits than for large installations, intended for these mammoth murals to be his masterpiece. There's also a set of allegorical murals by Pierre Puvis de Chavannes and the architecturally significant Bates Hall.

Opened to the public in 1972, the Johnson Building was designed by legendary architect Philip Johnson. The building, which houses the General Library, faces Boylston Street and is still referred to as the "new wing." (Granted, a better nickname might be the "ugly wing.") The Johnson Building has less knock-out art than the McKim Building, but it does have the tiled architectural frieze *The Goose Girl*, which is worth seeking out if you're wandering through the building. The BPL offers guided tours of both the old and new wings.

Internet

If you're ever stuck without Internet access, head over to the Central Library. Both the old and new wings have PCs available for use by the general public. (All computers have Internet connections and Microsoft Office software.) The first floor of the new wing also has "express" PCs that limit use to 15 minutes—handy for a quick e-mail hit. Both buildings are also equipped with Wi-Fi access.

For the Kids

Besides the weekly and seasonal programs it offers for everyone small from infants to teens, the Central Library has an outstanding collection of materials for even the youngest readers. Most of these materials can be found in the Margret and H.A. Rey Children's Room, named for the creators of that beloved, inquisitive simian, Curious George. The Children's Room also offers access to computers with Internet-filtering software, which is helpful for protecting fragile little minds. For more information, check the website or call 617-859-2328.

Restaurants

The Central Library now has two restaurants to sate you during long hours of research. Courtyard Restaurant, the fancier of the two restaurants, is set in a spacious room overlooking the courtyard in the center of the McKim Building. (Tip: Nip in for afternoon tea, served 2:30 pm to 4 pm on weekdays.) Next door to Courtyard Restaurant, Map Room Café serves breakfast, lunch, and snacks. For reservations at Courtyard Restaurant, or for additional information, call 617-385-5660. Note that food and drink are generally prohibited from the public areas of the Central Library, so chug your coffee before entering.

How to Get There—Driving

From the north or the south, take I-93 to Exit 26 (Storrow Drive). From Storrow Drive, take the Copley Square exit. The exit dead-ends at Beacon Street. Turn right on Beacon Street, drive four blocks to Exeter Street, and make a left. Drive along Exeter Street until you reach Boylston Street. The Central Library is on the corner of Boylston Street and Exeter Street.

From the west, take the Mass Pike (I-90 E) to Exit 22 (Prudential Center/Copley Square). Move to the right lane and follow the road in the tunnel toward Copley Square. The tunnel exits onto Stuart Street. Quickly move to the far left lane of Stuart Street and make a left at the next light onto Dartmouth Street. Drive through the next set of lights. The Central Library will be on the left.

Parking

The Central Library's location near Copley Square doesn't offer much in the way of street parking. If you're feeling unlucky, try the parking garage on Stuart Street between Dartmouth Street and Exeter Street.

How to Get There—Mass Transit

Take the T's Green Line to the Copley stop or the Orange Line to the Back Bay stop. From there, it should be pretty obvious: Look for the biggest, oldest, and grayest building around.

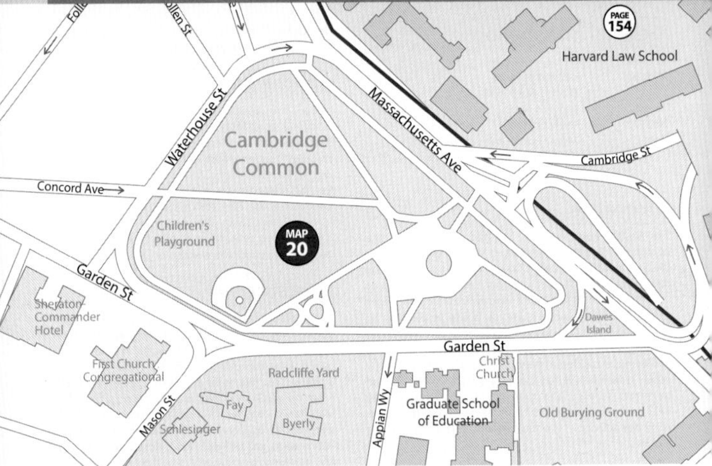

Overview

Cambridge Common was the center of rebel activity in the early years of the Revolution and has been a hub of political and social activity ever since. George Washington rallied the 16,000-man Continental Army under an elm tree on the green on July 3, 1775, and the area became the primary training ground for the troops.

William Dawes, along with Paul Revere and Dr. Samuel Prescott, rode his horse across the Common on his way to warn those in Lexington and Concord that "the regulars are coming" (not that "the British are coming"). While Revere inspired a famous poem and became the namesake of many American cities, Dawes was commemorated with some lousy bronze hoof prints in the pavement of the Common.

Three cannon that the colonists seized from the Lobsterbacks still sit by the flagpole. There's also a memorial to victims of the Irish Potato Famine.

Even with the addition of a playground and a softball field, this historical urban oasis remains an important place to voice ideas and protests. Just steps away from Harvard University, the Common's corner on Mass Ave has been used by activists protesting everything from the occupation of Iraq to the existence of SUVs.

Attractions

Relaxing and people-watching are, by far, the two best activities to undertake on the Common. With its prime location next to Harvard Square, you can feel like a Harvard student, without the excessive course fees and mandatory high IQ, though tree-shaded benches are available for reading if you want to play the part.

Cambridge Common is the focal point of the Cambridge Common Historic District, which also includes Christ Church, Old Harvard Yard, Massachusetts Hall, and Gannett House (the oldest surviving building on Harvard University's campus).

The park has a fenced-in playground, located on the corner of Garden and Waterhouse Streets, where kids can frolic safely. The playground was last renovated in 1990 (including the addition of a wooden climbing structure, swings, bridges, slides, and benches/picnic tables) and is recommended for parents with children aged one to ten.

Sports

There's a softball field, soccer fields, and designated areas for other light recreation along with bike paths for cyclists, skaters, joggers, and walkers. Despite the close link between afternoon softball games and booze, the rules forbid alcoholic beverages on the ball field.

General Information

NFT Map: 8
Address: 1st Ave, Charlestown, MA 02129
Phone: 617-242-5601 (Visitor Center); 617-242-5671 (USS Constitution)
Websites: http://www.nps.gov/bost/historyculture/cny.htm
www.cityofboston.gov/freedomtrail/ussconstitution.asp
www.charlestownonline.net/navyyard.htm
Hours: 10 am–4 pm, Thurs-Sun (Winter); 10 am–5:50 pm, Tues-Sun (Summer); 10 am–4 pm, Tues-Sun (Fall); free admission

Overview

The Charlestown Navy Yard is a must-see for anyone who likes big ships or US naval history. The two main attractions are the *USS Cassin Young* and "Old Ironsides" herself, the *USS Constitution*. The yard was established in 1800 as one of the first naval shipyards in the country, and the *Constitution* is almost as old as the country itself. When the Navy retired the yard in 1974, the yard became part of the Boston National Historic Park.

Attractions

Typical Fourth of July celebrations in Boston range from backyard barbecues to beach sunbathing, but the Navy Yard has its own unique tradition. Independence Day is celebrated with the customary turning of the *Constitution*—an annual practice in which the great vessel is tugged out of the dock and rotated to ensure uniform weathering. The *Cassin Young* has battle scars from its service in both World War II and the Korean War. The nearby Commandant's House, the oldest building in the Navy Yard, is no longer a private home, but an elegant museum, which is open to the public. The Navy Yard Visitor Center/Bunker Hill Pavillion also serves those visiting the nearby Bunker Hill Monument.

How to Get There—Driving

From the north, take I-93 S to Exit 28 (Sullivan Square/Charlestown), go under I-93, and follow signs to Sullivan Square. Bear left at the first traffic light and drive into the Sullivan Square rotary; take the second right onto Bunker Hill Street, turn right onto Chelsea Street, and make an immediate left onto Fifth Street. Drive one block (Fifth Street dead-ends) and turn left onto First Avenue.

From the south, take I-93 N to Exit 26 (Storrow Drive) and aim for the "North Station, USS Constitution" signs. Turn left onto Martha Road (which becomes Lomasney Way), left on Causeway Street, then left at N Washington Street, and get into the right lane as quickly as possible. At the end of the bridge, turn right onto Chelsea Street.

From the west, take the Mass Pike (I-90 E) to I-93 N, and follow the directions above.

Parking

Though public transportation is strongly recommended for this area, discounted parking with Boston National Historical Park validation is available from the Nautica Parking Garage across from the park's Visitor Center on Constitution Road.

How to Get There—Mass Transit

Visitors can take the MBTA Water Shuttle to Pier 4 at the Navy Yard from Long Wharf for $3. (See page 190 for more information.) Or follow the Freedom Trail from North Station.

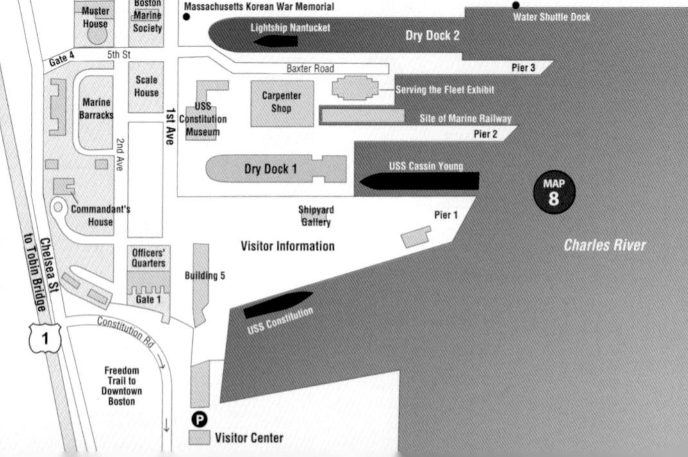

General Information

NFT Map: 3
Address: 147 Tremont St (b/w Temple Pl & West St)
Phone: 617-426-3115
Websites: www.bostonusa.com
www.cityofboston.gov/freedomtrail/bostoncommon.asp

Overview

One of the nation's oldest public parks, Boston Common was purchased by the Commonwealth of Massachusetts in 1634 to serve as livestock grazing ground. The city charged each household six shillings to pay for "the Commonage." (It was Tax-achusetts even back then!) People also used the Common to watch others being hanged at the gallows (like them cursed Quakers), for public meetings, and for military drills. The gallows were removed in 1817 and cow grazing was officially banned in 1830, around the time that urban cow ownership began falling out of fashion. In 1910, the Olmsted Brothers oversaw a massive landscape renovation, designating Boston Common as the anchor of the "Emerald Necklace," a system of connected parks that winds through many of Boston's neighborhoods. Boston Common is the beginning of the Freedom Trail and the Black Heritage Trail.

Situated across from the State House, Boston Common embodies the spirit of the city around it. Tourists, students, lunching suits, homeless Bostonians, and strolling older folks all share the park. On the lawn, squirrels and pigeons fight the latest chapter in their centuries-old gang war, while ducks enjoy free bread from park-goers. It is home to America's first and second subway stations (Park St and Boylston St), the Central Burying Ground, and the Robert Gould Shaw and Massachusetts 54th Regiment Memorial (a.k.a. the dudes from *Glory*).

Adjacent to the park is the Public Garden, former swampland that was filled in 1837. The nation's first botanical garden, the Public Garden's French style of ornamental beds and paths stand in sharp contrast to the Common's informal, pastoral English layout. This is where you can ride the famous Swan Boats and admire the *Make Way for Ducklings* sculpture.

Activities

The Freedom Trail is a 2.5-mile path through central Boston that passes by 16 of the city's historic landmarks. You'll find detailed route maps and information at the Visitor Center on Boston Common. Many of the sites along the red-painted line offer free admission, others "recommend" a donation, and some actually charge.

Frog Pond serves as a part-time ice-skating rink in winter and a splashing pool for children in summer. The smooth, paved paths that traverse the Common make it ideal for cyclists, rollerbladers, scooters, joggers, and walkers. Throughout the year the park hosts concerts, plays, political rallies, and other formal and informal gatherings.

How to Get There

Tremont, Beacon, Charles, Park, and Boylston Streets bound Boston Common. Parking is available, believe it or not, under the Common on Charles Street. By car, take the Mass Pike (I-90) to the Copley Square exit. Go straight at the off ramp onto Stuart Street. Take a left onto Charles Street by the Radisson Hotel.

By mass transit, take the Green Line or the Silver Line bus to the Boylston T stop at the corner of Boylston Street and Tremont Street. This stop is heavily used by tourists and locals, so expect crowds. Another equally bustling option is to take the Red Line or Green Line to the Park Street T stop at the northeastern edge of the Common.

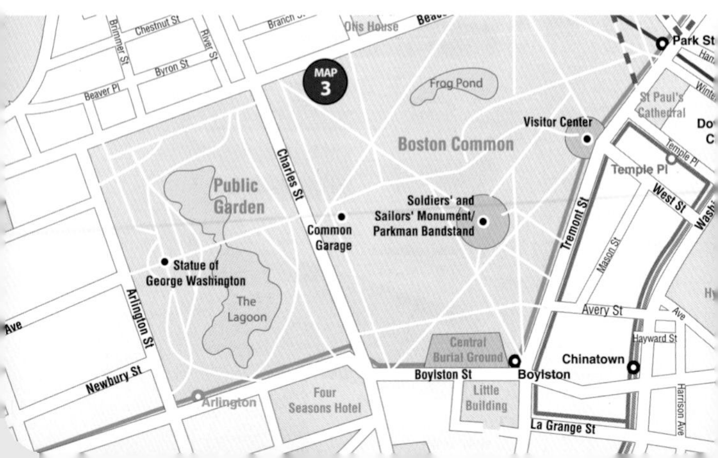

General Information

NFT Maps:	1, 2, 3, 4, 8
Address:	Visitor Center, 147 Tremont St, Boston, MA 02111
Freedom Trail:	www.thefreedomtrail.org
Black Heritage Trail:	www.afroammuseum.org/trail.htm
Walking Tours:	Available daily during spring/summer/fall, from Boston Common to Faneuil Hall, daily: Departs hourly, 11 am-4pm. From Faneuil Hall to Boston Common, daily: 10:30 am, 12:30pm, and 3:30 pm. ($12 adults, $6 children, cash only) ($12 adults, $6 children, cash only)
Audio Tours:	Available at the Visitor Center, or download an MP3 version for $15 from the Freedom Trail website.

Freedom Trail Overview

The Freedom Trail conveniently links several important colonial and post-colonial historical sites. Marked by a thick red path on the sidewalks, either painted or made of inlaid brick, the trail leads sightseers from the Visitor Center on Boston Common to the Charlestown Navy Yard on the opposite side of the Charles River. The 2.5-mile trek passes by 16 different sites, including the location of the Boston Massacre, Paul Revere's house, a couple of old cemeteries, and Bunker Hill. Walking tours led by costumed guides leave the Visitor Center or Faneuil Hall, and a complete trail walk usually lasts about 90 minutes. Audio tours are also available.

Trail Head: The Boston Common—America's oldest public park, 44-acre Boston Common is home to well-fed squirrels, pigeons, walkers, joggers, bikers, dogs, and ducks.

1. **The State House**—The Massachusetts state government sits here in this gold-domed building, the oldest on Beacon Hill, in fact. Tour Hours: Mon–Fri 10 am–3:30 pm; 617-727-3676.
2. **Park Street Church**—The Evangelical Church was constructed in 1809 and has since stood as a testament to Bostonian faith. Lucky passersby may even be treated to a tirade being given from the outdoor pulpit. 617-523-3383. Traditional worship: 8:30 am and 11 am.
   Contemporary worship: 4 pm.
3. **Granary Burying Ground**—An epitaph here reads "Revere's Tomb" near the resting places of both John Hancock and Samuel Adams, along with a giant monolith paying tribute to the family of Boston-born Ben Franklin. This is the city's third-oldest burial ground, the resting place of the victims of the Boston Massacre. Open daily 9:30 am-3:30 pm, Tues-Sat; 617-635-4505.
4. **King's Chapel**—The chapel site dates from 1688, and the current chapel was built in 1754 with the objective that it "would be the equal of any in England." The bell was made by Paul Revere. Summer hours: Mon, Thurs-Sat 10 am–4 pm; winter hours: 10 am-4 pm, Sat. Entry is free but there's a $2 "suggested" donation. Concerts on Tuesdays at 12:15 pm and Sundays at 5 pm. Services are held Wednesdays 12:15 pm and Sundays 11 am; 617-227-2155.

   King's Chapel Burying Ground—Older than the Granary and the final resting place of some of Boston's first settlers.
5. **Benjamin Franklin's Statue/Site of the First Public School**—Boston Latin School, founded in 1635, is still open (but it's since moved to the Fenway). The old high school is considered the top public school in Boston. A mosaic in the sidewalk marks its original site nearby to a statue of one of its famous students, Ben Franklin. Both are in the courtyard of Old City Hall, also worth a look.
6. **Old Corner Bookstore Building**—Built in 1718, this is one of Boston's oldest surviving structures. Once an apothecary, during the 19th century the building housed the publisher of classic New England titles *Walden* and *The Scarlet Letter*.
7. **Old South Meeting House**—"Voices of Protest," a permanent exhibit in the house, speaks of generations who made history under one roof, including Samuel Adams, William Dawes, Benjamin Franklin (and his parents and grandparents), Phillis Wheatley, and the instigators of the Boston Tea Party. Nov–Mar, 10 am–4 pm. Apr–Oct, 9:30 am–5 pm. Adults $5, students and seniors $4, children (6-18) $1, children under six free; 617-482-6439.
8. **Old State House**—The oldest surviving public building in Boston, its lush exterior will draw you inside where the Bostonian Society houses a library along with its museum of Boston's past.

   Library: Open for research by appointment only; call (617) 720-1713, ext 13. Daily use fee: non-members $10; free to members.

   Museum: 9 am–5 pm, extended hours in summer, closed New Year's Day, Thanksgiving, and Christmas Day. Adults $8.50; seniors (62+) and students, $7.50; members, youth (6-18), veterans, and US military are free ; 617-720-1713.
9. **Site of the Boston Massacre**—Cobblestones now mark this historic site outside the Old State House.
10. **Faneuil Hall**—Shopping mixed with history, with some eateries to boot. If you like touristy knick-knacks, this is the place to shop. The actual hall still holds public meetings and houses an armory museum. The Marketplace is open Mon-Sat, 10 am–9 pm and 11 am-5 pm on Sundays. Historical talks every thirty minutes, 9:30 am–4:30 pm. See page 126.
11. **Paul Revere House**—See how Boston's favorite patriot once lived. Keep in mind that when he lived there, the area wasn't filled with Italian restaurants. Apr 15–Oct 31, 9:30 am–5:15 pm. Nov 1–Apr 14, 9:30 am–4:15 pm. Closed Mondays in Jan–Mar and on Thanksgiving, Christmas Day, and New Year's Day. Adults $3.50, seniors and college students $3, children (5–17) $1; 617-523-2338.
12. **Old North Church**—"One if by land, two if by sea," goes the poem. And so two lanterns were placed in the Old North Church, the oldest church building in Boston, warning that the British were making their way across the Charles towards Lexington and Concord. The church has held services since 1723 and is the most visited historical site in Boston. Historic site hours: 10 am–4 pm (Tues-Sun), Jan–Feb; 9 am-5 pm, Mar-May; 9 am-6 pm, June–Oct; 10 am-5 pm, Nov-Dec; 617-523-6676.
13. **Copp's Hill Burying Ground**—The site began as a cemetery in the 1660s and was later used by the British as a strategic vantage point in the Battle of Bunker Hill. Open daily 9 am–5 pm.
14. **USS Constitution**—a.k.a. "Old Ironsides," America's oldest commissioned warship, with daily flag-raising and lowering ceremonies accompanied by cannon fire. Winter hours: Thurs–Sun, 10 am–4 pm. Summer hours: Tues–Sun: 10 am–6 pm. Tours depart every half hour; 617-242-5670. See Charlestown Navy Yard, page 119.
15. **Bunker Hill Monument**—A 221-foot granite obelisk commemorates the Battle of Bunker Hill—the first major battle of the American Revolution. The monument sits atop Breed's Hill, where the misnamed battle actually took place. Exhibitions at the visitor's center explain how the battle came to be and how it was won. Hours: Open daily 9 am–5 pm and 9 am-6 pm during July and August; 617-242-5641.

Freedom Trail & Black Heritage Trail

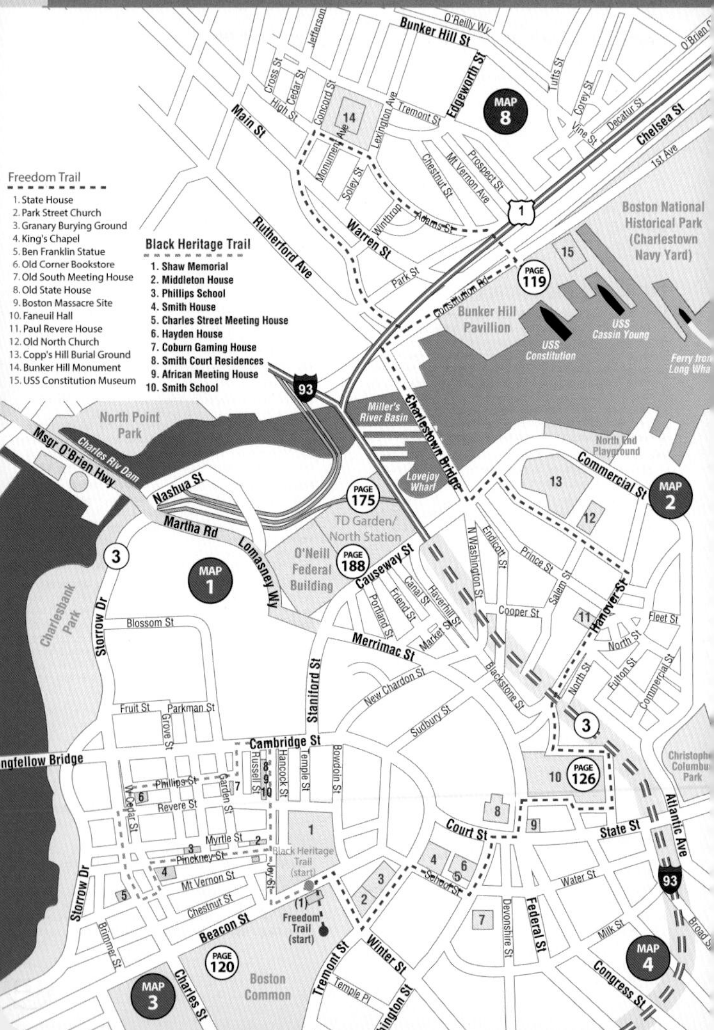

Freedom Trail
1. State House
2. Park Street Church
3. Granary Burying Ground
4. King's Chapel
5. Ben Franklin Statue
6. Old Corner Bookstore
7. Old South Meeting House
8. Old State House
9. Boston Massacre Site
10. Faneuil Hall
11. Paul Revere House
12. Old North Church
13. Copp's Hill Burial Ground
14. Bunker Hill Monument
15. USS Constitution Museum
Black Heritage Trail
1. Shaw Memorial
2. Middleton House
3. Phillips School
4. Smith House
5. Charles Street Meeting House
6. Hayden House
7. Coburn Gaming House
8. Smith Court Residences
9. African Meeting House
10. Smith School
Boston National Historical Park (Charlestown Navy Yard)
Bunker Hill Pavillion
USS Constitution
USS Cassin Young
Miller's River Basin
Lovejoy Wharf
North Point Park
North End Playground
TD Garden/ North Station
O'Neill Federal Building
Charlesbank Park
Boston Common
Black Heritage Trail (start)
Freedom Trail (start)
Christopher Columbus Park
PAGE 119
PAGE 175
PAGE 188
PAGE 126
PAGE 120
MAP 8
MAP 2
MAP 1
MAP 3
MAP 4
Bunker Hill St
Main St
Rutherford Ave
Warren St
Chelsea St
Charlestown Bridge
Commercial St
Hanover St
Causeway St
Merrimac St
Cambridge St
Court St
State St
Atlantic Ave
Beacon St
Tremont St
Charles St
Storrow Dr
Congress St
Federal St
Msgr O'Brien Hwy
Martha Rd
Nashua St
Lomasney Wy
Staniford St
Longfellow Bridge
Winter St

Black Heritage Trail Overview

Running north from the State House, this trail recognizes the historical significance of Boston's post-Revolution African-American community. Before being forced into the South End and Roxbury in the 20th Century, the first community of free African-Americans actually lived in Beacon Hill after the American Revolution, in what is now known as the North Slope. According to the first federal census in 1790, Massachusetts was the only state in the country without slaves. The Museum of African-American History is housed in two of the buildings on the Trail, the African Meeting House and the Abiel Smith School, which are open to visitors. Most of the historic homes on the Trail are private residences, closed to the public.

1. **Robert Gould Shaw and Massachusetts 54th Regiment Memorial**—Located on Boston Common across from the State House, this monument was built in 1897 in honor of the first all-black regiment that fought for the Union Army during the Civil War.

2. **George Middleton House**—(5–7 Pinckney St) George Middleton was the commander of an all-black military company during the Revolutionary War called the Bucks of America. His house, erected in 1797, is the oldest standing wooden structure on Beacon Hill. It is a private residence.

3. **The Phillips School**—(Anderson & Pinckney Sts) One of the first Boston public schools to be integrated (in 1855) as a result of the historic court case *Roberts v. The City of Boston*, which opposed the racial segregation of the city's schools.

4. **John J. Smith House**—(86 Pinckney St) John J. Smith was born free in Virginia in 1820 and eventually moved to Boston where he opened a successful barbershop that catered to many wealthy white customers from all over the city. His shop served as a haven for anti-slavery debates, fugitive slaves, and advocates for equal education rights.

5. **Charles Street Meeting House**—(Mt Vernon & Charles Sts) Built in 1807, the Charles Street Meeting House was originally the site of the segregated Third Baptist Church. After a failed attempt to desegregate the church, Timothy Gilbert and several other abolitionist sympathizers left to form the Free Baptist Church (now the Tremont Temple), the first integrated church in America. In 1876, the Meeting House was sold to the African Methodist Episcopal Church, which eventually left Beacon Hill for Roxbury in 1939, due to changing economic conditions in the area.

6. **Lewis and Harriet Hayden House**—(66 Phillips St) Lewis and Harriet Hayden ran a boarding house out of their home, which was also a stop on the Underground Railroad. Lewis Hayden was an ardent African-American abolitionist and community leader who served as a delegate for the Republican Convention, fought for women's rights, and helped found the Museum of Fine Arts.

7. **John Coburn Gaming House**—(2 Phillips St) Home to one of Boston's wealthiest African-Americans, clothier James Coburn, the gaming house was built in 1843. Serving Boston's white elite, it became one of the most successful black-owned businesses in the city. Coburn used the profits to finance several abolitionist groups in the community, including the Massasoit Guards. Founded as an all-black military company to support the state's troops in case of war, the Guards also patrolled Beacon Hill to protect African-Americans from slave catchers.

8. **Smith Court Residences**— (3, 5, 7, 7A, & 10 Smith Ct) Five remaining wooden houses located on Beacon Hill's north slope were all purchased by middle-class African-Americans from white landowners in the mid-1800s.

9. **The African Meeting House**—(8 Smith Ct) Founded as a response to racial discrimination in Boston's religious communities, the African Meeting House remains the oldest standing Black church building in the country. The structure was built using labor and donations from the African-American community. It was used for religious services, as a safe haven for political discussion, and as a makeshift school for black children until the Abiel Smith School came into existence. Following a six-year historic restoration, the building has been restored to its 1855 appearance. With the Abiel Smith School, it houses the Museum of African-American History.

10. **Abiel Smith School**—(46 Joy St) Built in 1834 as the first schoolhouse in America to educate black school children, the Abiel Smith School was consistently overcrowded and neglected by the city. Substandard conditions led to *Roberts v. Massachusetts* and the desegregation of schools in 1855. Hours: 10 am–4 pm, Mon–Sat. Closed Thanksgiving, Christmas, and New Year's Day. Small admission fee. 617-725-0022.

MAP 16
MAP 17
MAP 15
MAP 14
MAP 31
MAP 30
90
BROOKLINE
BOSTON
St Mary's St
Hawes St
Kent St
St Paul St
Harvard St
Beacon St
Coolidge Corner
Summit Ave
Brandon Hill
Fenway
Riverway Park
Riverway
Longwood
Back Bay Fens
Boylston St
Agassiz Rd
Park Dr
Fenway
Louis Prang St
Prudential
Symphony
Massachusetts Ave
Northeastern
Massachusetts Ave
Museum
Ruggles St
Ruggles
Brookline Ave
Washington St
Aspinwall Ave
Huntington Ave
Longwood Med Area
Brigham Cir
Brookline Village
Greenfort
Fenwood Rd
Tremont St
Roxbury Crossing
Malcolm X Blvd
Brookline Hills
Riverway
Back of the Hill
Boylston St
Jamaicaway
Cypress St
Olmsted Park
Willow Pond
S Huntington Ave
Heath St
Heath St
Jackson Square
Ward's Pond
Centre St
Columbus Ave
Perkins St
Warren St
Francis Parkman Dr
Jamaica Park
Jamaica Pond
Townsend St
Centre St
Stony Brook
Washington St
Quincy St
Green St
Green Street
Walnut Ave
George R White Schoolboy Stadium
Pond St
Main Gate
Pierpont Rd
Seaver St
Franklin Park
Jewish War Veterans Dr
Glen Ln
Franklin Park Zoo
Columbia Rd
Forest Hills St
Arborway
Centre St
Forest Hills
William J Devine Golf Course
Blue Hill Ave
Circuit Dr
Dairy Rd
Arnold Arboretum
South St
Morton St
Scarboro Pond
American Legion Hwy
Kilmer Park
Walter St
Bussey St
Washington St
Hyde Park Ave
Forest Hills Cemetery
Walk Hill St
Talbot Ave
Franklin Field

General Information

NFT Maps: 14, 15, 16, 17, 30, & 31
Address: Two Brookline Pl, Brookline, MA 02445
Phone: 617-232-5374
Websites: www.emeraldnecklace.org
www.cityofboston.gov/parks/necklace.asp

Overview

Known primarily for his work designing New York's Central Park (along with co-designer Calvert Vaux), celebrated landscape architect Frederick Law Olmsted also created a beautiful string of Boston parks when he moved to Brookline in 1883. Olmsted's Necklace was designed as an uninterrupted five-mile walkway from Back Bay to Franklin Park, where Bostonians could stroll barefoot and without worry. The Necklace has been broken up over the years, both by the construction of the Casey Overpass near Franklin Park and by the conversion of the Riverway, Jamaicaway, and Arborway from pleasant carriage paths to major roads carrying highway-amounts of traffic. The city and conservation groups are putting together a "master plan" for the severed sections of the Necklace and together are trying to balance path restoration with traffic concerns. Since the completion of the Rose Kennedy Greenway, where the Central Artery once stood, all of Boston's parks are finally linked into an actual, sorta-kinda necklace.

Franklin Park

Occupying 500 acres, Franklin Park is the Necklace's largest park and was originally designed as a country retreat in the vein of Central Park in New York. Named after Benjamin Franklin, the park encompasses the Zoo (617-541-LION), one of the first public golf courses in the country (617-265-4084), 100 acres of woodland, and the seven-acre Scarboro Pond. The Franklin Park Zoo (not part of Olmsted's original plan), which opened in 1911, is home to the "Butterfly Landing," a butterfly enclosure open seasonally from June through September. The zoo made headlines in 2003 when adolescent gorilla "Little Joe" escaped from his enclosure—twice. The first time, he stayed on site. The second time, he ended up at a bus stop in Roxbury. Zoo entry: Adults $17, children (2-12) $11, seniors (62+) $14, reduced price the first Sat of each month, 10 am–12 pm; winter hours (Oct 1–Mar 31), 10 am–4 pm; summer hours, 10 am–5 pm weekdays, and 6 pm weekends and holidays, admission is half price the Friday after Thanksgiving; www.zoonewengland.com.

Arnold Arboretum

The oldest arboretum in the country, Arnold Arboretum is named after its financier, whaling tycoon and horticulturalist James Arnold. Visitors come primarily to stroll amongst the exotic greenery, which includes bonsai and lilac trees. Because Arnold left most of his estate to Harvard and the school uses the arboretum as a nature museum, it seems only fair for the city to allow the grand university to rent the land for just a dollar a year. Open every day until dusk; the Visitor Center is open Apr-Oct 11 am–6 pm, Nov-Mar 12 pm–4 pm, and is closed Wednesdays and holidays. Entry is free!

Jamaica Park

Wealthy Bostonians of yesteryear built their summer homes in this spot, called "the jewel in the Emerald Necklace" because of the 60-acre sparkling Jamaica Pond. The largest and purest body of water in Boston, the glacier-formed pond is fed by natural springs and is 90 feet deep in some places. The pond is so clean that it serves as a back-up city reservoir. Joggers and dog-walkers share the 1.5 mile paved trail around the pond. Fishing is one of the most popular activities, and every year the City of Boston stocks the pond with trout, salmon, and indigenous pickerel, bass, hornpout, and perch. The boathouse rents canoes, sailboats, and rowboats, and, in winter, has a fireplace going. Around Halloween, the community organization Spontaneous Celebrations sponsors a lantern walk around the pond.

Olmsted Park

A joint project between the City of Boston and the Town of Brookline to link the two cities together, Olmsted Park showcases the landscape architect's unique design philosophy with a series of ponds and wooded paths that open onto expansive views that help you understand why Olmsted is the Boston Brahmin equivalent of a rock star. (The city boasts at least one Olmsted impersonator.) A great feature of the park is the human-made Muddy River, currently the site of a major dredging project. Leverett, Willow, and Ward's Ponds are more secluded and less crowded than nearby Jamaica Pond. A bike/pedestrian path system on the Brookline side from Jamaica Pond to Boylston Street (Route 9) was completed in 1997.

Riverway Park

Hidden below the busy street level is the narrowest park in the system and also the only one that is completely human-made. Riverway lies in the valley of the Muddy River (the boundary between Boston and Brookline) and features several small islands, wooded paths, and pretty footbridges. Its steep tree-lined banks protect visitors from the city bustle above. Footbridges connect the Boston and Brookline sides, but these are poorly lit at night.

Back Bay Fens

Olmsted's first phase of the Necklace in 1878, the Back Bay Fens was a sewage-infested saltwater marsh on the verge of extinction when he stepped in, transforming the swampy area into a meandering brackish creek. The creation of the Charles River Dam in 1910 turned the Fens into a freshwater marsh. Today, the Fens has quite a few notable attractions, including recreational facilities, the Kelleher Rose Garden, War Memorials, and the Victory Garden. The Victory Garden was created in 1941, in an effort to grow extra food for troops, and is currently tended to by local green thumbs who shell out a small annual fee to maintain personal plots. A former parking lot, the western end of the Fens was converted into green space. But it's a notorious local fact that more than mere gardening takes place on the grounds—think George Michael.

Rose Kennedy Greenway

Opened in late 2008, the Rose Kennedy Greenway, a 15-acre green space extending from Chinatown to the North End, stands upon what was once the Central Artery highway. This nuisance of a highway had torn through neighborhoods and displaced residents for over forty years, until the Big Dig came along and fixed everything (after it was finally fixed itself). A joint effort of the Massachusetts Turnpike Authority, the Commonwealth, the City of Boston, and various civic groups, the Greenway features gardens, plazas, fountains, and tree-lined walkways—a relaxing oasis tucked within the busy surrounding urban environment.

General Information

NFT Map: 2
Phone: 617-523-1300
Websites: www.faneuilhallmarketplace.com
www.faneuilhall.com
www.cityofboston.gov/freedomtrail/faneuilhall.asp
http://www.nps.gov/bost/historyculture/fh.htm

Faneuil Hall

Faneuil Hall was built as a food and produce market/meeting hall by Boston's wealthiest merchant, Peter Faneuil, in 1742. It's a historically poignant section of commercial property: At this location, Samuel Adams rallied for independence (prior to his interest in brewing beer), the doctrine of "no taxation without representation" was established, and George Washington and company celebrated our country's freedom. In later years, it was the site of abolitionist rallies. It's still both a commercial spot and a meeting place used by campaigning politicians, with shops in the basement and the first floor, the Great Hall on the second, and a museum on the third.

Since its inception, the Faneuil Hall Marketplace has been a major shopping arena, and it's now stocked with more than 100 stores and pushcarts and 17 sit-down restaurants as well as a gastronomic orgy of a food hall. The marketplace alone attracts more than 12 million visitors a year and hosts numerous events and festivals. Local talent includes jugglers, mimes (yes, those, too), magicians, bands, and the occasional strolling Ben Franklin. If you're looking to be entertained while you shop, Faneuil Hall is your place.

Four buildings make up the marketplace: Faneuil Hall, Quincy Market, North Market, and South Market. Touristy and crowded at times, it's still one of the best and most visually pleasing places to buy souvenirs, shop in a mall-like environment, and try any number of local dishes. Standard mall stores occupy most of North and South Market, while local vendors and souvenir slingers can be found in the Hall or at pushcarts in Quincy Market. The Hall and all pushcarts are open Monday through Saturday from 10 am to 9 pm, and from 11 am to 6 pm on Sundays. Shopping hours in the other marketplaces vary by vendor. The Hall and all shops are closed on Christmas.

Quincy Market

Located directly behind Faneuil Hall, Quincy Market is where you go to chow down. The food court runs the length of the building and far exceeds a typical food court in both variety and quality of offerings. Whatever you crave, it's hard to go away disappointed. It is usually crowded at lunch, especially during the field trip and leaf-peeping seasons, so avoid peak hours if you're in a rush. Various sit-down bars and restaurants and pushcarts encircle the food court around the perimeter. The North Market and South Market, which stand on either side of Quincy Market, have other places to sit for a meal, including the still-there Durgin Park.

Like many places in Boston, Quincy Market is built on landfill in what used to be Boston Harbor. Unlike other sections, when you're in Quincy Market, you're standing on bones. The butchers who used to occupy the wharves behind Faneuil Hall would let their unusable animal parts pile up, creating a sanitation nightmare. Then, someone had the bright idea of throwing the bones in the water, which eventually helped fill the wharf area and allowed for the construction of Quincy Market.

Museum

Ancient and Honorable Artillery Company Museum; 617-227-1638; http://www.ahac.us.com/

Located on Faneuil Hall's third floor, the museum and library showcase the history of the Ancient and Honorable Artillery Company. The oldest military organization in the US (and third-oldest in the world), this august body was established as the Military Company of Boston in 1637 and still holds military drills and participates in various ceremonial events. The museum proudly displays the company's artifacts. It is a unique collection that is well worth a visit for military and history buffs. The museum is open Monday–Friday, 9 am–3:30 pm.

How to Get There—Driving

From the south, take I-93 N to Exit 23 ("Government Center"). Upon exiting, follow the signs to the Aquarium. At Surface Road, turn left. Faneuil Hall will be on the right-hand side.

From the west, take the Mass Pike (I-90) to Exit 24B (I-93 N). From I-93, take Exit 23 ("Government Center") and follow the directions above.

From the north, take I-93 S to Exit 24A toward Government Center. Stay to the right, and follow the signs for Faneuil Hall. Immediately off the exit, turn right. Faneuil Hall will be directly in front of you.

Parking

There are over 10,000 parking spaces within a two-mile radius of Faneuil Hall. The 75 State Street garage near the intersection of State Street and Broad Street offers a discount on weekdays with validation from participation stores, and $16 parking after 5 pm daily, all day Saturdays and Sundays, and on select holidays.

How to Get There—Mass Transit

To get to Faneuil Hall Marketplace, take the T's Green Line to Government Center or Haymarket, the Blue Line to State or Aquarium, or the Orange Line to State or Haymarket.

Shopping

A Hat for Every Head (pushcart)
Ann Taylor
Bill Rodgers Running Center
Boston Logos (pushcart)
Boxers To Go (pushcart)
Build A Belt (pushcart)
Celtic Weavers
Coach
Cuoio
Fantasy Island (pushcart)
Harvest Fare (pushcart)
Head Games
La Cloche (pushcart)
Life is a Highway (pushcart)
Michal Negrin
Nightshirts To Go (pushcart)
Nine West
Orient Express (pushcart)
Orvis
Sacs (pushcart)
Sea Boston USA (pushcart)
Sock It To Me
Urban Outfitters
Victoria's Secret

Goods & Gifts

African Collections (pushcart)
Air Brush Tattoos (pushcart)
Anytime (pushcart)
Arman Time Company (pushcart)
Art for 'Em (pushcart)
Atmosphere (pushcart)
Belt Stop
Best of Boston
Boston Art Work (pushcart)
Boston Campus Gear
Boston Pewter Company
The Boston Sun Spot
Bostonian Society Museum Shop
Camera Center
Cheers Gift Shop
Christmas In New England
The Christmas Dove
Conversations (pushcart)
Crabtree & Evelyn
Crate & Barrel
Destination Boston
Every Bead of My Heart (pushcart)
Exotic Flowers
Funusual
Gateway News
Geoclassics
Godiva Chocolatier
Happy Hangups (pushcart)
Harley Davidson-Boston (pushcart)
Headlines of America (pushcart)
Henri's Glassworks
Illusions (pushcart)
Irish Eyes (pushcart)
Local Charm
Lokta Paper (pushcart)
Lucky Decor
Magnetic Chef (pushcart)
Museum of Fine Arts Store
Musically Yours (pushcart)
Newbury Comics
On the Edge
Origins
Pillow Pets (pushcart)
Sluggers Upper Deck Kiosk (pushcart)
Stuck on Stickpins (pushcart)
Sunglass Hut & Watch Station
Teeny Billboards (pushcart)
Yankee Candle Company
Zip It (pushcart)

Food

Al Mercantino
Ames Plow Tavern
Aris Barbeque
Bagelville
Bangkok Express
Berry Twist
Boston & Maine Fish Co
Boston Café
Boston Chipyard
Boston Chowda
Boston Kitchen
Boston Pretzel & Lemonade
Boston Rocks
Carol Ann's Bake Shop
Dick's Last Resort
The Dog House
Durgin Park
El Paso Enchilada
Fisherman's Net
Gourmet India
The Green Organic Bowl
Jen Lai Rice & Noodle Company
Joey's Gelateria
Kilvert & Forbes
Kingfish Hall
La Pastaria
McCormick & Schmick's
Megumi
Mija Cantina & Tequila Bar
MMMac & Cheese
The Monkey Bar
New York Deli
North End Bakery
Parris
Philadelphia Steak & Hoagie
Piccolo Panini
Pizzeria Regina
The Prime Shoppe
Quincy's Place
Salty Dog Seafood Grill & Bar
Sam's Café at Cheers
Slugger's Dugout
Sprinkles Ice Cream
Starbucks
Steve's Greek Cuisine
Ueno Sushi
Wagamama
Walrus and the Carpenter
West End Strollers
Zuma's Tex Mex Café

Bars & Entertainment

Cheers
Comedy Connection
Coogan's
Hard Rock Cafe
Jose MacIntyre's
Ned Devine's Irish Pub
Parris
The Monkey Bar
Trinity

Services

Bean Town Trolley Tours (pushcart)
BosTix Ticket Booth
City View Trolley Tours
Faneuil Hall Marketplace Information
Old Town Trolley Tours (pushcart)
Super Duck Tours (pushcart)

Nearby Bars

The Atrium Lounge
Bell in Hand Tavern
Black Rose
Dockside Restaurant & Bar
Hennessey's
McFadden's
Kitty O'Shea's
The Rack
The Place
Purple Shamrock
Sissy K's
Union Oyster House
Vertigo

Long Wharf & Rowes Wharf

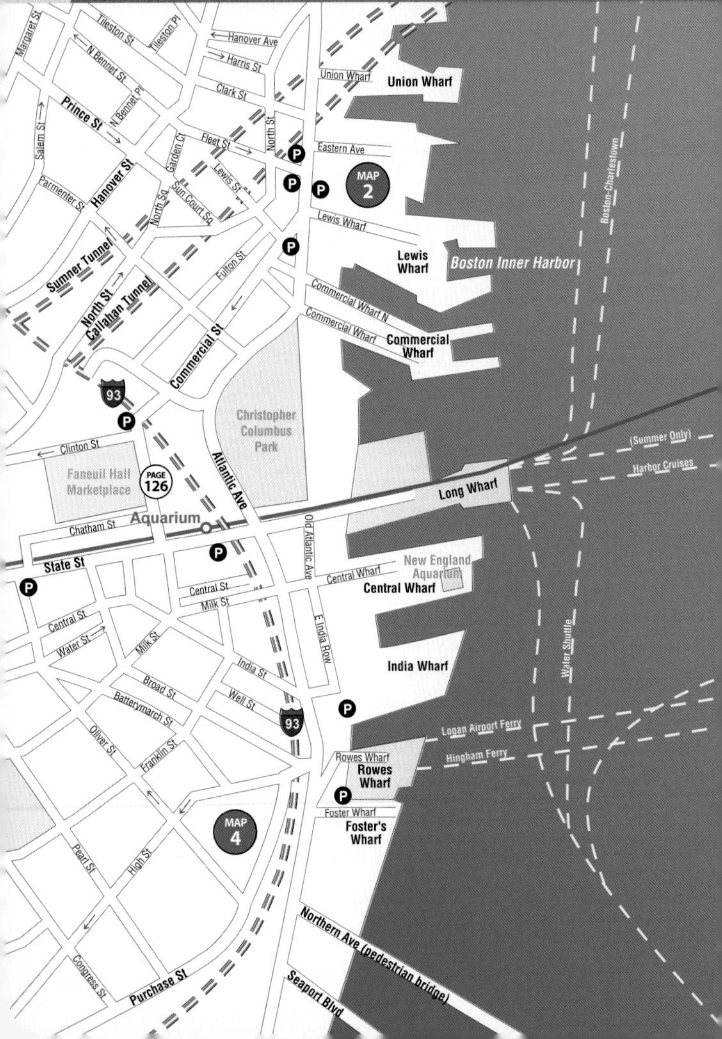

Margaret St
Tileston St
Tileston Pl
Hanover Ave
Harris St
N Bennet St
N Bennet Pl
Clark St
Union Wharf
Union Wharf
Prince St
Salem St
Fleet St
North St
Eastern Ave
Garden Ct
Lewis St
Hanover St
Parmenter St
MAP 2
North Sq
Sun Court Sq
Lewis Wharf
Boston-Charlestown
Sumner Tunnel
Fulton St
Lewis Wharf
Boston Inner Harbor
North St
Callahan Tunnel
Commercial Wharf N
Commercial Wharf
Commercial St
Commercial Wharf
93
Christopher Columbus Park
Clinton St
(Summer Only)
Harbor Cruises
Faneuil Hall Marketplace
PAGE 126
Atlantic Ave
Long Wharf
Aquarium
Chatham St
Old Atlantic Ave
State St
New England Aquarium
Central Wharf
Central St
Central Wharf
Milk St
Central St
Water St
E India Row
Milk St
India Wharf
India St
Broad St
Water Shuttle
Weil St
Batterymarch St
93
Logan Airport Ferry
Oliver St
Franklin St
Rowes Wharf
Hingham Ferry
Rowes Wharf
Foster Wharf
Foster's Wharf
MAP 4
Pearl St
High St
Northern Ave (pedestrian bridge)
Congress St
Purchase St
Seaport Blvd

Overview

Originally named Boston Pier, Long Wharf juts into Boston Harbor at the bottom of State Street, while Rowes Wharf is farther south, near Broad Street. In the 1700s, Long Wharf extended more than one-third of a mile into Boston Harbor, but the dumping of urban landfill has resulted in a significant portion of the pier being surrounded by land rather than water. Purportedly the oldest continually operating wharf in the US, Long Wharf is also the site of the oldest existing pre-Revolutionary War warehouse in Boston, the Gardiner Building, which has been the home of the Chart House restaurant since 1961.

Attractions

During the warmer months, stop by The Landing on Long Wharf for a drink in the sunshine. It's the perfect place to hang out and catch a Red Sox game on television after work or when you're waiting to board a ferry.

The New England Aquarium is located at nearby Central Wharf and operates an IMAX Theatre next door. The Aquarium allows scientists and researchers to study marine and aquatic habitats and to educate visitors about conservation issues. One of the most exciting events to participate in is a "release party," when an animal is returned to its natural habitat. Hours: 9 am–5 pm weekdays (6 pm summer), 9 am–6 pm weekends (7 pm summer). Closed Thanksgiving and Christmas Day. $24.95 adults, $17.95 children 3-11, $22.95 seniors (60+). www.neaq.org; 617-973-5200.

There are several whale-watching excursions that leave from the wharves. Whale-watching season starts in April and ends in the fall.

- **Voyager III** • Central Wharf • 617-973- 5281
- **Boston Harbor Cruises** • 1 Long Wharf • 617-227-4321
- **Massachusetts Bay Lines Whale Watch** • 60 Rowes Wharf • 617-542-8000

Long Wharf is also where you catch the Harbor Express boat to the Boston Harbor Islands. There are 34 islands in all, six of which are staffed and serviced by a free boat shuttle from the headquarters on Georges Island. These islands are still underutilized by locals and unfrequented by tourists. They vary in size, but most offer trails, old forts, diverse flora and fauna, camping (on Grape, Lovells, and Bumpkin), and great views of Boston and the harbor. Spectacle Island's past as a former quarantine island, glue factory, and garbage dump has been covered over with rubble from the Big Dig and transformed into an eco-friendly recreation spot. The island is now open to the public and features a visitor center and a café. The islands open seasonally, so check the website, www.bostonharborislands.org, or call 617-223-8666.

If you're prone to seasickness, or if watching whales isn't your bag, the newly-renovated Christopher Columbus Park is a short walk from Long Wharf. The playground for the little ones is top-notch, and its famous rose garden is dedicated to Rose Fitzgerald Kennedy. It's also a good viewing spot for the fireworks on First Night. Next door is Tia's, a popular after-work, meat market bar in the summer.

Architecture

Rowes Wharf features a commanding arch that looks out onto Boston Harbor. The Wharf is a mixed-use complex that has won numerous design awards, including the Urban Land Institute's "Award for Excellence." The complex is shared by the Boston Harbor Hotel, 100 luxury condominiums, and offices. There is a little-known observation area on the ninth floor named the Fosters Rotunda, offering views of both the city and harbor. Though not advertised, you can go through the hotel to gain access. In the summertime, a floating dock hosts outdoor concerts and movies under the stars.

Ferries

Both Long Wharf and Rowes Wharf serve as ferry terminals for the MBTA. F1 transports people to and from Rowes Wharf and Hingham Shipyard. F2 and F2H stop at Long Wharf, Logan Airport, and the Fore River Shipyard in Quincy. F2H also has limited service to Pemberton Point in Hull. F4, which travels to the Charlestown Navy Yard, also uses the Long Wharf terminus. The Harbor Express to Georges Island also leaves from Long Wharf. For more information on ferries, see page 190. For schedules and maps, go to www.mbta.com/schedules_and_maps/boats, or call 617-222-5000. You can also catch the high-speed catamaran ferry to Provincetown from Long Wharf. For schedules, rates, and area information visit www.bostonharborcruises.com/provincetown-ferry/default.aspx.

How to Get There—Driving

To Long Wharf from the north, take I-93 S, and get off at Exit 24A (Government Center/Aquarium). Follow signs to the Aquarium. From the south, take Exit 23 (Government Center) and follow signs to the Aquarium.

To Rowes Wharf from the north, take I-93 S and get off at Exit 23 (aim for South Station). Turn left onto Congress Street and immediately left onto Atlantic Avenue. The wharf is on the right, two blocks past the intersection of Congress Street and Atlantic Avenue.

From the south, take I-93 N to Exit 20, and follow signs to South Station. Once you drop onto Atlantic Avenue, proceed through the Congress Street intersection and drive two blocks. The wharf will be on your right.

Parking

There is *very* limited street parking in the area, so if you want to forego driving around to find a free spot, you should try one of the many parking garages that are all within walking distance of the various wharves. Parking fees can cost $25 or more, depending on how long you stay, though there are usually discounted rates on weekends and after 5 pm on weekdays. If you're willing to shell out the cash, here are a few nearby garages:

- **The Rowes Wharf building** features an underground discounted parking garage with an entrance on Atlantic Avenue.
- **Harbor Garage at the Aquarium**, 70 East India Row; 617-367-3847
- **Dock Square Garage,** 200 State St; 617-367-4373
- **Laz Parking,** 290 Commercial St; 617-367-6412
- **Fitz-Inn Parking,** 269 Commercial St; 617-367-1681
- **Central Parking,** 2 Atlantic Ave; 617-854-3365

How to Get There—Mass Transit

To Long Wharf, take the T's Blue Line to the Aquarium stop. To Rowes Wharf, take either the Blue Line to Aquarium or the Red or Silver Line to South Station.

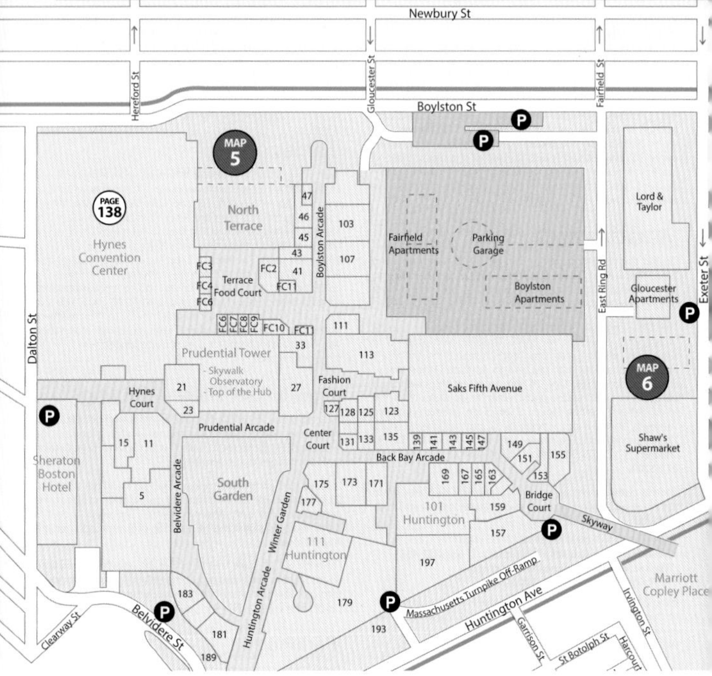

Stores

1 PF Chang's China Bistro
5 US Post Office
11 Ann Taylor Loft
15 Au Bon Pain
17 Tossed
19 Best of Boston
21 St Francis Chapel
23 Dunkin' Donuts
27 Ann Taylor
33 Jasmine Sola
39 Godiva
41 Free People
43 GameStop
45 Florsheim Shoes
46 Travel 2000
47 Truffles Fine Confections
103 Legal Sea Foods
107 Sephora
111 F Carriere
113 Talbots Collection/ Talbots Kids/ Talbots Mens
123 Olympia Sports
125 Chico's
127 The Body Shop
131 Alpha Omega
133 Johnston & Murphy
135 Aldo
139 Sunglass Hut
141 Teavana
143 Papyrus
145 Landau Collections
147 Optical Shop of Aspen
153 L'Occitane
155 California Pizza Kitchen
159 Crane & Co
163 Lacoste
165 Yankee Candle
167 Swarovski
169 Arden B
171 Levenger
173 J Jill—The Store
175 Club Monaco
175A Charles David
177 Franklin Covey
179 Barnes & Noble
181 The Sharper Image
183 Sovereign Bank
187 Cold Stone Creamery
189 The Cheesecake Factory
193 Applebee's
197 FitCorp

Food Court

FC1 Qdoba Mexican Grill
FC2 Panda Express
FC3 Pizzeria Regina
FC4 Poulet Rotisserie Chicken
FC5 Boston Chowda
FC6 Flamers
FC7 Gourmet India
FC8 Sakkio Japan
FC9 Ben & Jerry's
FC10 Paradise Bakery & Café
FC11 Louis Barry Florist

General Information

NFT Maps: 5 & 6
Address: 800 Boylston St, Boston, MA 02199
Phone: 1-800-SHOP-PRU or 617-236-3100
Website: www.prudentialcenter.com

Overview

The Prudential Center opened in 1965 and, at 52 stories, reigned as the city's tallest building until the 60-story John Hancock Tower was completed eleven years later. With the exception of the top two floors, which house an observation deck and a restaurant, the Prudential Tower is used mainly as office space. The Prudential Mall (not be confused with the more highbrow Copley Place mall, attached to the Prudential Mall by a natty skywalk) was opened in the 1990s on the lower floors and houses almost 50 shops, including Saks Fifth Avenue and numerous restaurants and services. The "Pru" is also home to several apartment buildings and is connected to the Hynes Convention Center and the Sheraton Boston Hotel. If you're not in the mood for the maddening crowd, avoid the mall, which is always teeming with tourists, hardcore browsers, and convention attendees.

Skywalk and Top of the Hub

The Prudential Tower gives you two options for catching its spectacular views: Skywalk Observatory and Top of the Hub restaurant. Both offer breathtaking sights of Boston and its suburbs, as well as the harbor, Blue Hill, and—way off in the distance—Cape Cod. (By default, the Prudential Center became the best place to see Boston from on high after the observatory at the John Hancock Tower closed following September 11.) The Skywalk is open daily from 10 am until 10 pm (8 pm in the winter). Skywalk tickets cost $15 adults, $13 seniors (62+) and students, and $10 children (6th grade and under). As you walk around the Skywalk, focus on the huge windows, which are marked to help you locate some of the more well-known features of the Boston skyline.

Top of the Hub offers a somewhat more cost-effective viewing experience, and one that's two floors above the Skywalk, at that. Entrees are pricey, but juice and cocktails from the bar are fairly priced and served with a spectacular view. And if you're acrophobic, a little nip might be exactly what you need to be able to relax and enjoy the view as you peer down at the city or across at the top of the John Hancock Tower with beverage in hand. The restaurant and lounge get busy at night, especially when the jazz band is playing. A semi-casual but "anti-slob" dress code is in effect.

How to Get There—Driving

From the north, take I-93 S to Exit 26 (Storrow Drive) and follow it to the Copley Square exit on the left. Take a right onto Beacon Street and follow it to Exeter Street. Make a left onto Exeter Street and the Prudential Center Garage will be four blocks down on the right.

From the west, follow the Mass Pike (I-90 E) into Boston. Get off at Exit 22 (Copley Square/Prudential Center) and follow the signs for Prudential Center. This will take you directly to the Prudential Center Garage entrance on your right.

From the south, take I-93 N to Exit 26 (Storrow Drive) and follow to the Copley Square exit on the left. Take a right onto Beacon Street and follow it to Exeter Street. Take a left onto Exeter Street. The Prudential Center Garage will be four blocks down on the right.

If you get lost, try this: Look up. Find the giant building that says "Prudential" on top. Drive towards it.

How to Get There—Mass Transit

The Green Line will take you to the Prudential T stop on Huntington Avenue (E train only; FYI: Only the doors of the first car open for this stop), the Copley stop on Boylston Street at Dartmouth Street, and the Hynes/ICA stop on Newbury Street at Mass Ave. The Orange Line and the MBTA Commuter Rail both stop at Back Bay Station, just across the street from Copley Place and a short walk away.

Overview

Originally one of the least fashionable streets of Back Bay, Newbury Street has undergone quite a transformation, morphing into Boston's most popular shopping area and an excellent place to hang out and strut your stuff.

A beautiful stretch of real estate featuring late 19th- and early 20th-century architecture, Newbury Street runs eight blocks from the Public Garden west to Massachusetts Avenue. The cross streets run alphabetically from east to west, starting with Arlington, then Berkeley, Clarendon, etc. Stores pack the buildings along Newbury, which were originally designed for residential use, making for a lot of oddly shaped, quirky boutiques. The good shopping extends to either side of Newbury St with trendy stores and big name designers lining Boylston Street and many of the cross roads. Though the area features shops for all ages and tax brackets, the ambiance of Boston's most famed street may make an indulgence in $300 shoes or a $15 martini seem perfectly sensible.

In the summertime, the cafés spill out onto the sidewalk, providing a perfect spot from which to partake in unparalleled people-watching. The street is a veritable human car crash; the "hippest" elements of every age group, from 80-year-olds to eight-year-olds, interact and fight for space (and attention) on the same small sidewalk.

For an updated list of shops, see www.newbury-st.com.

History

The whole of Back Bay was swampland until about 1870, when workers completed a massive filling project. As a result, Back Bay is the only neighborhood in Boston to benefit from a modern urban planning. Streets actually cross each other at 90-degree angles, and at no point is there a rotary or an eight-way intersection. Fluctuations in the water table, however, are rotting the wooden planks on which most of the area's structures sit. The result: Back Bay is sinking.

The architecture on Newbury Street is fairly uniform, since most of the development occurred during the same half-century. Emmanuel Church, designed by Alexander Esty in 1862, was the first building completed on Newbury Street. The Church of the Covenant, built in 1865, houses some spectacular stained glass windows and its steeple was once described by Oliver Wendell Holmes as "absolutely perfect." Its Emmaus Window shines even in the dimmest of lights.

How to Get There—Driving

Newbury Street is easy to get to. From I-93 take Exit 26 to Storrow Drive. Take the exit for Arlington Street, and proceed up Arlington until you hit Newbury Street (right turn only, one-way). Newbury Street lies between Boylston Street and Commonwealth Avenue, so if you get twisted around use these larger streets as landmarks.

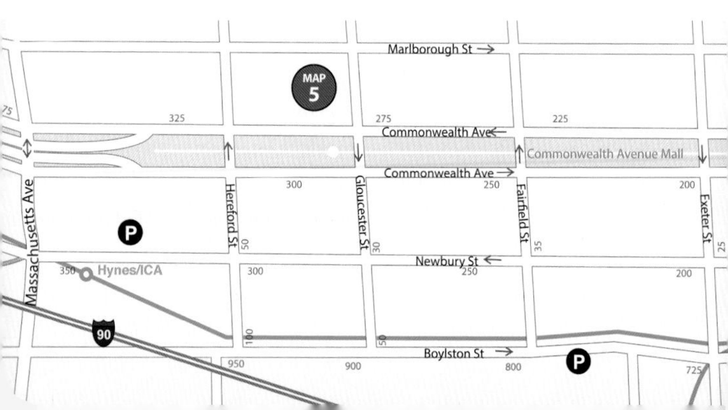

How to Get There—Mass Transit

From the T's Green Line you can get off at the Arlington stop, the Copley stop, or the Hynes/ICA stop. Note that the Green Line's E train breaks off the main track at Copley, so use the B, C, or D train to get to Hynes/ICA.

Shopping

Unless you have bionic feet, a shopping day on Newbury Street is going to leave your dogs barking. Luckily, the layout of the veritable brownstone mall that is Newbury Street is laid out in such a way that the most expensive boutiques are found near the Boston Public Garden end of Newbury Street, with shops gradually becoming cheaper and funkier by the time you collapse at Mass Ave.

Newbury Street probably wouldn't have gotten to where it is today without the support of some of the heavy-hitter and high-end chain stores, so you can't damn them for being there. And, as a result, their presence also gave the nearby little guy a steady stream of patrons. Some of the better (read: less ostentatious) chains here include: **Urban Outfitters** (361), **Patagonia** (346), **Puma** (333), **Johnny Cupcake**s (279), **1154 Lill Studio** (220), **Lush** (166), and **O & Company** (161). Unfortunately, between retail space progression and the down economy, the chains appear to be taking more than their fair share lately, so enjoy the hidden gems while they're still around. Check out **Mastu** (259), **Army Barracks** (173), **Trident Booksellers & Café** (138), **Condom World** (332), **Envi-Eco Fashion Boutique** (164), **Poor Little Rich Girl** (166), **Newbury Yarns** (164), **Queen Bee** (85), **Paperchase** (172), **Too Timid** (297), and **Dress** (221), to name a few.

Restaurants

If you don't stop to eat on Newbury Street, you're missing half the fun. Even if you've dropped most of your cash on shopping, you can still afford to stuff your face with good cheap eats like **Upper Crust** (222), **Steve's Greek** (316), **Snappy Sushi** (144), **Bottega Fiorentina** (264), **Boloco** (247), **JP Licks** (352), and **Kashmir** (279). Or pick up a little piece of prepared food heaven at **DeLuca's Market** (239). But if your coffers still have a little silver left in 'em, splurge at **Stephanie's on Newbury** (190), **Tapeo Restaurant & Tapas Bar** (268), **Capital Grille** (359), or **Bouchee** (159). Either way, you'll never make it on this street without some fuel in your belly.

Nightlife

Even if you only go to one store, a trip to Newbury Street will most certainly merit a nightcap (even if it's still day time). Unfortunately, there seems to be a dearth of boozin' spots specifically on this street. Fortunately, a great deal exists on adjacent streets (see Map 5 and 6). In the meantime, the best waterin' holes 'round these parts include the martini bar at **Sonsie** (327), and **Bukowski Tavern** at the end of the line on 50 Dalton Street.

All addresses are on Newbury Street

Clothing

A Pea in the Pod • 10 • maternity wear
AG Adriano Goldschmied • 201 • men's and women's clothing
Akris Boutique • 16 • shoe store
Alan Bilzerian • 34 • designer clothes
Alan Rouleau Couture • 73 • custom tailoring
Aldo • 180 • shoes and leather goods
Allen Edmonds • 36 • shoes and cedar products
American Apparel • 138 • men's and women's clothing
American Eagle Outfitters • 201 • youth clothes
Ana Hernandez Bridal • 165 • bridal boutique
Ann Taylor • 18 • women's clothes
Anthropologie • 203 • For the wealthy hipster.
Aria Bridesmaids • 39 • custom dresses
Army Barracks • 328 • military duds
Banana Republic • 28 • men's and women's clothing
Barbour by Peter Elliot • 134 • men's and women's clothing
BCBG Max Azaria • 71 • women's designer clothing
Bebe • 349 • women's clothing, accessories
Bella Bridesmaid • 163 • wedding clothing
Best of Scotland • 115 • sweaters at mill prices
Betsey Johnson • 201 • designer clothes
Betsy Jenney of Boston • 114 • women's unusual designer clothes
Blue Jeans Bar • 85 •
Borelli • 73 • high-end fashion
The Boston Baked Bean • 291 • keychains and more
Boutique Giorgio Armani • 22 • clothes
Boutique Longchamp • 139A • French handbags
Brooks Brothers • 46 • classy clothing for men and women
Burberry Limited • 2 • clothes for men and women
Calypso • 114 • women's clothing
Camper Shoes • 139 • shoes
Ceri • 31 • women's clothing
Chanel • 5 • clothing and accessories
Classic Tuxedo • 223 • ummm…?
The Closet • 175 • consignment; men's and women's clothing
Cole-Haan • 109 • men's and women's clothing
Cuoio • 115 • European shoes for women
Daniela Corte Fashion • 91 • women's fashion
Designer Shoes • 125 • designer shoes
Diesel • 339 • clothing
DKNY • 37 • clothing
Dress • 221 • women's clothing
Easter Wings • 244 • women's clothing
Ecco Newbury Street • 216 • shoes
Emporio Armani • 210-214 • men's and women's clothing
Envi-Eco Fashion Boutique • 164 • womens fashion accessories
Fiandaca • 73 • couture clothing
Flair Bridesmaid Boutique • 129 • wedding clothing
Footstock • 133 • shoes
French Connection • 208 • men's and women's clothing
G-Star Raw • 348 • men's and women's clothing
Guess? • 80 • clothing
H&M • 100 • men's and women's clothing
Hempest • 207 • hemp clothing
I Boutique • 251 • men's and women's clothing
In the Pink • 133 • women's clothing
Intermix • 186 • women's clothing
Jasmine Sola Shoes • 329 • shoes
Jessica McClintock • 201 • women's cocktail attire
John Fluevog Shoes • 302 • shoes
Johnny Cupcakes • 279 • men's and women's clothing
Juicy Couture • 12 • women's clothing
Karmaloop Boston • 160 • men's and women's clothing
Kate Spade Shoes • 117 • shoes, purses, etc.

Kenneth Cole Productions • 128 • shoes
Lester Harry's • 115 • bedding, children's and infant's clothing
Life is Good • 285 • men's and women's clothing
Lingerie Studio • 264 • lingerie
LF Stores • 353 • women's clothing
Loro Piana • 43 • men's and women's clothing, accessories, tailoring and alteration
Lucky Brand • 229 • denim
Luna Boston • 286 • accessories and handbags
Maha Barson • 127 • women's clothing
Marc Jacobs • 81 • fashion
Matsu • 259 • handbags
Max Mara • 69 • women's clothing
Mudo • 205 • clothing
Nanette Lepore • 119 • women's clothing
Niketown • 200 • everything Nike
Oilily • 31 • Dutch clothing for women and children
Oilily Women's • 32 • women's clothes
Patagonia • 346 • clothing for the great outdoors
Pavo Real Boutique • 115 • women's clothing and accessories
Petit Bateau • 171 • women's clothing
Players of Newbury • 250 • women's clothing
Puma • 333 • wildlife
Queen Bee • 85 • women's clothing
Ragg & Bone • 111 •
Ralph Lauren • 95 • clothing
Reiss • 132 • men's and women's clothing
Relic • 116 • men's and women's clothing
Riccardi Boutique • 116 • clothing
Rugby Ralph Lauren • 342 • men's and women's clothing
Sean Store • 154 • men's clothing
Second Time Around Collections • 176 & 219 • new and consignment clothes
Serenella • 134 • European women's clothes
Soudee • 293 • fashion
Stel's • 334 • men's and women's clothing, accessories, and jewelry
Steve Madden • 324A • shoes and handbags
Stil • 170 • women's clothing
Technical • 230 • skate style and art
Timberland • 201 •
Thom Brown of Boston • 337 & 331 • shoes
Ugg • 75 •
United Colors of Benetton • 140 • women's clothing
Urban Outfitters • 361 • clothing
Valentino • 47 • men's and women's clothing
Vera Wang • 253 • wedding clothing
Victoria's Secret • 82 • fig leaves
Whim Boutique • 253 • men's and women's clothing

Restaurants

29 Newbury • 29 • new American food
Ben & Jerry's • 174 • ice cream
Boloco Inspired Burritos • 247 • burritos
Boston Baked Bean • 291 • gourmet gifts
Bouchee • 159 • American and French food
Bostone Pizza • 225 • pizza
The Capital Grille • 359 • steak house
Charley's Eating & Drinking Saloon • 284 • American food
Ciao Bella • 240 • Italian food
Daisy Buchanan's • 240 • bar
Emack & Bolio's Ice Cream • 290 • ice cream
Emporio Armani Café • 214 • Italian cuisine
Espresso Royale Café • 286 • coffee house
The Jewel of Newbury • 254 • Italian food
Kashmir • 279 • Indian food
L'Aroma Café • 85 • coffee shop
Marcello's Restaurant • 272 • Persian, Italian
Pazzo • 268 • Italian food
Piattini Wine Café • 226 • Italian food
Scoop • 177 •
Scoozi • 237 • pizza and sandwiches
Shino Express Sushi • 144 • Japanese food
Sonsie • 327 • international cuisine
Stephanie's on Newbury • 190 • American food
Steve's • 316 • Greek-American food
Tapeo • 268 • Spanish food
Tealuxe • 108 • tea bar
Thai Basil • 132 • Thai food
The Upper Crust • 222 • pizza
Wisteria House • 264 • Chinese-American cuisine

Gifts & Miscellaneous

1154 Lill Studio • 220 • handbags
A Touch of France Gallery • 173 • art gallery
Acme Fine Art • 38 • bought and sold modern American art
Aldo Accessories • 184 • accessories, handbags, jewelry
Alfred J. Walker Fine Art • 162 • art gallery
Alpha Gallery Inc • 38 • art gallery
Andrea Marquit Fine Arts • 38 • art gallery
Arden Gallery • 129 • art gallery
Atelier Janiye • 165 • jewelry
Aurum • 293 • jewelry
Axelle Fine Arts • 91 • art gallery
Back Bay Oriental Rugs • 154 • rugs
Barbara Krakow Gallery • 10 • art gallery
Bauer Wines Spirits • 330 • liquor store
Beadworks • 167 • make your own jewelry
Beth Urdang Gallery • 14 • art gallery
Bliss • 121 • home furnishings, cooking and dining
Brodney Antiques & Jewelry • 145 • antiques and jewelry
Cartier • 40 • jewelry
CD Spins • 324 • music and records
Chase Gallery • 129 • art gallery
Childs Gallery • 169 • art gallery
Cohen's Fashion Optical • 179 • sunglasses and glasses
Comenos Fine Arts • 9 • art gallery
Commonwealth Fine Art • 236 • art gallery
CoSo Artist's Gallery • 158 • art gallery
Crush Boutique • 264 •
Dajuli Sparkles • 304 • jewelry
Diptyque • 123 • French perfumery
Domain Home Fashions • 7 • furniture
Dona Flor • 246 • home ceramics
Dorfman Jewelers • 24 • jewelry
Down to Basics • 249 • bedding
DTR Modern Galleries • 167 • art gallery
Erwin Pearl • 4 • jewelry
European Watch Co • 232 • watch repair and shop
Fairy Shop • 302 • Fairies, bubbles, incense, jewelry, you name it
Family Treasures Bookstore • books and magazines
Felicia's Cosmetics • 314 • cosmetics
Firefly Jewelry and Gifts • 270 • jewelry and gift shop
Firestone and Parson • 8 • antique jewelry
Fresh • 121 • bath products
Galerie d'Orsay • 33 • art gallery
Gallery NAGA • 67 • art gallery
Guido Frame Studio • 118 • ready-to-frame prints
The Guild of Boston Artists • 162 • art gallery
Hope • 302 • unique gift shop
Howard Yezerski Gallery • 14 • art gallery
International Poster Gallery • 205 • poster art gallery
Inviting Company • 213 • stationery
Judi Rotenberg Gallery • 130 • art gallery
Judy Ann Goldman Fine Art • 14 • art gallery
Kiehl's • 112 • beauty products
Kitchen Arts • 161 • kitchen tools
Kitty World • 279 • Hello Kitty heaven
Knit and Needlepoint • 11 • crafts and sewing supplies

L'Attitude Gallery Sculpture Garden • 218 • art gallery
Lalo Treasures • 255 • jewelry
Lanoue Fine Art • 160 • art gallery
Lavender Home & Table • 173 • home and garden, bedding, antiques
Lipstick • 293 •
Lululemon • 337 •
Lush Cosmetics • 166 • beauty products
M-A-C Newbury • 112 • beauty products
Madura Company • 144 • home furnishings, bedding
Marcoz Antiques • 177 • Antiques
Martin Lawrence Gallery • 77 • art gallery
Mayan Weavers • 268 • Native American crafts
Mercury Gallery • 8 • art gallery
Miller Block Gallery • 14 • art gallery
Needlepoint of Back Bay • 125 • crafts and sewing
Newbury Comics • 332 • music and video store
Newbury Fine Arts Gallery • 29 • art gallery
Newbury Visions • 215 • sunglasses and glasses
Newbury Yarns • 164 • crafts and sewing supplies
Nielsen Gallery • 179 • art gallery
O & Company • 161 • olive oil store
O'Brien Stephen B • 268 • art gallery
Pageo • 33 • Jewelry
Pepper Gallery • 38 • art gallery
Pierre Deux • 109 • gourmet gifts and home accessories
Poggenpohl Boston Showroom • 135 • designer kitchens
Pottery Barn • 122 • home décor
Pratesi Linens • 110 • bed and bath linens
Prem-La • 211 • home and garden
Pucker Gallery • 171 • art gallery
Q Optical • 287 • glasses and sunglasses
Richardson-Clarke Gallery • 38 • art gallery
Robert Klein Gallery • 38 • art gallery
Robert Marc Newbury Street • 35 • glasses and sunglasses
Royka's Fine Arts Antiques Gallery • 213 • antiques
SAC Gallery • 175 • art gallery
Sarkis Sajonian • 273 • jewelry
Shu Uemura • 130 • beauty products
Simon Pearce Glass • 115 • glassware
Small Pleasures • 142 • jewelry
So Good Jewelry • 349 • jewelry
Solstice • 168 • glasses and sunglasses
St George Gallery • 245 • art gallery
Sunglass Hut International • 182 & 86 • sunglasses store
Swiss Watch Boston • 217 • timepieces
Teuscher Chocolates of Switzerland • 230 • chocolates
Time & Time Again • 249 • watch store
Timeless Teas • 85 • tea
Trident Booksellers and Café • 338 • bookstore and café
VOSE Galleries of Boston Inc. • 238 • art gallery
Waterworks • 103 • bathroom accessories

Boston Convention & Exhibition Center

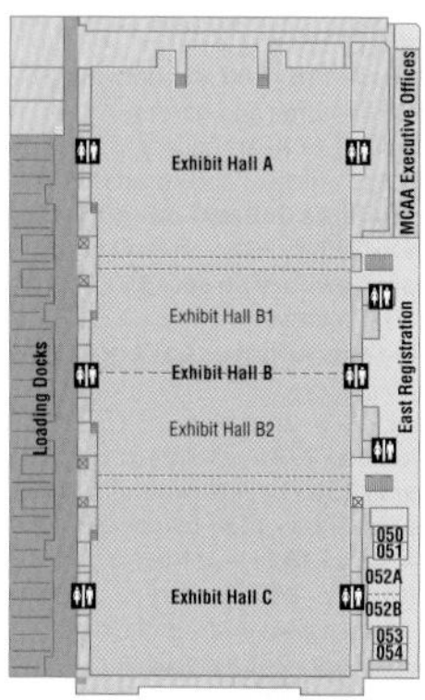

EXHIBIT LEVEL

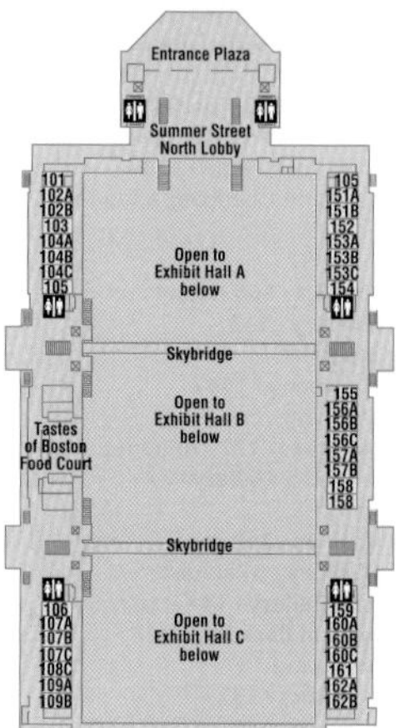

MEETING LEVEL 1

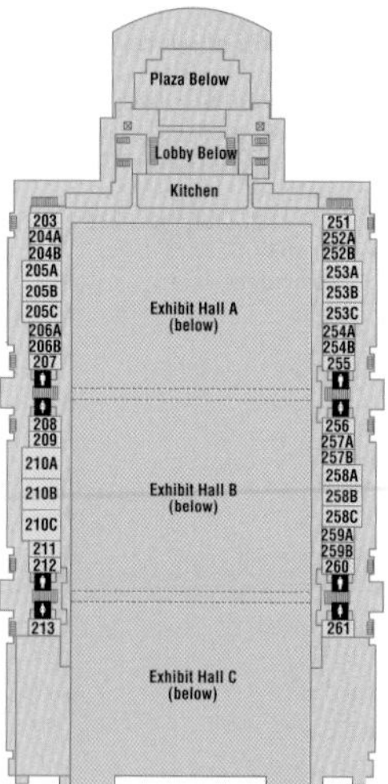

MEETING LEVEL 2

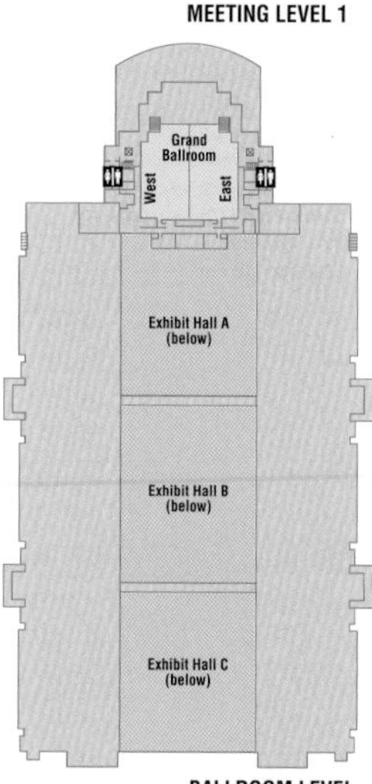

BALLROOM LEVEL

General Information

NFT Map: 10
Address: 415 Summer St,
Boston, MA 02210
Phone: 617-954-2000
Fax: 617-954-2299
Websites: massconvention.com
www.advantageboston.com

Overview

It took longer than expected to complete (what doesn't in this town?) and was plagued by cost overruns and contractor squabbling, but the Boston Convention & Exhibition Center finally opened in June 2004. In our humble opinion, it was worth the wait. Designed by noted architect Rafael Viñoly, the BCEC, which stands near Fort Point Channel on Summer Street (about a half-mile from South Station), is a stunning addition to the South Boston waterfront landscape.

Put simply, the BCEC is gargantuan. With 516,000 square feet of contiguous exhibition space, 160,000 square feet of flexible meeting space, more than 80 meeting rooms, and a 40,000-square-foot grand ballroom, the building covers an overall area of 1.7 million square feet. The BCEC now holds the coveted title of New England's Largest Man-Made Space and is big enough to hold 16 football fields.

The new complex is the centerpiece of the city's initiative to attract more convention business to Boston. As the old real estate mantra goes, it's all about "location, location, location," and a prime selling point for the BCEC is its proximity to both South Station and Logan Airport. Only two miles from Logan, the BCEC is closer to its city airport than the convention center of any other American city.

Services

The BCEC is used for large-scale conferences, meetings, and exhibitions. To schedule an event and be assigned a personal coordinator, contact the sales department at 617-954-2411 or sales@massconvention.com.

Catering services at the BCEC are provided by Levy Restaurants. If you are planning a catered event, contact Levy at 617-954-2382.

How to Get There—Driving

The BCEC is easy to reach from the Mass Pike (I-90). From the Pike, take Exit 25 (South Boston). Turn right onto Congress Street, then right onto D Street, then the second right onto Summer Street. The BCEC will be immediately on the left. It's hard to miss.

From the south, take I-93 N, get off at Exit 20, follow the signs to I-90 E and Exit 25. Follow the directions above.

From the north, take I-93 S, get off at Exit 23 (Purchase Street/South Station), proceed straight onto Purchase Street at the end of the exit ramp, and take a left onto Summer Street at South Station. Drive about a mile down the road to D Street and make a right.

Parking

If you must drive, you'll probably be dropping your car in a garage or fenced parking lot. The establishments listed below are the closest to the BCEC.

LAZ Parking• 10 Necco St, 617-426-1556
Fitz-Inn Auto Parks • 30-60 Necco St, 617-426-1556
Farnsworth Parking Garage • 17-31 Farnsworth St, 617-737-8161
Stanhope Garage • 338 Congress St, 617-338-5657
Stanhope Garage • 381 Congress St, 617-426-5326
Fanpier Parking Lots • 28 Northern Ave, 617-737-0910
Transpark • 390 Congress St, 617-737-3363
Transpark • 25 Northern Ave, 617-451-7732

How to Get There—Mass Transit

The Silver Line stops at the BCEC (alight at the World Trade Center stop, escalate to the top entrance, and traverse the bridge). To connect to the Silver Line from points other than Logan Airport, take the T's Red Line to South Station. The BCEC is only a few hundred yards away from South Station, so if you want to stretch your legs, take a stroll across Fort Point Channel instead of transferring to the Silver Line.

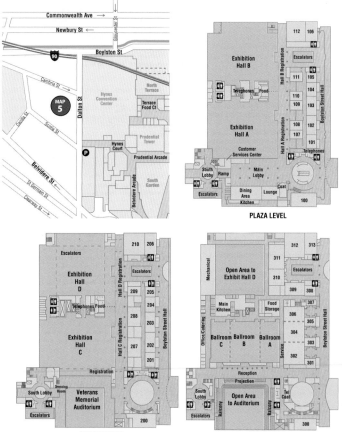

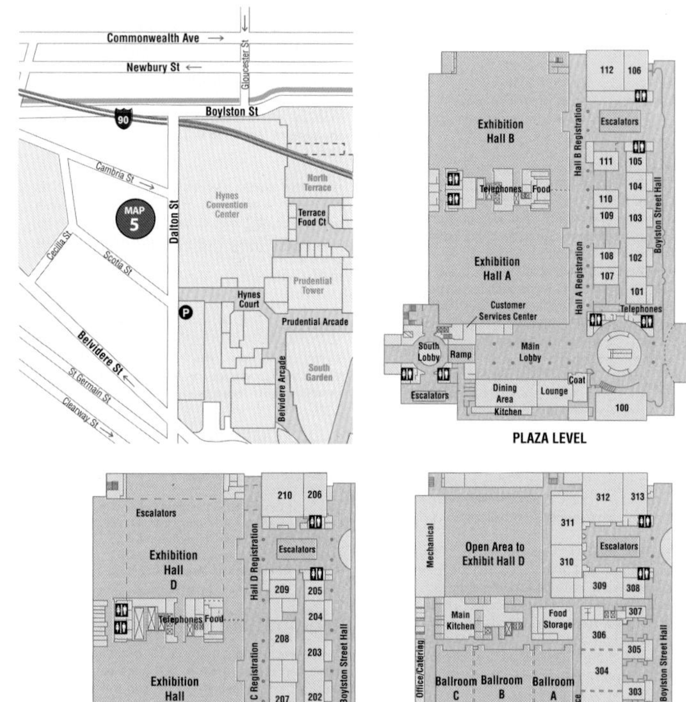
Commonwealth Ave
Newbury St
Gloucester St
Boylston St
90
Cambria St
MAP 5
Dalton St
Hynes Convention Center
North Terrace
Terrace Food Ct
Cecilia St
Scotia St
Prudential Tower
Hynes Court
Prudential Arcade
Belvidere St
St Germain St
Clearway St
Belvidere Arcade
South Garden
Exhibition Hall B
Hall B Registration
112
106
Escalators
111
105
104
Telephones
Food
110
109
103
Boylston Street Hall
Exhibition Hall A
Hall A Registration
108
102
107
101
Customer Services Center
Telephones
South Lobby
Ramp
Main Lobby
Escalators
Dining Area
Lounge
Coat
Kitchen
100
PLAZA LEVEL
210
206
Escalators
Exhibition Hall D
Hall D Registration
Escalators
209
205
Telephones
Food
204
208
203
Exhibition Hall C
Hall C Registration
207
202
201
Registration
South Lobby
Dressing Room
Veterans Memorial Auditorium
Escalators
200
SECOND LEVEL
312
313
Mechanical
Open Area to Exhibit Hall D
311
Escalators
310
309
308
Main Kitchen
Food Storage
307
306
Office/Catering
305
Ballroom C
Ballroom B
Ballroom A
304
Boylston Street Hall
Service
303
302
301
Reception
Projection
South Lobby
Open Area to Auditorium
Tel
Coat
Balcony
Balcony
Escalators
300
THIRD LEVEL

General Information

NFT Map: 5
Address: 900 Boylston St, Boston, MA 02115
Phone: 617-954-2000
Websites: massconvention.com
www.advantageboston.com

Overview

The John B. Hynes Veterans Memorial Convention Center is a relatively small center, with just 176,480 square feet of exhibit space, a 25,000-square-foot ballroom, and 38 meeting rooms. The Hynes is conveniently located in Back Bay with many hotels, historical sites, and tourist attractions within close proximity. Only a short walk from the Green Line's Hynes Convention Center stop.

Once the big name in town for would-be conventioneers, the Hynes Convention Center now plays second fiddle to the Boston Convention and Exhibition Center (see page 204). Because the Hynes adjoins the Prudential complex and sits in the midst of a few thousand hotel rooms, it continues to attract convention business, focusing on mid-size meetings (think the American Association of Immunologists and the National Council of Teachers of Mathematics) and letting the biggest fish (like the International Boston Seafood Show) swim to the Southie Starship.

Services

The Hynes is used for conferences, meetings, exhibitions, and most other events where groups of people gather. (Word to the wise: Stay far, far away during CollegeFest.) To schedule an event and be assigned a personal coordinator, contact the sales department by phone at 617-954-2411, or by email at sales@massconvention.com.

Catering services at the Hynes are provided by Levy Restaurants. If you are planning a catered event, contact Levy at 617-954-2382.

How to Get There—Driving

The Hynes is only four miles from Logan Airport. Two major roadways, I-93 and the Mass Pike (I-90), will deliver you close to the venue. From I-93, take Exit 26 B (Storrow Drive). Follow Storrow Drive for about two miles to the Fenway/Kenmore exit and head towards Fenway. Continue to the first set of lights and merge left onto Boylston Street.

From the Mass Pike, take Exit 22 (Prudential/Copley Place), stay left as you exit, and turn onto Huntington Avenue. At the next set of lights (Belvidere Street), take a right, follow the curve, and bear right onto Dalton Street. At the lights, turn right onto Boylston Street.

The main entrance to the Hynes is at 900 Boylston Street and is easily accessible to taxis and buses via an access lane, which is set apart from Boylston Street.

Parking

There are numerous parking garages within a three-block walk of the Hynes, totaling more than 4,400 spaces. There is metered parking available around the Hynes and adjacent streets, but these spots are hard to come by.

- **Prudential Center Parking Garage**, 800 Boylston St, 2–10 hours for $36, and the daily maximum is $39. 617-236-3060.
- **Copley Place Parking Garage**, 100 Huntington Ave (corner of Huntington Ave & Dartmouth St), $9 for the first half hour with an increase of $4 for every additional half hour, $30 for 3–10 hours, but only $10 for three hours with validation. Maximum day rate is $35. 617-369-5025.
- **Boston Marriott Hotel Copley Place**, 100 Huntington Ave, self-parking $35 per day, valet parking, $41 per day. 617-236-5800.
- **Westin Copley Place Parking Garage**, 10 Huntington Ave, $16 for up to 1 hour; $24 for 1-3 hours, $32 for 3-5 hours, $36 for 5-8 hours, $46 for 8-24 hours, $48 for overnight. 617-262-9600.
- **Colonnade Hotel Parking Garage**, 120 Huntington Ave, $12 for the first hour, with a $4 increase every additional hour; $24 for 3–12 hours. $36 for overnight parking. 617-424-7000.
- **Back Bay Hilton Hotel Parking Garage**, 40 Dalton St, $5 for 1/2 hour, $12 for 1 hour, $20 for 1–2 hours. $22 for 2–3 hours, $24 for 3–12 hours, $35 for overnight parking, $39 for overnight parking with valet service. 617-236-1100.

How to Get There—Mass Transit

The subway stops just two blocks away from the Hynes. Take the Green Line (B, C, or D train) to the Hynes Convention Center stop. Once you get off the subway, exit at any entrance and follow signs to the Hynes.

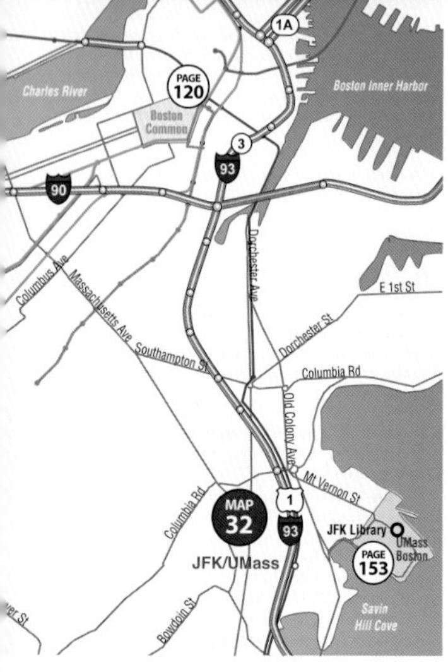

General Information

NFT Map: 32
Address: Columbia Point
Boston, MA 02125
Phone: 617-514-1600
Website: www.jfklibrary.org
Hours: 9 am–5 pm daily except Thanksgiving, Christmas, and New Year's Day
Research Library is open M–F 8:30–4:30 by appointment
Admission: Adults $12, seniors and students $10, children $9, free for children 12 and under

Overview

The John F. Kennedy Library and Museum, dedicated to our 35th president on October 20, 1979, houses 25 multimedia exhibits examining the life and work of JFK, his administration, his family, and his legacy. The library is one of thirteen presidential libraries administered by the National Archives and Records Administration, a federal government agency. The library draws approximately 200,000 visitors each year.

The library, which overlooks Boston Harbor from windswept Columbia Point, was designed by architect I.M. Pei (who also designed the Christian Science Center next to the Pru). The centerpiece of the complex is a nine-story concrete tower fronted by a glass-enclosed pavilion. The adjacent Stephen E. Smith Center, used for educational programs and conferences, opened in 1991. Outside on the lawn sits *Victura*, JFK's 26-foot sloop.

What's Inside

The JFK Library holds 8.4 million pages of presidential papers, 180,000 still photographs, six million feet of film and videotape, and 15,000 catalogued museum objects. The library also houses the world's most comprehensive collection of the papers and mementos of Ernest Hemingway, but they are available to professional researchers only. If you are a scholar who seeks access to Papa's papers, check the library's website to review the restrictive rules.

The library's Centennial Room displays rotating exhibits showcasing the Kennedy White House's embrace of cultural values and the arts. Visitors can watch a 17-minute film about the Kennedy administration before entering the main exhibit space. On weekends, the 2 pm showing of the introductory film is replaced by a 30-minute film about JFK's brother/attorney general, Robert F. Kennedy. Visitors can also watch a 20-minute film about the Cuban Missile Crisis.

A museum café serves light meals and snacks from 9 am to 5 pm, and the gift shop is open during visiting hours.

How to Get There—Driving

The JFK Library is off Morrissey Boulevard next to the UMass Boston campus. From the north or the south, take I-93 to Exit 14 (Morrissey Boulevard) and follow the signs. From the west, take the Mass Pike (I-90) east to the intersection with I-93. Take the exit toward I-93 S, get off I-93 at Exit 14, and follow the signs. The library provides free on-site parking.

How to Get There—Mass Transit

Take the T's Red Line to the JFK/UMass stop. A free shuttle bus runs between the T stop and the library. Shuttle buses run every 20 minutes between 8 am and 5 pm.

General Information

Cape Cod Chamber of Commerce:
508-362-3225; www.capecodchamber.org
Wellfleet Bay Wildlife Sanctuary:
508-349-2615; www.massaudubon.org/Nature_Connection/Sanctuaries/Wellfleet/index.php
Cape Cod National Seashore Salt Pond Visitor Center:
508-349-3785; www.nps.gov/caco

Overview

Thanks to the eternal appeal of picturesque beaches, fried seafood, and miniature golf, Cape Cod is one of New England's most popular getaway destinations. Separated from mainland Massachusetts by the Cape Cod Canal, the region is located on the portion of the state that looks like a strong, flexing arm. There are only two roads that cross the canal, both via bridge; those Cape Cod Canal Tunnel stickers on locals' cars are just a mind game played on the out-of-towners.

The Cape is composed of 15 towns, with a permanent population of roughly 230,000 that swells to over 550,000 in the summer months. The islands of Martha's Vineyard and Nantucket are not officially part of Cape Cod, but are generally considered the same destination region. Each town has its own character: Bustling and bawdy Provincetown is home to a large and proud gay community, while Falmouth is a more tranquil, wooded locale.

Highlights and Essentials:

•Beaches—With a total of 559.6 miles of coastline, the Cape is perhaps most well-known for its beaches, many of which are open to the public for a modest daily parking fee. The northern ocean water resists warming though, so swimming is generally, let's say, refreshing.

• Seafood—Fried clams, twin lobsters, steamers, baked stuffed quahogs…need we say more?

• Christmas Tree Shops—The merchandise sold at this thriving retail chain can be best described as discount "stuff." The company has expanded beyond its Cape Cod origins, but there is no better place to go when you need picture frames, beach toys, or souvenir tchotchkes.

• Miniature Golf—The Cape has elevated mini-golf landscaping to a fine art. Whether you prefer putting in a serene garden setting or braving darkened caves in a pirate-inspired golf adventure, Cape Cod has something for you.

• Lighthouses—If you have time to visit a lighthouse or two, we recommend the Nobska Point Lighthouse at Woods Hole, an oft-photographed white tower at the southwestern tip of Cape Cod, the Cape Cod (Highland) Lighthouse in North Truro, or the Chatham Lighthouse on the southeastern corner of the Cape.

• Whale Watches—Hop aboard a whale watch voyage out of Wood's Hole, Hyannis, or Provincetown to experience the truly breathtaking phenomenon of cruising alongside some of the world's largest and most powerful creatures.

The Towns

The Cape, about 70 miles in length, is often divided into three regions:

The Upper Cape—The first area you reach after crossing the canal, the Upper Cape includes the towns of Falmouth, Mashpee, Sandwich, and Bourne. For the best views and smoothest journey, avoid the highways and take surface routes, such as 28A, that take you close to the water. Film buffs might consider a visit to Woods Hole, where part of the movie *Jaws* was filmed.

The Mid Cape—Continuing eastward, the next area you will reach includes Dennis, Yarmouth, and Barnstable, a town containing seven villages: Hyannis, Osterville, Centerville, Cotuit, West Barnstable, Barnstable Village, and Marstons Mills. Almost 70% of the Cape's permanent population resides in the Hyannis area, so the downtown remains busy throughout the year, and it is about the only place in the area to find such national chains as Barnes and Noble or Old Navy. If such conventional commercialism isn't on your vacation itinerary, take the Old King's Highway (Route 6A) to stay in the Cape mood.

The Outer Cape—Home of the peaceful Cape Cod National Seashore, Nickerson State Park, and the quiet towns of Brewster, Orleans, Eastham, Wellfleet, Chatham, Harwich, and Truro, it's difficult to imagine the spectacle sitting at the tip of the Outer Cape: Provincetown. At land's end sits one of the most "out" towns, where gay couples are as plentiful as seagulls, and the prevailing aesthetic can best be described as "flamboyant." After a day in the sun, cruise into P-town for a night of revelry. Gay or straight, the town knows how to party. For full effect, visit during Carnival in August. More information is available at www.provincetown.com.

The Islands—Martha's Vineyard and Nantucket each possess a distinct feel. Martha's Vineyard is known for great beaches, ocean vistas, and the annual (and controversial) Monster Shark Tournament. It's even better known for its well-heeled rich folk and the Kennedy Compound. Nantucket, only three and a half by fourteen miles, is a quaint New England destination where tourists roam the cobble-stoned streets year-round. In addition to shops and galleries, the downtown is home to the Nantucket Whaling Museum. The best way around the island is to rent a moped or a bicycle but remember to pack a lunch if you head to the beaches because there are no restaurants or snack bars.

The Outdoors

Sculpted dunes, haunting marshlands, and miles of hiking trails make the Cape an ideal area for outdoor exploration. If the water calls, you can splash about at one of the Cape's many bay or ocean beaches, take a boat out to sea, dive or snorkel in the bay, canoe or kayak, parasail, kiteboard, or enjoy one of the whale- or seal-watching excursions offered.

Flora and fauna enthusiasts come here to explore the lush plant and animal life at the Cape's many sanctuaries. The Audubon Society's Wellfleet Bay Wildlife Sanctuary is the only sanctuary with a visitor's center. It boasts 1,000 acres of woodlands, wetlands, and grasslands that attract an exciting variety of wildlife, including songbirds and shorebirds. Five miles of scenic trails wind through

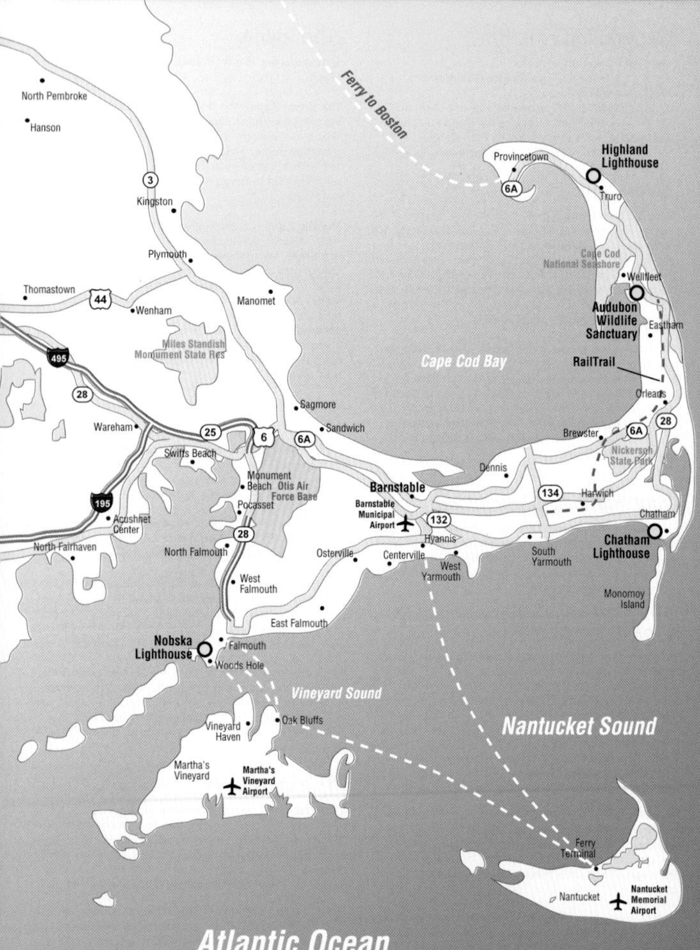

Ferry to Boston
North Pembroke
Hanson
3
Kingston
Plymouth
Thomastown
44
Wenham
Manomet
Miles Standish Monument State Res
495
28
Wareham
25
6
6A
Sagmore
Sandwich
Swifts Beach
Monument Beach
Otis Air Force Base
Pocasset
195
Acushnet Center
North Fairhaven
28
North Falmouth
West Falmouth
East Falmouth
Nobska Lighthouse
Falmouth
Woods Hole
Barnstable
Barnstable Municipal Airport
132
Hyannis
Osterville
Centerville
West Yarmouth
South Yarmouth
Dennis
134
Harwich
Brewster
6A
28
Nickerson State Park
Orleans
Chatham
Chatham Lighthouse
Monomoy Island
Cape Cod Bay
RailTrail
Eastham
Audubon Wildlife Sanctuary
Wellfleet
Cape Cod National Seashore
Truro
Highland Lighthouse
Provincetown
6A
Vineyard Sound
Oak Bluffs
Vineyard Haven
Martha's Vineyard
Martha's Vineyard Airport
Nantucket Sound
Ferry Terminal
Nantucket
Nantucket Memorial Airport
Atlantic Ocean

the various habitats, while the newly renovated Nature Center includes "green" elements such as solar heating and composting toilets. Inside the nature center, you'll find two 700-gallon aquariums that feature the underwater worlds of the salt marsh and tidal flats. Other sanctuaries on the Cape include Long Pasture near Barnstable, Skunknett River near Osterville, Sampson's Island (accessible only by private boat from local marinas and town landings), and Ashumet Holly near Falmouth. The Cape Cod National Seashore Salt Pond visitor center in Eastham offers guided tours and nature walks through the salt marshes.

Monomoy Island, established in 1944 as a National Wildlife Refuge, is a barrier island that sits ten miles south of Chatham. It is prime habitat for migratory birds and a seal population that has grown in recent years. It is not uncommon to sit on Nauset beach to the north and see seals swimming regularly along the shoreline, which wasn't the case ten years ago. Monomoy has hiking trails and bird watching opportunities as well as commercial boat tours for seal-watching. Check out www.fws.gov/northeast/monomoy.

Sports

Cape Cod is an ideal location for sport fishing. Charters and tours are available and, for those looking to have a little fun on the water, ships such as the *Yankee* offer party cruises, perfect for those who hate lugging around a heavy cooler. Be warned: Drinking and waves are not always the best combo.

Golf is also popular here. There are a dozen or so courses on the Cape, varying in price, size, and level of difficulty. Dennis Pines and Dennis Highlands are two highly-respected municipal courses where a challenging game can be had for a reasonable price, and Highland Links in Truro is perched atop sheer bluffs that overlook the ocean.

Biking is another favorite pastime in the area, with free trails including the epic 22-mile RailTrail at Cape Cod National Park. The trail runs along the bed of a defunct railroad (hence the name) from Dennis (get on at Route 134 just south of Exit 9 from Route 6) to the South Wellfleet General Store.

Diehard baseball fans shouldn't miss the 104-year-old Cape Cod League, where top college athletes are recruited to play in the summer, many of whom go on to the majors. Thurman Munson, "Nomah" Garciaparra, Jason Varitek, and other stars once played for one of the league's ten teams. Attending one of their early evening games is what summer is all about. Bring your beach chair, grab a hot dog, and watch the little kids scramble for foul balls.

Arts and Culture

Though better-known for its natural splendor, Cape Cod also boasts a thriving arts community. Every summer, the Cape Cod Melody Tent in Hyannis hosts popular music and comedy acts ranging from Willie Nelson to Lewis Black. In Dennis, the Cape Playhouse mounts theatrical productions such as *Guys and Dolls* and *Thoroughly Modern Millie*.

Galleries, studios, specialty museums, and whimsical artisan shops are to be found on almost every corner. For help navigating, download the Cape Cod, Nantucket, or Martha's Vineyard ArtsApp from the Cape Cod Chamber of Commerce website (www.capecodchamber.org/artsapp). For something a little more analog, try to locate a copy of Arts and Artisans Trails, a book featuring self-guided tours of the Cape and Islands that highlight the best of the area's arts scene.

Ever since Henry David Thoreau penned *Cape Cod*, the region has also been the full-time or summer home of a number of notable authors. Literary greats Norman Mailer and Kurt Vonnegut, and the mystery maven Mary Higgins Clark have been among the Cape's more notable literary residents over the years.

If you aspire to join this tradition, check out the Fine Arts Work Center in Provincetown, where summer workshops in painting, drawing, and writing could help you find your hidden muse.

How to Get There

By Car: The only two driving routes onto Cape Cod are via the overburdened Bourne and Sagamore bridges. This limited access has traditionally resulted in multi-mile gridlock on Friday evenings and Saturday mornings. The Sagamore Rotary has recently been replaced with a direct ramp known as the flyover, intended to tame the traffic. Plan to travel outside of the peak times and slowdowns should be minimal. Once on the Cape, most places are easily drivable, though downtown areas such as Hyannis and Provincetown can get a bit tangled up.

By Ferry: Avoid traffic and cut down on gas expenditures by hopping a ferry to Provincetown or the Islands. Bringing along a car or bike generally increases the fare, but the price may be a bargain if you have limited patience for the traffic that driving across the Canal can entail. Keep your eyes peeled for Secretary of State John Kerry in the summertime. At 6'4", he's hard to miss.

Bay State Cruise Company • 617-748-1428 •
www.boston-ptown.com
Boston-Provincetown. May–October.
Round-trip fare: $46 on weekend excursion ferry, $62-$83 on daily fast ferry. $12 for bikes.

Boston Harbor Cruises Provincetown Fast Ferry •
617-227-4321 • www.bostonharborcruises.com
Boston-Provincetown. May–October.
Round-trip fare: $63–$83. $7 for bikes.

Hy-Line Cruises • 800-492-8082 • hylinecruises.com
Hyannis-Martha's Vineyard. High-speed ferry, April–October. Standard ferry, May–October.
Hyannis-Nantucket, High-speed ferry year-round.
Standard ferry, May–October.
Martha's Vineyard-Nantucket. June–September
Round-trip fare: $45–$77. $7 for bikes.

Island Queen Ferry • 508-548-4800 • www.islandqueen.com
Falmouth Harbor- Martha's Vineyard. June–September.
Round-trip fare: $8–$20. $8 for bikes.

Steamship Authority • 508-693-9130 •
http://steamshipauthority.com
Woods Hole-Martha's Vineyard. Year-round.
Hyannis-Nantucket, Year-round.
Woods Hole-Martha's Vineyard round-trip fare:
$8-$16. $8 for a bike. $85–$155 for a car.
Hyannis-Nantucket round-trip fare:
$34–$67. $14 for a bike. $280–$450 for a car.

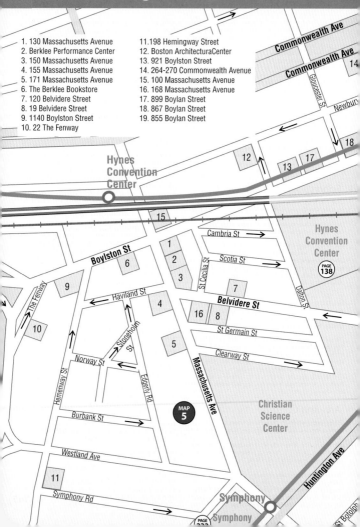

Berklee College of Music

1. 130 Massachusetts Avenue
2. Berklee Performance Center
3. 150 Massachusetts Avenue
4. 155 Massachusetts Avenue
5. 171 Massachusetts Avenue
6. The Berklee Bookstore
7. 120 Belvidere Street
8. 19 Belvidere Street
9. 1140 Boylston Street
10. 22 The Fenway
11. 198 Hemingway Street
12. Boston ArchitecturaCenter
13. 921 Boylston Street
14. 264-270 Commonwealth Avenue
15. 100 Massachusetts Avenue
16. 168 Massachusetts Avenue
17. 899 Boylan Street
18. 867 Boylan Street
19. 855 Boylan Street

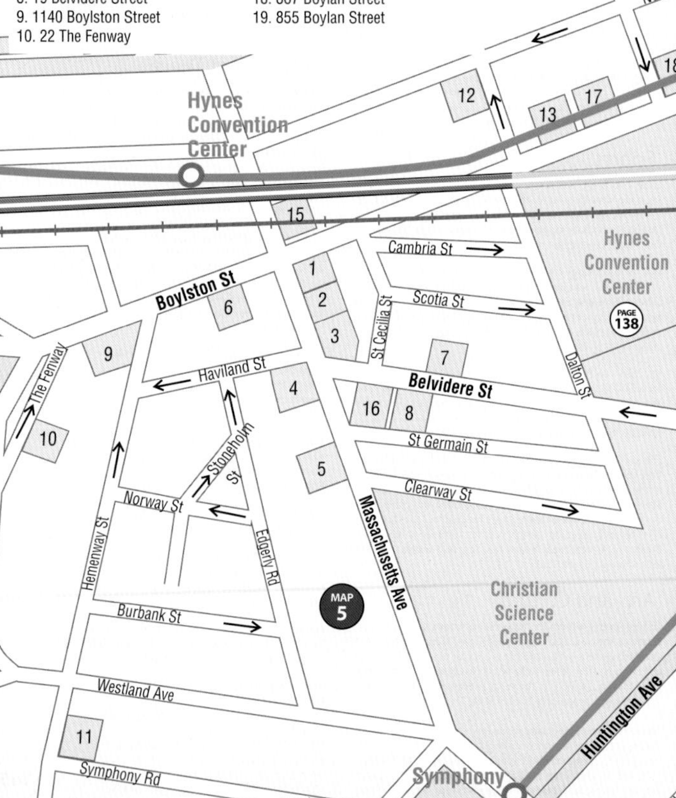

General Information

NFT Map: 5
Address: 1140 Boylston St, Boston, MA 02215
Phone: 617-266-1400
Website: www.berklee.edu

Overview

Berklee is the largest independent music college in the world and calls itself the "premier institution for the study of contemporary music." Founded in 1945 by pianist and MIT-trained engineer Lawrence Berk, the school became accredited in 1973. Berklee offers four-year degrees as well as diploma programs that allow students to forego the liberal arts and focus exclusively on music. Facilities include more than 250 private practice rooms. In addition to performance, students study Music Business/Management, Music Education, and Music Therapy. During the summer, the school offers specialized programs including Berklee in Los Angeles.

The college enrolls close to 4,000 students, with the highest percentage (about 26%) of international students of any college in the United States from more than 70 different countries. The student body is a funky, diverse lot, with many musicians from Japan, Korea, Germany, Switzerland, and Brazil. They tend to congregate on Mass Ave, particularly outside the Berklee Performance Center where bedraggled musical geniuses stand around with their instruments. Tracy Bonham, Melissa Etheridge, Patty Larkin, Branford Marsalis, Howard Shore, and Aimee Mann are among Berklee's notable alumni. Furthermore, Berklee was the first college to recognize the guitar as a principal instrument and develop a curriculum for it back in the '60s.

Tuition

Currently, tuition fees hover around $35,000 and housing will run you an extra $17,000 or so per year.

Sports

There are no college-level athletics at Berklee, but student clubs do offer soccer, basketball, softball, and yoga, among others. Nearby fitness facilities, including the YMCA, the Tennis and Racquet Club, and Boston Kung-Fu Tai-Chi Institute offer discounted rates for students. Much more popular than sports are the 350-plus student music ensembles in an impressive range of styles.

Culture on Campus

Housed in the historic Fenway Theater, the 1,220-seat Berklee Performance Center (BPC) stands as one of the finest concert halls on the East Coast. Located at 136 Massachusetts Avenue near the intersection with Boylston Street, the BPC offers numerous performances by major concert promoters as well as faculty and student concerts throughout the year. To attend a performance, check out the Event Calendar at www.berklee.edu/BPC or call the box office at 617-747-2261.

Departments

Admissions 617-747-2047
Financial Aid .... 617-747-2274 or 800-538-3844
Registrar 617-747-2240
Housing 617-747-2292
Alumni Relations 617-747-2236
Berklee Performance Center 617-747-2474
Library 617-747-2258

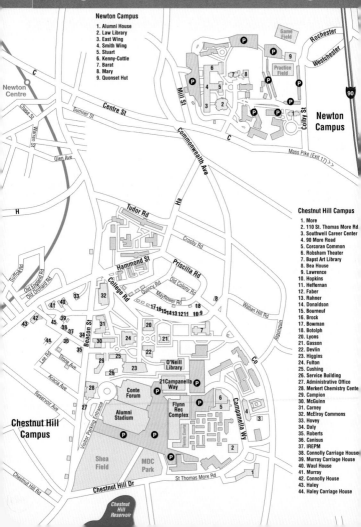

Newton Campus

1. Alumni House
2. Law Library
3. East Wing
4. Smith Wing
5. Stuart
6. Kenny-Cottle
7. Barat
8. Mary
9. Quonset Hut

Game Field
Practice Field
Rochester
Westchester
Newton Centre
Centre St
Sumner St
Chase St
Warren St
Glen Ave
Mill St
Commonwealth Ave
Colby St
Newton Campus
Mass Pike (Exit 17) >>
90

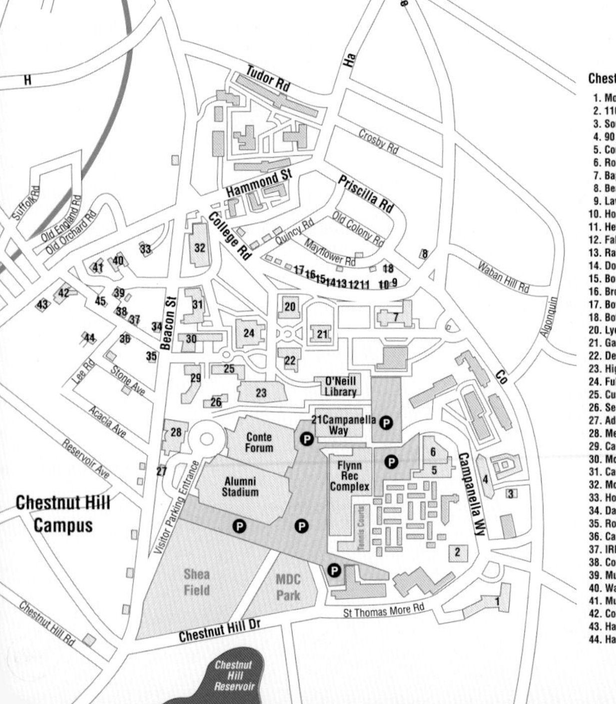

General Information

Main Campus: 140 Commonwealth Ave, Chestnut Hill, MA 02467
Newton Campus: 885 Centre St, Newton Center, MA 02459
Phone: 617-552-8000
Website: www.bc.edu

Overview

It all began one day in Paris in 1534, when a group of students at the University of Paris got together and decided to combine their devotion to God with their commitment to bettering society. They called themselves the Society of Jesus, or the Jesuits. A few centuries later, in 1863, three Jesuits opened a college in the South End and cleverly named it Boston College. The college began with just 22 students, but even then the Jesuit profs envisioned a grander institution that would integrate intellectual development with religious and ethical growth.

Over the past century-and-a-half, the school has drifted a bit, both geographically and ethically. Once located in Boston proper, the school now sits six miles to the west, sprawling over 117 acres in Chestnut Hill and another 40 in Newton. And while the college is still officially Jesuit through and through, today's 14,500 undergraduates and graduate students students come from 80 countries and all 50 states and all religions and creeds.

In the past BC perhaps had a bit of a Doug Flutie-style chip on its shoulders, what with Boston's competitive and crowded academic scene. Often overlooked is BC's excellent academic reputation. Its eight colleges and schools offer degree programs in more than fifty fields of study, and the school continues to be ranked as one of the best universities in the country by *U.S. News & World Report*.

Tuition

Currently, undergraduate tuition, room and board and fees amount to around $57,000.

Sports

Supporting 31 varsity and 38 club and intramural sports, Boston College boasts a diverse and strong athletic department. The varsity teams all compete at the NCAA Division I level. The BC Eagles football program is strong and the team continues to reach bowl games. The biggest game every year is against Notre Dame. The men's hockey team has been perennially successful, winning the national championship in 2001 and losing in the semifinals of the Frozen Four in 2004. In 2008 and 2012, however, Boston College won, much to BU's chagrin. In 2010 Boston College won the Beanpot, which is a hockey tournament amongst Boston colleges.

Culture on Campus

The Robsham Theater Arts Center is Boston College's creative center. Built in 1981, the theater seats 591 people. The building also includes a black box theater that seats 150–200 people. The three main departments housed in the facility are the Department of Theater Arts, the Robsham Dance and Theater Company, and the Boston Liturgical Dance Ensemble. The university presents four faculty-directed and two student-directed productions each year, and 20 musical and dance groups perform throughout the year. BC also has its share of improv and sketch comedy troupes including one that puts on comedic, part-improv murder mysteries once per semester. Worth checking out to get a better sense of the school's culture is the (now archived) website for "The BC" (the-bc.com), a send-up of "The OC" that is set at the Heights (local-speak for BC's Chestnut Hill campus). Download one of the show's commercials such as "Jon Bon Jesuits" for an hysterical, rocking-good time.

Another source of culture at Boston College is the McMullen Museum of Art. Located on the first floor of Devlin Hall, the museum is housed in one of the many Neo-Gothic buildings on the main campus. Aside from its notable permanent collection, the museum has frequent exhibitions of international and scholarly importance from all periods and cultures. The museum is free and open to the public. Hours: Mon–Fri 11 am–4 pm and Sat–Sun 12 pm–5 pm.

Departments

Undergraduate Admissions................ 617-552-3100
A&S Graduate Admissions................. 617-552-3265
Carroll Graduate School of Management... 617-552-3920
Connell School of Nursing................. 617-552-4928
Law School Admissions 617-552-4350
Lynch School of Education 617-552-4214
Graduate School of Social Work............ 617-552-4024
Student Services.......................... 617-552-3300
Athletic Departments and Tickets......... 617-552-GoBC
O'Neill Library............................ 617-552-4470

General Information

NFT Map: 16
Address: One Silber Way, Boston, MA 02215
Phone: 617-353-2000
Website: www.bu.edu

Overview

If you really want to go to school *in* Boston, BU is the school for you. Consisting of a strip of buildings along Commonwealth Avenue, BU's campus doesn't win any points for style, beauty, or landscape architecture (since that would require having a clearly defined landscape). Aside from several thousand red banners on the lampposts that say "Boston University," and a larger than usual concentration of jaywalking young folk along Comm Ave, there's little indication that you've even entered BU's domain.

The fourth-largest private university in the country, the school's "campus" is the learning center for all students and the residence of many of its 30,000 undergraduates and grad students. The upshot of the ill-defined BU campus is that its students are truly living in the city. BU students make the best of the little green space they have. "The Beach," a strip of greenery on the inbound side of Storrow Drive (which runs along the Charles), is a springtime hotspot for socializing and sunbathing.

When the university was founded in 1839, it was intended to be a theological school for ministers of the Methodist Episcopal Church. As the years went by, the university expanded its curriculum in order to accommodate the needs and interests of its growing student population. Today, there are 11 schools and colleges and over 250 different degree programs. Boston University students represent all 50 states, as well as 140 countries. BU also holds the distinction of having the most property owned by a non-government institution in the City of Boston. The university also boasts a bevy of outspoken alumni including Howard Stern, Bill O'Reilly, and Rosie O'Donnell (who didn't graduate).

Longtime president and infamous curmudgeon John Silber stepped down in 1996 after more than thirty years of leading the school to wherever he pleased. His replacement, former NASA chief Daniel Goldin, was called off the job even before he began his first day due to conflicting ideas about how the university should be run. Goldin said he took the job on the condition that Silber would not occupy a seat on the board of trustees. The Executive Committee balked at this stipulation and, after a little mud was slung, Goldin's termination was signed, thereby embarrassing the university in national headlines. Following the reign of an interim president since the resignation of Jon Westling in 2002, BU's tenth and current president, Robert A. Brown, was inaugurated to the post in April 2006.

Tuition

Undergraduate tuition costs run at about $51,000 per year with room board and fees. Graduate student tuition, fees, and expenses vary by college.

Sports

Notwithstanding the termination of the university's football program in 1997, the Terriers have quite an impressive athletics department. With 24 NCAA Division I varsity sports, Boston University provides a rich environment for sports lovers. The department prides itself on its equal emphasis on women's and men's varsity sports. The men's varsity ice hockey team is, by far, the most popular sports team at BU, with the most enthusiastic community support. There is fierce competition every year for the Beanpot—the "New England Invitational" tournament. BU has won the Beanpot 29 times, with Boston College being their biggest rival for the title. The university's hockey and basketball teams play in the Agganis Arena, a spiffy new facility that also hosts other sporting and entertainment events.

Culture on Campus

The first university to have a music program, BU remains committed to the arts. The Boston University Art Gallery is located at 855 Commonwealth Avenue. Although the gallery has no permanent collection, the architecture of the building is like an exhibit unto itself. Alluding to both the Classical and the Medieval, the columns that adorn the façade are a rare beauty and have attracted many people on that basis alone. You would never guess that the building is actually a converted Buick dealership. If this piques your interest, you'll be happy to learn that the gallery is open and free to the public, but only during the academic school year: Tues–Fri 10 am–5 pm and Sat–Sun 1 pm–5 pm.

Departments

Undergraduate Admissions................617-353-2300
Graduate Admissions 617-353-2696
Graduate School of Management..........617-353-9720
School of Medicine........................617-638-4630
School of Law.............................617-353-3100
School of Education.......................617-353-4237
School of Public Health....................617-638-4640
School of Social Work 617-353-3765
Athletic Department and Ticket Office 617-353-GoBU
Mugar Memorial Library...................617-353-3732

Building Legend

1. 1019 Commonwealth Ave (major residence)
2. Case Athletic Center
3. West Campus (major residence)
4. Office of Housing
5. Fitness and Recreation Center
6. 10 Buick St (major residence)
7. Center for English Language and Orientation Programs
8. Comptroller; Financial Assistance; Registrar; Student Health Services
9. College of General Studies
10. College of Fine Arts; University Art Gallery
11. School of Hospitality Administration; Metropolitan College Academic departments and other programs
12. Boston University Academy
13. George Sherman Union; Dean of Students; Student Activities Center; Howard Thurman Center
14. Mugar Memorial Library;University Information Center
15. School of Law
16. Metropolitan College; Summer Term
17. School of Theology; University Professors Program
18. Marsh Chapel
19. Photonics Center
20. College of Arts and Sciences
21. School of Social Work
22. Graduate School of Arts and Sciences
23. The Tsai Performance Art Center
24. The Castle
25. Warren Towers (major residence)
26. Office of Information Technology
27. College of Engineering
28. Sargent College of Health and Rehabilitation Sciences
29. College of Communication
30. School of Education
31. Morse Auditorium
32. Biological and Physics Research Buildings
33. The Towers (major residence)
34. Chancellor's Office; President's Office; Provost's Office; Development and Alumni Relations
35. School of Management
36. 575 Commonwealth Ave (major residence)
37. Metcalf Science Center
38. Admissions Reception Center
39. Kenmore Classroom Building
40. Shelton Hall (major residence)
41. International Students and Scholars Office; Career Services; Disability Services; Judicial Affairs & Student Safety
42. University Computers
43. Barnes & Noble at BU; Asian Archeology & Cultural History
44. Hotel Commonwealth
45. Miles Standish Hall (major residence)
46. Danielsen Hall (major residence) (off map)
47. Agganis Arena

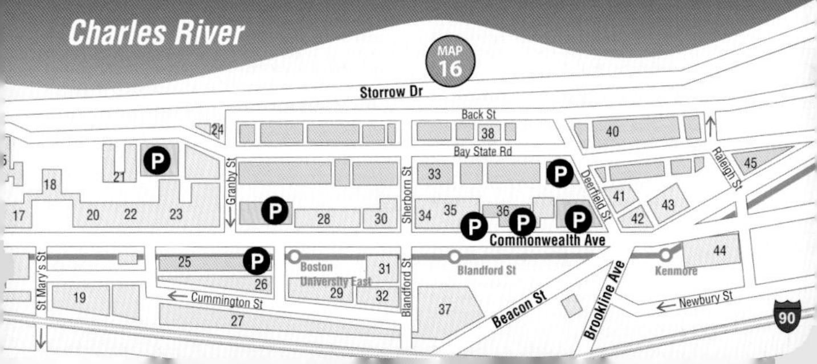

General Information

NFT Maps:	3 & 6
Address:	120 Boylston St, Boston, MA 02116
Phone:	617-824-8500
Website:	www.emerson.edu

Overview

Emerson College is the country's only comprehensive college or university dedicated solely to communication and the arts in a liberal arts context. In close proximity to Boston's Theater District, Emerson is near all of the city's major media interests. Founded as a small oratory school in 1880, Emerson has expanded its curriculum over the years to include other forms of communication. Today, Emerson specializes in communications, marketing, communication sciences and disorders, journalism, the performing arts, the visual and media arts, and writing, literature, and publishing. Emerson also operates semester-study programs in Los Angeles and the Netherlands. There is also a thriving continuing education department, recently renamed the Department of Professional Studies and Special Programs, which offers—besides communications classes—certificate programs in media, publishing, and screenwriting.

The college enrolls about 3,000 full-time undergraduates and 1,000 graduate students, many of whom can be found sporting funky haircuts and smoking outside Emerson buildings between classes. Students take pride in their award-winning radio station, WERS (88.9 FM). Most alumni go on to pursue careers in the communications and entertainment fields. Notable alumni include talk show host Jay Leno, actor Denis Leary, comedian Steven Wright, and entrepreneur and make-up artist Bobbi Brown.

Tuition

Undergraduate tuition fees are about $35,000. Room and board adds about $14,000. Add on books, service fees, activity fees, and personal expenses. Graduate student tuition, fees, and expenses vary by the number of credits taken.

Sports

Although Emerson does have an athletic department, it has never been one of the school's top priorities. Since most of the students attending Emerson College are interested primarily in the fields of communications and performing arts, sports are considered nothing more than a lighthearted diversion. Still, Emerson College sponsors 13 men's and women's varsity teams that compete in the NCAA's Division III.

Culture on Campus

Because Emerson considers itself an arts school, it takes great pride in its theater. The aptly named Majestic Theatre was built in 1903 as an opera house. In 2001, the college closed the theater temporarily for renovation and reopened its doors in 2003. Today, the historic venue seats 1,200 people and has become an integral part of the campus. Not only does it provide a venue for all types of productions by Emerson students, it also serves the greater New England community. It hosts more operas than any other theater in New England and is the top stop for most touring dance companies. To visit the theater or check out a performance, go to the theater box office located at 219 Tremont Street in Boston or visit the website: cutlermajestic.org.

Departments

Undergraduate Admissions Office 617-824-8600
Graduate Admissions Office 617-824-8610
Majestic Theatre 617-824-8000
Athletics Department 617-824-8690
Fitness Center.................................... 617-824-8692
Library... 617-824-8668

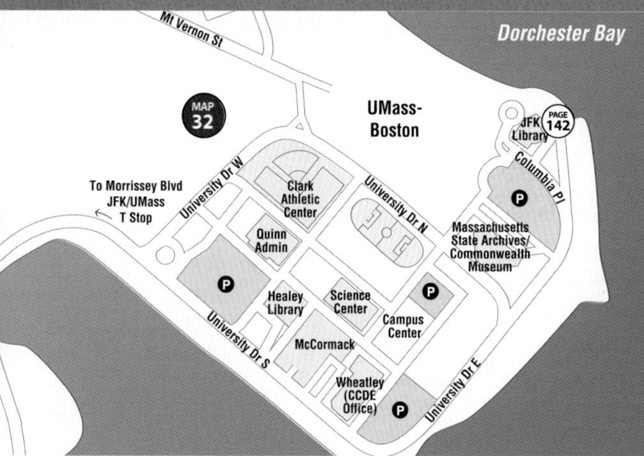

General Information

NFT Map:	32
Address:	100 Morrissey Blvd, Boston, MA 02125
Phone:	617-287-5000
Website:	www.umb.edu

Overview

The University of Massachusetts Boston is one of five UMass campuses. The campus opened in 1982 when UMass acquired Boston State College. The university has been described as a sensibly priced, high-quality college that provides excellent academic programs to people from all walks of life. UMass Boston aims "to bring technical, intellectual, and human resources to the community."

The school's most famous alum is Boston Mayor Thomas M. Menino. Not exactly renowned for his oratory skills, he is nevertheless a well respected champion of the low-income neighborhoods. Menino graduated from UMass Boston at the age of 45 in 1988 with a degree in community planning. UMass Boston's campus, which has been described as a "concrete jungle," is only three miles from downtown Boston and is pretty easy to reach by public transportation. (Take the Red Line to JFK/UMass Station, then jump on the shuttle buses, which run almost constantly.)

While on campus, be sure to check out the Campus Center—simply look for the most modern-looking (and attractive) building on campus. A graceful building featuring huge windows that overlook magnificent Boston Harbor, the Center makes it easy to forget that the rest of the campus is pockmarked by bomb-shelteresque architecture. Also, a trip to campus should always include a quick walk or drive over to the JFK Presidential Library, which shares Columbia Point Peninsula with UMASS Boston.

Tuition

Undergraduate tuition runs about $28,000 per year for outsiders, and around $14,000 for staties. Graduate tuition costs run at about $28,000 per year for out-of-towners and $14,000 for in-state residents.

Sports

UMass offers 14 varsity sports, including basketball, soccer, lacrosse, and ice hockey. All teams compete in the NCAA's Division III. The Beacon Fitness Center is open to all students and staff free of charge. The UMass teams are called the Beacons, carry the slogan "Follow the Light," and have been named All-Americans 64 times in seven sports. UMass Boston provides a community service program which offers, for free or at very low cost, the use of all athletic facilities and coaches to the general public.

Culture on Campus

Often considered a commuter-centric school, UMass Boston is nonetheless a mini-mecca of culture, offering everything from rampant community-service opportunities to myriad student-run publications. The current Performing Arts Department is actually a conglomerate of three previously separate theater arts, music, and dance departments. Music courses provide grounding in music theory, history, and performance. Private music lessons are also available for one credit. The college Jazz Band, Chamber Orchestra, and Chamber Singers all give public performances at the end of each semester.

Departments

Undergraduate Admissions	617-287-6100
Graduate Admissions	617-287-5700
Graduate College of Education	617-287-7600
College of Nursing & Health Sciences	617-287-7500
Performing Arts Department	617-287-5640
Athletic Department	617-287-7801
Healey Library	617-287-5900
Honors Program	617-287-5520
Campus Center	617-287-4800

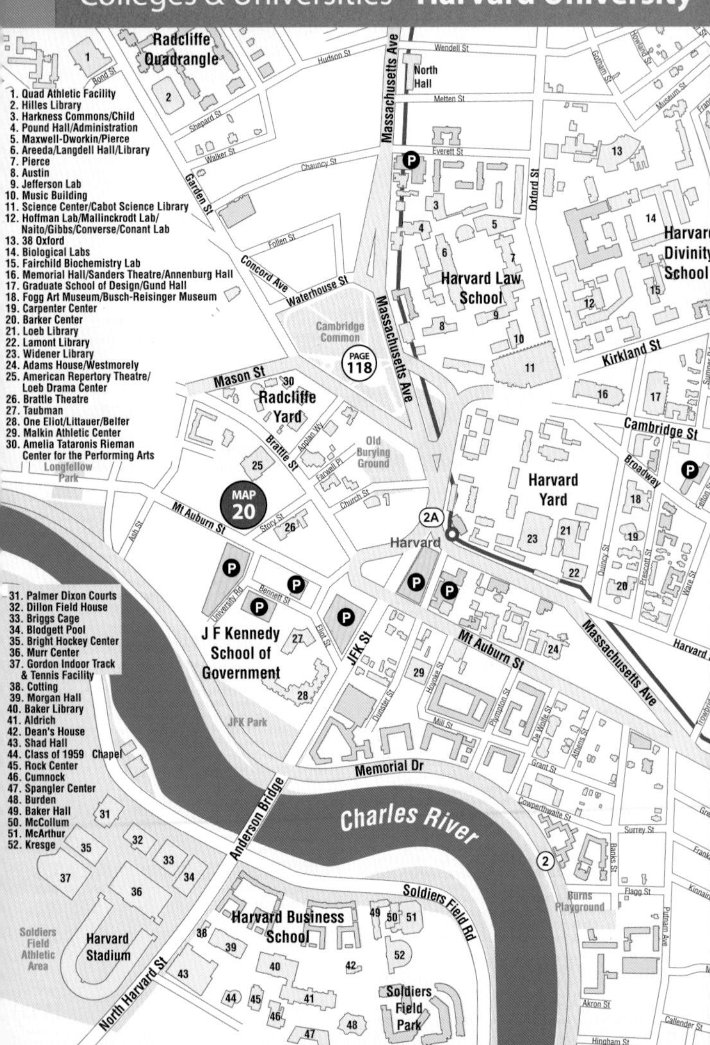

1. Quad Athletic Facility
2. Hilles Library
3. Harkness Commons/Child
4. Pound Hall/Administration
5. Maxwell-Dworkin/Pierce
6. Areeda/Langdell Hall/Library
7. Pierce
8. Austin
9. Jefferson Lab
10. Music Building
11. Science Center/Cabot Science Library
12. Hoffman Lab/Mallinckrodt Lab/ Naito/Gibbs/Converse/Conant Lab
13. 38 Oxford
14. Biological Labs
15. Fairchild Biochemistry Lab
16. Memorial Hall/Sanders Theatre/Annenburg Hall
17. Graduate School of Design/Gund Hall
18. Fogg Art Museum/Busch-Reisinger Museum
19. Carpenter Center
20. Barker Center
21. Loeb Library
22. Lamont Library
23. Widener Library
24. Adams House/Westmorely
25. American Repertory Theatre/ Loeb Drama Center
26. Brattle Theatre
27. Taubman
28. One Eliot/Littauer/Belfer
29. Malkin Athletic Center
30. Amelia Tataronis Rieman Center for the Performing Arts
31. Palmer Dixon Courts
32. Dillon Field House
33. Briggs Cage
34. Blodgett Pool
35. Bright Hockey Center
36. Murr Center
37. Gordon Indoor Track & Tennis Facility
38. Cotting
39. Morgan Hall
40. Baker Library
41. Aldrich
42. Dean's House
43. Shad Hall
44. Class of 1959 Chapel
45. Rock Center
46. Cumnock
47. Spangler Center
48. Burden
49. Baker Hall
50. McCollum
51. McArthur
52. Kresge
Radcliffe Quadrangle
Harvard Law School
Harvard Divinity School
Radcliffe Yard
Harvard Yard
J F Kennedy School of Government
Harvard Business School
Harvard Stadium
Soldiers Field Park
Soldiers Field Athletic Area
Cambridge Common
Old Burying Ground
Longfellow Park
JFK Park
Burns Playground
North Hall
Charles River
Harvard
PAGE 118
MAP 20
Massachusetts Ave
Garden St
Concord Ave
Waterhouse St
Mason St
Brattle St
Mt Auburn St
Kirkland St
Cambridge St
Broadway
Oxford St
JFK St
Memorial Dr
Anderson Bridge
Soldiers Field Rd
North Harvard St
Hudson St
Wendell St
Metten St
Everett St
Chauncy St
Shepard St
Walker St
Follen St
Bond St
Gotham St
Howland St
Museum St
Sumner Rd
Felton St
Quincy St
Prescott St
Ware St
Harvard St
Trowbridge St
Appian Wy
Farwell Pl
Church St
Story St
Ash St
University Rd
Bennett St
Eliot St
Dunster St
Holyoke St
Plympton St
De Wolfe St
Athens St
Mill St
Grant St
Cowperthwaite St
Surrey St
Banks St
Flagg St
Putnam Ave
Akron St
Callender St
Hingham St

General Information

NFT Map: 20
Address: University Hall, Cambridge, MA 02138
Phone: 617-495-1000
Website: www.harvard.edu

Overview

You've probably heard quite a bit about Harvard. Chances are, you associate it with academic excellence, cutting-edge research, red brick, and students with at least two roman numerals after their names.

That stereotype hits the nail at least partly on the head. Founded in 1636, Harvard remains the richest and most revered university in the country (and perhaps even the world). True to myth, its pool of 19,000+ undergrads and grad students include children of royalty, famous actors, heirs, heiresses, and an assortment of other fortunate sons and daughters. But the truth is that these folks are more the exception than the rule. Harvard's deep pockets have allowed it to offer generous scholarships and increase the cultural and financial diversity of its student population (and to allow such great intellectuals like Conan O'Brien to attend). The same loot also helps them net world-class professors in each of its 11 schools and colleges.

With the goal of properly housing and educating "the best of the best" in all fields from arts and humanities to business and technology, Harvard is hungry for more than just talented minds. The university continues to gobble up land in Cambridge and across the river in Allston, disgruntling some locals.

Perhaps Harvard needs more space for its livestock. A phrase coined to mock the local accent states that you cannot "pahk the cah in Havahd Yahd," since automobile traffic is prohibited there. However, an old contract clause allows each full professor to pasture one cow in the Yard. Assistant faculty members are allowed a sheep. Luckily for Harvard, no professor in recent memory has taken advantage of this opportunity.

In early 2007, Harvard made news yet again by naming its first female president, historian Drew G. Faust.

Tuition

Undergraduate tuition, room, board, and college fees amount to about $56,000. Graduate school tuition varies depending on the program.

Sports

Athletics at Harvard began around 1780, when a small group of students began challenging each other to wrestling matches, thereby starting an early version of *Fight Club*. Since then, the spirit of athletic competition has remained integral to the Harvard experience. Harvard introduced its crew team in 1844, and won its first championship just two years later. Since then, the men's heavyweight and lightweight crew teams have won 15 championships between them and the women's lightweight crew team has won five championships. Years ago, Harvard was a football powerhouse, always ranked among the top ten in the nation. Harvard still consistently tops the Ivy League, and games against the likes of Yale continue to fill century-old Harvard Stadium on fall afternoons. The men's tennis team has also been a source of pride in the athletic department, consistently producing top-class players, many of whom have gone on to play professionally. In the fall of 2004, the team captured their second consecutive Eastern College Athletic Conference title.

Not all jocks are dumb: Since 1920, Harvard athletes have netted 46 Rhodes Scholarships.

Not all nerds suck at sports: More than 100 Harvard athletes have participated in the Olympics.

Culture on Campus

Harvard boasts four art museums (free every day after 4:30 pm and from 10 am until noon on Saturdays), each showcasing art from different parts of the world. The university also runs an extensive music and theater program. Music department performances are held in the prestigious Sanders Theater, renowned for its acoustics and design. Aside from hosting most of the orchestral and choral performances by Harvard groups, Sanders Theatre is also a popular venue for professional groups such as the Boston Philharmonic, the Boston Chamber Music Society, and the Boston Baroque.

Harvard's various dance troupes perform at the Amelia Tataronis Rieman Center for the Performing Arts.

The country's only not-for-profit theater company housing a resident acting company and an international training conservatory, the American Repertory Theater (A.R.T.) operates out of the Harvard University campus.

A building shaped suspiciously like "Linguo, the Grammar Robot" of *Simpsons* fame houses the offices of the Harvard Lampoon on Mt Auburn Street. Graduates of this famed humor publication have gone on to work for *Saturday Night Live*, *The Simpsons*, and *The Office*.

Departments

Undergraduate Admissions................617-495-1551
Graduate School of Arts and Sciences.......617-495-1814
Graduate School of Education..............617-495-0740
Kennedy School of Government............617-495-1100
Harvard Crimson...........................617-576-6565
Harvard Law School........................617-495-3100
Harvard Medical School....................617-432-1000
Harvard Business School...................617-495-6000
Athletics Department Ticket Office....877-GO-HARVARD
or 617-495-2211
Sanders Theatre............................617-496-2222

General Information

NFT Maps: 26 & 27
Address: 77 Massachusetts Ave, Cambridge, MA 02139
Phone: 617-253-1000
Website: www.mit.edu

Overview

Just down the Chuck River from Harvard, MIT is one of the top tech schools in the world. The school's 1022 faculty and over 11,000 slide-rule-bearing graduate and undergraduate students inhabit a 168-acre "factory of learning" that features both neoclassical domes and some of the most aggressively modernist buildings in Boston (including the Stata Center, designed by world-renowned architect Frank Gehry).

MIT profs are infamous for assigning massive amounts of work, but some students can't seem to get enough of engineering, spending their downtime planning and executing "hacks," technically elaborate pranks. A frequent target of hackers is MIT's Great Dome. In 1994, a replica of an MIT police cruiser appeared atop the dome. In 1996, it was adorned with a gigantic beanie cap complete with a fully functioning propeller. Just before the release of *Star Wars Episode One: The Phantom Menace*, students decorated the dome to look like the robot R2-D2. Harvard is another frequent target of hackers. During a 1990 Harvard-Yale football game, players and spectators alike were surprised when an 8.5' x 3.5' rocket-propelled banner with the letters MIT sprang up from under the end zone as Yale lined up to kick a field goal.

Tuition

Undergraduate tuition fees, room, and board total about $54,000.

Sports

Whoever said science nerds can't play sports was totally right. Nevertheless, they keep trying, posting moderate success in both Division II and III. Believe it or not, MIT actually boasts the largest

number of NCAA-sponsored programs in the nation, and the coaches and students have received numerous awards for sports excellence. The heavyweight crew squads and the men's cross-country and track teams have garnered accolades for the university.

Culture on Campus

In a time when art and technology are often indistinguishable, it's not hard to believe that MIT has a happening arts program, too. We highly recommend a visit to the MIT Museum. Holographic images, scientific photographs, and mechanical sculptures with names like "Untitled Fragile Machine" show just how beautiful math-type stuff can be.

The Wiesner Building (designed by I.M. Pei and housing the Media Laboratory) opened in 1985 and was used, for much of its first decade, to explore digital video and multimedia. The Media Lab allows for interdisciplinary research, and the developing focus of study is on how electronic information affects our daily lives—how we use it to think, express, and communicate ideas. Many of the Media Lab's research projects are made possible through corporate sponsorship, and the lab fosters a positive relationship between academia and industry.

According to the MIT website, the Media Lab "houses a gigabit fiber-optic plant that connects a heterogeneous network of computers, ranging from fine-grained, embedded processors to supercomputers." Unfortunately, in its role as an academic research laboratory, the Media Lab is not able to accommodate visits from the general public.

Departments

Undergraduate Admissions....................... 617-253-4791
Graduate Admissions 617-253-2917
School of Humanities, Arts, and Social Sciences ... 617-253-3450
School of Engineering............................ 617-253-3291
School of Science 617-253-8900
Sloan School of Management 617-253-2659
Office of the Arts................................. 617-253-4003
Athletic Department 617-253-4498

E55. Eastgate
E60. Arthur D Little Building
E70. Badger Building
N4. Albany Garage
N9. Superconducting Test Facility
N10. High Voltage Research Lab
N16. Cooling Tower & Oil Reserve
N16A. 60 Albany Street
N42. Information Services & Technology
N51. Design Fabrication Group
N52. MIT Museum
N57. Library Storage Annex
NE18. 1 Cambridge Center
NE20. 3 Cambridge Center
NE25. 5 Cambridge Center
NE30. Broad Institute
NE46. 400 Technology Square
NE47. 500 Technology Square
NE48. 700 Technology Square
NE49. 600 technology Square
NE80. Hill Building
NW10. Edgerton House
NW12. Nuclear Reactor Laboratory
NW13. 144 Albany Street
NW14. Francis Bitter Magnet Lab
NW15. Francis Bitter Magnet Lab
NW16. Plasma Science & Fusion Center
NW17. Plasma Science & Fusion Center
NW20. Albany St Generator Shelter
NW21. Plasma Science & Fusion Center
NW22. Plasma Science & Fusion Center
NW30. 224 Albany Street
NW61. Random Hall
NW62. Volvo Garage
NW86. 70 Pacific Street Dormitory
W1. Ashdown House
W2. 311 Memorial Drive
W4. McCormick Hall
W5. Green Hall
W7. Baker House
W8. Pierce Boathouse
W11. Kosher Kitchen
W13. Bexley Hall
W15. MIT Chapel
W16. Kresge Auditorium
W20. Stratton Student Center
W31. Du Pont Athletic Gymnasium
W32. Du Pont Athletic Gymnasium
W33. Rockwell Cage
W34. Johnson Athletics Center
W35. Zesiger Sports & Fitness Center
W45. West garage
W51. Burton-Conner House
W53. Carr Indoor Tennis Facility
W59. Heinz Building
W61. MacGregor House
W70. New House
W71. Next House
W79. Simmons Hall
W84. Tang Hall
W85. Westgate
W89. Campus Police
W91. Information Services & Technology Operations
WW15. Mail Services (off map)

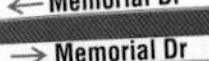

Northeastern University

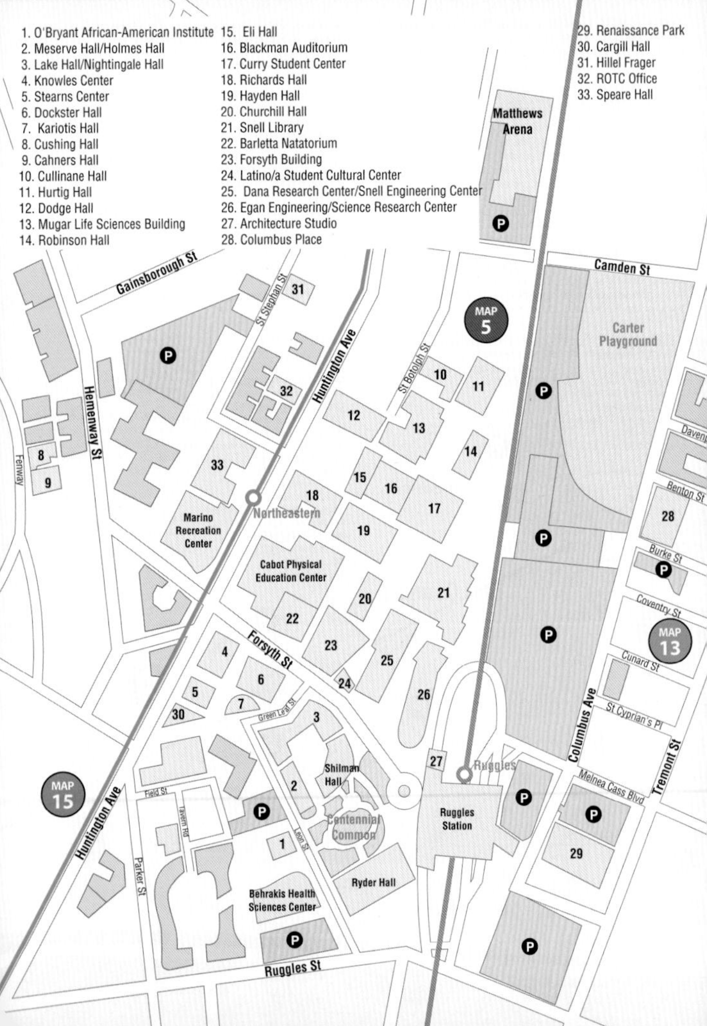

1. O'Bryant African-American Institute
2. Meserve Hall/Holmes Hall
3. Lake Hall/Nightingale Hall
4. Knowles Center
5. Stearns Center
6. Dockster Hall
7. Kariotis Hall
8. Cushing Hall
9. Cahners Hall
10. Cullinane Hall
11. Hurtig Hall
12. Dodge Hall
13. Mugar Life Sciences Building
14. Robinson Hall
15. Eli Hall
16. Blackman Auditorium
17. Curry Student Center
18. Richards Hall
19. Hayden Hall
20. Churchill Hall
21. Snell Library
22. Barletta Natatorium
23. Forsyth Building
24. Latino/a Student Cultural Center
25. Dana Research Center/Snell Engineering Center
26. Egan Engineering/Science Research Center
27. Architecture Studio
28. Columbus Place
29. Renaissance Park
30. Cargill Hall
31. Hillel Frager
32. ROTC Office
33. Speare Hall
Matthews Arena
Camden St
Carter Playground
MAP 5
Gainsborough St
St Stephan St
Huntington Ave
St Botolph St
Hemenway St
Fenway
Marino Recreation Center
Northeastern
Cabot Physical Education Center
Forsyth St
Green Leaf St
Shilman Hall
Centennial Common
Ruggles
Ruggles Station
Ryder Hall
Behrakis Health Sciences Center
Ruggles St
Field St
Tavern Rd
Parker St
Leon St
MAP 15
Davenport
Benton St
Burke St
Coventry St
MAP 13
Cunard St
St Cyprian's Pl
Columbus Ave
Melnea Cass Blvd
Tremont St

General Information

NFT Maps: 5, 13, & 15
Address: 360 Huntington Ave, Boston, MA 02115
Phone: 617-373-2000
Website: www.northeastern.edu

Overview

Northeastern University has come a long way from being a commuter school with a fairly unimpressive urban campus. In recent years, the university has emerged as an important national research institution with sparkly new academic, athletic, and residential facilities. NU originally began as a five-year school with an academic model called "Practice-Oriented Education," a program that combines education and internships (co-op) and is alternatively dubbed "real-life learning" by school officials. The school added more four- and five-year options, along with online study for a number of degrees.

Founded in 1898 as a part-time night school, Northeastern is located on more than 67 acres along Huntington Avenue and served by three Green Line E train stops. The current enrollment at NU is approximately 16,300 full-time undergraduate students and around 4,800 graduate students with a male-to-female ratio that is pretty evenly matched. However, cultural diversity isn't something for which the university is known. The most popular degree programs on offer are in Business, Health, and Engineering/Technology. The University Honors Program is also a big draw for potential undergrads.

Tuition

Undergraduate tuition costs run at about $40,700 per year with room and board adding up to an additional $13,600. Books, lab fees, and personal expenses are, as always, extra. Graduate student tuition and fees vary by college, as do individual online courses.

Sports

The Northeastern Huskies compete in Division I with varsity teams in nine men's and ten women's sports. The school's various teams had their finest collective performance ever in the 2002-03 season. The Huskies sent four teams to the NCAA playoffs and won a total of seven conference titles—Northeastern's most ever in both categories. Every February, men's hockey takes part in the Beanpot, the largest college sporting event in Boston

Culture on Campus

While Northeastern University doesn't offer much in the way of the arts, it is located in a prime spot for cultural enrichment. Huntington Avenue, also known as "Avenue of the Arts," runs through the urban campus, making it easy to visit the neighborhood museums. Among the most notable are the Isabella Stewart Gardner Museum, a ten-minute walk from the center of campus, and the Museum of Fine Arts (page 326), a four-minute walk from the main quad. Massachusetts College of Art is also located just a few T stops away and Symphony Hall (BSO, anyone?) is next door. Thai, soul food, and pizza abound—whether you walk or T it, you can hit anywhere from five to infinite restaurants with one stone.

For on-campus entertainment, afterHOURS, the campus's late-night club, welcomes various musical acts, ranging from local unknowns to bigger names like Gavin DeGraw. Additionally, the Curry Student Center is a magnet for Huskies in search of a bite (the Food Court includes everything from a salad bar to a Taco Bell) or an e-mail fix.

Departments

Admissions 617-373-2200
(TTY) 617-373-3768
Library.............................. 617-373-2350
Registrar............................ 617-373-2300
Athletics Department 617-373-2672
Athletics Ticket Office 617-373-4700

Undergraduate:

Admissions 617-373-2200
College of Arts & Sciences 617-373-3980
Bouvé College of Health Sciences..... 617-373-3321
College of Business Administration ... 617-373-3270
College of Computer & Information Science 617-373-2462
College of Criminal Justice 617-373-3327
College of Engineering 617-373-2152
School of Engineering Technology.... 617-373-7777
School of Nursing 617-373-3649

Graduate:

Bouvé College of Health Sciences...617-373-2708
College of Arts & Sciences..........617-373-3982
College of Business Administration .617-373-5992
College of Computer & Information Science 617-373-2464
College of Criminal Justice 617-373-3327
College of Engineering.............617-373-2711
Law School 617-373-2395
School of Professional & Continuing Studies............617-373-2400

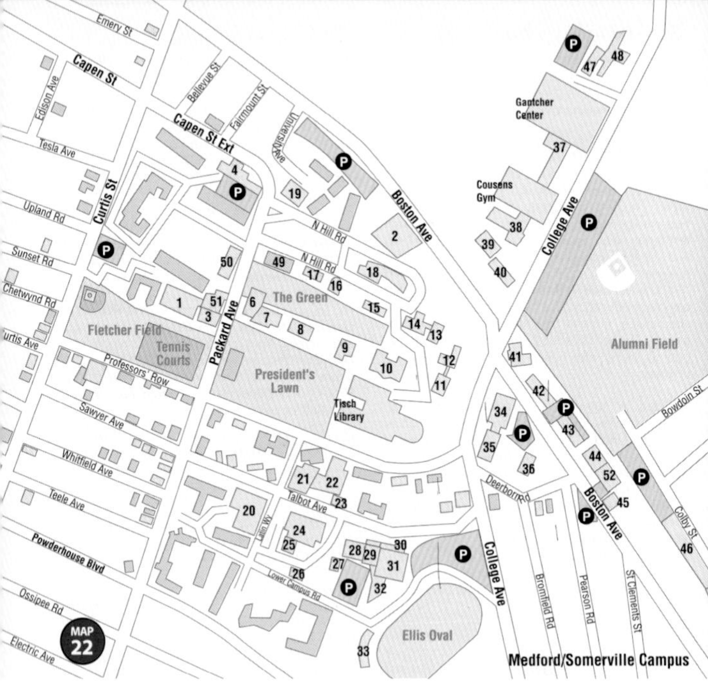

1. Mugar Hall
2. Dowling Hall
3. Goddard Hall
4. Granhoff Family Hillel Center
6. Dana Lab
7. Barnum Hall
8. Ballou Hall
9. Goddard Chapel
10. Eaton Hall
11. Miner Hall
12. Paige Hall
13. Lincoln-Filene Center
14. Braker Hall
15. East Hall
16. Packard Hall
17. Bendelson Hall
18. Central Heating Plant
19. Lane Hall
20. Dewick-MacPhie Hall
21. Bookstore
22. Elizabeth Van Huyson Mayer Campus Center
23. 55 Talbot Ave
24. Pearson Chemical Laboratory
25. Michael Lab
26. Academic Computing Building
27. Costume Shop
28. Jackson Gym
29. Baltch Arena Theatre
30. Remis Sculpture/ Leir Hall
31. Cohen Auditorium
32. Aidekman Arts Center
33. Baronian Field House
34. Anderson Hall
35. Robinson Hall
36. Bromfield-Pearson
37. Hamilton Pool
38. Halligan Hall
39. 177 College Ave
40. Office Services
41. Curtis Hall
42. Psychology Building
43. Bray Laboratory
44. Central Services
45. Bacon Hall
46. Science and Technology Center
47. Eliot-Pearson Child Development Center
48. Eliot-Pearson Children's School
49. West Hall
50. Olin Center
51. Cabot Center
52. Scene Shop

General Information

NFT Map:	22
Tufts Admin Building:	169 Holland St, Somerville, MA 02144
Medford/Somerville Campus:	Medford, MA 02155
Boston Campus:	136 Harrison Ave, Boston, MA 02111
North Grafton Campus:	200 Westboro Rd, North Grafton, MA 01536
Tufts General Phone:	617-628-5000
Website:	www.tufts.edu

Overview

There's a perception that Tufts is a school for kids who didn't get into Harvard, just two Red Line stops away. This is (mostly) not true. Tufts possesses academic prowess in its own right, especially in its engineering, veterinary, international relations, and science departments. The Fletcher School is the country's oldest graduate school of international affairs, and its prestige and strong curriculum draw students from across the globe. To boot, Tufts boasts a kick-ass study-abroad program (pick a continent, any continent) and a laudable community-service focus.

The university has three campuses. The main Medford/Somerville campus is where approximately 5,500 students, mostly liberal arts undergrads, live and learn. The Medford/Somerville campus also houses the School of Engineering, the Graduate School of Arts and Sciences, and the School of Special Studies. Tufts prides itself on diversity: A whole center is devoted to lesbian, gay, bisexual, and transgender students, and on any given day the "viewpoints" section of *The Tufts Daily*—the school's impressive and professional-looking student newspaper—will have several pieces about the LGBT community. As touchy-feely as campus politics may be, though, academics remain pretty hardcore.

The centrally located Boston campus houses the School of Medicine, School of Dental Medicine, Sackler School of Graduate Biomedical Sciences, Jean Mayer USDA Human Nutrition Research Center on Aging, and The Gerald J. and Dorothy R. Friedman School of Nutrition Science and Policy.

Tuition

Undergraduate tuition fees total around $43,600. Room and board cost an additional $12,000. Books, service fees, activity fees, and personal expenses are extra. Graduate student tuition, fees, and expenses vary by college.

Sports

If you ever find yourself at Tufts University and, more specifically, in the office of the Athletic Director, you might notice a peanut butter jar with ashes in it. Don't be frightened; it's only Jumbo. Jumbo is the elephant mascot of Tufts University. P.T. Barnum, of the Barnum and Bailey Circus, was one of the University's original trustees. His prize act was an elephant named Jumbo, who was hit by a train and killed in 1885. His stuffed body was donated to Tufts, where it was stored in a museum on campus that eventually became a student lounge. Sadly, however, the museum burned in 1975 and Jumbo went up with it. The ashes in the jar are said to be those of Jumbo, though university officials say they have no evidence that that is the case. Luckily, they have his tail in a cardboard folder in their archives. (Extra trivia fun: Jumbo also has the honor of being the only mascot mentioned in *Webster's*. Take that, Ivy Leaguers.)

If that isn't enough to attract you to the sports, then maybe the recent successes of the golf and women's sailing teams will pique your interest.

There's also an old campus joke: "What's Brown and Blue and loses every weekend?" Answer: "The Tufts football team." It's not really funny, but often accurate.

Culture on Campus

If sports aren't your thing, cultural activities are plentiful at Tufts. In the Aidekman Arts Center on the Medford/Somerville campus, you'll find the Tufts University Art Gallery. Again, the mantra seems to be diversity, diversity, and more diversity. The Gallery's mission is to explore art through all of its cultural complexities.

Over 70 students make up the Tufts Symphony Orchestra, which performs regularly throughout the school year. A capella groups abound, ranging from all-male to all-Jewish. The Department of Drama and Dance is where all of the performing artists can be found. Its students—a tight-knit, talented group— perform regularly at the Balch Arena Theater. Lately, though, music has been taking center stage on the Medford Campus: In February 2007, the $27-milion, 55,000-square-foot Granoff Music Center opened to campus-wide accolades.

Departments

Undergraduate Admissions	617-627-3170
Graduate and Professional Studies	617-627-3395
The Fletcher School	617-627-3040
School of Medicine	617-636-7000
School of Dental Medicine	617-636-6828
Sackler School of Graduate Biomedical Sciences	617-636-6767
School of Nutrition and Science Policy	617-636-3737
School of Veterinary Medicine	508-839-5302
School of Engineering	617-627-3237
Athletics Department and Ticket Office	617-627-3232
Balch Arena Theater	617-627-3524
Tufts Symphony Orchestra	617-627-4042
Tisch Library	617-627-3460

Continuing Education in Boston

Harvard, MIT, Boston College…the city of Boston has long been associated with academic achievement. But even if you're not ready to matriculate at one of the city's famed institutions of higher learning, Boston is a great place to learn everything and anything from basic Arabic to authentic Italian cooking.

For those looking to change careers—or simply get ahead in a current position—many of the area's renowned schools offer continuing education or professional development classes. Tuition at Harvard Extension School is very reasonable and comes with unbeatable name recognition. Even community colleges like North Shore Community College, Bunker Hill, and Quincy College (Red line accessible) offer credited and non-credited courses from everything like computers to feng shui.

Those who are feeling less cerebral can try gymnastics at Cambridge's Jam'nastics or take a golf lesson at CityGolf. Got an urge to indulge your creative side? Explore painting or sculpture with a studio art class at the MFA or learn the craft of glass-blowing at Diablo Glass and Metal.

Adrenaline junkies can hop the commuter rail and head out to Trapeze School, hidden in the Jordan's Furniture complex in suburban Reading.

Continuing Education and Professional Development

Boston College Woods College of Advancing Studies, www.bc.edu, 617-552-3900, 140 Commonwealth Ave, Chestnut Hill

Boston Language Institute, www.bostonlanguage.com, 617-262-3500, 648 Beacon St, Boston

Boston University Metropolitan College, www.bu.edu/met, 617-353-6000, 755 Commonwealth Ave, Boston

Bunker Hill Community College, www.bhcc.mass.edu/, 617-228-2000, 250 New Rutherford Ave, Boston

Harvard Extension, www.dce.harvard.edu/extension, 617-495-4024, 51 Brattle St, Cambridge

MIT, www.mit.edu/education/professional, 617-253-1000, 77 Massachusetts Ave, Cambridge

North Shore Community College, www.northshore.edu/, 978-762-4000, 1 Ferncroft Rd, Danvers

Northeastern University, www.ace.neu.edu, 617-373-2000, 360 Huntington Ave, Boston

Quincy College, www.quincycollege.edu/, 617-984-1700, 150 Newport Ave, Quincy

Little Bit of Everything

Boston Center for Adult Education, www.bcae.org, 617-267-4430, 5 Commonwealth Ave, Boston

Cambridge Center for Adult Education, www.ccae.org, 617-547-6789, 42 Brattle St, Cambridge

Arts and Lifestyle

Beadworks, www.beadworksboston.com, 617-247-7227, 167 Newbury St, Boston and 617-868-9777, 23 Church St, Cambridge

Boston Wine Tasting Classes, www.invinoveritas.com, 617-784-7150, 1354 Commonwealth Ave, Allston

Cambridge School of Culinary Arts, www.cambridgeculinary.com, 617-354-2020, 2020 Massachusetts Ave, Cambridge

Diablo Glass and Metal, www.diabloglassandmetal.com, 617-442-7444, 123 Terrace St, Boston

Grub Street Writing Center, www.grubstreet.org, 617-695-0075, 160 Boylston St, Boston

Massachusetts College of Art, www.massart.edu, 617-879-7000, 621 Huntington Ave, Boston

Mudville Pottery Classes, www.nanhamilton.com/mudville/mudville/, 617-623-9191, 181 Pearl St, Somerville

Museum of Fine Arts, www.mfa.org, 617-267-9300, 465 Huntington Ave, Boston

Spark Craft Studios, www.sparkcrafts.com, 617-718-9132, 50 Grove St, Somerville

Athletics and Dance

Boston Sailing Center, www.bostonsailingcenter.com, Lewis Wharf, Boston

CityGolf Boston, www.citygolfboston.com, 617-357-4653, 38 Bromfield St, Boston

Fred Astaire Dance Studios, www.fadsboston.com, 617-247-2435, 179 South St, Boston

GottaDance Cambridge, www.gottadance.org, 617-864-8675, 11 Garden St, Cambridge and 7 Temple St, Cambridge

Green Street Studios, www.greenstreetstudios.org, 617-864-3191, 185 Green St, Cambridge

Jam'nastics, www.jamnastics.org, 617-354-5780, 199 Columbia St, Cambridge

Trapeze School, http://boston.trapezeschool.com, 781-942-7800, 50 Walkers Brook Dr, Reading

Overview

Bostonians love that dirty water, but we like clean water even better. This fact is best reflected by the Boston Harbor Project. Thanks to over $3 billion spent cleaning it up, the Hub's harbor is no longer on that shameful list of the country's dirtiest waterways, but it's still a work in progress. So while you may still hear that damn Standells' song coming from every bar on Lansdowne Street, you no longer need to worry about your genetic makeup should you go for a swim in the Charles. However, NFT does not recommend donning your speedos and goggles just yet. Instead, consider more appropriate activities as reflected in the slew of yacht clubs and boating centers that decorate the coastline and upriver all the way to Watertown.

A perfect place to start is at one of Boston Harbor's 34 beautiful islands, which have been collectively designated a National Recreation Area. Nine of the islands are either fully or partially accessible to the public and are a great, affordable getaway within 10-miles of downtown Boston. For the most part, amenities consist of composting toilets, but if you come prepared, the islands are great for a picnic or a camping excursion (www.bostonharborislands.org). On George's Island (Boston Harbor Cruises) you will find historic Fort Warren, a former Civil War prison replete with ghost—the wife of a Civil War inmate nicknamed "Lady in Black." The trails across 48-acre Lovell's Island pass through dunes, forests, and the ruins of Fort Standish. There's a supervised swimming beach, some picnic areas, and 11 campsites. Little Brewster Island is the home of Boston Light, the oldest continually used lighthouse site in America (1716), While not open to casual visitors, private boaters and tours are welcomed, call for specifics (617-223-8666). If your boss is scheduling a Survivor-style teamwork safari or if your kids are looking for that Kevin Bacon, *White Water Summer* role model, chances are you're heading to privately owned Thompson Island. If you want to venture a bit farther out, consider Buzzards Bay to the south. Touching more than 280 miles of the Massachusetts coastline, the bay stretches from Rhode Island Sound to the Cape Cod Canal. Calmer waters inside the bay make for good sailing conditions.

Back on the Charles (don't even *think* about pronouncing the "r"), crew is a popular sport, particularly among the local colleges and universities. Many of the clubs and organizations offer instruction to the general public. The Head of the Charles Regatta, held every fall, is the world's largest two-day rowing event. The race schedule includes single and team events and draws competitors from around the world. Check out www.hocr.org for more information.

The nonprofit Community Boating Inc. (located between the Charles/MGH Red Line stop and the Hatch Shell) offers summer kayaking, windsurfing, and sailing lessons for kids aged 10–18. (Participants must be able to swim 75 yards.) Visit www.community-boating.org for more information.

If you're looking for waves but find the Harbor a bit intimidating, check out the Jamaica Pond Boat House (617-522-5061) for mini-sailboat and rowboat rentals. At around 68-acres, the pond is the purest and largest body of water within city limits and the only date-friendly glacial-kettlehole in town. It's also a great place to watch kamikaze drivers on the Jamaicaway. As they scream expletives and give each other the finger, you can fish in the liberally stocked pond and gloat. If that isn't relaxing, what is? Visit www.jamaicapond.com for further information.

Boston is also home to the CRASH—B World Indoor Rowing Championships, held annually in February at Agganis Arena at Boston University. More information is available at www.crash-b.org.

Sailing/Boating Centers	Address	Phone	Website
Boston Harbor Cruises	1 Long Wharf, Boston	617-227-4321	www.bostonharborcruises.com
Boston Harbor Sailing Club	58 Batterymarch St, Boston	617-720-0049	www.bostonharborsailing.com; moorings/hire/lessons racing/clothing
Boston Harbor Shipyard & Marina	256 Marginal St, East Boston	617-561-1400	www.bhsmarina.com; moorings/lessons
Boston Sailing Center	The Riverboat at Lewis Wharf	617-227-4198	www.bostonsailingcenter.com; hire/courses/lessons/racing
Community Boating	21 David Mugar Way, Boston	617-523-1038	www.community-boating.org; sailing lessons
Courageous Sailing Center	One 1st Ave, Charlestown	617-242-3821	www.courageoussailing.org; lessons/racing
Jamaica Pond Boat House	Jamaicaway at Pond St, Jamaica Plain	617-522-5061	www.jamaicapond.com; sailing/rowing
Lincoln Sailing Center	PO Box 492, Hingham	781-741-5225	www.lincolnsailing.org; non-profit/lessons/sailing/rowing
MIT Sailing	134 Memorial Dr, Cambridge	617-253-4884	http://sailing.mit.edu; lessons/racing
Piers Park Sailing	95 Marginal St, East Boston	617-561-6677	www.piersparksailing.org; hire/lessons/racing/sale
UMass Boston Waterfront Recreationt	100 Morrissey Boulevard, Boston, Fox Point Dock.	617-287-5404	www.UMB.edu/marineops

Yacht Clubs	Address	Phone	Website
Bass Haven Yacht Club	10 McPherson Dr, Beverly	978-922-9712	www.basshavenyachtclub.com
Boston Yacht Club	1 Front St, Marblehead	781-631-3100	www.bostonyc.org
Braintree Yacht Club	9 Gordon Rd, Braintree	781-843-9730	N/A
Corinthian Yacht Club	1 Nahant St, Marblehead	781-631-0005	www.corinthianyc.org
Danversport Yacht Club	161 Elliott St, Danvers	978-774-8620	www.danversport.com
Eastern Yacht Club	47 Foster St, Marblehead	781-631-1400	www.easternyc.org
Hull Yacht Club	5 Fitzpatrick Wy, Hull	781-925-9739	www.hullyc.org
Jeffries Yacht Club	565 Sumner St, East Boston	617-567-9656	www.jeffriesyachtclub.com
Jubilee Yacht Club	126 Water St, Beverly	978-922-9611	www.jubileeyc.net
Metropolitan Yacht Club	39 Vinedale Rd, Braintree	781-843-9882	www.metyc.com
New Bedford Yacht Club	208 Elm St, South Dartmouth	508-997-0762	www.nbyc.com
Old Colony Yacht Club	235 Victory Rd, Dorchester	617-436-0513	www.oldcolonyyc.com
Peninsula Yacht Club	671 Summer St, Boston	617-464-7901	www.pycboston.org
Plymouth Yacht Club	34 Union St, Plymouth	508-746-7207	www.plymouthyachtclub.org
Sandy Bay Yacht Club	5 T Wharf, Rockport	978-546-9433	www.sandybay.org
South Boston Yacht Club	1849 Columbia Rd, South Boston	617-268-6132	www.southbostonyc.com
Squantum Yacht Club	646 Quincy Shore Dr, Quincy	617-770-4811	www.squantumyc.org
Wianno Yacht Club	101 Bridge St, Osterville	508-428-2232	www.vsb.cape.com/~wianno/
Winthrop Yacht Club	649 Shirley St, Winthrop	617-846-9774	www.win-yc.org

Rowing Clubs	Address	Phone	Website
Community Rowing (Apr–Oct)	600 Pleasant St, Watertown	617-923-7557	www.communityrowing.org
Whaling City Rowing Club	5 Dover St, New Bedford	508-517-1251	www.whalingcityrowing.org

General Information

City of Boston Bicycling:	www.cityofboston.gov/bikes
City of Cambridge Bicycling:	www.cambridgema.gov/CDD/Transportation/gettingaroundcambridge/bybike.aspx
MassBike:	www.massbike.org
Charles River Wheelmen:	www.crw.org
Hubway (Bike Share):	www.thehubway.com
Rubel BikeMaps:	www.bikemaps.com
Bike to Bridge Boston:	www.hubonwheels.org

Overview

The city's streets are narrow and congested, and short-tempered, bike-hating drivers abound. Make no mistake, Boston is tough for cyclists.

That said, Boston and the surrounding cities are making efforts to increase the accessibility and safety of bike transportation, and it's a great way to explore the city. Relatively flat and compact, it's generally quicker to get around on a bike, and you'll find, even in the middle of winter, hardy cyclists trekking through the city, delivering packages, and heading to class. Bike-only or mixed-use bike/pedestrian paths run through most of the area's parks, paralleling major roads such as the Riverway, Storrow Drive, and Memorial Drive. While getting "doored" is a serious threat in Central Square, a much-needed repaving of Mass Ave has smoothed the bike lane connecting Boston to Harvard. In 2011, Hubway, the Boston-area bike share program, launched and it continues to expand its fleet of bike stations both in Boston and into neighboring cities.

Brookline has recently added a lane in its streets specifically for bikes, making it a much less stressful option for riding. While it isn't perfect, and there is a chance of getting "mirrored", it is 1000 times better than having to contend with cars in a shared lane or pedestrians on a sidewalk

Danger lurks around every non-perpendicular corner. To avoid catastrophe, have your best cycling wits about you and be especially wary of:

- **Drivers**—Boston drivers reserve some of their most venomous roadrage for cyclists. They're also notoriously self-centered, erratic, prone to underestimate your speed, and quick to double-park to dash in for liquor or donuts.
- **Potholes**—They can sneak up on you, especially at night. The bigger ones will swallow you whole, while bumping over the little ones lead to nasty bruises in the nether regions.
- **Trolley Tracks**—Green Line tracks will flip you over and buckle your wheel, especially in parts of Mission Hill, Jamaica Plain, and in Cleveland Circle. If you're going to cross the tracks, take them at a 90-degree angle.
- **Bridge**s—All the bridges across the Charles are narrow and heavily trafficked.
- **Pedestrians**—They jaywalk into your path, they text while doing so, and they can't hear your screams because their iPod is set to volume level "jet engine." Also, keep in mind that even if they can hear you scream "On your left," 99% of them will step directly to the left to ensure that you die.

If you plan on biking in Boston and you have a brain that you'd like to keep, invest in a helmet and a battery-powered red light to place below your seat or on your back. Front lights and rear reflectors are the law after dark.

The city offers many options for recreational riding, including the popular 11-mile Minuteman Bikeway through Lexington and the 17-mile Charles River Bikeway growing past Watertown. Shorter but handy for commuting, the Southwest Corridor sends you from Northeastern along the Orange Line to Forest Hills. Recent funding should improve one of the serious flaws of the Boston bike system: a lack of cross-trail connections, crossing lights, or route markings. This makes them less than ideal for outing with small children. Of particular danger to families are the many bridge intersections along the south Charles River Bikeway. If light jogging traffic doesn't bug you, another great option is the 38-mile-long Boston Harborwalk, which runs through Dorchester, Charlestown, and East Boston among other communities. The smooth pavement, picturesque views, and prohibition of cars make it an excellent choice for a long ride.

For something a little longer and farther away, the Bay Circuit Trail winds its way 150 miles from Newburyport on the North Shore to Duxbury on the South Shore, creating a "C" shape around Boston. Cycling enthusiasts refer to it as "Boston's outer Emerald Necklace." You'll find the boy racers skipping the summer crowds on the Minuteman for spins around Concord and many of the cycle shops sponsor club teams. The Charles River Wheelmen is one of the nation's oldest bicycle clubs with a year round calendar of rides and site full of cue sheets.

For the distance riders, the BMB (Boston-Montreal-Boston) ride draws randonneurs from across the country for the grueling 90 hour, 1,200K ride.

Rubel BikeMaps produces maps of riding paths and trails throughout the Greater Boston area and is well worth the six bucks. You'll likely want both the Boston map and the Eastern Mass map. They can be purchased at most bike shops, bookstores, or on the Rubel website. Take it to the State House with MassBike, the primary lobbying and bicycle advocacy group in the state. They maintain an extensive website of all things pedal-powered in Massachusetts. Bike to Bridge Boston is a new addition to the city and organizes free tours to offbeat Boston during the summer. DIY guides to biking Jewish Boston, the Underground Railroad, and other routes are on their web site, and they organize a city bike rally and ride in early October

Bikes and Mass Transit

Bikes are allowed on the Red, Orange, and Blue Lines, on the MBTA Commuter Rail with some limitations, on all busses equipped with bike racks, and on the MBTA ferries at all times. Bikes (with the exception of folding bikes) are not permitted on the Green Line and the Mattapan Trolley. Bikes are allowed on the Silver Line only if a bike rack is available. On the subway and commuter rail, bikes are permitted during non-rush hours (roughly before 7am, between 10am–4pm, and after 7pm). Bikes are allowed at all subway stations except Park Street, Downtown Crossing (except to transfer), and Government Center. Crosstown buses are equipped with bike racks and can be used at any time. Other bus services do not provide racks and bikes are not permitted on board.

If you're traveling on commuter rail, wait for the conductor's instructions before entering or exiting the train. On subways, head for the rear of the train. You're only allowed to enter the last carriage and, even then, there's a two-bikes-per-carriage limit. There is no additional fee for bikes on any public transportation. See the MBTA website for (www.mbta.com/riding_the_t/bikes) for more information.

Bike Shops and Makers

Boston's got a great variety of shops. While most will have a low-end city cruiser or two, it's worth getting to know your local shops for their specialties, whether the high-end racing bikes at ATA or fixies at Beacon Street. Oddly enough, Boston's most famous shop and mechanic, Sheldon Brown, are way out in West Newton at Harris Cyclery. However, if you don't mind getting your hands dirty, we applaud the rent-by-the-hour stands and geniuses at Broadway Bicycle School.

• Ace Wheelworks •
145 Elm St, Somerville • 617-776-2100

• Back Bay Bicycles •
362 Commonwealth Ave, Boston • 617-247-2336

• Bicycle Bill's •
253 North Harvard St, Allston • 617-783-5636

• Bicycle Exchange •
2067 Massachusetts Ave, Cambridge • 617-864-1300

• Bikes Not Bombs •
284 Amory Street, Jamaica Plain • 617-522-0222

• Cambridge Bicycle •
259 Massachusetts Ave, Cambridge • 617-876-6555

• Community Bike Supply •
496 Tremont St, Boston • 617-542-8623

• Ferris Wheels Bicycle Shop •
66 South St, Jamaica Plain • 617-524-2453

• International Bicycle Center •
89 Brighton Ave, Brighton • 617-783-5804t

• Superb Bicycle •
842 Beacon St • 617-236-0752

• Urban AdvenTours •
103 Atlantic Ave • 617-670-0637

When out on the road, what's better than showing off some Yankee ingenuity? Boston's been a center of bike fabrication since Columbia popularized the ready-made bike in 1877. Here are some sweet hand-crafted builders welding new traditions:

• A.N.T. •
24 Water St, Holliston • 508-429-3350

• Independent Fabrication •
86 Joy St, Somerville • 617-666-3609

• Seven Cycles •
125 Walnut St, Watertown • 617-923-777

Overview

If you like the idea of lowering your center of gravity and darting around at high speeds on tiny wheels or thin blades, then Boston is the place for you. The city is jam-packed with parks and rinks that accommodate inline skaters in the summer and ice skaters in the winter.

Inline Skating

Boston drivers are no more sympathetic to skaters than they are to bikers. If you're skating for recreation, it is probably best to stick to the numerous places designated for outdoor activities. A favorite haunt of Boston skaters is Harvard's Arnold Arboretum (125 Arborway, Jamaica Plain, 617-524-1718), which offers one of the most scenic (and hilly) skates in the area. The best thing about this place is that skaters are welcome everywhere. There are two or three miles of paved paths and you don't have to worry about cars (although you might find yourself dodging strollers, cyclists, and fellow skaters, particularly on sunny weekends).

Boston Common (see page 188) is another popular skating destination, but the pedestrian traffic on the Common makes skating quite challenging. The Common is usually crowded with meandering tourists and fast-walking business folk who don't take too kindly to being mowed down by skaters. The upside, though, is that you can take in some impressive cityscapes as you zip around. The best way to get there is to take the T to Park Street. Note: Wearing skates on the T is prohibited.

For a great view of the bridges that stretch over the Charles River, try the Charles River Bike Path. The trail runs along both sides of the river between the Galen Street Bridge in Watertown and River Street Bridge in Boston, and from the Science Museum to Watertown Square. The path is about 8.5 miles each way.

Beacon Hill Skate Shop (135 Charles St S, 617-482-7400) rents top-of-the-line inline skates, roller skates, and ice skates. Rentals cost $10/hour, $15/day, and $20 overnight. Beacon Hill Skate Shop accepts cash only and requires you to leave a credit card as a deposit. All rentals come with safety equipment.

Ice Skating

Even on crisp winter days, when the cold makes it almost unbearable to be outside, Boston Common's famous Frog Pond entices many Bostonians to bundle up and head out for some good, old-fashioned ice skating—either that or some good, old-fashioned heckling from the sidelines. Skating is free for children 13 and under and $5 for everyone else. Skate rental is $5 for children and $9 for everyone else. Lockers are available for $2. Regulars might consider buying individual season passes for $150 or a family pass for $250. Lunchtime passes are valid Mon–Fri, 11 am to 2 pm (holidays excluded), and cost $100. Frog Pond is open Sun–Thurs 10 am-9 pm (except Mon when the rink closes at 5 pm) and Fri–Sat 10 am–10 pm. For more information, call 617-635-2120.

The Larz Anderson Park in Brookline is a great back-up option when Frog Pond gets too crowded (and it will be). Larz Anderson Park is located on a former 64-acre estate and is the largest park in Brookline. In addition to the outdoor skate rink, the park has picnic areas, ball fields, and an incredible view of Boston. The only downside is that the skating rink is only open a few months every year, from December to February. Skating fees cost $5 for adult residents and $7 for adult non-residents and reduced daily skating rates are available for seniors, students, veterans, and disabled skaters. Skate rentals are $6. The rink is open Tues and Thurs 10 am–12 pm, Fri 7:30 pm–9:30 pm, Sat–Sun 12 pm–5 pm. For more information, call 617-739-7518.

Ice Skating Rinks

If you have your own skates, you might opt for one of the following rinks run by the Department of Conservation and Recreation, where skating in the winter is free. Call rinks for hours of operation:

Bajko Memorial Rink,
75 Turtle Pond Pkwy, Hyde Park, 617-364-9188
Jim Roche Community Ice Arena,
1275 VFW Pkwy, West Roxbury, 617-323-9532
Daly Memorial Rink,
1 Nonantum Rd, Brighton, 617-527-1741
Devine Memorial Rink,
995 Morrissey Blvd, Dorchester, 617-436-4356
Emmons Horrigan O'Neill Memorial Rink,
150 Rutherford Ave, Charlestown, 617-242-9728
Flynn Skating Rink,
2 Woodland Rd, Medford, 781-395-8492
Kelly Outdoor Skating Rink,
1 Marbury Ter, Jamaica Plain, 617-727-7000
LoConte Memorial Rink,
3449 Veterans Pkwy, Medford, 781-395-9594
Murphy Memorial Rink,
1880 William J Day Blvd, South Boston, 617-269-7060
Porazzo Memorial Rink,
20 Coleridge St, East Boston, 617-567-9571
Reilly Skating Rink,
355 Chestnut Hill Ave, Brighton, 617-277-7822
Skating Club of Boston,
1240 Soldiers Field Rd, Brighton, 617-782-5900
Simoni Memorial Rink,
155 Gore St, Cambridge, 781-982-8166
Steriti Memorial Rink,
561 Commercial St, Boston, 617-523-9327
Veterans Memorial Rink,
570 Somerville Ave, Somerville, 617- 623-3523

Skateboarding

The Charles River Skatepark, 40,000 square feet of pipes, ramps, and rails, will be constructed at North Point Park along the Charles River where Cambridge meets Charlestown. Ongoing issues are still causing delays with construction here, so the original goal of a 2010 opening is long gone. If it ever gets finished, it will be one of the largest skateparks in the country, perfect for catching air like Tony Hawk or busting backside lipslides like Ryan Sheckler. Until the mythical park opens, the best option in Boston is the Reservation Skatepark in Hyde Park. The park is small, but it does have a very nice pool setup and a few good sets of stairs. The park is just steps away from the Hyde Park stop on the Providence/Stoughton commuter rail line.

Gear

Beacon Hill Skate Shop,
135 Charles St S, Boston, 617-482-7400
Orchard Skate Shop,
156 Harvard Ave, Boston, 617-782-7777

General Information

Boston Parks and Recreation Office
Phone: 617-635-4505
Hotline: 617-635-PARK
Website: www.cityofboston.gov/parks

Cambridge Recreation Department
Phone: 617-349-6200
Website: www.cambridgema.gov

Department of Conservation and Recreation (Division of Urban Parks)
Phone: 617-626-1250

Outdoor Courts—Open to the Public

These public courts operate on a first-come, first-served basis. Most courts are not equipped with lights, so get there early to get your game in. Although many courts are in good condition, some have pretty major divots, à la the Boston Garden's parquet floor, making the ball spin in unexpected directions. Courts are managed by the city or the town recreation department, or by the Commonwealth's Department of Conservation and Recreation's Division of Urban Parks (DCR). Until recently, the DCR was the Metropolitan District Commission (MDC), so the courts might still be labeled with the wrong acronym. Don't let it affect your game! Many locals also use the well-maintained school courts in the university-rich area. Each school has a different policy regarding outsiders depending on season, location, and the mood of the athletic director on a particular day. Contact the schools or just take your chances.

Tennis Courts	*Address*	*Type*	*# of Courts*	*Map*
Charlesbank Park (DCR)	Boylston St & Charles St	Public	4	1
North End Park (DCR)	Commercial St & Cooper St	Public	2	2
Boston Common	Boylston St & Charles St	Public	2	3
Pagoda Park	Kneeland St	Public	1	4
Cook Street Playground	Hill St & Cook St	Public	1	8
Porzio Park	Maverick Sq	Public	2	9
Boston Athletic Club	653 Summer St	Private		11
Marine Park (DCR)	Day Blvd	Public	1	11
Clifford Playground	Norfolk Ave & Proctor St	Public	1	12
Carter Playground	Columbus Ave & Camden St	Public	5	13
Jeep Jones Park	King St	Public	1	13
Malcolm X Park	Dale St & Bainbridge St	Public	2	13
Trotter School Playground	Humboldt Ave & Waumbeck St	Public	1	13
Mission Hill Deck (DCR)	Southwest Corridor Park	Public	2	14
South Street Mall	South St & Carolina Ave	Public	2	14
Stony Brook Deck (DCR)	Southwest Corridor Park	Public	2	14
Amory Clay Tennis Courts	Amory St	Public		16
Longwood Playground Park	Newall Rd off Kent St	Public	3	16
Waldstein Playground	37 Dean Rd	Public	8	17
Rogers Park	Lake St & Foster St	Public	2	18
Coolidge Playground	Kenwood St b/w Harvard St & Columbia St	Public	1	19
Devotion Playground	Steadman St off Harvard St	Public	3	19
Driscoll School	Westbourne St	Public	2	19
Ringer Playground	Allston St & Griggs Pl	Public	2	19
Anderson Courts	Pemberton St & Haskell St	Public		22
George Dilboy Field (DCR)	Alewife Brook Pkwy	Public	2	22
Saxton J Foss Park (DCR)	McGrath Hwy & Broadway	Public	2	24
Hoyt Field	Western Ave & Howard St	Public		27
Riverside Press Park	River St & Memorial Dr	Public		27
Harvard Street Park	Harvard St & Clark St	Public		28
Joan Lorentz Park at Cambridge Public Library	Broadway & Ellery St	Public		28
Hunt Playground	Blue Hill Ave & Almont St	Public		31

Public Courses

Public Courses	Address	Phone	Par	Fees (WD/WE)	Map
Fresh Pond Golf Course	691 Huron Ave	617-349-6282	35/70	$30 WD / $36 WE	
Presidents Golf Course	357 W Squantum St, Quincy	617-328-3444	70	$35 WD / $44 WE	
Putterham Meadows Golf Club	1281 W Roxbury Pkwy, Chestnut Hill	617-730-2078	71	$35 WD / $38 WE	
William J. Devine Golf Course	1 Circuit Dr, Dorchester	617-265-4084	72	$23-26 WD / $29-34 WE	

Driving Ranges

Driving Ranges	Address	Phone	Fees (WD/WE)	Map
City Golf Boston	38 Bromfield St	617-357-4653	$10/bucket	3

Bowling

First and foremost, if you prefer tenpin over candlepin bowling than you are clearly not from Boston. If you are trying to fit in with the cutters or if want your girlfriend to think you're the real life Will Hunting, then you better learn how to hit those skinny sticks. On the other hand, if you are comfortable admitting that you were born in upstate New York and that you collected Don Mattingly cards when you were a kid, then embrace the tenpin, no one will think less of you for it (yeah, right).

All kidding aside, bowling has become hip and bowling has become expensive. Take **Kings (Map 16)**, for instance. Go there on a Friday night and it's filled with people who wouldn't have been caught dead bowling on a Friday night back in high school. Then there's **Lucky Strike Lanes (Map 16)** with a friggin' dress code. If that's your idea of bowling, by all means, have at it. If you're an old-school bowler, the kind that embraces leagues and finds no kitsch value in a button up short sleeve with your name in cursive on it (your real name), then you must head straight to **Lanes & Games,** order yourself a Bud and some steak tips, and get out your lucky glove. Another similar option is **Sacco's Bowl Haven (Map 22)** in Somerville (candlepin only). And here's one of those moments that remind you why you bought this little awesome book in the first place—**Boston Bowl Family Fun Center (Map 32)** on Morrissey Boulevard is open all night! You read correctly: In the squarest late-night town in America, where your options are your buddy's stained futon or the South Street Diner, Boston Bowl has you covered 24 hours a day.

Bowling Lanes

Bowling Lanes	Address	Phone	Fees	Map
King's Boston	50 Dalton St	617-266-2695	$5.50/game, $4/shoes	5
Central Park Lanes	10 Saratoga St	617-567-7073	$2.50/game, $1/shoes	9
South Boston Candlepin	543 E Broadway	617-464-4858	$3.50/game, $1.50 shoes	11
Lucky Strike Lanes	145 Ipswich St	617-437-0300	$4/game, $3/shoes	16
Sacco's Bowl Haven	45 Day St	617-776-0552	$3/game, $2/shoes	22
Boston Bowl (24 hrs)	820 Morrissey Blvd,	617-825-3800	$4.95/game, $4.25/shoes	32
Lanes & Games	195 Concord Tpke	617-876-5533	$4.75/game, $2.75/shoes	n/a

Billiards

Billiards	Address	Phone	Fees	Map
Boston Beer Works	112 Canal St	617-896-2337	$10/hr	2
King's Boston	50 Dalton St	617-266-2695	$14/hr	5
4 X 4 Billiards	1260 Boylston St	617-424-6326	$12/hr	15
Big City	138 Brighton Ave	617-782-2020	$10/hr	19
Sacco's Bowl Haven	45 Day St	617-776-0552	$7.50/hr	22
Flat Top Johnny's	One Kendall Sq, Bldg 200	617-494-9565	$12/hr	26
Boston Bowl (open 24hrs)	820 Morrissey Blvd	617-825-3800	$13/hr	32
Columbia Billiard CO	Columbia Rd	617-265-1828	$6.60/hr	32

General Information

Phone: 617-236-1652

Website: www.baa.org

Overview

One of the great perks that comes with living in Boston is Patriots' Day, a little gem of a holiday that is celebrated on the third Monday of April. Schools and most jobs get the day off, opening the door for the best athletic day of the year in Beantown. The Sox play an 11:05 a.m. home game, the Bruins and/or Celtics usually have a playoff game, and the Boston Marathon draws the best distance runners in the world to the hub. The Marathon's history goes back to the 19th century, making it the oldest annual road race in the world. Today, nearly 25,000 people ran in the Marathon, which boasts one of the most famous and peculiar courses in the world.

The race stretches from Hopkinton to Copley Square, and features plenty of unique hills and obstacles. Anyone preparing to run the race (props to you for running a qualifying time) should take into account the legendary Newton hills that rear their heads around the 19th mile, and the Cleveland Circle train tracks that must be crossed at the 23rd mile. There is usually a wind at your back when you are running, making the race a bit more tolerable. Boston's weather varies so much in April that in 2011, the winning time for the marathon was a record setting 2:03:02 and in 2012, it was nearly 10 minutes slower, at 2:12:52. Runners can expect temperatures from the 40s to mid-90s, making training very difficult.

If running is not your thing, and you want to watch one of the best races in the country, there are plenty of great options for viewing the race. Obviously, the finish line is the prime spot, but if you don't like waking up at 5:00 in the morning on a day off from work, there are better options. Kenmore Square has plenty going for it. It's only a mile away from the finish, there are plenty of great places to eat and it's shady on one side. It gets very loud at around 2 p.m. as thousands of Sox fans stream out from Fenway Park to support the runners as they make the final push towards the finish line. Coolidge Corner in Brookline is also a great spot, and Heartbreak Hill is easily the most dramatic spot on the course. If you know someone running in the race, you might want to set up there to help will them up the slope.

The weekend leading up to Patriots' Day is a blast. The Sports and Fitness Expo at the Seaport World Trade Center is a must for any runner. All of the top names in the fitness business are eager to show off their new creations and hand out tons of free swag at the convention, which runs on the Friday, Saturday and Sunday leading up to the big race. The Marathon begins on Patriots' Day Monday ("Marathon Monday") at 9 a.m., so be sure to set up by 11:00 if you're spectating in Boston.

How to Get There—Driving

This would be a pretty touristy move if there ever was one. Don't drive, for the love of all things holy, just don't. If you HAVE to, take I-93 to exit 6, and follow signs to the Braintree Red Line T station. If you're watching in Newton or Brookline, driving shouldn't be that bad, as long as you give yourself an extra half hour for traffic. Take I-95 to exit 19 or 20, depending on where you want to watch.

Parking

Good luck. A ton of roads are shut down along the race route, so spots are very scarce, try to get lucky and find a meter, but it's basically a lost cause.

How to Get There—Mass Transit

Ahh—now we're talking. Take the green line to Arlington if you're planning on watching from the finish line, or Kenmore if you're going to Kenmore Square (note that Copley is closed on Marathon Monday). Take the C train to the stop of your choice if you're planning on watching in Brookline (it runs parallel to the race). The D train will get you to Newton. If you're coming in from out of town, take the commuter rail to Back Bay and walk to the Arlington T stop, or simply walk a block and you're at the finish line. Fares run from $2 to $8.75.

Hiking in Boston

While it may not be the greatest city for driving, Boston is a great walking city. Whether you're in the mood for a casual stroll or a major trek, the city offers a surprisingly wide array of hikes and walks from which to choose. The trails closest to the city tend to be more scenic walks than hikes—appropriate for strolling students or families who want to get out and about in the city. If you're hungering for some real hiking, you'll need to be prepared for a drive. Boston's outskirts offer plenty of rigorous hiking trails with breathtaking views of the city and a taste of Massachusetts nature. If none of that is hardcore enough for you, the White Mountains of New Hampshire are just a Zipcar (see page 193) away.

Boston Harbor Islands

Seven miles from downtown Boston, this cluster of pretty much undiscovered islands is a great day trip to walk among historical forts and bucolic landscapes, birdwatch, or do some beachcombing. The inexpensive ferry from Long Wharf drops you off at Georges Island, where you can explore Fort Warren, a former Civil War prison that supposedly has its own ghost, "The Lady in Black." From there you can take free shuttles to the other islands. Peddocks Island has the longest coastline of all the islands and the most diverse set of trails. Grape Island takes you through forests, orchards, and rocky shoreline. Lovells has nice sand dunes and swimming beaches. Ferry service runs six times a day to Spectacle Island, a former dump site, which has been refurbished with excavated dirt from the Big Dig. It features a renewable energy visitor center, electric cars, a marina, beaches, and five miles of trails. There is camping on Peddocks, Grape, Lovells, and Bumpkin, but you must pack in and pack out everything yourself. Ferries to Spectacle Island and Georges Island operate from 9 am until sunset in the summer. Roundtrip tickets cost $15 for adults, $11 for seniors (65+), $9 for children (ages 4-11), and children under 4 ride for free. For more information, go to www.bostonharborislands.org or call 617-223-8666 for schedules.

HarborWalk

With the cleaning up of Boston Harbor (though we still wouldn't swim in it) and the removal of the Central Artery, the waterfront has become more beautiful and accessible to pedestrian traffic. Finally realizing that people are attracted to a picturesque waterfront, Boston decided to capitalize on its coastal setting and incorporate it into the life of the city. The HarborWalk is a multi-use attraction consisting of walkways, parks, benches, artwork, restaurants, and swimming spots extending from Chelsea to Neponset. Currently 38 miles long, it is 80% complete and meanders through diverse waterfront neighborhoods with views of the Harbor Islands and Boston skyline. A don't miss highlight is the Institute of Contemporary Art (ICA), with its glass structure perched over the waterfront. It is really quite pleasant on warm summer nights to wander among the boats and the lights of the city and revisit neighborhoods from a whole new perspective. With the Rose Kennedy Greenway complete (and catching flack for not having enough people on it), feel free to give that a stroll from where it parallels the Harbor Walk on Atlantic Ave. The signs might be the best part—especially the one that speaks directly to your pooch.

Arnold Arboretum

Harvard's Arnold Arboretum, located in Jamaica Plain, occupies 265 acres and boasts a dizzying array of woody plants, more than 700 of which are over 100 years old. You can take a free guided tour of the grounds (call 617-524-1718 for tour schedules) or amble along the three-mile trail at your own pace. The arboretum welcomes dogs as long as they're kept on a leash. The botanical haven is just two blocks away from the Forest Hills T stop (Orange Line) and parking is available outside the main gate (although spots can be hard to come by on certain days, such as Sundays and summer holidays). Restrooms are located next to the entrance gate in the Hunnewell Visitor Center. The grounds are open every day of the year during daylight hours. For more information, visit www.arboretum.harvard.edu.

Fresh Pond Reservation

This is a favorite of local residents and Harvard students. Located just one mile from the university and six miles from downtown Boston, the Fresh Pond Reservation offers a rather easy 2.25-mile paved trail around comely Fresh Pond, the 155-acre reservoir. The trail has become a hot spot for joggers, cyclists, and skaters. If you take your dog, be sure to check out the pooper-scooper dispensers! But it's not just the athletic types that reap the benefits of the reservation—the reservoir provides drinking water to many residents and businesses in Cambridge. To reach the reservation by train, take the Red Line to Alewife (last stop). By car, follow Route 2 east or west to Fresh Pond Parkway. The reservation lies on the corner of Huron Avenue and Fresh Pond Parkway. You'll find the best entrance to the reservation directly across from Wheeler Street. Parking in the reservation is reserved for cars with a Cambridge permit. There is parking after hours at the Tobin School, or take bus #72, #74, #75, or #78. For more information, visit www.friendsoffreshpond.org or call 617-349-6319.

Mount Auburn Cemetery

Hailed as America's first landscaped cemetery and a National Historic Landmark, Mount Auburn provides two miles of leisurely walking, alternating between paved walkways and unpaved footpaths, and is considered one of the best birding spots in the state. Aside from the 86,000 graves, the cemetery is home to over 5,000 native and foreign trees. Located just 1.5 miles west of Harvard Square, the cemetery can be reached via Route 2 or 3 to Route 16 at the Mount Auburn/Brattle Street intersection on Fresh Pond Parkway. If you follow Mount Auburn Street (Rte 16) west for two blocks, you will reach the entrance. Contact the Friends of Mount Auburn Cemetery (617-547-7105) for information about guided tours and lectures or visit their website at www.mountauburn.org. No dogs allowed.

Forest Hills Cemetery

Jamaica Plain's Forest Hills Cemetery is overshadowed in popularity (perhaps unfairly) by Mount Auburn Cemetery. Established in 1848, it's one of the country's oldest burial grounds, featuring 275 acres of beautifully sculpted landscape. The cemetery offers books, brochures, and maps to help visitors create their own tours of the grounds and its famous residents, including Eugene O'Neill and e.e. cummings. One of its most impressive features is Lake Hibiscus, which hosts the Buddhist-inspired lantern lighting festival held annually in the summer season. Another highlight is the Sculpture Path, a revolving exhibit of work by contemporary local and national artists. The cemetery is located conveniently next to the Forest Hills T stop. If you're driving, take the Arborway east over the Casey Overpass and follow signs for the cemetery exit, located on the right on Shea Circle. The grounds are open year-round during daylight hours. For more information, visit www.foresthillscemetery.com or call 617-524-0128.

Hammond Pond Reservation

Hammond Pond is located behind a suburban mall in Chestnut Hill—an unlikely place to find a reservation. You can see the department stores as you hike through the 114 acres of woodlands. It's also one of the few outdoor places in Boston where you can rock climb. The best place to start is at the entrance to the reservation, located on the left of Hammond Pond at the north side of the parking lot. Walk through the metal gate and remain on the wide main path through the woods. If you're interested in rock climbing, you'll see rocks to your left a little way along the path. If climbing rocks is not your thing, continue on for two miles of easy walking or try fishing in the pond. Hammond Pond Reservation can be reached by foot from the Chestnut Hill T stop. Hammond Pond Reservation is open year-round during daylight hours. For more information, call 617-698-1802.

Breakheart Reservation

Hidden amidst strip malls and fast-food joints along Route 1, this 640-acre hardwood forest is a treasure for hikers lucky enough to stumble across it. The reservation offers many miles of scenic views and plenty of strenuous trails to get your heart pumping. Fishing, bird watching, cross-country skiing, swimming, and biking are other attractions that lure nature lovers out to Breakheart. As there's really no way to get to there by mass transit, you'll have to drive. Take Route 1 to the Lynn Fells Parkway exit towards Melrose and Stoneham. Turn right onto Forest Street, and follow the signs to Breakheart Reservation. A good place to begin your hike is on the paved Pine Tops Road, located next to the parking lot adjacent to the headquarters building. For more information, call 781-233-0834.

Skyline Trail

This seven-mile trail is located in Blue Hills Reservation (near Milton), the largest open space within 35 miles of Boston. The Skyline Trail winds through rocky hills and provides scenic views of the city. With an elevation gain of 2,500 feet, this hike is not for the faint of heart. This is a strenuous hike that will take at least half a day. But don't fret! If you're not up for a real workout, there are plenty of less challenging trails in the park and the color-coded trail map available at the headquarters building will help you find your way around. To get there, take Route I-93 to Exit 3 towards Houghton's Pond. After exiting, turn right at the stop sign onto Hillside Street and travel about a mile until you reach Houghton's Pond. The trail is open year-round from sunrise until sunset. Also in the Reservation is the Ponkapoag Pond trail, a four-mile loop around the pond, the highlight of which is a boardwalk trail (two miles roundtrip) through a rare Atlantic white cedar swamp. It's fun and different, but be warned: Wear waterproof shoes. Seriously. The boardwalk is made up of half submerged logs.

Middlesex Fells Reservation Eastern Section

Located seven miles north of Boston, Middlesex Fells is a 2,060-acre reservation where you'll find some of the area's most challenging hikes, many of which are considered some of the Boston area's best kept secrets. (If anyone asks, you didn't hear about it from us.) Middlesex Fells is off I-93 past the Stone Zoo. Parking is available on Pond Street. The beginning of the trail is located on the south side of Pond Street and begins behind a Virginia Wood sign near Gate 42. The trail is approximately 5.5 miles long, but can be extended to 16 miles if you connect trails. All of the hikes in this area are fairly strenuous and involve climbing and descending rocky slopes.

Moose Hill Wildlife Sanctuary

This is the oldest and second-largest Massachusetts Audubon Society (MAS) sanctuary. Moose Hill covers 1,984 acres that teem with wildlife and offers more than 25 miles of well-marked trails. One trail in particular, the Warner Trail, provides an exceptional view of the surrounding area from 491 feet. (You have to earn the view by climbing up Bluff Head.) Admission is $4 for adults, $3 for seniors and children aged 3–12. Members enter for free. Trails are open daily from dawn to dusk. The best way to get to Moose Hill is off of Route 128/I-95 S. Take Exit 10. At the end of the ramp, make a left; then travel a quarter-mile and turn right onto Route 27 towards Walpole. After half a mile, turn left onto Moose Hill Street. Follow the MAS signs to the parking lot on the left. Find your way to the Visitor Center. All of the trails stem from there. For more information call 781-784-5691.

Walden Woods

Henry David Thoreau's account of his two-year stay in Walden is credited with sparking the conservation movement. Though nestled between railroad tracks and busy Route 2, Walden Pond is still a peaceful and pleasant setting for an afternoon walk no matter what season. The 102-foot deep Walden Pond is just one part of the 2680-acre Walden Woods. There is an easy loop trail around the pond, which passes by the site of Thoreau's house (a replica sits in the parking lot). If you get too hot, you can always stop for a quick dip. Easy interconnecting trails link up with the neighboring Walden Woods and Lincoln Conservation Trust. The main parking area is on Route 126 off of Route 2. Parking ($5) is limited to 350 spaces and fills up quickly on hot summer days. If there is no ranger at the gate, you will need exact change for the annoying automated ticket machine, inevitably causing longer delays than dealing with a live person. On crowded days, there are designated times of the day when they let people in. Call ahead at 781-259-4700, and visit www.walden.org for more information.

General Information

City of Boston Swimming:	www.cityofboston.gov/bcyf/facilities.asp
Department of Conservation Resources:	www.mass.gov/eea/state-parks-beaches/pools-beaches-boating
MIT Zesiger Center:	mitrecsports.com/index.php/aquatics
YMCA of Greater Boston:	www.ymcaboston.org
New England Masters Swimming:	www.swimnem.org

Overview

With your swimming options including universities, the oldest Y in the country, and local gyms, it's easier to skip the many poorly maintained pools of the city with their odd hours. While the city's pools are the cheapest option (meaning free), they're only open from mid-June to mid-August. You'll find the city's website provides little help in locating pools and the only way to get schedules is to call each pool directly. For serious lap swimmers, the largest indoor pool in Boston is at **MIT's Zesiger Center (Map 27)**, running short course all winter and changing lanes to a 50 m for the summer. Day passes are available. New England Masters maintains a comprehensive listing on swimming clubs, workout locations, and stroke clinics. There are also YMCAs scattered around the metro area.

In the summer, the DCR operates many outdoor swimming and wading pools and public beaches along the Bay and at local ponds. Their website lists the hours and locations. The most famous wading pool is the Frog Pond in Boston Common. If fighting for pool space amongst hordes of screaming children is not your thing, favorite alternatives include taking a dip in Walden Pond in Concord (get there early, as the parking lot fills up fast) and strolling the busy beaches at Revere and Wollaston, which can be accessed by the Blue and Red Lines respectively. The Standells might "love that dirty water," but ongoing efforts to improve the once dangerous water quality of the Charles River continue, and the Charles River Swimming Club held its first ever one-mile swim in 2007 to demonstrate its safety (toxic algae postponed it in 2006), but recreational swimming is not encouraged, especially after a heavy rain. For those of you with a little extra cash burning some holes in your designer swim trunks, the **Colonnade Hotel (Map 6)** has a rooftop pool that has a $50 weekday pass for the public. It's like a club scene up there though, so make sure to spray tan on some abs if you're on the flabbier side.

Where to Swim

Where to Swim	*Address*	*Phone*	*Fees*	*Map*
Lee Memorial Wading Pool	Charles St	617-523-9746	Free	1
Boston Harbor Island National Park Beach	ferry leaves from Long Wharf outside Marriott Hotel, State St	617-223-8666	Free (but unavoidable $10–12 ferry ticket)	2
Mirabella Pool	585 Commercial St	617-635-5235	$10 adults, kids under 5 free	2
Boston Chinatown Neighborhood Center Pool	Ash St	617-635-5129	$75 per year, $30 children	4
Huntington Avenue YMCA	316 Huntington Ave	617-536-6950	Membership $55.60 per month. Plus $100 joining fee	5
Colonnade Hotel	120 Huntington Ave	617-424-7000	$30 per day pass	6
Blackstone Community Center	50 W Brookline St	617-635-5162	$25 per year, children $5	7
Charlestown Community Center	255 Medford St	617-635-5169	$25 per year adults, $5 children	8
Harborside Community Center	312 Border St	617-635-5114	$25 per year adults, $5 children	9
Paris Street Pool	113 Paris St	617-635-5125	$20 per year adults, $5 children	9
Condon Community Center	200 D St	617-635-5100	$5 adults, $3 youth	10
Curley Community Center	1663 Columbia Rd	617-635-5104	$25 per year	11
Madison Park Community Center	55 New Dudley St	617-635-5206	$10 per year adults, $4 children	13
Curtis Hall Community Center	20 South St	617-635-5193	$25 per year adults, $5 children	14
Hennigan Community Center	200 Heath St	617-635-5198	$25 per year adults, $5 children	15
Clougherty Pool	Bunker Hill St	617-635-5173	Free	16
Dealtry Memorial Pool	114 Pleasant St	617-923-0073	Free	16
Kirrane Aquatic Center	60 Tappan St	617-713-5435	$5 adults, $3 students	17
Brighton-Allston Swimming & Wading Pool	380 N Beacon St	617-254-2965	Free	18
Oak Square YMCA	615 Washington St	617-782-3535	$58/month	18
Reilly Memorial Swimming Pool	Chestnut Hill Ave	617-277-7822	Free	18
Artesani Wading Pool	Soldiers Field Rd	-	-	19
McCrehan Memorial Swimming & Wading	356 Rindge Ave	617-354-9154	Free	22
Vietnam Veterans Memorial	Carter St	617-884-9630	Free	25
Cambridge Family YMCA	820 Massachusetts Ave	617-661-9622	$48 per month & $50 joining fee	27
Veterans Memorial Swimming & Wading	719 Memorial Dr	617-354-9381	Free	27
Zesiger Sports and Fitness Center	120 Vassar St	617-452-3690	$12 per day adults, $7 children	27
Mason Pool	176 Norfolk Ave	617-635-5241	$10 per year (adult), $5 (under 18)	28
Cass Memorial	120 Washington St	617-445-0062	Free	
Moynihan Wading Pool	920 Truman Pkwy		Free	
Olsen Swimming & Wading	95 Turtle Pond Pkwy	617-364-9524		

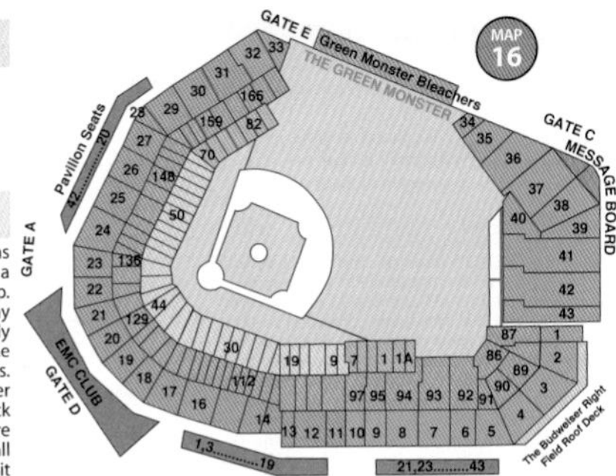

General Information

NFT Map: 16
Address: 4 Yawkey Wy
Boston, MA 02215
Phone: 617-REDSOX9
(617-733-7699)
Website: boston.redsox.mlb.com

Overview

It would be only the slightest of exaggerations to say that, in Boston, the Red Sox are a religion and Fenway Park is a house of worship. Situated just outside Kenmore Square, Fenway Park is a place where the reputedly unfriendly locals find fellowship in their deep love of the Sox and an even deeper hatred of the Yankees. In fact, Red Sox Nation is still (and will forever be) gloating over the historic 2004 comeback win against the evil men in pinstripes before crushing the St. Louis Cardinals in the Fall Classic. Yet, our gloating increased quite a bit in 2007, as the Sox once again brought home the World Series Trophy with a four game sweep of the Colorado Rockies, while the Yankees were at home washing their uniforms. That's two World Series wins in four seasons, after an 86-year drought. Boston is truly in its baseball renaissance.

Despite this devotion, even the most die-hard fan cannot deny two basic truths: Fenway is old and Fenway is small. Fenway Park celebrated it's 100th anniversary in 2012 The first game at Fenway Park, played on April 20, 1912, got bumped off the front page of the newspapers by the breaking news of the Titanic sinking a few days earlier. With only 37,493 seats, it is the smallest park in the majors, though management has recently added a few thousand more seats in some very creative locations to expand capacity.

With age, however, comes a rich sense of history, and the dusty corners of Fenway have more personality than perhaps any other park in the game. The best-known of these character traits is the towering Green Monster, the 37-foot left field wall whose odd location can turn pop flies into homers and homers into singles. Marking the right field foul line is Pesky's Pole, named for Sox legend Johnny Pesky. On the manually operated scoreboard in left field, Morse Code dots and dashes spell out the initials of Red Sox owner Tom Yawkey and his wife.

Walking on Yawkey Way before a game is one of the best experiences you can have in Boston. Make sure to arrive at the game at least 45 minutes before first pitch, so you can experience the action around the park, which includes a live band, plenty of souvenir shops, and some of the best hot dogs in the world, "Fenway Franks" (Fenway Park sells more hot dogs than any other park in the country). Note, only ticketed fans are allowed on Yawkey Way before games.

Truly patriotic citizens of Red Sox Nation should take the Fenway Park tour. A tour leaves from Yawkey Way every hour Mon–Sun 9 am–5 pm. On game days, the last tour is offered 3 hours before the start of the game (so 4 p.m. for a 7 p.m. game). Tours are $16.00 for adults, $14.00 for seniors, and $12.00 for children and students. Tickets for tours can be purchased at the Gate D Ticket Booth on the corner of Yawkey Way and Van Ness Street. When the booth is closed, they are available at the team store on Yawkey Way. Tours last for 50 minutes.

How to Get There—Mass Transit

Take the Green Line to Kenmore and follow the crowd to the ballpark. The MBTA Commuter Rail's Worcester/Framingham line also goes to Yawkey, a short walk from Fenway Park. There's also a free game-day-only shuttle that connects Gate B at Fenway Park with the Ruggles stop, served by the T's Orange Line and the MBTA Commuter Rail's Providence/Stoughton, Needham, and Franklin lines. Subway fare is $2; commuter rail fares range from $2 to $11, with a $3 surcharge if you buy tickets aboard the train.

How to Get Tickets

Always difficult to score, the first places to try for individual game and season ticket information, are the Red Sox box office at 877-REDSOX9 and the team's website. Ticket prices range from $12 bleacher seats to $312 dugout box seats. If you are willing to wait in line, a great way to get tickets is to head to the gate E window around 2 and a half hours before game time (4:40 on weeknights). Tickets that had been held for players' families are sold at face value at the window. It's the only way to get face value seats on a whim the day of a game. Fans are allowed to start lining up five hours before game time (2 p.m. on weeknights, but you would only need to wait that long for a marquee game, such as the first Yankee game, or opening day), and tickets go on sale two hours before first pitch. Everyone that wants to go to the game must be on hand to buy a ticket, holding places in line is strictly prohibited. There is a "scalp free" zone at gate B on game days, where ticket holders can sell extra seats to fans at face value. Red Sox personnel are on hand to observe every sale.

A good tip for getting tickets is showing up to the game after an inning and a half or so, say 7:40 for a 7:10 game, when scalpers slash prices severely, prices can get as low as $15 for $55 tickets. Another good tip is to look for standing room tickets either down the first base line or on the Budweiser right field roof deck. The tickets are only $20-$30 and can usually be purchased the day of the game at the Red Sox ticket office. The Bud Deck has especially great views, better than the Green Monster, so $30 is well worth it.

General Information

Address: One Patriot Pl
Foxborough, MA 02035
Phone: 508-543-1776
Websites: www.gillettestadium.com
www.patriots.com
www.revolutionsoccer.net

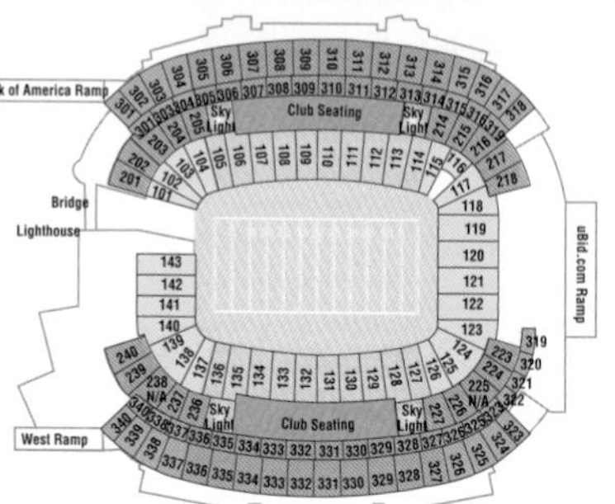

Upper Level, Corner/End Zone
Upper Level, Sideline
Mezzanine Level, Corner/End Zone
Lower Level, Corner/End Zone
Lower Level, Sideline
* N/A=Non-Alcoholic Section

Overview

As far as NFL franchises go, the New England Patriots were a joke until Bill Parcells took over as head coach in 1993 and Robert Kraft bought the team in 1994. The team continued to play in a mediocre stadium until 2002. Old Schaefer/ Sullivan/Foxboro Stadium was an unsightly, obsolete, charmless concrete slab, but the Pats sent it packing in style. The last game at Foxboro Stadium was the hotly debated "Snow Bowl" vs. the Oakland Raiders. Depending on your loyalties, QB Tom Brady either fumbled or "tucked" the ball during a key late-game possession. (It was a tuck.) The Pats won, propelling them to victory in Super Bowl 36.

The 2002 season was ushered in by the opening of Gillette Stadium, where the Patriots proved that their first championship season was no fluke, winning two more Super Bowls over the next three years. The stadium has been accessorized with a 12-story lighthouse and a replica of the Longfellow Bridge at one end of the field. A high definition screen, nearly 1,300 square feet in size, hangs over each end zone.

With a seating capacity of over 68,000, Gillette Stadium does triple duty, also acting as the home of Major League Soccer's New England Revolution and a major concert venue. It can be a good place to catch big names like the Rolling Stones or U2. Gillette also hosts the biggest annual country music festival in the northeast during the last weekend of August, with perennial headliner Kenny Chesney and a loaded lineup of Nashville talent. Given the size of the stadium, make sure to bring a pair of binoculars if you have anything but the best seats.

On non-game days, the Hall At Patriot's Place is a great destination for any football fan. Located steps away from the stadium, with an entrance through the team's pro shop, the hall of fame has plenty of interactive exhibits as well as relics from throughout Patriots history in a state-of-the-art facility that was opened in 2008. Some notable exhibits include the team's three Super Bowl trophies, the infamous snow plow from 1982 and a film chronicling the Pats' rise to the top of the football world. The Hall opens at 10 a.m. every day and closes at 7 p.m. every day except for Saturday, when it closes at 9 p.m. Admission is $10 for adults, $7 for seniors and $5 for children aged 12 or younger. For more information, visit www.thehallatpatriotplace.com.

Patriot Place, the gigantic mall that's sprung up around the stadium, is now in full swing, with every option imaginable for you to purchase on your way in or out of a game. The movie theater there, which has an adults only section, recently kicked Justin Bieber out for being underage, proving that the Patriots always make good decisions.

How to Get There—Driving

From Boston, take I-93 S to I-95 S; take I-95 S to Exit 9 (Wrentham) onto Route 1 S. Follow Route 1 S approximately three miles to Gillette Stadium (on the left).

Parking

The lots open four hours before Pats games, three hours before concerts and other events, and two hours before Revolution games, leaving plenty of time for tailgating—an opportunity fans use to the fullest. The lots tend to fill up well before game time, so make sure you give yourself ample time to get there. Pre-game Route 1 traffic is legendary, so give yourself at least 90 more minutes than you think you'll need when heading out to the game, even more in bad weather. General Seating ticket holders should enter lot P2, P5, or P10 from Route 1. Follow signs for "General Stadium Parking." Disabled parkers and limos should head for P2, buses for P5, and RVs for P10. For Patriots games, car parking costs $40, RV and limo parking costs $125, and bus parking costs $200. Prices vary for other Gillette events.

How to Get There—Mass Transit

MBTA commuter rail trains leave South Station for Foxboro Station on game days. A round-trip ticket costs around $12. The train departs from the stadium 30 minutes after the game. For more information and a complete schedule, visit www.mbta.com/riding_the_t/patriots/

How to Get Tickets

With the Pat's Dynasty status firmly cemented as the team of the Century, and the Greatest Football Team to Ever Exist (fact), you're going to have some ticket troubles, especially since Tom Brady is still throwing bombs. To get on the season ticket waiting list, visit the Patriots' website and have $100 a seat on hand for a deposit. For regular tickets (or concert tickets), call Ticketmaster at 617-931-2222 or visit www.ticketmaster.com. Game tickets range from $59 to $125. The ubiquitous scalpers can be found roaming the parking lots and entrances to the stadium. StubHub.com, eBay, and Craiglist also accommodate folks who are selling and buying tickets, but be careful—season ticket holders have been known to lose their seats after being caught selling extra tickets online.

General Information

NFT Map: 1
Address: 150 Causeway St
Boston, MA 02114
Phone: 617-624-1000
Celtics: 617-854-8000
Bruins: 617-624-1900
Websites: www.tdgarden.com
www.nba.com/celtics
bruins.nhl.com

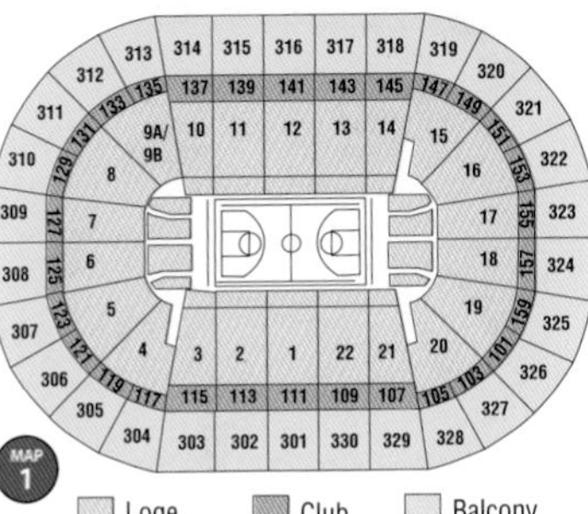

Overview

Greater Boston's long regional sports nightmare is over. Once again Celtics and Bruins fans can accurately say that their teams compete in "the Garden." The original Boston Garden, which opened in 1928, earned the adoration of Bostonians as the arena in which Bird, McHale, and Parish propelled the Celts to dynasty status. In footage of the team's 1984 NBA finals victory over the Lakers, fans crowd the sidelines and rush the court with time left on the clock. Bruins games could be even less civil and, correspondingly, even more fun.

As the 1980s drew to a close, however, both the Celtics and the Garden lost a bit of their luster. The team began a slow decline from glory and the venue grew more and more decrepit. Finally in 1995, the FleetCenter was constructed next door and both the Celtics and the Bruins said goodbye to their old stomping grounds. The new name took years to catch on among the area's stubborn traditionalists. When Fleet was acquired by Bank of America, the new parent company sold the naming rights—for $6 million a year—to TD Banknorth, who promptly restored the proper name. Then in 2009 TD Banknorth became TD so now we have TD Garden. Can we just replace TD with "Boston" and get this over with! The 17,565-seat (18,624 for basketball) TD Garden has all that you would expect from a modern arena—rocket-launched t-shirts, overpriced food and beer, luxury box TVs, and airline and casino promotions during timeouts—but still holds on to touches of tradition, including the Celts' legendary parquet floor. Nonetheless, even with the relative success of the Celts and Bs in recent years, the new venue just doesn't seem to inspire the same sort of love as did its dilapidated predecessor. Having said that, the Celtics NBA Record 17th Banner now hangs from these new rafters, hopefully ushering in a new dynasty for our boys in Green. Even more fitting was the fact that we won it against those old purple and gold Lakers, at home, proving once again that in NBA history it's Celtics first, Lakers a solid and distant second. Just don't remind us what happened during the rematch in 2010.

The Bruins, the only major league team in Boston (the Revolution? They don't count!), that was left without a recent championship, has fully cemented Boston as Titletown, USA by bringing the Stanley Cup home in 2011 with a victory over the Vancouver Canucks. That's seven, count them again dear god, seven major championships in 10 years. To break that down further, that's the Pats with three, the Sox with two, and the C's and B's with one each. We've had so many championship parades that people are lining up for the next one already, just to get a good spot. BEST. CITY. EVER.

In addition to sporting events, the TD Garden hosts the circus and concerts by artists ranging from Beyonce to U2. It is also home to the sports museum, which houses many of the most important pieces from the old Garden, including Larry Bird's locker, and the Bruins' penalty box. For more info, go to www.sportsmuseum.org.

How to Get There—Driving

Driving to the Garden is no more difficult than getting any place else in Boston by car—which is to say that it is quite difficult. From the north, take I-93 S to Exit 26A (Leverett Circle/Cambridge). Follow the signs (if construction hasn't relocated them) towards North Station/TD Garden. Take a right at the end of the ramp; the arena will be on your left. From the south, take I-93 N to Exit 26 (Storrow Drive). After the exit, keep left and follow the signs (see above warning) for TD Garden. Watch out, it's a left-hand exit. The Garden will be on your left.

Parking

Parking is provided directly underneath the Garden in the North Station garage, which charges $30 for events. The lot doesn't block cars in, so it's a pretty good option. It will fill up, as it only has 1,200 spaces. The T is the way to go, it's cheaper and you don't have to show up an hour early for a game. Unlike Fenway Park, before a game, you're staring at a hardwood floor or a clean sheet of ice, when can get old after around 90 seconds.

How to Get There—Mass Transit

The TD Garden sits atop the North Station commuter rail station, which services the northern suburbs. Directly underneath is a new "superstation" that finally puts North Station's Green Line and Orange Line T stops in the same location. The Charles/MGH Red Line stop and the Bowdoin Blue Line stop are less than a ten-minute walk away. Commuter rail fares range from $2 to $11, with a $3 surcharge if you buy the ticket on board the train.

How to Get Tickets

To get Celtics season tickets, call 866-4CELTIX or visit the Celtics' website. They offer full-season, half-season, and multi-game packages. Individual ticket prices range from $25 nosebleed seats to $275 courtside seats. The mid-range $55 end-court seats offer an excellent value.

To get Bruins season tickets call 617-624-BEAR or visit the Bruins' website. The Bs offer full-season, half-season, and ten-game packages, with individual ticket prices ranging from $26 to $101, topping out with the mysteriously un-priced Premium Club. (If you have to ask, you can't afford them.) Craigslist is a good option the night before a game. You can probably find tickets at face value or below.

If you don't have tickets but have cash to burn, scalpers can be found on Causeway Street on game days.

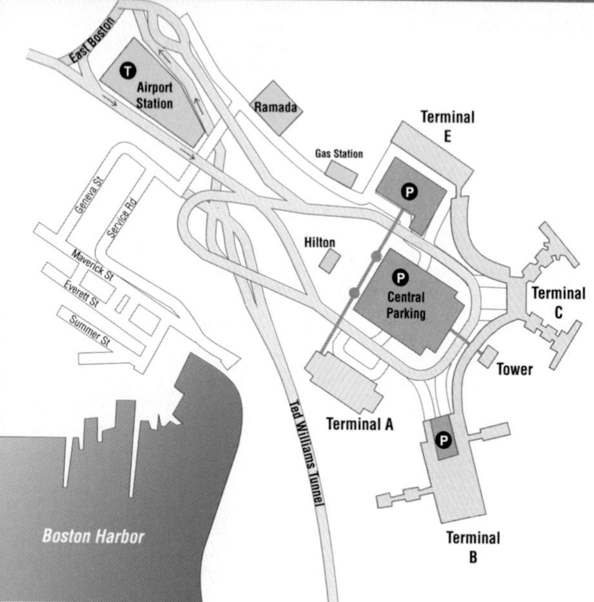

Airline	Terminal	Phone Number
Aer Lingus	E	800-474-7424
Air Canada/ Air Canada Jazz	B	888-247-2262
Air France	E	800-237-2747
AirTran	C	800-247-8726
Alaska Airlines	B	800-252-7522
Alitalia	E	800-223-5730
American (except int'l arrivals)	B	800-433-7300
American (int'l arrivals only)	E	800-433-7300
American Eagle	B	800-433-7300
British Airways	E	800-247-9297
Cape Air	C	800-352-0714
Copa Airlines	E	800-359-2672
Delta Air Lines	A	800-221-1212
Delta Connection/Com Air	A	800-354-9822
Delta Shuttle	A	800-221-1212
Finnair	E	800-950-5000
Iberia	E	800-772-4642
Icelandair	E	800-223-5500
Japan Airlines	E	800-525-3663
JetBlue (except int'l arrivals)	C	800-538-2583
JetBlue (int'l arrivals only)	E	800-538-2583
Lufthansa	E	800-645-3880
PenAir	B	800-448-4226
Porter Airlines	E	800-619-8622
SATA	E	800-762-9995
Southwest Airlines	E	800-435-9792
Spirit Airlines	B	800-772-7117
Sun Country	E	800-359-6786
Swiss	E	877-359-7947
TACV	E	866-359-8228
United	C	800-241-6522
United Express	C	800-241-6522
US Airways	B	800-428-4322
US Airways Express	B	800-428-4322
US Airways Shuttle	B	800-428-4322
Virgin America	B	877-359-8474
Virgin Atlantic	E	800-862-8621

General Information

Website:	www.massport.com/logan-airport
Customer Service:	617-561-1800
Ground Transportation Info:	800-23-LOGAN
Logan Lost and Found:	617-561-1714
Parking Office:	617-561-1673

Overview

The country's 12th busiest airport (according to Bureau of Transportation Statistics), Logan International Airport features all the serpentine security lines and two-mile gate runs of most major airports and is located in an area of the country where weather can ground planes at any time of the year. But thanks to the completion of the Big Dig and the extension of the Silver Line, getting to Logan is now much easier.

Jutting into the harbor from East Boston, Logan opened in 1923 as the "temporary occupant" on landfill originally intended to be a port. By 1939, flying contraptions had proven their worth and the site was made permanent. The airport is named after Lt. General Edward Lawrence Logan, a local and a Harvard grad who served in the Spanish-American War, the Massachusetts House of Representatives, and the Senate.

The decade-long Logan Modernization Project yielded new and improved Terminals A and C, a new T station, an extended Silver Line, a new international arrivals hall serving Terminal E, standardized and improved signage, and improved access to the Central Parking Garage. In 2009, Health Magazine ranked Logan as the 8th healthiest airport in the country. Terminal A is the world's first airport terminal certified by the U.S. Green Building Council for using the highest green construction standards, with a heat reflecting roof, low-flow faucets, waterless urinals, self-dimming lights, and recycled construction materials.

If good planning or bad weather leaves you with time to kill before your flight, you can grab a gourmet snack at Todd English's Bonfire or one of the three Legal Seafood locations, relax in one of 50 wooden rocking chairs (16 decorated by local artists), or just spend an hour letting yourself be hypnotized by the rhythmic movements of billiard balls through the kinetic sculpture in Terminal C.

How to Get There—Driving

To get to Logan from the west, take the Mass Pike (I-90) E through the Ted Williams Tunnel until the highway ends. From the south, use I-93 N and take Exit 20 to I-90 E. From the north, take I-93 S and follow the signs to the Callahan Tunnel. Check www.massport.com for traffic and construction updates.

Parking

Hourly and daily parking are available at Central Parking Garage, Terminal B Garage, and Terminal E Parking Lots 1 and 2. Rates range from $3 to $24 during the day and $36 to $48 a day for overnight parking. The Economy Parking lot charges a daily rate of $27 and a weekly rate of $108.

How to Get There—Mass Transit

Seriously, do yourself a favor by taking the T. It's a quick ride on the Blue Line from downtown to the Airport stop. A free shuttle bus that runs 4am–1am (and prevents 7 tons of emissions from polluting the atmosphere every year by running on compressed natural gas), will take you from the T stop to your terminal. Or take the Red Line to South Station and transfer to the Silver Line bus, which stops at each airport terminal. If you're coming in from the 'burbs, check out the Logan Express buses that service Braintree, Framingham, Peabody, and Woburn. A Park-and-Ride system is in place, and although the prices for parking and buses vary, they will always be cheaper than taking a cab, especially with the Mass(ive) Pike and tunnel tolls. If you're downtown near the water, the MBTA's Harbor Express water taxi can get you from Long Wharf to the airport in less than ten minutes.

How to Get There—Taxi

It's hard to get to Logan from anywhere except Eastie for less than $20. Boston Cab: 617-536-5010; Checker Taxi: 617-536-7000; City Cab: 617-536-5100; Green Cab (Somerville): 617-623-6000; Cambridge Cab: 617-776-5000.

Rental Cars

Advantage	800-777-5500
Alamo	800-327-9633
Avis	800-831-2847
Budget	800-527-0700
Dollar	800-800-4000
Hertz	800-654-3131
National	800-227-7368
Enterprise	800-325-8007 (off-airport)
Thrifty	800-367-2277 (off-airport)

Hotels

Courtyard Boston Tremont • 275 Tremont St • 617-426-1400
Embassy Suites • 207 Porter St • 617-567-5000
Hampton Inn • 230 Lee Burbank Hwy • 781-286-5665
Hilton • 85 Terminal Rd • 617-568-6700
Holiday Inn • 225 McClellan Hwy • 617-569-5250
Hyatt • 101 Harborside Dr • 617-568-1234 • 800-633-7313
Marriott Long Wharf • 296 State St • 617-227-0800
Omni Parker House • 60 School St • 617-227-8600
Hilton Boston Downtown •
89 Broad St • 617-556-0006

History

The story begins just after World War II. When the good people at the Massachusetts Department of Public Works noticed the increasing popularity of automobiles and the stream of people leaving the city for the suburbs, they decided to make plans to build some major highways. The first highway to be completed was I-93, the Central Artery, hailed at the time as "a futuristic highway in the sky."

It soon became apparent that I-93 totally sucked. It was ugly, disruptive to neighborhoods, and boasted a high accident rate due to the excessive number of entry and exit ramps along the 1.5-mile stretch through the city. Recognizing that the Central Artery was a disaster, community groups fought successfully to stop other major highway projects. Two plans that never came to fruition were the Inner Belt (unbuilt I-695), which would have taken traffic around I-93 via a new, ten-lane BU bridge, and the Southwest Corridor Highway (unbuilt I-95), which would have run from the 93/128 split up through Hyde Park and JP to central Boston.

While averting construction of two new highways was a small victory for city dwellers, I-93 was still operating at triple its capacity, resulting in traffic jams at most hours of the day. The solution to the congestion was to dig a highway under the city—a solution that rather resembled performing open-heart surgery on a fully awake patient. Planning the project took the entirety of the 1980s and construction finally began in September 1991. After fifteen years and almost fifteen billion dollars, the project is officially finished. Hallelujah!

What Is the Big Dig?

As most Bostonians know, the substantially completed "Central Artery/Tunnel Project" was, as the Massachusetts Turnpike Authority puts it, "the largest, most complex and technologically challenging highway project ever." The most important element of the Big Dig is the routing of I-93 from the Central Artery to a new (and leaky) tunnel. Other major aspects of the Dig include the extension of the Mass Pike to Logan Airport through the Ted Williams Tunnel, the construction of the beautiful Leonard P. Zakim Bunker Hill Memorial Bridge (yeah, it's a ridiculously long name), the erection of the Leverett Circle Connector Bridge, and a complete overhaul of the roads and traffic patterns around Logan Airport. The 2006 opening of the Albany Street off-ramp from I-93 S marked the point when all of the Dig's tunnels and bridges and their connection and ramps to surface roads were open to general traffic. But when exactly does a civil engineering project of this magnitude "end"? Is it when the last orange pylon is removed from the road, or when the litigation finally wraps up? The I-93 tunnel (O'Neill Tunnel) sprouted a leak in 2004 shortly after opening to traffic. In its design for the tunnel, contractor Bechtel/Parsons Brinckerhoff recommended an approach that had never been used for another highway tunnel in the US, rejecting the more conventional design of lining the huge slurry walls with a concrete "tunnel box" in favor of making the slurry walls the tunnel's *only* walls. When the tunnel construction later necessitated waterproofing, the lack of interior walls caused some major problems. While the leaky walls and the endless construction are causes of concern and ennui for the daily commuters, the faulty bolts that fasten the concrete ceiling tiles are another issue all together. In July 2006, a woman was killed by one such tile falling on her car in the I-90 connector on her way to Logan Airport, a tragic event that lead to comprehensive inspections within the tunnels and the discovery of dangerous structural flaws and evidence of negligence. After extensive closings and traffic rerouting, the tunnel ceiling tiles have all reportedly been reinforced, though, and we are told that travel is once again wet and safe, but the loss of human life has added an unfortunate and serious undertone to Big Dig's already infamous story.

Park Development

In December 2007, the Big Dig was officially completed, with the final price tag ringing up at $14.8 billion (not including interest which could raise the "real" cost to around $24 billion—ouch!), which Bostonians may end up paying for via toll and mass transportation rate hikes. Either way, someone has to pay the piper . . . er, digger. On a more positive note, the old elevated 93 was finally demolished, leading to a great deal more walking traffic from Faneuil Hall to the North End via the lovely Rose Kennedy Greenway, a 15-acre green space extending from Chinatown to the North End. Post-Dig park construction included pedestrian-friendly spots along the Fort Point Channel, in the Wharf District, and in the North End.

General Information

Mass Highway Department:	www.massdot.state.ma.us/highway/Main.aspx
Massport:	www.massport.com
Big Dig:	www.massdot.state.ma.us/highway/TheBigDig.aspx

Overview

The first bridge built in the American colonies (a pile bridge, incidentally) was completed in 1662, connecting Cambridge and Brighton. It stood where the Larz Anderson Bridge stands today. Fast-forward 350 years and you'll find no fewer than ten bridges spanning the Charles River from the Inner Harbor to Brighton, including the Boston University Bridge, the Harvard Bridge (a.k.a. the Mass Ave Bridge), and the Longfellow Bridge (with its salt-and-pepper-shaker towers), all of which offer great views of the skyline. (The view from the BU Bridge is our favorite.) Other bridges further upstream cross the river at River Street, Western Avenue, JFK Street/North Harvard Street (the Larz Anderson Bridge), and Gerry's Landing Road/Soldiers Field Road (the Eliot Bridge).

The Hub's new pet landmark is the Leonard P. Zakim Bunker Hill Memorial Bridge. No postcard of the Boston skyline seems complete without the Zakim, which connects downtown Boston with Charlestown. Perhaps the only Big Dig undertaking worth its salt, the Zakim is the widest cable-stayed bridge in the world, with soaring towers designed to reflect nearby Bunker Hill Monument. The bridge gives off a luminous glow at night, adding to its impressive appearance. According to the *Portsmouth Herald*, some call it the "Bill Buckner Bridge" as traffic passes through an inverted Y-shaped structure like the ball that passed through the legs of the Red Sox first baseman during the 1986 World Series. Poor Bill Buckner. Unlike the other bridges crossing the Charles, the Zakim is unfortunately not open to pedestrians. The Charlestown Bridge, now somewhat overshadowed by the Zakim, connects the North End and Charlestown and was once the scene of many Irish/Italian gang fights.

The old green lady crossing the Mystic River and connecting Charlestown with Chelsea is the Tobin Bridge. The three lanes on the lower level of the Tobin run northbound; the three lanes on the upper level run southbound. Drivers heading south on the Tobin must pay a toll (30 cents with a resident commuter permit and $3 for everyone else).

The Evelyn Moakley Bridge, built in the mid-1990s over the Fort Point Channel to divert traffic from the historic-but-decaying Northern Avenue Bridge, is itself decaying at an alarmingly fast pace. Be careful walking across the bridge at high tide.

And remember: The Callahan Tunnel takes you to the airport (no toll) and the Sumner Tunnel takes you from the airport (yes, toll).

Bridge	*Engineer (E); Architect (A)*	*Length*	*Opened*
Boston University Bridge	Desmond and Lord (A) John Rablin (E)		1928
Charlestown (N Washington St) Bridge			1901
Congress Street Bridge			1930
Eliot Bridge	Maurice Witner (A) Burns & Kennerson (E)		1950
Evelyn Moakley Bridge	Ammann & Whitney (A) Modern Continental (E)	800′	1996
Harvard Bridge	William Jackson (E)	364.4 smoots, one ear	1891
Larz Anderson Bridge	Wheelright, Haven, and Hoyt (A) John Rablin (E)		1915
Leverett Circle Connector Bridge	HNTB Corporation (E)	830′	1999
Longfellow Bridge	Edmund M. Wheelwright (A) William Jackson (E)	1,768′	1906
Malden (Alford St) Bridge		2420′	
Northern Avenue Bridge		636′	1908
River Street Bridge	Robert Bellows (A) John Rablin (E)	330′	1926
Summer Street Bridge	John Cheney (A) William Jackson (E)		1899
Tobin Memorial Bridge	JE Grenier Co (A)	1,525′	1950
Weeks Footbridge	McKim, Mead, and White (A) John Rablin (E)		1924
Western Avenue Bridge	John Rablin (E)	328′	1924
Leonard P. Zakim Bunker Hill Bridge	Christian Menn (designer) Miguel Rosales (A) HNTB Corporation (E)	1,457′	2002

Tunnel	*Engineer*	*Length*	*Opened*
Callahan Tunnel			1961
O'Neill Tunnel	Bechtel/Parsons Brinckerhoff (E)		2003
Sumner Tunnel			1934
Ted Williams Tunnel	Jacobs Engineering Group (designer) Bechtel/Parsons Brinckerhoff (E)	8,500′	1995

General Information

Websites:
Boston: with: www.cityofboston.gov/parking
Brookline: www.brooklinema.gov
Cambridge: www2.cambridgema.gov/traffic
Somerville: www.ci.somerville.ma.us
Mass. RMV: www.massrmv.com
Phones:
Boston: 617-635-4680
Brookline: 617-730-2177
Cambridge: 617-349-4700
Somerville: 617-666-3311

Overview

Boston drivers have somehow made order out of chaos. We offer very few signs, have roadways simultaneously labeled both North and South (causing you to believe you've found the nexus of the universe), and claim, with pride mind you, the most aggressive road-ragers in the entire Northeast. Driving in the city itself is done more by "feel" than by specific directions, as every trip becomes an adventure in side streets, wrong turns, and clusterf**ks. And don't even ask about the endless civil war between drivers, bikers, and pedestrians.

The road system (if you can call it that) in Boston grew organically as the city expanded, not, as legend has it, out of cow paths (though it's a reasonable misconception). Little, if any, urban planning took place. The result is the chaos of today: an exasperating, exhilarating tangle of streets that are a source of pride to those who master them. The only exception to this pandemonium is Back Bay, which was given the benefit of foresight in its planning when this former marshland was filled and developed in the 1850's. The result: a grid-like pattern and alphabetized street names. But where's the fun in that?

State legislation prohibits the majority of national auto insurance providers from doing business in Massachusetts, though it's easy to just assume that they'd be insane to insure Bostonian drivers in the first place. But as a rule, we are both aggressive and competent. We know precisely how far we can push the envelope on sudden lane changes and risky passing maneuvers.

The novice may find himself reduced to tears on the side of the road, but the initial challenge makes the eventual mastery that much more satisfying.

Learn the Vocabulary

The Boston Turnaround: the act of turning one's car a full 180 degrees in the middle of the street with no regard for oncoming traffic in either direction.

The Boston Creep: the act of executing a turn by slowly creeping one's car into the middle of an intersection, which eventually leads to a complete blockage of both lanes of oncoming traffic. This allows the driver to successfully negotiate the turn—or cause an accident.

Rotary: Known in other parts of the country as a roundabout or traffic circle. Usually, vehicles already in the rotary have right-of-way. But no one in Boston follows this rule. Watch out.

Square: A location at which several feeder streets connect in odd formations and strange angles (see Harvard or Davis). Squares are rarely, if ever, square.

Masshole: From the mouths of out-of-staters, a derogatory term. For a true Boston driver, a label worn with pride.

Registry of Motor Vehicles (RMV): Known in other parts of the country as the DMV. The main RMV is in Chinatown, but other, equally disgruntled branches exist in Watertown, Cambridge, and the suburbs. You will have to pay the RMV $100 to become an officially licensed Masshole if you're changing from out-of-state.

Survival Tips

Be aggressive: You're never gonna make it in this town without a thick skin. Seriously, we will run you off the road.

Pay it forward: If you want people to let you in, you have to let them in—once in a while.

Be wary of cabs and buses: They WILL cut you off if you don't gun it.

Be color blind: A yellow light (and the first ten seconds of a red light) are considered the functional equivalent of a green light. This goes both ways though, so be careful. But the faster you gun it, the less honks you'll hear.

Trust your instincts: If you think that unlabeled street is the one you want, it probably is. If you think that guy is going to cut you off, he probably will. Tailgate the lady in front of you as a preventative measure.

You will get lost: Resistance is futile. A GPS won't save you. Neither will Google Maps. Leave yourself some extra time. We promise, one day it will start making sense. Or you'll have a nervous breakdown and never drive again.

General Information

Websites:
Boston: www.cityofboston.gov/parking
Brookline: www.brooklinema.gov
Cambridge: www.cambridgema.gov/Traffic/index.cfm
Somerville: www.ci.somerville.ma.us

Phones:
Boston: 617-635-4680
Brookline: 617-730-2230
Cambridge: 617-349-4700
Somerville: 617-625-6600

Overview

When parking within the city, you'll need time, patience, and a sixth sense for parking spots that are *about* to open up. With a few notable exceptions (near Fenway during Sox games comes to mind), careful circling of a target area will eventually yield results. If patience fails, a willingness to pay the outrageous fees at a parking garage is also helpful. There are, however, bargains to be found; the rates at the Post Office Square garage are amazing considering its location and the Cambridgeside Galleria charges only $2 per hour.

Depending on where you live, and whether parking in Boston causes you to regularly lose your temper, you might want to reconsider even owning a car. To relinquish driving is to lower your blood pressure considerably. The North End and Allston are crowded neighborhoods with narrow streets jam-packed with parked cars. When it snows (and it will snow), Boston residents become fiercely protective of their parking spots, illegally using traffic cones, lawn chairs, and other assorted paraphernalia to claim their freshly shoveled out spaces. Fisticuffs over disputed parking spots are not unheard of. Somerville, Cambridge, and Brookline, however, aren't quite as bad for parking, in part due to vast "resident-only parking" zones, plus the fact that there is no overnight parking allowed in Brookline. Remember, if you own a car and live in the city, always lock your doors, tuck in your mirrors, and remove any valuables. The Club ain't a bad investment, either.

Ultimately, if you live in Boston and own a car, you will receive *at least* one ticket a month. Maybe there was street cleaning the night before. Maybe there was a parking ban because of snow. Or maybe you got towed because there's a construction project and you missed the half-hidden "Tow Zone" sign that workers positioned conveniently on the sidewalk under a discarded pizza box. It doesn't matter what you do and how careful you are—*they will get you*—so just add it to the monthly budget.

How to Get Permits

In Somerville, take a current bill or bank statement with your address and your registration to 133 Holland Street. In Boston, take your registration and a current bill with your address to City Hall, Room 224, at Government Center. All Brookline wants is $25 and, apparently, they don't care where you live. Brookline Town Hall is at 333 Washington Street. In the People's Republic of Cambridge, you need your registration saying that either you or your car (it's not clear which) weighs less than 2.5 tons and proof of residency (other than a lease). You can visit the website, download the form, and send copies of the above with a check for $25 to: Traffic, Parking & Transportation, City of Cambridge, 344 Broadway, Cambridge, MA 02139.

Towing

Cars get towed for snow emergencies, street cleaning, and other emergency violations, so keep an eye out for Nor'easters, third Thursdays, and massive construction. If your car gets towed, it'll cost you at least $100 to get it back.

The Boston BTD Tow Lot is located at 200 Frontage Road, near the Andrew T stop in Dorchester/Southie where you can hail a cab or hoof the .8 miles to the tow lot. Another option is to take the Red Line to the Broadway stop and then walk .8 miles to the lot.

Brookline, Somerville, and Cambridge use private, commercial lots to store your newly towed car. Call one of the numbers above, and they'll (hopefully) be able to tell you where your car is.

The Somerville tow lot is, for reasons unknown, Pat's Auto Body on McGrath Highway near Union Square.

Cambridge either has a top-secret tow lot, or it rotates. If your car gets towed, they ask you to call the police (617-349-3300), who will presumably then tell you where your car is.

Brookline has a similarly clandestine car imprisonment system. A call to their transportation/parking office should unearth your car.

Tickets

Because it allows them to take your money immediately, all four places offer online ticket payment. Tickets are dispensed for offenses such as double-parking, expired meters, non-resident parking on a resident-only street, street cleaning violations, and the city/town needing money. Regardless of the city, you're looking at about 50 bucks per infringement.

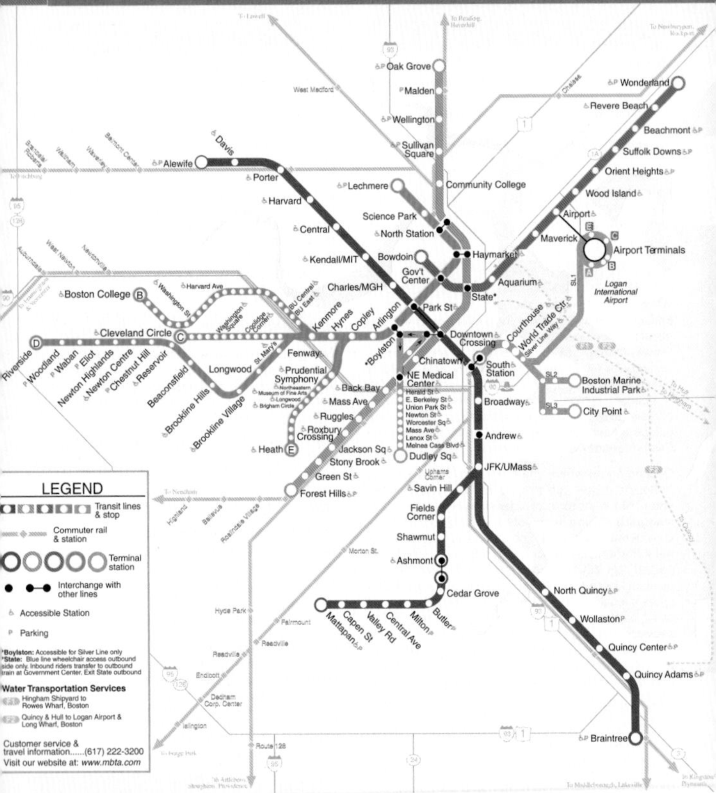

General Information

Website: www.mbta.com
Phone: 617-222-5000

Overview

Maps of the T show its four subway lines (Red, Orange, Blue, and Green) and the Silver Line (the T's mash-up of a subway line and a bus). All of the T lines except the Green Line's B train move you across the city at a decent clip. But if you need to get from Davis Square (Somerville) to Cleveland Circle (Brighton), well…it's not easy. Despite the proximity of the two places, you have to go downtown on one line (Red) and back out on another (Green)—an 11-mile trip connecting destinations that are 6.5 miles apart. Another T peeve is that the last trains depart from stations between midnight and 1 am, even though last call at Boston bars is between 1 and 2 am. (Some Redcoat traditions live on.) Late-night revelers are left to shell out for cabs.

The Red Line: The T's flagship line, the Red Line runs from Alewife in Cambridge through Davis Square, Harvard Square, MIT, the Esplanade (where you can admire the sparkling new Charles/MGH station,) the Common, Southie, and Dorchester. At the JFK/UMass stop, the line splits in two: The Ashmont train goes to Dorchester (with a connecting trolley to Mattapan), and the Braintree train runs through Quincy. A fun game to play on the Red Line: Bet with your friends about which student riders and professorial-looking types will get off at which university stops.

The Green Line: This is the oldest operational subway in the country, and it shows. Not a grown-up subway like the Red, Orange, and Blue Lines, the Green Line features light-rail "trolleys"—130-foot-long green Twinkies—that shoot you beneath the city of Boston before emerging onto streets and getting stuck in traffic.

The Green Line runs from Lechmere in Cambridge as far as Kenmore in Boston. Stops along the way include the Museum of Science, TD Garden, Faneuil Hall, the Common, Back Bay, and Fenway Park. At Kenmore, the B (Boston College), C (Cleveland Circle), and D (Riverside) trains diverge and emerge from the ground as trolleys. The E train parts ways two stops back at Copley. The B is the slowest train because god forbid the Boston University kids walk anywhere. Lots of stops + lots of red lights = long rides. The B takes you through BU, Allston, Brighton, and as far as Boston College. The C runs along Beacon Street through Coolidge Corner (in Brookline) to Cleveland Circle (in Brighton). When getting off the train at Cleveland Circle, note the trolley making a wide circular turn through four-way traffic, which, inexplicably, leads to a lot of accidents. The D runs through Fenway and Brookline Village to Chestnut Hill before hitting several Newton neighborhoods. The E (Heath Street) train splits before Kenmore at Copley and services Symphony Hall, Mission Hill, Northeastern University, the Museum of Fine Arts, and Longwood Medical Area. Don't believe the maps that tell you E trains terminate at Forest Hills. This service was "temporarily" suspended in 1986—meanwhile, the 39 bus will take you from Heath Street to Forest Hills.

Somerville residents have been patiently waiting for the arrival of a long-promised, but controversial, extension of the Green Line. This extension, which would take the Green Line from Lechmere through exhaust-clogged Union Square to West Medford, is now expected in 2016-2017—but that delayed date will most likely be pushed back.

The Orange Line: The Southwest Corridor Park and the Orange Line follow a path originally designed for the extension of I-95 through Boston. Community groups defeated the proposal in 1979, convincing officials to put a subway and park on the land instead. The Orange Line runs from Oak Grove in Malden to Forest Hills in Jamaica Plain. Stops along the way include Sullivan Square, Bunker Hill Community College, TD Garden, Faneuil Hall, Downtown Crossing, Chinatown, New England Medical Center, Back Bay/South End, as well as a few stops in Roxbury and Jamaica Plain.

The Blue Line: Who rides the Blue Line? MBTA ridership figures show a little over 55,000 daily boardings on the Blue Line, compared to 154,000 on the Orange, 210,500 on the Red, and about 205,000 on the Green. Running from Bowdoin Street downtown to Wonderland in Revere, this is the line you want to ride if you're going fishing, flying, or betting on horses. On your way east, you'll pass the Aquarium, Logan Airport, Suffolk Downs, and Revere Beach before winding up at Wonderland. The stations at Aquarium and Logan have been renovated and made more accessible; other stations on the Blue Line are due to get the same treatment over the next couple of years.

The Silver Line: Now the most convenient way to the airport, this is actually a high-speed bus line. Don't ask.

Parking

Your chances of finding parking increase as you move further away from downtown, but generally only end cap stations and suburban stations provide day parking. Garages and lots fill up quickly on weekdays. Prices vary. Parking in resident-only spots will result in a ticket and, in some areas, a keying.

Fares and Passes

In 2007, the MBTA replaced subway tokens with the magnetic-stripe CharlieCard and the paper CharlieTicket. (The "Charlie" moniker was taken from the Kingston Trio's 1959 hit, "Charlie on the MTA.") A subway ride costs $2 using the CharlieCard, and $2.50 with the paper CharlieTicket. The monthly subway/bus "Linkpass" costs $70, and reduced fares are available for seniors, people with disabilities, and junior-high and high school students. Children under 11 ride free when accompanied by an adult. Passes are sold at certain T stops and in some stores, however—the T has stated that it will no longer give away the rechargeable plastic CharlieCard, and will instead charge a fee for new and replacement cards. To find out where to buy a pass or to purchase one online, visit www.mbta.com.

MBTA Buses

Website: www.mbta.com
Phone: 617-222-3200

Every day, intrepid T bus drivers pilot their behemoth vehicles down too-narrow streets filled with angry drivers, errant pedestrians, unfortunate bikers, and, in the winter, ice and snow. (A simple "thank you" to the driver as you get off the bus isn't too much to ask.) MBTA buses run everywhere the subway doesn't, and some places it does. Usually at least one of any bus route's end points is a subway station. The T also runs several popular express buses from outlying neighborhoods to downtown along the Mass Pike and other highways.

The T is in the process of replacing the bulk of its aging diesel fleet with new Compressed Natural Gas (CNG) buses. Identifiable by their blue strip and the low roar of their engines, the new buses reduce emissions by up to 90 percent and, so far, are cleaner on the inside as well (just give them a few years). Some buses on busy routes feature low floors and articulated midsections, such as those used along the Silver Line and JP's 39 bus.

In 2005, the MBTA discontinued its popular but unprofitable Night Owl service (is a public service supposed to be profitable, anyway?). The Night Owl used to run buses along the subway routes until 2:30 am on Friday and Saturday nights, helping late-night partiers with a lift home. There is still no word from the MBTA on whether this service will ever reappear.

With a fare increase in June 2012, buses cost $2 if you use the paper Charlie Ticket or $1.50 if you use the plastic Charlie Card. The fares on the express buses are also different depending on if you use the ticket ($4.50 for inner express buses and $6.50 for outer express) or card ($3.50 for inner express and $5 for outer express). Monthly bus passes are $48 and subway/bus combos cost as little as $70 for a subway/local bus packages, while express bus combos are either $110 or $168. Students, seniors, and disabled persons can purchase monthly passes at reduced rates. Bus passes can be bought at several T stations or online at www.mbta.com. And you should be able to pick up a Charlie Card at customer service booths in T stations or buy a pre-loaded one at the T's website.

Silver Line

Website: www.mbta.com/schedules_and_maps/subway/lines/default.asp?route=SILVER
Phone: 617-222-3200

Although the Silver Line appears on the MBTA's subway map, it is actually a high-speed bus line (a "state-of-the-art Bus Rapid Transit system," no less) that, according to the MBTA, "combines the quality of rail transit with the flexibility of buses." The MBTA's public relations materials may be as gassy as the CNG used by some of the new buses, but in fact the new system provides much-needed additional public transport options for Roxbury residents, and is proving handy to airport travelers, Moakley Courthouse staff, and people working at construction sites along the waterfront. It's also a convenient way to get to the Bank of America Pavilion for concerts or to one of the many Seaport district restaurants, like the Legal Test Kitchen or Anthony's Pier Four, for dinner and drinks.

The Silver Line is being constructed in three phases. Completed Phase I runs between Downtown Crossing and Dudley Square in Roxbury. Phase II, also completed, runs from South Station to Logan Airport, Boston Marine Industrial Park, and City Point. (The MBTA is waffling on its original plan to extend the Silver Line to the Andrew T stop in South Boston/Dorchester.

Phase III is scheduled to be completed in 2016, but because there hasn't yet been a decision taken on how the buses will actually get into the tunnel, it's anyone's guess when Phase III will go on-line.

The Silver Line Waterfront fare follows the above fare structure for the subway (subway passes are valid) and the Silver Line Washington Street follows that of the bus (bus passes are valid), with Charlie Tickets and Cards in effect for both.

Cambridge EZRide

Website: www.charlesrivertma.org/program_ezride.htm
Phone: 617-839-4636

Cantabrigians who traverse the Charles each morning on their daily commute should check out the EZRide bus service, whose cheery sky-blue coaches run through Cambridge to North Station. The EZRide route begins in Cambridgeport and passes through University Park, Kendall Square, and East Cambridge, making a dozen or so stops along the way.

EZRide operates Monday through Friday only, and does not run on holidays. Service in the morning runs from approximately 6:15 am to 10:45 am; afternoon service runs from approximately 3:30 pm to 7:30 pm. A limited midday service is also available, from Kendall Square to Pacific Street, from about 11 am until 3 pm.

A trip on EZRide costs $2. Students, seniors, disabled persons, and children aged 5–11 traveling with an adult pay 50 cents. Flashing an MIT ID lets you ride for free.

Greyhound

Website: www.greyhound.com
Phone: 800-231-2222

Greyhound buses leave from the South Station bus terminal (map 4) and they'll take you *anywhere*. It ain't the Concorde, but it'll eventually get you to one of its 3,700 stations across North America. Round-trip tickets to New York usually cost $55–$65 round-trip to Washington DC is $132–$142, and Boston to Philadelphia is $92–$118 round-trip.

South Station is on Atlantic Avenue, one block down from Summer Street. The bus terminal is the taller building behind the rail building.

To get to South Station from the Mass Pike (I-90), take Exit 24A. This exit drops you onto Atlantic Avenue—the bus terminal is on the right side. From I-93 N, take Exit 20 and follow signs for Downtown and South Station. At the lights, continue straight onto Atlantic Avenue.

From I-93 S, take Exit 23 onto Purchase Street, make a left on Kneeland Street, continue to the end of the street, and then take a left onto Atlantic Avenue. On-street parking is scarce. If you're pinched, try the bus terminal's parking garage. The entrance is on Kneeland Street.

The Red Line T line has a stop at South Station, also the end point for the southern routes of the commuter rail. Walk through the train station and past the tracks to reach the bus station entrance.

Chinatown Buses

If you want to get to New York City for really cheap, take a Chinatown bus. A round-trip ticket will cost you around $30 on Boston Deluxe or on Sunshine Travel. The quality of Chinatown buses can be hit or miss, but the price is right. In 2013, two of the best known Chinatown bus companies, Fung Wah and Lucky Star, were forced to shut down due to safety issues. Sadly, their shutterings may be permanent.

If you take a late Chinatown bus from NYC, you will get into Boston after the T closes, meaning you'll have to pay for a cab that will cost more than the 200-plus-mile journey from New York.

Boston Deluxe
www.gotobus.com/bostondeluxe/; 617-354-2101
Christian Science Plaza, 175 Huntington Ave (Map 5)
Pick up the Boston Deluxe near the Prudential Center for trips to New York City and Hartford. New York-bound buses depart Friday through Sunday at 8:30 am, 11 am, 1 pm, 4:30 pm, 6 pm, and 10:30 pm and drop off at Broadway and 32nd Street as well as E 86th Street and Second Avenue. Buses to Hartford depart Friday to Sunday at 8:30 am, 11 am, 1 pm, 6 pm, and 10:30 pm and drop off at 365 Capitol Avenue (Charter Oak Supermarket). Both routes cost $30 round-trip.

Sunshine Travel
www.sunshineboston.com;
617-328-0862 or 617-695-1989
31 Harrison Ave, Boston (Map 4);
McDonald's Plaza, Fields Corner, Dorchester (Map 32)
Along with buses departing hourly for NYC ($15 each way, $25 for the 2 am bus), Sunshine Travel offers two-, three-, and four-day tours to places like Tennessee (four days, $178), Chicago (four days, $269), Washington DC (three days, $118), Niagara Falls (two days, $105), and destinations in eastern Canada ($128–$278). Buses to the Mohegan Sun casino in Connecticut depart five times daily, picking up in Dorchester, Boston, and Quincy. Round-trip tickets cost $10, and you'll receive a $20 gambling voucher and a $15 dining voucher if you're 21 years of age or older.

Bolt Bus

Website: www.boltbus.com/
Phone: 1-877-BOLTBUS

Bolt Bus provides service between Boston and New York City, and connecting service to Philadelphia, Baltimore, Cherry Hill, and Washington DC out of New York. Round-trip tickets to New York run about $30, although the earlier you book your trip, the more the price goes down (it can go as low as $1!). Each bus includes free wireless internet, three extra inches of legroom per seat, and power outlets throughout.

Megabus

Website: www.megabus.com/us/
Phone: 877-GO2-MEGA

Megabus provides service from Boston to Hartford and New York, and connecting service from New York to Albany, Atlantic City, Baltimore, Buffalo, Niagra Falls, Philadelphia, Rochester, Syracuse, Toronto, and Washington. As with Bolt Bus, the earlier you book, the less you're likely to pay. Round trip tickets to New York round out to about $36 (maximum). Many locations of Megabus stops are on public streets (usually either outside train stations or transportation hubs), college campuses, or at park-and-ride lots. All Megabus buses are equipped with free Wi-Fi.

Go Buses

Website: www.gobuses.com
Phone: 855-888-7160
Alewife Bus Station (Map 22),
Alewife Brook Parkway, Cambridge

Go Buses (formerly World Wide Bus) is another option for taking the bus to NYC by offering service out of Alewife Station in Cambridge—a far less crowded, busy option than South Station. Buses to New York (with a stop in Newtown on the way out of town) depart six times a day Monday-Thursday, eight times a day on Fridays and Sundays, and five times a day on Saturdays. Round-trip tickets cost around $30-$60, depending on the time of day. All Go Buses are equipped with free WiFi and power outlets in every seat.

Transit • MBTA Commuter Rail

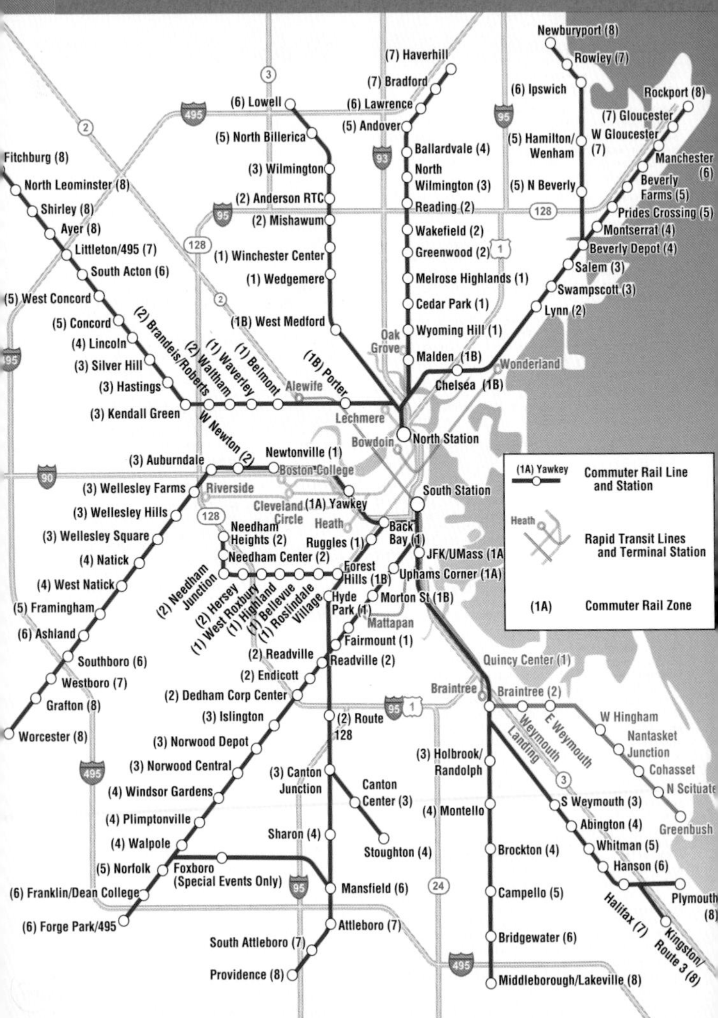

General Information

Website: www.mbta.com
Phone: 617-222-3200 or 800-392-6100

Overview

The commuter rail is a series of train lines that service the outer limits of Greater Boston, the suburbs, and points as far out as Worcester and Providence, Rhode Island. Northbound routes leave from North Station, and southbound routes depart from South Station. Compared to the commuter rail systems of other East Coast cities, Boston's trains make for a relatively pleasant experience. Massachusetts is working to renovate all of the stations, outfitting them with new platforms, electronic signaling, and new ramps and elevators to make them handicapped accessible. As with any major transit network, there are occasional (read: daily) delays on the commuter rail. Still, a ride on the rails is 1,000 percent less stressful than driving in and out of the city every day.

The commuter rail is also a great option for day-trippers going in either direction. Taking the train allows inbound visitors to enjoy, rather than just get lost in, the city. City-dwellers who want to escape the familiar urban landscape can head up to Gloucester for a day at the beach, venture to Plymouth for a history lesson, or just explore a new city down in Providence.

If you're looking at the commuter rail map for the first time, you might think that the lack of a connection between North Station and South Station is a mistake. Well, it may be a mistake, but not on the part of the mapmakers. To get from one station to another, you'll have to use the T (and transfer to a second T), take a cab, or walk. Seriously. For additional information about North Station and South Station, see the next page.

In the long term, Gov. Deval Patrick has pledged to bring commuter rail service back to the cities of New Bedford and Fall River by 2016.

Parking

Parking is available at every commuter rail station except Back Bay, Belmont Center, Chelsea, JFK/UMass, Morton Street, Porter Square, River Works, Ruggles, Silver Hill, Uphams Corner, Waverley, Windsor Gardens, and Yawkey. Rates vary, with some as low as $1 per day.

Fares and Passes

Commuter rail tickets range in price from $2 to $11. Each destination is assigned a zone number that determines the price of your ticket. Tickets can be purchased on the train, but depending on how busy the train is and the ticket-taker's mood, a surcharge may be added to the price. Kids 5–11, high school students, seniors, and disabled persons ride for half-price. Children under five and blind people ride free. The cost of monthly passes ranges from $70 to $345, depending on the zone. Some monthly passes offer varying perks like free subway, bus, and ferry use. Passes are sold at certain T stops and other locations (usually a local shop close to the station), as well as online at www.mbta.com. If you're buying your ticket at a T stop, be sure to look up your zone number ahead of time on the MBTA website. And make sure you're boarding a commuter rail train and not an Amtrak train. (This happens more often than you'd think.)

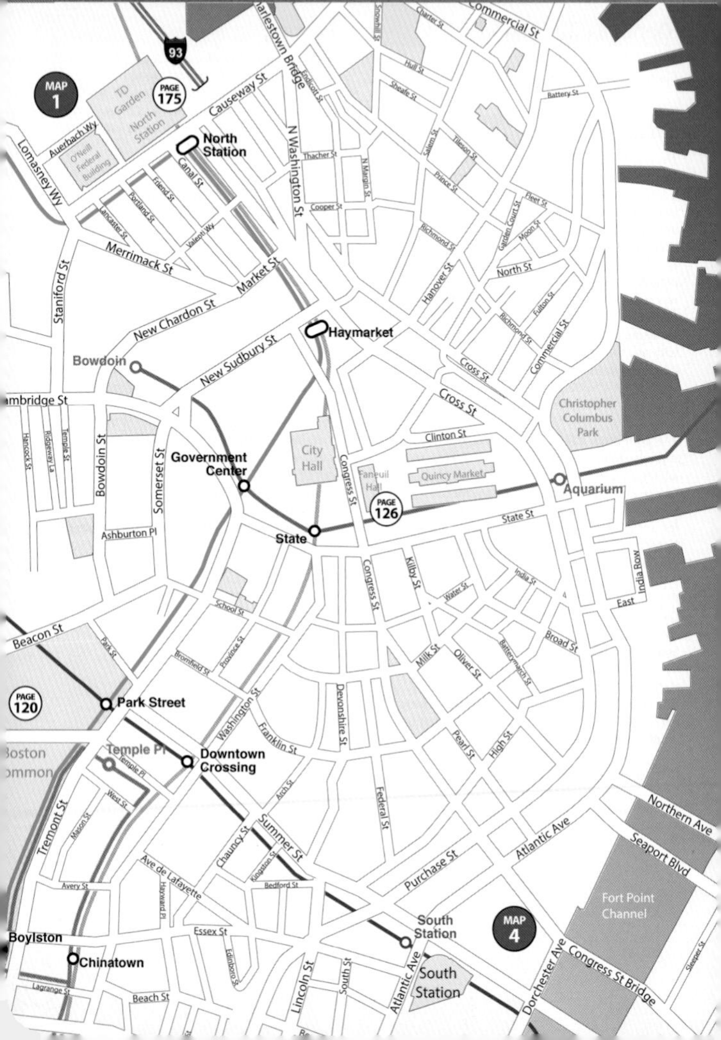

MAP 1
PAGE 175
TD Garden
North Station
O'Neill Federal Building
North Station
Haymarket
Bowdoin
Government Center
State
Aquarium
PAGE 126
City Hall
Faneuil Hall
Quincy Market
Christopher Columbus Park
Park Street
PAGE 120
Downtown Crossing
Boston Common
Boylston
Chinatown
South Station
MAP 4
Fort Point Channel
Commercial St
Charter St
Snowhill St
Hull St
Sheafe St
Battery St
Charlestown Bridge
Endicott St
Causeway St
Auerbach Wy
Lomasney Wy
Canal St
Friend St
Portland St
Lancaster St
Valenti Wy
Merrimack St
Market St
N Washington St
Thacher St
Cooper St
N Margin St
Salem St
Tileston St
Prince St
Fleet St
Garden Court St
Moon St
Richmond St
Hanover St
North St
Fulton St
Richmond St
Commercial St
Cross St
Cross St
Staniford St
New Chardon St
New Sudbury St
Cambridge St
Hancock St
Ridgeway La
Temple St
Bowdoin St
Somerset St
Clinton St
Congress St
State St
Ashburton Pl
Congress St
Kilby St
India St
Water St
India Row
East
School St
Beacon St
Park St
Bromfield St
Province St
Broad St
Milk St
Oliver St
Batterymarch St
Devonshire St
Washington St
Franklin St
Pearl St
High St
Temple Pl
Temple Pl
West St
Arch St
Federal St
Northern Ave
Seaport Blvd
Tremont St
Mason St
Summer St
Chauncy St
Kingston St
Atlantic Ave
Purchase St
Ave de Lafayette
Avery St
Hayward Pl
Bedford St
Essex St
Edinboro St
Lincoln St
South St
Atlantic Ave
Dorchester Ave
Congress St Bridge
Sleeper St
Lagrange St
Beach St

General Information

NFT Maps: 1 & 4
Websites: www.amtrak.com (Amtrak)
www.mbta.com (MBTA)
Amtrak: 800-872-7245 (800-USA-RAIL)
MBTA: 617-222-5215

Overview

North Station and South Station are the main Amtrak and MBTA Commuter Rail depots in Boston. North Station, near the North End and underneath TD Garden, sits above the T's new "superstation" that (finally) connects the Green Line and Orange Line. South Station, on Atlantic Avenue and Summer Street at the gateway to South Boston, is served by MBTA and Amtrak and also has a bus terminal, a food court in the domed arrival hall, a bar, a newsstand, and a bookstore.

Traveling between Stations

There is a one-mile gap between the two Amtrak stations. The North Station stop is on the Orange and Green Lines of the MBTA subway, and the South Station stop is on the Red Line. Yes, it *is* crazy that the stations aren't on the same line and don't directly connect to each other. No, they're *not* going to do anything to correct the problem in the near future. Yes, they *could* have rolled it into the Big Dig project, since they were digging under the city anyway. No, we *don't* know why they didn't. And yes, it *does* seem odd that they spent billions to improve automobile transportation while ignoring public transportation. As it stands, travelers going from New York to Maine have to get off the train at South Station and either take a cab, take two subway trains, or walk to get to North Station to continue their journey. Where's "Amtrak Joe" Biden when you need him?

How to Get There—Driving

Both stations are located off I-93 in downtown Boston. For North Station, take Exit 26 (Storrow Drive), and for South Station, take Exit 23 (Purchase Street/South Station). To get to South Station from the Mass Pike (I-90), take Exit 24B to Atlantic Avenue.

Parking

The MBTA says there's no parking at either station, but "street or private parking may exist." Helpful, huh? In fact, both North Station and South Station are served by nearby, expensive parking garages, and neither station offers much in the way of street parking. Lovely.

How to Get There—Mass Transit

North Station is on the T's Green and Orange Lines. South Station is on the Red Line.

Amtrak

Amtrak trains leave out of North Station and South Station going north to Portland, Maine and south to NYC and beyond. When you go north, they call it the Downeaster (that's Mainer for "near Canada"). When you go south, they call it a bunch of things, including "the Federal," "the Acela," and the mundanely titled "Regional." The Acela is Amtrak's flagship route, offering "high-speed" service from South Station to NYC, Philly, and DC, with stops along the way. On a good day, the Acela chugs from Boston to New York in 3.5 hours, which is still only slightly faster than a bus and, at $100 a ticket, costs much more than taking one of the Chinatown buses or Greyhound.

Baggage Check

Three items of baggage weighing up to 50 lbs each may be checked up to 30 minutes prior to train departure. For an additional fee of $10 per bag, three additional pieces can be checked. Each passenger is allowed two carry-on items on board. No dangerous, fragile, valuable items, animals, or household goods can be checked. Bikes, skis, and other odd-shaped equipment usually count as one checked bag and should not be carried aboard the train. With the exception of service animals, all pets are prohibited on Amtrak trains.

How to Get Tickets

To purchase train tickets, call Amtrak or visit their website. The website sometimes offers discounts for purchasing online, so it's worth checking the website before heading to the station.

Going to New York

One-way fares start at $62 and the journey takes about 4.5 hours from South Station. You could cut an hour off your commute by riding express on the Acela, but the comfort and convenience will cost ya ($100 or more).

Going to Philadelphia

One-way fares start at $60 and the ride takes about six hours. Fares on the speedier Acela Express start at $115 and cut about an hour off of the journey.

Going to Washington DC

A trip to Washington on the regular Amtrak train will cost you at least $65 and will take you between eight and nine hours. Acela Express tickets start at $124 and the trip takes between six and seven hours.

CHARLESTOWN
MAP 8
46
Navy Yard
45
43
F4
22
Charles River
EAST BOSTON
Commercial Wharf
19
MAP 9
18
MAP 1
16
East Boston Piers
Long Wharf
Boston Marina
BOSTON
15
68
Aquarium
Logan International Airport
14
1
Boston Inner Harbor
Rowes Wharf
F2/F2H
Logan Airport
PAGE 176
Courthouse
MAP 2
7
9
8
F1
Fort Point Channel
World Trade Center
5
4
MAP 10
F1
Fleet Boston Pavilion (summer only)
F2/F2H
2
Reserved Channel
Boston Harbor
SOUTH BOSTON
MAP 11
Pleasure Bay
Black Falcon Terminal
F2H only
Pemberton Point (limited service)
HU
Dorchester Bay
F2/F2H
F1
Commuter Boats
Limited Service
Inner Harbor Ferries
Ferry Station
Rowes Wharf Water Taxi
City Water Taxi
Fore River Shipyard
QUINCY
Hingham Shipyard
HINGHAM

General Information (Ferries)

MBTA: www.mbta.com/schedules_and_maps/boats/; 617-222-5215
Boston Harbor Cruises: www.bostonharborcruises.com/commuter-boat-services; 877-733-9425

Overview

The MBTA Commuter and Excursion Boat Service connects Boston to Logan Airport and is one of the best routes in and out of Charlestown and other shore side communities. One thing that makes the T boat better than any other form of Boston transportation is the fun factor. On a nice day, paying three bucks for a quick jaunt across the harbor feels like a steal. And on any day, not having to deal with Boston traffic is priceless. The views of the city from the water are gorgeous, and since the routes are in the Inner Harbor, the ride remains relatively smooth even in bad weather. There is also that delicious old-time feeling that comes with ferrying across the harbor. You'll want to keep in mind that boat schedules are more limited than bus schedules (particularly on weekends) and are more susceptible to disruptions due to inclement weather.

Most ferries operated by the MBTA leave from Long Wharf and travel to the Charlestown Navy Yard (F4), the Fore River Shipyard in Quincy (F2), and Pemberton Point in Hull (F2H). The F1 boat travels between Rowes Wharf and Hingham Shipyard.

The F2 and the F2H boats, catamarans operated by Boston Harbor Cruises, stop at Logan Airport, but not at all times of the day—check the MBTA website for timetables. During rush hour (and decent weather) the Boston Harbor Cruises is a sensible choice for getting to the airport. It takes a mere seven minutes to get to the airport dock from Long Wharf and about 25 minutes from Quincy and Hull. From the airport dock, take the free Water Shuttle bus 66 to the terminals. The 66 bus takes about 15 minutes to visit all terminals and return to the dock.

All ferry stops are accessible to wheelchair users. Bicycles can also be taken on board for free.

Parking

Parking for commuter ferry stops in the Inner Harbor is available only on the street or in a garage. Parking in Quincy costs $1 for a day and $6 overnight. In Hingham, parking costs $1 for a day and $1.75 overnight. Free parking is available at Hull High School.

Fares

A trip on a boat between destinations in the Inner Harbor costs $3 (pay a crewmember when boarding the boat). Trips from Hull, Quincy, and Hingham to the Inner Harbor (Rowes Wharf or Long Wharf) cost $8 ($4 for kids, seniors, and disabled persons). Trips from Quincy and Hull to Logan Airport on the Boston Harbor Cruises are $13 ($7.50 for seniors, students, and kids 5–11). Pay a crewmember when boarding the boat.

General Information (Water Taxis)

City Water Taxi: www.citywatertaxi.com; 617-422-0392
Rowes Wharf Water Taxi: www.roweswharfwatertransport.com/RWWT_2010/HOME.html; 617-406-8584
Massport: www.massport.com/logan-airport/Pages/WaterTransport.aspx; 800-23-LOGAN

Overview

On the charmed waters of the Inner Harbor, two water taxi companies ply their trade. During the warmer months, water taxis provide an enjoyable way to cross the Inner Harbor. Both water taxi companies stop at the Logan Airport dock.

City Water Taxi

City Water Taxi offers direct service to the entire Boston waterfront, year-round, with enclosed boats that are heated when the weather is bad. (Mon–Sat 7 am–10 pm; Sun 7 am–8 pm). In addition to the airport dock, City Water Taxi serves 16 other points, including Bank of America Pavilion, Fan Pier, Charlestown Navy Yard, Black Falcon Terminal, and all the major wharves in the Inner Harbor. (To get to the Boston Convention and Exhibition Center, aim for the World Trade Center.) To catch a City Water Taxi from the airport, take Massport's 66 bus to the airport dock. Use the call box at the dock to call for a boat if there isn't one already there. From other destinations, call City Water Taxi to arrange a pick-up.

Tickets are sold on board the boat. Fares to downtown points and Logan Airport cost $10 one-way and $17 round-trip. There is a $20 minimum to Charlestown, North Station, and Black Falcon Terminal, but if you have a traveling companion, the fare is $15 each.

Rowes Wharf Water Taxi

Also operating year-round, Rowes Wharf Water Taxi provides on-call service to 31 points in the Inner Harbor (from Nov 2–April 1, service runs 7 am–7 pm; from April 2–Nov 1, service runs from 7 am–10 pm Mon–Sat and 7 am–8 pm on Sun). After-hours service is available upon request. Rowes Wharf Water Taxi serves 17 different docks and now operates a Seaport Express providing weekday service between Rowes Wharf, Central Wharf, and the Seaport World Trade Center for $1.70. For the complete schedule, look online. To hail a boat from the airport dock, use the company's call box; from other destinations, give them a call from your own phone.

Tickets are sold on board. The fare costs $10 one way and $17 round-trip.

Car Rental

Map 1 • Beacon Hill / West End

Avis	3 Center Plz	617-534-1400

Map 2 • North End / Faneuil Hall

Enterprise	1 Congress St	617-723-8077

Map 3 • Downtown Crossing / Park Square / Bay Village

Hertz	30 Park Plz	617-338-1500

Map 4 • Financial District / Chinatown

Alamo	270 Atlantic Ave	617-557-7179
Hertz	Summer St & Atlantic Ave	617-338-1503
National	270 Atlantic Ave	617-557-7179

Map 5 • Back Bay (West) / Fenway (East)

Enterprise	800 Boylston St	617-262-8222
Hertz	39 Dalton St	617-338-1506

Map 6 • Back Bay (East) / South End (Upper)

Avis	100 Clarendon St	617-534-1404
Dollar	110 Huntington Ave	617-578-0025
Hertz	10 Huntington Ave	617-338-1506

Map 9 • East Boston

Affordable	84 Condor St	617-561-7000
Alamo	6 Tomahawk Dr	617-561-4100
Avis	202 Porter St	617-561-3500
Budget	20 Tomahawk Dr	617-497-3733
Enterprise	2 Tomahawk Dr	617-561-4488

Map 12 • Newmarket / Andrew Square

Enterprise	230 Dorchester Ave	617-268-1411

Map 13 • Roxbury

Enterprise	17 Melnea Cass Blvd	617-442-7500

Map 18 • Brighton

Hertz	1686 Commonwealth Ave	617-232-1892

Map 19 • Allston (South) / Brookline (North)

Adventure Vehicle	27 Harvard Ave	617-783-3000
Budget	95 Brighton Ave	617-497-3608
Enterprise	292 Western Ave	617-783-2240
Enterprise	996 Commonwealth Ave	617-738-6003
Hertz	414 Cambridge St	617-787-2894
U-Save Auto	25 Harvard Ave	617-629-3091

Map 20 • Harvard Square / Allston (North)

Avis	1 Bennett St	617-534-1430
Hertz	24 Eliot St	617-338-1520
Thrifty	110 Mt Auburn St	617-876-2758

Map 23 • Central Somerville / Porter Square

Hertz	646 Somerville Av	617-625-7958

Map 24 • Winter Hill / Union Square

Americar	190 Highland Ave	617-776-4640l

Map 25 • East Somerville / Sullivan Square

Enterprise	37 Mystic Ave	617-625-1766

Map 27 • Central Square / Cambridgeport

Budget	20 Sidney St	617-577-7606
Enterprise	25 River St	617-547-7400

Map 28 • Inman Square

Adventure Vehicle	72 Prospect St	617-623-6408
U-Save Auto	70 Prospect St	617-625-6704

Map 30 • Roslindale

Enterprise	4009 Washington St	617-327-6688

Zipcar General Information

Website: www.zipcar.com
Phone: 617-933-5070

Background

Zipcar rents out cars by the hour. The company, which now runs similar services in DC, New Jersey, New York, and elsewhere, was founded at MIT: "People would achieve transportation nirvana by having a transit pass and a Zipcard in their pockets. The result would be reduced congestion, fewer auto emissions, more green space, and a revolution in urban planning." That's Cantabrigians for "Give us $9/hr, we'll give you a Jetta." This seems like the smartest idea on wheels if you live in congested areas like the North End, Allston, or Harvard Square and you need to get somewhere the T can't take you. For infrequent drivers, the $25 application fee and minimum annual fee of $60 still make Zipcar service cheaper than owning a car.

How It Works

If you're 21 or older, in possession of a valid driver's license, and you've completed the online application, all you need to do is call or go online to reserve one of the hundreds of cars available at zipcar.com. (You get to choose from a fleet of BMWs, Minis, pick-ups, and others.) Your Zipcard unlocks the car that has been reserved for you, which you pick up at the most convenient of their many locations. Cars must be returned to the same spot where they were picked up. The car unlocks when a valid Zipcard is held to the windshield; your card will only open the car during the time you have reserved it.

Costs

The cost of Zipcar varies depending on the pick-up location, but rates start at $8.25 an hour. A reservation for 24 hours, the maximum amount of time that a car can be reserved, starts at about $84. The first 180 miles are free; each additional mile costs about 45 cents. Membership costs are additional. Make sure to return your car on time, as Zipcar charges exorbitant hourly late fees on unreturned cars. The best part: gas and insurance are included with every reservation.

If you've just moved to Boston and need a crash course on the "sights," you must check out the **Freedom Trail** (see page 189). Yes, it's touristy, but it's the best self-guided tour of Revolution-era Boston and gives you the skinny on aspects of Boston colonial history that every resident should know. To gain a better appreciation of just where it is you live, hit the top of the **Prudential Tower (Map 5)** for a bird's eye view, which will show you that Boston has a lot more hills and water than you might have suspected. For a more human perspective, get familiar with the Charles River with a stroll along the **Esplanade (Map 6)**, or, for a walk with an impressive view of Beacon Hill and Back Bay, cross the **Harvard Bridge (Map 26)** and take a stroll along Memorial Drive in Cambridge. For a nice rest, grab a snack in Harvard Square, and find a tree in **Harvard Yard (Map 20)** under which to chill.

If winter keeps you from strolls outside, there's plenty to see indoors. The **Museum of Fine Arts (Map 15)** (see page 326) is world-class. Across the street, the **Isabella Stewart Gardner Museum (Map 15)** has a first-rate collection, and the setting (inspired by a 15th-century Venetian palace) is stunning. The ornate interior of **Trinity Church (Map 6)** and the Sargent Murals of the **Boston Public Library (Map 6)** (see page 185) are also impressive. Boston's best concert halls are in the neighborhood, so why not catch a show at internationally acclaimed **Boston Symphony Hall (Map 5)** or one of the many free shows at the New England Conservatory's **Jordan Hall (Map 5)**. For rock music, comedy and high-quality musical theater head to the Wilbur and Wang theaters in the Theater District near the Boylston Green Line T stop. The Orpheum, near the Park Street T station, is home to national and international acts in a seated, classic concert hall setting. You'll also not want to overlook the many museums of Harvard, notably the **Fogg Art Museum (Map 20)** (focusing on Western art) and the **Natural History Museum (Map 20)** (with its brilliant glass flowers).

If you've already checked out Boston's big hits, there are plenty of quirky spots to fill your time. See the skull of Phineas Gage, the 19th century medical oddity who survived a thirteen-pound rod of steel shot through his brain at the **Warren Anatomical Museum (Map 15)**. **The Boston Athenaeum (Map 1)** has a true crime account bound with the skin of it's author. If that's not to your sense of everlasting life, you could sip coffee in the North End and wander over to see if Peter Baldassari is home and his folksy **All Saints Way (Map 2)** is open. Roxbury has the only scale Nubian tomb at the **Museum of the National Center for Afro-American Artists (Map 13)**. The Mapparium at the **Christian Science Center(Map 5)** highlights the ambitions of Mary Baker Eddy and her clean-living movement. Those with a more criminal bent can find mobster haunts like "Whitey" Bulger's old Southie **liquor store (Map 10)** or the garage of the **Brink's Job (Map 2)** in the North End.

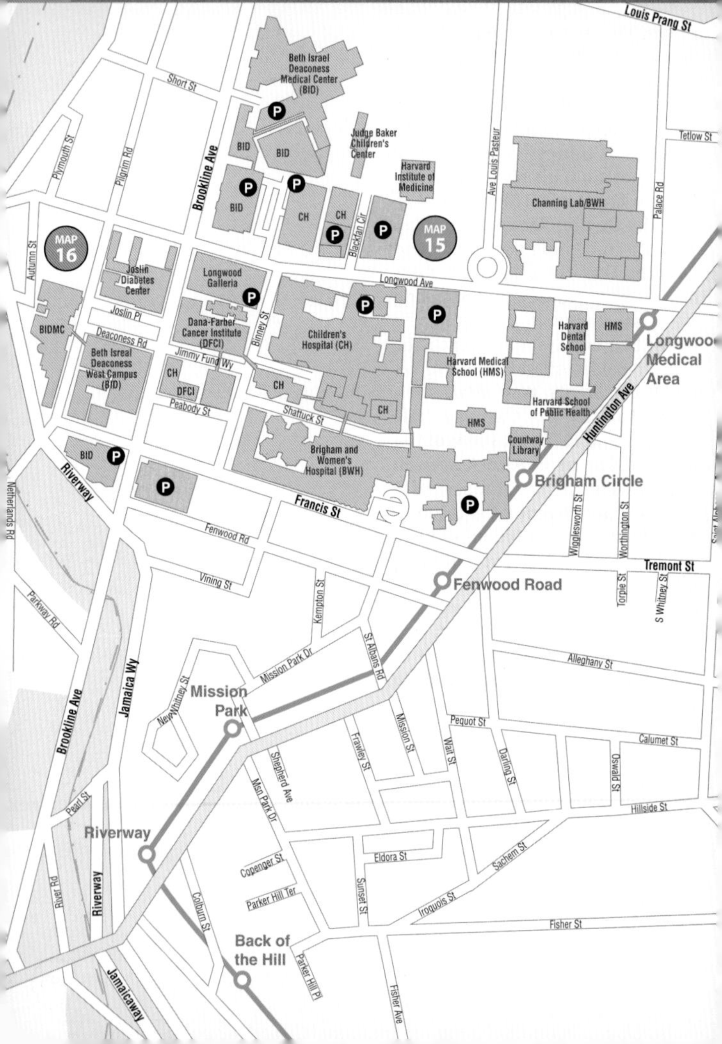

Louis Prang St
Beth Israel Deaconess Medical Center (BID)
Short St
P
Judge Baker Children's Center
BID
BID
Tetlow St
Plymouth St
Pilgrim Rd
Brookline Ave
Harvard Institute of Medicine
Ave Louis Pasteur
P
P
Channing Lab/BWH
BID
Palace Rd
CH
CH
Blackfan Cir
P
P
MAP 15
MAP 16
Autumn St
Joslin Diabetes Center
Longwood Galleria
Longwood Ave
P
P
P
Joslin Pl
BIDMC
Binney St
Harvard Dental School
HMS
Dana-Farber Cancer Institute (DFCI)
Children's Hospital (CH)
Longwood Medical Area
Deaconess Rd
Beth Isreal Deaconess West Campus (BID)
Jimmy Fund Wy
Harvard Medical School (HMS)
CH
DFCI
CH
Peabody St
Harvard School of Public Health
CH
Shattuck St
HMS
Huntington Ave
Countway Library
BID
P
Brigham and Women's Hospital (BWH)
Brigham Circle
Riverway
P
Francis St
P
Netherlands Rd
Wigglesworth St
Worthington St
Fenwood Rd
Tremont St
Vining St
Fenwood Road
Torpie St
S Whitney St
Parkway Rd
Kempton St
Alleghany St
St Albans Rd
Mission Park Dr
Jamaica Wy
New Whitney St
Mission Park
Brookline Ave
Pequot St
Mission St
Frawley St
Wait St
Darling St
Calumet St
Shepherd Ave
Oswald St
Msn Park Dr
Pearl St
Hillside St
Riverway
Eldora St
Sachem St
Copenger St
River Rd
Riverway
Colburn St
Parker Hill Ter
Sunset St
Iroquois St
Fisher St
Back of the Hill
Parker Hill Pl
Jamaicaway
Fisher Ave

Hospitals

Boston's medical facilities rank among the best in the world. Many medical firsts happened in Boston, including the:

- First public demonstration of anesthesia during surgery, at Massachusetts General Hospital (1846).
- First identification and analysis of appendicitis, at Massachusetts General Hospital (1886).
- First surgical procedure to correct a congenital cardiovascular defect, performed by Dr. Robert Gross (1938).
- First successful fertilization of a human ovum in a test tube, by researchers at Peter Bent Brigham Hospital (1944).
- First successful pediatric remission of acute leukemia, achieved by Dr. Sidney Farber (1947).
- First isolation of the polio virus, at Children's Hospital (1948).
- First successful kidney transplant, at Peter Bent Brigham Hospital (1954).
- First demonstration of the effectiveness of an oral contraceptive, by Dr. John C. Rock (1959).

The Longwood Medical Area (see map on the facing page) compresses a dozen medical institutions into a handful of blocks below Mission Hill. These institutions, including **Brigham and Women's Hospital (Map 15)**, **Beth Israel Deaconess Medical Center (Map 16)**, **Children's Hospital (Map 15)**, **Dana-Farber Cancer Institute (Map 15)**, **Joslin Diabetes Center (Map 16)**, the **CBR Institute for Biomedical Research (Map 16)**, and Harvard's medical, dental, and public health schools, comprise what is probably the world's leading center for health care and medicine.

Massachusetts General Hospital (Map 1), which opened in 1811, is the oldest and largest hospital in New England. Each year MGH admits over 45,000 in-patients, processes over 76,000 emergency visits, and, at its West End main campus and four satellite facilities, handles more than 1.5 million outpatient visits.

Mount Auburn Hospital (Map 21) is a Harvard Medical School teaching hospital and the most prominent hospital in Cambridge.

Emergency Rooms	*Address*	*Phone*	*Map*
Massachusetts Eye and Ear Infirmary	243 Charles St	617-523-7900	1
Massachusetts General Hospital	55 Fruit St	617-726-2000	1
Tufts Medical Center	750 Washington St	617-636-5000	3
Boston Medical Center	1 Boston Medical Ctr Pl	617-638-8000	7
Brigham and Women's Hospital	75 Francis St	617-732-5500	15
Children's Hospital	300 Longwood Ave	617-355-6000	15
Beth Israel Deaconess Medical Center	330 Brookline Ave	617-667-7000	16
St Elizabeth's Medical Center	736 Cambridge St	617-789-3000	18
Mount Auburn	330 Mt Auburn St	617-492-3500	21
CHA Somerville Hospital	230 Highland Ave	617-591-4500	23
The Cambridge Hospital	1493 Cambridge St	617-665-1000	28

Other Hospitals	*Address*	*Phone*	*Map*
Boston Shriners Hospital	51 Blossom St	617-722-3000	1
Spaulding Rehabilitation Hospital	125 Nashua St	617-573-7000	1
Jewish Memorial Hospital & Rehabilitation Center	59 Townsend St	617-989-8315	13
Arbour Hospital	49 Robinwood Ave	617-522-4400	14
Dana-Farber Cancer Institute	44 Binney St	617-632-3000	15
Immune Disease Institue	220 Longwood Ave	617-734-9500	15
New England Baptist Hospital	125 Parker Hill Ave	617-754-5800	15
VA Boston-Jamaica Plain Campus	150 S Huntington Ave	617-232-9500	15
Joslin Diabetes Center	1 Joslin Pl	617-732-2400	16
Franciscan Hospital for Children	30 Warren St	617-254-3800	18
St Elizabeth's Medical Center	736 Cambridge St	617-789-3000	18
The Boston Center	14 Fordham Rd	617-783-9676	19
Youville Hospital & Rehabilitation Center	1575 Cambridge St	617-876-4344	28

Post Offices & Zip Codes

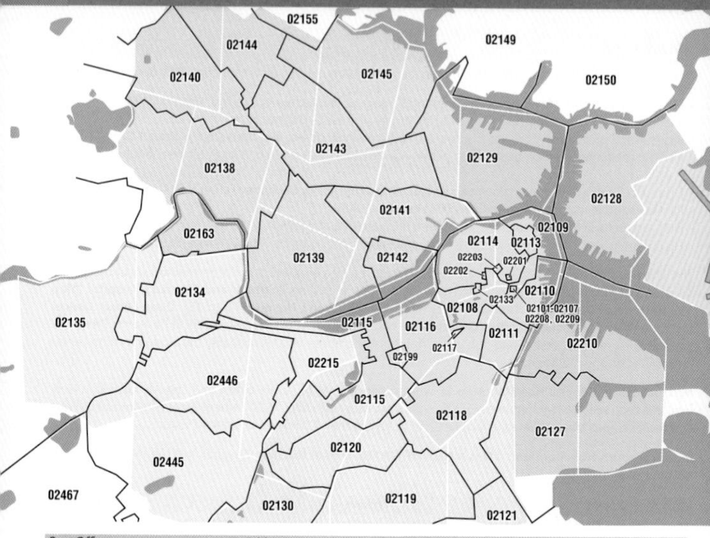

Post Offices	Address	Phone	Zip Code	Map
Charles Street	136 Charles St	617-723-7434	02114	1
John F Kennedy	25 New Chardon St	617-523-6566	02114	1
State House	24 Beacon St	617-742-0012	02133	1
Hanover Street	217 Hanover St	617-723-6397	02113	2
Lafayette	7 Ave de Lafayette	617-423-7822	02111	4
Milk Street	31 Milk St	617-482-1956	02109	4
Astor	207 Massachusetts Ave	617-247-2429	02115	5
Prudential Center	800 Boylston St	617-267-4164	02199	5
Back Bay	133 Clarendon St	617-587-5260	02117	6
Cathedral	59 W Dedham St	617-266-0989	02118	7
Charlestown	23 Austin St	617-241-5322	02129	8
East Boston	50 Meridian St	617-561-3900	02128	9
South Boston	444 E 3rd St	617-269-9948	02127	10
Roxbury	55 Roxbury St	617-427-4898	02119	13
Jamaica Plain	655 Centre St	617-524-3620	02130	14
Mission Hill	1575 Tremont St	617-566-2040	02120	15
Kenmore	11 Deerfield St	617-437-1113	02215	16
Brookline	1295 Beacon St	617-738-1649	02446	17
Brookline Village	207 Washington St	617-566-1557	02445	17
Brighton	424 Washington St	617-254-5026	02135	18
Allston	47 Harvard Ave	617-789-3769	02134	19
Soldiers Field	117 Western Ave	617-354-0131	02163	19
Harvard Square	125 Mt Auburn St	617-876-3883	02138	20
West Somerville	58 Day St	617-666-2255	02144	22
Porter Square	1953 Massachusetts Ave	617-876-5599	02140	23
Somerville	237 Washington St	617-666-2332	02143	24
Winter Hill	320 Broadway	617-666-5225	02145	24
East Cambridge	303 Cambridge St	617-876-8558	02141	26
Kendall Square	250 Main St	617-876-5155	02142	26
MIT	84 Massachusetts Ave	617-494-5511	02139	26
Cambridge	770 Massachusetts Ave	617-575-8700	02139	27
Inman Square	1311 Cambridge St	617-864-4344	02139	28
Uphams Corner	551 Columbia Rd	617-287-9626	02125	32

General Information

All Emergencies: 911
Crime Stoppers: 800-494-TIPS
Boston Area Rape Crisis Center (BARCC): 617-492-RAPE
State Police: 617-727-7775
Boston: www.ci.boston.ma.us/police
Brookline: www.brooklinepolice.com
Cambridge: www.ci.cambridge.ma.us/~CPD/
Somerville: www.ci.somerville.ma.us

Police Stations	*Address*	*Phone*	*Map*
District A-1	40 New Sudbury St	617-343-4240	1
District D-4	650 Harrison Ave	617-343-4250	7
District A-7	69 Paris St	617-343-4220	9
District C-6	101 W Broadway	617-343-4730	10
District B-2	135 Dudley St	617-343-4270	13
District E-13	3345 Washington St	617-343-5630	14
Brookline Police Department	350 Washington St	617-730-2222	17
District D-14	301 Washington St	617-343-4260	18
Somerville Police Department	220 Washington St	617-625-1600	24
Cambridge Police Department	125 6th St	617-349-3300	26

Though Boston is chiefly known for its college-town feel, there is plenty for the younger set to enjoy. You're bound to find something to hold the attention of your little ones among the many, MANY museums and parks.

The Best of the Best

- **Best Kid-Friendly Restaurant:** Full Moon (344 Huron Ave, Cambridge, 617-354-6699). Full Moon is the brainchild of two restaurateurs who also happen to be moms. The result is a restaurant that features a sophisticated menu with an extensive wine list for adults and a tasty assortment of kids' tried-and-true favorites. With sippy cups, toy buckets at every table, and a play area stocked with pretty much every toy imaginable, Full Moon gives you "grown-up dining with a kid-friendly twist."
- **Quaintest Activity:** Swan Boats in the Public Garden (Public Garden, Boston, 617-522-1966). Owned and operated by the same family for over 120 years, the swan boats have directly inspired two children's classics: Robert McCloskey's *Make Way for Ducklings* and E.B. White's *The Trumpet of the Swan*. The people-paddled boats can hold up to 20 passengers during the 15-minute cruise around the lagoon and under the world's smallest suspension bridge. An inexpensive and adorable treat for all. Open April–Sept.
- **Funnest Park:** Rafferty Park (799 Concord Ave, Cambridge). One of the area's best-hidden playgrounds, this wooded park provides tons of fun stuff for older children, including a new metal climbing structure with a twisty slide, wobbly bridge, boat-shaped sand box, and a mini schoolhouse with a chalkboard roof. Basketball hoops, tennis courts, and a baseball field reside next door.
- **Best Rainy Day Activity:** Children's Museum (300 Congress St, Boston, 617-426-8855). This world-renowned museum—reopened in spring 2007 after a pricey and well-received renovation and expansion—has designed early learning experiences for kids of all ages with its inventive hands-on exhibits. Permanent exhibits include the Japanese House, where children experience the culture of Kyoto, Japan through a replica of a silk merchant's house, as well as a Hall of Toys, in which children can look at toys of the past, but not touch.
- **(The World's Only) Curious George Store :** Re-opened in April 2012 at the same iconic, fork-in-the-road spot at 1 JFK Street. Only Curious George store still has plenty of children's and young adult books, exclusive apparel and, yes, toys.
- **Cutest Event:** The Annual Ducklings Day Parade (Boston Common). Held every year on Mother's Day, the parade commemorates Robert McCloskey's children's book *Make Way for Ducklings* set on Boston Common. Children come dressed as their favorite duckling character and ready to parade.
- **Neatest Store:** Irving's Toy and Card Shop (371 Harvard St, Brookline, 617-566-9327). Since 1939, Irving's has been a favorite neighborhood source for ice cream, candy, and little nostalgic toys galore. This small store is packed with everything you never knew you needed from kazoos, to jacks, to tiny plastic farm animals.

Shopping Essentials

- **Nine Months Maternity and Infant Wear** (mom & baby clothes) 272 Newbury St, Boston, 617-236-5523
- **Barefoot Books Store** (kids' books) 1771 Massachusetts Ave, Cambridge, 617-349-1610
- **Black Ink** (stamps):
  101 Charles St, Boston, 617-723-3883
  5 Brattle St, Cambridge, 617-497-1221
- **Boing!** (toys) 729 Centre St, Jamaica Plain, 617-522-7800
- **Calliope** (toys & kids' clothes) 33 Brattle St, Cambridge, 617-876-4149
- **The Children's Book Shop** (kids' books) 237 Washington St, Brookline, 617-734-7323
- **Co-op for Kids at the Harvard Co-op** (kids' books) 1400 Massachusetts Ave, Harvard Square, Cambridge, 617-499-2000
- **Discovery Channel Store** (educational gifts) 40 South Market Building, Faneuil Hall, 617-227-5005
- **Eureka! Puzzles and Games** (endless supply of brain-teasers and boardgames)1349 Beacon Street, Coolidge Corner, 617-738-7352
- **Henry Bear's Park** (kids' books & toys) 361 Huron Ave, Cambridge, 617-547-8424
- **KB Toys** (toys) 100 Cambridgeside Pl, Cambridgeside Galleria, Cambridge, 617-494-8519
- **Oilily** (up-scale kids' clothes) 32 Newbury St, Boston, 617-247-9299
- **PriKidz** (tween girls' clothes and accessories) 1378 Beacon Street Suite B, Coolidge Corner, 617-682-0998
- **The Red Wagon** (kids' toys & clothes) 69 Charles St, Boston, 617-523-9402
- **Stellabella Toys** (toys)
  1360 Cambridge St, Inman Square, Cambridge, 617-491-6290
  1967 Massachusetts Ave, Porter Square, Cambridge, 617-864-6290
- **Under Henry Bear's Park**
  (additional location) 19 Harvard Street, Brookline, 617-264-2422

Parks for Playing

Kids need fresh air. And singing into the rotating fan doesn't count. Take them out for a swing. In addition to the roomy Boston Common and Cambridge Common, Boston boasts many smaller neighborhood parks:

- **Alden Playground** (Oxford St and Sacramento St, Cambridge). A great neighborhood playground located in the shadow of Baldwin School and Lesley University, this toddler and big-kid-friendly park includes a mini-track, jaw-dropping climbing equipment, and what may be the World's Coolest Slide.
- **Charlesbank/Esplanade Playground** (Charles St at Longfellow Bridge). This large play area features several climbing structures, slides, and swings for all ages with a nearby snack bar, open during the summer months.
- **Christopher Columbus Park** (Atlantic Ave & Commercial Wharf, Boston). One large climbing structure dominates this playground that is mostly geared towards the six-and-under set.
- **Clarendon Street Playground** (Clarendon St & Commonwealth Ave, Boston). This fenced and gated area provides ample scope for the imagination of children of all ages. The park features several climbing structures, slides, swings, and a sand area, along with a larger, open area for games of tag and soccer.
- **Constitution Beach** (Orient Heights, East Boston). Lifeguarded swimming areas, a bathhouse with a snack bar, tennis courts, and a playground with lots of climbing and sliding prospects make this a great destination to take the kids.
- **Emerson Park** (Davis Ave & Emerson St, Brookline). The Park boasts one of the town's oldest spray pools, with lots of trees for shade and a casual open space for tag.
- **Green Street Playground** (Green St, Jamaica Plain). On summer days, the city turns on the water, and kids in bathing suits splash around in the fountains. Families set up picnics around the periphery, and there is a sandy jungle gym and swingset area nearby.
- **Huron Avenue Playground** (Huron Ave, Cambridge). This newly renovated play area has two climbing structures for children of all ages, as well as a play train and spray fountain for the summer months. The lack of tree shade may bother some parents.

- **Langone Park** (Commercial St, Boston). The park features a brand-new playground with multi-age, multi-level climbing structures, and a swing set hovering on the edge of the harbor, great for that flying-across-water feeling. There are also three bocce courts and a baseball field.
- **Larz Anderson Park** (Newton, Avon, & Goddard Sts, Brookline). The largest park in Brookline holds an enclosed playground, picnic areas, ball fields, and an outdoor skating rink open December though February.
- **Millennium Park** (VFW Pkwy & Gardner St, West Roxbury). This park is larger than the Boston Common and TD Banknorth Garden combined and located on the site of the former Gardner Street landfill. The park provides picnic areas, play structures, and hiking and walking trails, as well as access to the river for boating and fishing.
- **Myrtle Street Playground** (Myrtle St & Irving St, Boston). Situated at the top of Beacon Hill, this playground features several climbing structures, a glider, a fire pole, swings, and a crazy daisy.
- **Public Garden** (Between Arlington St & Charles St, Boston). The first public botanical garden in the US, the Public Garden has 24 acres of flowers and green in the middle of the bustling city. Among the park's winding pathways and tranquil lagoon are the prized bronze statues of a mama duck and her brood commemorating Robert McClosky's famous children's book, *Make Way for Ducklings*.
- **Rafferty Park** (799 Concord Ave, Cambridge). One of the area's best-hidden playgrounds, this wooded park provides tons of fun activities for older children, including a new metal climbing structure with a twisty slide, wobbly bridge, boat-shaped sand box, and a mini-schoolhouse with a chalkboard roof. Basketball hoops, tennis courts, and a baseball field reside next door.
- **Raymond Street Park** (Walden St & Raymond St, Cambridge). Located on the shady side of the field, this playground is split up into two sections: one sandy, sunken area for the younger toddlers and one area for older children, equipped with a large climbing structure. Play gear ranges from a bridge to swing sets, including one handicapped swing seat.
- **Stoneman Playground** (Fairfield Ave & Massachusetts Ave, Cambridge). This playground is divided into a toddler area and an older children's space, with entertaining activities for both groups. Supervised model sailboat racing and fishing takes place on Sundays in the summer months.

Rainy Day Activities

It rains in Boston. A lot. It's also one of the windiest cities in the country. Foul weather can drench even the highest aspirations for outdoor fun. Here are some dry alternatives:

Museums with Kid Appeal

- **Museum of Afro-American History** (46 Joy St, Boston, 617-725-0022). The first publicly-funded grammar school built for African-Americans now has interactive exhibits for kids. www.afroammuseum.org
- **Children's Museum** (300 Congress St, Boston, 617-426-8855). This world-renowned museum, freshly renovated, has designed early learning experiences for children of all ages with its inventive hands-on exhibits. Permanent exhibits include the Japanese House, where children get to experience the culture of Kyoto, Japan through a replica of a silk merchant's house, as well as a Hall of Toys where children can look at toys of the past, but not touch. www.bostonkids.org
- **New England Aquarium** (Central Wharf, 617-973-5200). Among the many exhibits you'll find here are the sea lion show and a supervised hands-on demonstration that allows children to touch sea stars, snails, and mussels. Whale-watching trips and summer classes are also offered through the aquarium. www.neaq.org
- **Larz Anderson Auto Museum** (Larz Anderson Park, 15 Newton St, Brookline, 617-522-6547). Located in the grand Carriage House, the museum features an extensive exhibit on the history of the automobile, as well as America's oldest car collection. www.mot.org
- **Museum of Science** (Science Park, 617-723-2500). This award-winning interactive science museum features permanent and changing exhibits, including a Virtual Fish Tank, where children see life through the eyes of a fish. The museum also houses the Charles Hayden Planetarium, featuring sky and laser shows, and the five-story IMAX Mugar Omni Theater. Various science classes are also available. www.mos.org
- **Harvard Museum of Natural History** (26 Oxford St, Cambridge, 617-495-3045). This museum has great educational programs and exhibits for little explorers interested in botany, zoology, and geology. The Sunday afternoon programs and lectures are highly recommended for families with middle school children. www.hmnh.harvard.edu

Other Indoor Distractions

- **The Clayroom** (1408 Beacon St, Brookline, 617-566-7575). Paint your own pottery place. Great for parties. www.clayroom.com
- **Lanes and Games** (195 Concord Tpke, Rte 2, Cambridge, 617-876-5533). Candlepin bowling and ten-pin lanes for the whole family. www.lanesgames.com
- **Puppet Showplace Theater** (32 Station St, Brookline, 617-731-6400). This 100-seat theater has been staging shows for Boston's young brood for over 30 years. The company stages classic puppet shows, as well as many original productions. Shows are recommended for children five and older. Great for parties. www.puppetshowplace.org

Outdoor and Educational

For when you've come to realize your children are a little too pale from sitting inside and playing video games all day.

- **Boston Duck Tours** (departure points: Prudential Center and Museum of Science, information: 617-267-DUCK). The Boston Duck is an original WWII amphibious landing vehicle that takes guests on an 80-minute tour (rain or shine) around the city by land and by sea. Kids are encouraged to quack at passersby. Tickets are sold inside the Prudential Center and Museum of Science beginning at 8:30 am. An additional ticketing location is at Faneuil Hall. Operating season: March 27th–Nov 26th. www.bostonducktours.com
- **Zoo New England** (1 Franklin Park Rd, Boston, 617-541-LION). The zoo holds all the standard zoo fare, plus the Butterfly Landing exhibit, a tented outdoor area where you can walk among more than 1,000 butterflies in free flight. (Smaller but still fun is the other Zoo New England site, Stone Zoo, in suburban Stoneham.) Adults: $9.50, seniors: $8, children (2–12): $5.50, under 2: free, and half-price tickets the first Sat of each month 10 am–12 pm. www.zoonewengland.com

Classes

Boston kids can participate in any number of structured activities that could help to mold and shape them like the blobs of clay that they are.

- **Boston Ballet School** (19 Clarendon St, Boston, 617-695-6950). Ballet classes for kids ages three and up. www.bostonballet.org
- **Boston Casting** (129 Braintree St, Suite 107, Allston, 617-254-1001). Acting classes for kids ages five and up. www.bostoncasting.com
- **Boston Children's Theatre** (321 Columbus Ave (Studio/Office), Boston, 617-424-6634). "Theatre for children by children," this theatre group has children involved in all phases of production. The theatre also offers acting classes and a summer creative arts program, in which kids learn stage combat, clowning, and juggling. www.bostonchildrenstheatre.org
- **Brookline Arts Center** (86 Monmouth St, Brookline, 617-566-5715). A non-degree school for the visual arts, the Brookline Arts Center offers classes for children ages two to teen in subjects ranging from jewelry-making to sculpture. www.brooklineartscenter.com
- **The Brookline Ballet School** (1431 Beacon Street, Brookline, 617-879-9988). Ballet as well as other dance and fitness classes. www.brooklineballet.com
- **Cambridge Multicultural Arts Center** (41 Second St, Cambridge, 617-577-1400). A program designed for Cambridge residents to promote cross-cultural interchange using dance, music, writing, theater, and the visual arts. www.cmacusa.org
- **Community Music Center of Boston** (34 Warren St, Boston, 617-482-7494). A music program designed to promote musical development through experimental learning for kids of all ages. The center also offers visual arts classes, summer programs, and individual instruction. www.cmcb.org
- **The Dance Complex** (536 Massachusetts Avenue, Central Square, 617-547-9363). Volunteer-based, artist-run organization located in historic Odd Fellows Hall. www.dancecomplex.org
- **French Library and Cultural Center** (53 Marlborough St, Boston, 617-912-0400). French classes for children ages three to ten. www.frenchlib.org
- **Full Moon** (344 Huron Ave, Cambridge, 617-354-6699). This kid-friendly restaurant offers cooking classes for parents and children ages three and up. www.fullmoonrestaurant.com
- **Grace Arts Project** (Grace United Methodist Church, 56 Magazine St, Cambridge, 617-864-1123). The program offers non-sectarian classes in music.
- **Grub Street Writers, Inc.** (160 Boylston St, Boston, 617-695-0075). Boston's only private writing school offers workshops and summer courses for young adults. www.grubstreet.org
- **Happily Ever After** (799 Concord Ave, Cambridge, 617-492-0090). The classes use fitness with creative stories and games for children aged three to six. Great for birthday parties. www.evergreendayschool.org
- **Hill House** (127 Mt. Vernon St, Boston, 617-227-5838). A non-profit community center that offers activities such as inline skating, karate, and youth soccer teams to downtown residents. www.hillhouseboston.org
- **John Payne Music Center** (kids' and adults' classes and ensembles with patient teachers) (9 Station Street, Brookline, 617-277-3438). Kids and adult classes and ensembles with patient teachers. www.jpmc.us
- **Isis Maternity** (Two Brookline Pl, Brookline, 781-429-1599; 397 Massachusetts Ave, Arlington, 781-429-1598; 110 2nd Ave, Needham, 781-429-1597). The brainchild of Boston-area moms and health professionals, each Isis Center offers classes to stimulate everyone from the newly born to those about to bop into kindergarten. Infant massage, anyone? www.isismaternity.com
- **Jeanette Neill Children's Dance Studio** (261 Friend St, Boston, 617-523-1355). Since 1979, the program has offered children ages three to 12 an "intelligent dance alternative" with its focus on education, not preparation. www.jndance.com
- **Jose Mateo's Ballet Theatre** (Old Cambridge Baptist Church, 400 Harvard St, Cambridge, 617-354-7467). A professional performance company that provides ballet instruction for children ages three through 18. www.ballettheatre.org
- **Longy School of Music** (1 Follen St, Cambridge, 617-876-0956). Music instruction for children ages 1 to 18. www.longy.edu
- **Made By Me in Harvard Square** (1685 Massachusetts Ave, Cambridge, 617-354-8111). A paint-your-own-pottery studio. Great for birthday parties. www.made-by-me.com
- **Make Art Studio** (44 N Bennett St, Boston, 617-227-0775). Children ages four to 13 are encouraged to "choose their own medium" with guidance and instruction in small, age-appropriate classes.
- **Mudflat Studio** (149 Broadway, Somerville, 617-628-0589). For the past 30 years, the studio has offered hand-building, pot throwing, and individual workshops for children ages four and up. www.mudflat.org
- **Museum of Fine Arts** (465 Huntington Ave, Boston, 617-267-9300). The museum offers weekday and Saturday instruction that combines gallery study and creative expression for children ages five to 18. www.mfa.org/learn/index.asp?key=3117
- **New School of Music** (25 Lowell St, Cambridge, 617-492-8105). Newborns and up are provided with musical instruction for all levels of interest and skill, as well as musical theater classes for the older kids. www.cambridgemusic.org
- **North Cambridge Family Opera** (23 North St, Cambridge, 617-492-4095). Adults and children ages seven to 14 can participate in theatrical and operatic production. www.familyopera.com
- **North End Music and Performing Arts Center** (Paul Revere Mall, between Hanover St and Unity St, Boston, 617-227-2270). The center offers classes in music, language, and the performing arts to North End residents. www.nempac.org
- **New England Conservatory** (290 Huntington Ave, Boston, 617-585-1130). Music lessons for kids ages four and up at the oldest independent school of music in the US. www.newenglandconservatory.edu
- **Oak Square YMCA** (615 Washington St, Brighton, 617-782-3535). The center offers instruction in swimming, gymnastics, basketball, and art as well as after school programs for kids of all ages. www.ymcaboston.org
- **The Skating Club of Boston** (1240 Soldiers Field Rd, Brighton, 617-782-5900). Classes for skaters and hockey players of all levels. www.scboston.org
- **Topf Center for Dance Education** (551 Tremont St, Boston, 617-482-0351). The center provides underserved youth access to classes in jazz, tap, ballet, hip hop, and African dancing. www.topfcenter.org
- **Upon a Star** (441 Stuart St, Studio 4, Boston, 617-797-5562). Music and movement classes for children ages 14 months to three. www.uponastar.net
- **Wang YMCA of Chinatown** (8 Oak St W, Boston, 617-426-2237). Activities ranging from swimming instruction to music and art classes for children of all ages. www.ymcaboston.org
- **Wheelock Family Theatre** (180 The Riverway, Boston, 617-879-2147). The Theatre offers classes for kids ages four to 17. www.wheelock.edu/wft

For more information, visit www.gocitykids.com

Overview

The Boston Public Library, founded in 1848, was the first publicly supported municipal library in the United States, and is the only public library in the United States that is also a Presidential library, that of John Adams. It is also the first library to open and operate neighborhood branches. By far the coolest looking branch, the **Honan-Allston (Map 19),** was designed by Machado & Silvetti Associates, Inc. and features tree guards and bike racks created by artist Rich Duca. The BPL now operates 27 branch libraries, each of which offers free wireless Internet access. Check out the details on the BPL's website. If you're looking for a getaway in Copley Square, the Italian courtyard is the perfect place to sit down with a book or a bagged lunch. For more information on the BPL's main branch and just how much cultural heat it's packing check out BPL Central Library **(see page 185)**.

Brookline, Cambridge, and Somerville have their own public libraries, which are part of the Minuteman System. The Brookline Public Library houses government documents, Russian and Chinese materials, Brookline high school yearbooks and newspapers, well-stocked CD collection, DVDs, videos, new books, and local newspapers. The **Cambridge Public Library's Main Library (Map 28)** has occupied the same building since 1889. After moving to a temporary location while the building underwent renovations and an expansion, it reopened to the public 2009. The library now has seating for over 200 patrons, 100 public computers, both a Children's Room and a Teen Room, and WiFi throughout. Most noteworthy in the new addition is the Cambridge Room, which houses the CPL's Archives and Special Collections. Here you'll find historic maps, photographs, city directories and other genealogy resources, and the Historic Cambridge Newspaper Collection. Neat. The 93-year old **Somerville Public Library (Map 24)** holds its own serving its community by providing access to all kinds of information, in analog and digital form, via its three branches. Both Cambridge and Somerville libraries offer residents free passes to visit the Children's Museum, Harvard University Museum of Natural History, the JFK Library and Museum, the Museum of Fine Arts, the New England Aquarium, the Roger Williams Park Zoo, and others. To reserve FREE tickets, call 617-623-5000 (Somerville) or 617-349-4040 (Cambridge). For more information about hours, collections, and special events, check the library websites.

Library	*Address*	*Phone*	*Map*
Boston Public Library - West End	151 Cambridge St	617-523-3957	1
Boston Public Library - North End	25 Parmenter St	617-227-8135	2
The Mary Baker Eddy Library	200 Massachusetts Ave	617-450-7000	5
Boston Public Library - Central	700 Boylston St	617-536-5400	6
Boston Public Library - Kirstein Business	700 Boylston St	617-859-2142	6
Boston Public Library - South End	685 Tremont St	617-536-8241	7
Boston Public Library - Charlestown	179 Main St	617-242-1248	8
Boston Public Library - East Boston	276 Meridian St	617-569-0271	9
Boston Public Library - South Boston	646 E Broadway	617-268-0180	11
Boston Public Library - Dudley	65 Warren St	617-442-6186	13
Boston Public Library - Connolly	433 Centre St	617-522-1960	14
Boston Public Library - Jamaica Plain	12 Sedgwick St	617-524-2053	14
Boston Public Library - Parker Hill	1497 Tremont St	617-427-3820	15
Brookline Public Library	361 Washington St	617-730-2370	17
Boston Public Library - Brighton	40 Academy Hill Rd	617-782-6032	18
Boston Public Library - Faneuil	419 Faneuil St	617-782-6705	18
Boston Public Library - Honan-Allston	300 N Harvard St	617-787-6313	19
Brookline Public Library - Coolidge Corner	31 Pleasant St	617-730-2380	19
Cambridge Public Library - Boudreau	245 Concord Ave	617-349-4017	21
Cambridge Public Library - O'Neill	70 Rindge Ave	617-349-4023	22
Somerville Public Library - West	40 College Ave	617-623-5000	22
Somerville Public Library	79 Highland Ave	617-623-5000	24
Somerville Public Library - East	115 Broadway	617-623-5000	24
Cambridge Public Library - O'Connell	48 Sixth St	617-349-4019	26
Cambridge Public Library - Central Square	45 Pearl St	617-349-4010	27
Cambridge Public Library	449 Broadway	617-349-4040	28
Cambridge Public Library - Valente	826 Cambridge St	617-349-4015	28

Websites

Boston Gay Men's Chorus • www.bgmc.org
Now in its 24th year, the BGMC, through its collaboration with The Boston Pops, was the first gay chorus in the world to be recorded with a major orchestra on a major label.

craigslist • http://boston.craigslist.org
General community site (for straights, gays, and everyone else) that offers heavily trafficked "men seeking men" and "women seeking women" sections, as well as other community-related listings and information.

EDGE Boston • www.edgeboston.com
Gay Boston news and entertainment.

Gay & Lesbian Advocates & Defenders (GLAD) • www.glad.org
New England's leading legal rights organization dedicated to ending discrimination based on sexual orientation.

Greater Boston Business Council • www.gbbc.org
Promotes the vitality of Boston's LGBT business and professional community.

Out In Boston • www.outinboston.com
Local news and events, personal ads, business ads, chat, and community message boards.

PinkWeb • www.pinkweb.com
The LGBT yellow pages for New England and beyond.

Provincetown Business Guild • www.ptown.org
A gay and lesbian guide to P'town.

Publications

Bay Windows—New England's largest gay and lesbian newspaper is a weekly publication that prints local, national, and international news as well as community events and guides. www.baywindows.com.

Boston Spirit Magazine—Free glossy bimonthly magazine www.bostonspiritmagazine.com.

In Newsweekly—News and entertainment weekly, including a calendar of events and a club guide. www.innewsweekly.com.

Bookstores

Calamus Bookstore • 92B South St, Boston • 617-338-1931 • www.calamusbooks.com

Sports

Beantown Softball League • www.beantownsoftball.com
LGBT softball since 1978.

Boston Bay Blades • www.bayblades.org/boston
For rowers and scullers.

Boston Boasts Squash League • www.bostonboasts.com
The country's oldest and largest gay and lesbian squash league.

Boston Gay Basketball League • www.bgbl.com
The country's largest LGBT basketball league.

Boston Strikers • www.bostonstrikers.com
Indoor and outdoor soccer league for gay and straight players of all levels.

Cambridge-Boston Volleyball Association • www.gayvolleyball.net
Indoor league with three levels of play.

Chiltern Mountain Club • www.chiltern.org
New England's largest LGBT outdoor recreation club.

East Coast Wrestling Club • www.eastcoastwrestlingclub.org
Gay men's wrestling group for athletes of all abilities.

FLAG Flag Football • http://flagflagfootball.tripod.com/flagflagfootballonline
Plays a full fall season and an abbreviated spring season.

FrontRunners Boston • www.mindspring.com/~frontrunners/index.htm
Welcomes joggers, walkers, and runners of all experience levels.

PrideSports Boston • 617-937-5858 • www.geocities.com/pridesportsboston
Gay & lesbian athletic alliance with more than 20 sports clubs.

Health Centers & Support Organizations

Boston Alliance of Gay Lesbian Bisexual and Transgender Youth • 617-227-4313 • www.bagly.org
For young people 22 and under.

Dignity Boston • 617-421-1915 • www.dignityboston.org
An inclusive community of LGBT Catholics.

Fenway Community Health • 7 Haviland St, Boston • 617-267-0900 • www.fenwayhealth.org
Provides high-quality medical and mental health care to Boston's gay and lesbian community; also a leader in HIV care.

Gay Men's Domestic Violence Project • 800-832-1901 • www.gmdvp.org
Offers shelter, guidance, and resources to allow gay, bisexual, and transgender men in crisis to remove themselves from violent situations and relationships; also operates a 24-hour free-of-charge crisis center.

MassEquality • 617-878-2300 • www.massequality.org
Grassroots advocacy group defending equal marriage rights for same-sex couples.

The Network • 617-423-SAFE • www.thenetworklared.org
Provides information and resources for battered lesbian, bisexual, and transgendered women.

Annual Events

Boston Pride Week • 617-262-9405 • www.bostonpride.org
Begins on a Friday in June with a flag raising at City Hall; the parade and festival usually take place on the Saturday of the following weekend.

Boston Gay/Lesbian Film/Video Festival • 617-267-9300 • www.mfa.org
Usually held in May at the MFA.

Mass Red Ribbon Ride • 617-450-1100 • www.massredribbonride.org
This bike ride across the state raises money for AIDS organizations. Takes place annually in August.

Venues – Lesbian

- **Aria** (Saturdays) • 246 Tremont St, Boston • 617-417-0186
- **Dyke Night Productions** • www.dykenight.com
- **Midway Cafe** (Sundays) • 3496 Washington St, Jamaica Plain • www.midwaycafe.com
- **Milky Way Lounge** (Sundays) • 284 Amory St, Jamaica Plain • 617-524-6060• www.milkywayjp.com
- **The Modern** (Thursdays) • 36 Lansdowne St, Boston • www.lesbiannightlife.com
- **Toast** (Fridays) • 70 Union Sq, Somerville • 617-623-9211 • www.toastlounge.com
- **Tribe** (at **Felt**) • 533 Washington St, Boston • 617-350-5555 • www.tribenightclub.com

Venues – Gay

- **The Alley** • 14 Pi Aly, Boston • 617-263-1449 • www.thealleybar.com
- **Club Cafe** • 209 Columbus Ave, Boston • 617-536-0966 • www.clubcafe.com
- **Eagle** • 520 Tremont St, Boston • 617-542-4494
- **Flaunt** (Saint Nightclub) • 90 Exeter St, Boston • 617-236-1134
- **Fritz** • 26 Chandler St, Boston • 617-482-4428 • www.fritzboston.com
- **Heroes** (Saturdays at **Toast**) • 70 Union Sq, Somerville • 617-623-9211 • www.toastlounge.com
- **Add House of Blues** Boston-15 Lansdowne Street, Boston • 888-693-2583 • http://www.houseofblues.com/venues/clubvenues/boston/
- **Jacques Cabaret** • 79 Broadway St, Boston • 617-426-8902 • www.jacquescabaret.com
- **Machine** (Thurs–Sat) • 1256 Boylston St, Boston • 617-226-2986 • www.ramrodmachine.com
- **Paradise** • 180 Massachusetts Ave, Cambridge • 617-868-3000 • www.paradisecambridge.com
- **Ramrod** • 1254 Boylston St, Boston • 617-226-2986 • www.ramrodmachine.com
- **Rise** (members only, after-hours) • 306 Stuart St, Boston • 617-423-7473 • www.riseclub.us
- **Shine Restaurant & Lounge** • 1 Kendall Sq, Cambridge • 617-621-9500 • www.shinecambridge.com
- **Venu** (Wednesdays) • 101 Warrenton St, Boston • 617-695-9500

After years of suffering from a shortage of hotel accommodations, Boston's hotel market has finally warmed up. Developers, encouraged by an improving economic climate and continued high demand for rooms, have moved forward with several large projects, most of which are located on or near the waterfront, where developers hope to leverage locations close to the Boston Convention & Exhibition Center. But it's not all just about harbor views and cafeteria-sized restaurants—boutique hotels are also popping up in various locations around town. Newcomers in the boutique market include **Hotel 140 (Map 6)** (a historic building in the shadow of the Hancock Tower), sleek **Nine Zero (Map 3)** (on Tremont Street), the **The Boxer (Map 1)** (near North Station), and the **Beacon Hill Hotel (Map 1)** (on Charles Street, near the Common). **Loews Boston Hotel (Map 6)** has opened in the fully renovated former headquarters of the Boston Police Department. **The Hampton Inn & Suites (Map 12)** (near Newmarket Square), may not be as luxurious as Loews Boston, but its suites are a decent option for long-term stays, and its proximity to I-93 and the Mass Pike make it easy to get to other locations. For visitors largely confined to happenings at the Boston Convention Center, the **Westin Boston Waterfront (Map 4)** and the **Seaport Hotel (Map 11)** are safe, convenient bets.

But Boston residents shouldn't let tourists have all the fun. Even if you're not staying the night, it's worth popping into one of Boston's classic hotels to soak up the atmosphere. The lobby of the **Fairmont Copley Plaza (Map 6)** exudes luxuriousness, as does its acclaimed restaurant, the OAK Long Bar and Kitchen. For those looking for a respite from retail therapy on nearby Newbury Street, the **Eliot Hotel (Map 5)** on Commonwealth Avenue can rejuvenate even the weariest shopper. Genteel rivals the **Four Seasons (Map 3)** and the **Taj Boston (Map 3)** (formerly home to the oldest Ritz Carlton in the country) both overlook the Public Garden. (The Bristol Lounge at the Four Seasons serves what many argue is the city's best-known high tea.) Across the Common, towards the financial district, the **Omni Parker House (Map 3)** stands as a Boston institution and a literary landmark (and has been known to flaunt its claim to fame as the birthplace of Parker rolls and Boston Cream Pies). Chic boutique newcomer Liberty Hotel, at the former Charles Street Jail right next to present-day Charles/MGH T stop, offers stunning atrium and hopping bar/lounge. The **Langham Hotel (Map 4)**, located smack dab in the middle of Boston's high-finance hub, offers a chocolate buffet on Saturdays that is To Die For. If you're killing time in Back Bay, check out the charming and cozy lobby of the **Lenox Hotel (Map 6)**. Playing up its proximity to techie heaven MIT is the lovely **Royal Sonesta Hotel Boston (Map 26)**, with great views of the Charles River and the Boston skyline. In Harvard Square, the **Charles Hotel (Map 20)** offers nightly jazz at the Regattabar as well as organic fine dining at Henrietta's Table. And if you're suffering from wanderlust of the spirit, ask about the weekend retreats at the **Monastery of the Society of St. John the Evangelist (Map 20)**. For another low-cost option, check into the new HI-Boston hostel in the Theatre District/Chinatown with plenty of free perks and programs.

Marriott's Custom House (Map 2) is located in one of Boston's most prominent historic landmarks, the Custom House Tower. The original Custom House building, completed in 1847, was described by Walt Whitman as "the noblest form of architecture in the world." The tower was added in 1915. The open-air observation deck on the 26th floor is open to the public and offers prime views of the harbor and the open spaces created by the demolition of the Central Artery.

Whether you're booking for yourself or the in-laws, call the hotels to ask about specials and check websites such as hotels.com, Orbitz, Hotwire, Travelocity, and All-Hotels for discounts. Maybe you'll get lucky.

Hotel	*Address*	*Phone*	*Price*	*Map*
Beacon Hill Hotel	25 Charles St	617-723-7575	$$$	1
The Boxer	107 Merrimac St	617-624-0202	$$	1
Liberty Hotel	215 Charles St	617-224-4000	$$$$	1
Marriott's Custom House	3 McKinley Sq	617-310-6300	$$$$	2
Four Seasons Hotel	200 Boylston St	617-338-4400	$$$$$$	3
Nine Zero Hotel	90 Tremont St	617-772-5800	$$$	3
Omni Parker House	60 School St	617-227-8600	$$$	3
Taj Boston	15 Arlington St	617-536-5700	$$$$	3
The Langham Hotel	250 Franklin St	617-451-1900	$$$$	4
Westin Boston Waterfront	425 Summer St	617-532-4600	$$$	4
Eliot Hotel	370 Commonwealth Ave	617-267-1607	$$$	5
Fairmont Copley Plaza Hotel	138 St James Ave	617-267-5300	$$$$$	6
Hotel 140	140 Clarendon St	617-585-5600	$$	6
Lenox Hotel	61 Exeter St	617-536-5300	$$$	6
Loews Boston Hotel	154 Berkeley St	617-266-7200	$$$$	6
Hampton Inn & Suites Boston Crosstown Center	811 Massachusetts Ave	617-445-6400	$$	7
Seaport Hotel	1 Seaport Ln	617-385-4000	$$$	11
Monastery of the Society of St John the Evangelist	980 Memorial Dr	617-876-3037	$	20
Charles Hotel	1 Bennett St	617-864-1200	$$$$	20
Royal Sonesta Hotel Boston	40 Land Blvd	617-806-4200	$$$	26

And this is good old Boston.
The home of the bean and the cod.
Where the Lowells talk to the Cabots,
And the Cabots talk only to God.

—John Collins Bossidy (a toast given at a Harvard alumni dinner in 1910)

Useful Phone Numbers

General Info	411
Emergencies	911
Boston Globe	617-929-2000
Boston Herald	617-426-3000
Boston Public Library	617-536-5400
Boston City Hall	617-635-4000
Brookline Town Hall	617-730-2000
Cambridge City Hall	617-349-4000
Somerville City Hall	617-625-6600
Boston Board of Elections	617-635-4635
Brookline Town Clerk	617-730-2010
Cambridge Board of Elections	617-349-4361
Somerville Board of Elections	617-625-6600, ext. 4200
Boston Police Headquarters	617-343-4200
Keyspan Energy Delivery	617-469-2300
NStar	617-424-2000
Comcast	888-633-4266
Verizon	800-256-4646
Red Sox Ticket Line	877-733-7699

Websites

www.beantownbloggery.com—
Anything and everything beantown.
www.boston.com—Website of the *Boston Globe*.
www.boston.craigslist.org—
Classifieds in almost every area, with personals, apartments for rent, musicians, job listings, and more.
www.boston.citysearch.com—
Portal channeling the Yellow Pages.
www.boston-online.com—
Forums and fun facts; guide to Boston English.
www. bostonist.com—
About Boston and everything that happens in it.
www.cambridgema.gov—
Cambridge government resources.
http://cheapthrillsboston.blogspot.com—
Perfect for those on an NFT salary.
www.cityofboston.gov—Boston government resources.
www.ci.somerville.ma.us—
Somerville government resources.
www.eatanddestroy.com—Amazing Boston food blog.
thephoenix.com/boston—Boston Phoenix, now online only.
www.universalhub.com—Info hub for the Hub.
www.universalhub.com—Info hub for the Hub.

We're the First!!!

- America's first public park (Boston Common, 1634)
- America's first college (Harvard, founded in 1636)
- America's first public school (Boston Latin, 1645)
- America's first public library (Boston Public Library, 1653)
- America's first post office (Richard Fairbanks' Tavern, 1639)
- America's first regularly issued newspaper (*Boston News-Letter*, 1704)
- America's first lighthouse (Boston Harbor, 1716)
- First flag of the American colonies raised on Prospect Hill (January 1, 1776)
- America's first published novel (*The Power of Sympathy* by William Hill Brown, 1789)
- First demonstration of surgical anesthesia (1845)
- First telephone call (Alexander Graham Bell, 1876)
- America's first subway (1897)
- First person-to-person network email (BBN Technologies, 1971)
- First "First Night" New Year's celebration (1976)

Boston Timeline

A timeline of significant Boston events (by no means complete)

1620 Mayflower arrives in Plymouth.
1630 Dorchester founded by Gov. John Winthrop.
1630 City of Boston chartered.
1634 Boston Common, first public park in America, opens.
1636 Harvard College opens.
1639 America's first canal cut near Dedham.
1645 Boston Latin School, first public school in America, opens.
1692 Witchcraft trials begin in Salem.
1693 Society of Negroes founded.
1704 First regularly issued American newspaper, the *Boston News-Letter*.
1706 Benjamin Franklin born.
1716 First American lighthouse built (Boston Harbor).
1770 Boston Massacre.
1773 Boston Tea Party.
1775 Revolutionary War begins at Lexington and Concord.
1775 Battle of Bunker Hill.
1776 First flag of the American colonies raised on Prospect Hill in Somerville.
1776 British evacuate Boston.
1780 John Hancock becomes first elected Governor of Massachusetts.
1788 Massachusetts ratifies Constitution.
1795 The "new" State House built.
1796 John Adams, of Quincy, elected second president.
1806 African Meeting House, first church built by free African-Americans, opens.
1820 Maine separates from Massachusetts.
1824 John Quincy Adams elected sixth president.
1826 Union Oyster House opens.
1831 William Lloyd Garrison publishes first abolitionist newspaper, the *Liberator*.
1837 Samuel Morse invents electric telegraph machine.
1845 Sewing machine invented by Elias Howe.
1846 Boston dentist William T.G. Morton publicly demonstrates the use of anesthesia in surgery.
1846 From 1846 to 1849, 37,000 Irish people flee the Potato Famine for Boston.
1860 From 1860 to 1870, the Back Bay is filled in, greatly increasing the landmass of Boston.
1863 University of Massachusetts at Amherst chartered.
1868 From 1868 to 1874, Boston annexes Charlestown, Brighton, Roxbury, West Roxbury, and Dorchester.
1872 *Boston Globe* prints its first newspaper.
1872 Great Fire.
1876 First telephone call by Alexander Graham Bell.
1877 Helen Magill becomes first woman Ph.D. in US (at BU).
1882 John L. Sullivan becomes bare-knuckle boxing champ.
1886 *Irish Echo* newspaper founded.
1888 Construction begins on new building for Boston Public Library.
1892 JFK grandfather John F. "Honey Fitz" Fitzgerald elected to state senate.
1894 Honey Fitz elected to US Congress.
1896 First US public beach opens in Revere.
1897 First American subway opens.
1900 Symphony Hall opens.
1901 Boston Red Sox play first game against New York Yankees.
1903 Red Sox (then the Americans) win first World Series.
1906 Honey Fitz becomes first Boston-born Irish-American mayor.
1912 Fenway Park opens.
1914 James Michael Curley elected mayor for the first time.

1915 Custom House Tower completed, tallest building in Boston at time.
1919 Great Molasses Flood kills 21 in the North End.
1920 Red Sox owner Harry Frazee sells Babe Ruth to Yankees for $100,000.
1920 Irish-Italian gang fights begin.
1924 Boston Bruins play first game.
1924 World's first mutual fund established.
1927 Sacco and Vanzetti wrongly executed for robbery shootings.
1928 Boston Garden opens.
1928 First computer invented at MIT.
1929 Bruins win their first Stanley Cup trophy.
1934 JFK's father, "Old Joe" Kennedy, named SEC chairman.
1941 Ted Williams hits .406, last player to hit over .400.
1942 Fire at Cocoanut Grove nightclub kills 491 people.
1946 JFK elected to Congress.
1946 Boston Celtics play first game.
1946 Red Sox lose World Series after tragic player error.
1947 Microwave oven invented at Raytheon.
1947 Polaroid camera invented.
1947 Dr. Sidney Farber introduces chemotherapy.
1950 Red Auerbach becomes Celtics coach.
1952 Boston Braves play final game in Boston, move to Milwaukee.
1956 Celtics draft Bill Russell.
1957 Massachusetts Turnpike opens.
1958 Celtics win first of 16 championships.
1958 Demolition of the West End neighborhood begins.
1959 Central Artery opens.
1960 Boston Patriots play first game.
1960 John F. Kennedy elected 35th president.
1960 Ted Williams homers in last at-bat for Red Sox.
1962 From 1962 to 1964, Boston Strangler kills 13 women. Albert DeSalvo is convicted and killed in prison.
1963 JFK assassinated in Dallas.
1964 Prudential Tower built.
1965 Havlicek steals the ball! Celtics win championship.
1966 Bobby Orr plays first game as a Bruin.
1966 Edward W. Brooke becomes first African-American elected to US Senate since Reconstruction.
1967 Red Sox's "Impossible Dream" season ends in defeat.
1971 First e-mail sent by BBN Technologies.
1973 John Hancock building, tallest in Boston, nears completion—giant windows start falling out.
1974 Federal court declares "*de facto* segregation" of Boston public schools; orders desegregation by busing. Demonstrations and violence ensue.
1975 Carlton Fisk hits 12th inning Game 6 homer, does baseline foul pole dance. Sox go on to lose Game 7.
1975 Gangster Whitey Bulger begins relationship with FBI agents, reign as Boston's biggest crime lord.
1976 First "First Night" New Year's celebration.
1978 Blizzard of '78 paralyzes Southern New England.
1978 Bucky Dent! Sox lose to Yanks.
1986 Celtics draft pick Len Bias dies of a drug overdose.
1986 Red Sox lose World Series Game 6 to Mets after excruciating 10th inning error, go on to lose Game 7.
1987 Big Dig construction begins in Charlestown.
1988 Cleanup of Boston Harbor begins.
1988 Governor Michael Dukakis runs for president, rides tank, loses to Bush the First.
1993 Celtics captain Reggie Lewis dies.
1993 Former Mayor Ray Flynn named ambassador to Vatican.
1993 Thomas M. "Mumbles" Menino elected Boston's first Italian-American mayor.
1995 Boston Garden closes; FleetCenter opens.
1995 Whitey Bulger goes on the lam after his FBI handlers are indicted.
1998 *Boston Globe* columnists Patricia Smith and Mike Barnicle fired over fabrications and plagiarism, respectively.
2001 Jane Swift becomes first female governor of Massachusetts.
2001 Planes that destroy NYC World Trade Center leave Logan Airport.
2002 After a 0-2 start, New England Patriots win their first Super Bowl.
2002 Ted Williams dies, cryogenically frozen in two pieces.
2002 Catholic clergy sexual abuse scandal explodes; Cardinal Bernard Law resigns amid controversy.
2003 Billy Bulger forced to resign as UMass president due to controversy about his gangster brother, Whitey.
2004 Supreme Judicial Court rules that gay couples have the right to marry.
2004 Demolition of Central Artery.
2004 Sox win World Series for first time since 1918.
2005 Patriots win their third Super Bowl in four years.
2006 Massachusetts elects Deval Patrick, first black Governor of the state.
2007 Sox end three year drought by winning the World Series (again!).
2008 Cetics beat Lakers for record 17th NBA championship.
2009 Ted Kennedy passes; crowds gather the funeral procession.

15 Essential Boston Movies

The Boston Strangler (1968)
The Thomas Crown Affair (1968)
Love Story (1970)
The Paper Chase (1973)
Between the Lines (1977)
The Verdict (1982)
The Bostonians (1984)
Glory (1989)
Far and Away (1992)
Good Will Hunting (1997)
A Civil Action (1998)
Monument Ave (1998)
Next Stop, Wonderland (1998)
Mystic River (2003)
The Departed (2006)
Gone Baby Gone (2007)
The Town (2010)

15 Essential Boston Songs

"Boston" — The Byrds
"Charlie on the MTA" — The Kingston Trio
"Dirty Water" — The Standells
"Down at the Cantab" — Little Joe Cook & the Thrillers
"Government Center" — Jonathan Richman
"Highlands" — Bob Dylan
"I Want My City Back" — The Mighty Mighty Bosstones
"Massachusetts" — The Bee Gees
"Roadrunner" — Jonathan Richman
"Rock and Roll Band" — Boston
"Sweet Baby James" — James Taylor
"Tessie" — Dropkick Murphys
"The Ballad of Sacco & Vanzetti" — Joan Baez
"Twilight in Boston" — Jonathan Richman
"UMass" — The Pixies

15 Essential Boston Books

All Souls, Michael Patrick McDonald
The Autobiography of Benjamin Franklin
Black Mass, David Lehrer and Gerard O'Neill
The Bostonians, Henry James
Dark Tide: The Great Boston Molasses Flood of 1919, Stephen Puleo
Faithful, Stewart O'Nan and Stephen King
The Handmaid's Tale, Margaret Atwood
The House of the Seven Gables, Nathaniel Hawthorne
Infinite Jest, David Foster Wallace
John Adams, David McCullough
Johnny Tremain, Esther Forbes
Little Women, Louisa May Alcott
Make Way for Ducklings, Robert McCloskey
The Trumpet of the Swan, E.B. White
Walden, Henry David Thoreau

Overview

There's always something going on in Boston—the list below is just a smattering of the hundreds of annual parades, festivals, and wing-dings. Note that dates change from year to year, so as always, it's a good idea to check an event's website when making plans. Now get out and enjoy!

- **First Night** • Dec 31/Jan 1 • www.firstnight.org • Family-oriented First Night got its start in Boston. Celebrate the new year with live performances, interactive events, and in most years, bitter cold. The purchase of a First Night Button gains you admission to participating performance centers.
- **Chinese New Year** • Early Feb • Fireworks, parades, and special banquets in Chinatown.
- **Boston Wine Expo** • Mid-Feb • www.wine-expos.com/boston • Largest consumer wine event in the country, with a long bill of celebrity chefs to boot.
- **Black History Month Music Celebration** • Feb • www.berkleebpc.com • A series of concerts at the Berklee Performance Center.
- **Winter Restaurant Week** • Early March • www.restaurantweekboston.com • Local eateries offer specially priced lunches and dinners. A chance to sample meals you could never otherwise afford!
- **Boston Flower and Garden Show** • Mid-March • www.masshort.org • Flower and craft exhibition at the Seaport World Trade Center.
- **Evacuation Day** • Mar 17 • British troop withdrawal from Boston was the perfect excuse for infamous Mayor Curley to make St. Paddy's Day an official holiday for all Suffolk County municipal workers. Gotta love the Irish.
- **St. Patrick's Day Parade** • March• www.saintpatricksdayparade.com/boston • Marching through Southie since 1737.
- **Red Sox Opening Day** • Early Apr • www.redsox.com • Unofficial holiday.
- **Boston Marathon/Patriots Day** • Apr 15 • www.baa.org • Pseudo local holiday with the 117th running of the marathon and an early Red Sox game.
- **Wake Up the Earth Festival** • May 4 • spontaneouscelebrations.org • Hippies and children alike enjoy stilt walking, puppets, live bands, and community bonding in Jamaica Plain.
- **MayFair** • First Sunday in May • www.harvardsquare.com/mayfair/ • Harvard Square festival featuring everything from Literary tours to indie rock to Morris dancers.
- **Lilac Sunday at the Arnold Arboretum** • Early May • www.arboretum.harvard.edu • Follow the perfume of the lilac and the hippie in a Morris dancing outfit. Fun atmosphere at the Arnold Arboretum for families and friends.
- **Walk for Hunger** • Early May • www.projectbread.org • 20-mile walk whose proceeds fund over 400 emergency food programs each year.
- **Anime Boston** • May 24–26 • www.animeboston.com • Japanese animation convention at the Hynes Convention Center.
- **Street Performers Festival** • Late May • Faneuil Hall carnival that's especially fun for kids. Magicians, sword swallowers, and lil' one activities like the Kid's Kazoo Parade.
- **Feast of the Madonna di Anzano** • Early June • www.anzanoboston.com • Procession and gala feast in the North End Italian community.
- **WUMB Music Festival** • Early June • www.wumb.org/folkfest • Pickin' and grinnin'.
- **Scooper Bowl** • Early June • www.jimmyfund.org • World's biggest all-you-can-eat ice cream festival. Proceeds go to the Jimmy Fund.
- **Boston Gay Pride Parade** • Early/Mid June • www.bostonpride.org • New England's largest, capping a week of pride events.
- **Cambridge River Festival** • Mid June • Summer-starting festival along Memorial Drive between JFK Street and Western Ave, featuring music, food, art, kid-stuff.
- **Dragon Boat Festival** • Early/Mid June • www.bostondragonboat.org • Celebration of Chinese Dragon Boat racing at the Weeks footbridge, on Memorial Drive. Races, food, activities all day long.
- **Bloomsday** • Jun 16 • www.artsandsociety.org • Celebration of James Joyce's *Ulysses* at BU.
- **Bunker Hill Parade** • Around June 17 • www.charlestownonline.net • Celebration of Bunker Hill Day in Charlestown.
- **Boston Globe Blues and Jazz Festival** • Late Jun • Jazz and blues on the waterfront.

- **Boston Harborfest** • Early July • www.bostonharborfest.com • Over 200 events celebrating Boston's colonial and maritime history through reenactments, concerts, and historical tours.
- **Boston's Fourth of July** • Guess • www.july4th.org Ridiculously crowded Boston Pops concert and fireworks on the Esplanade.
- **French Cultural Center's Bastille Day** • Mid July • Block party in Back Bay with paid admission, crêpes and occasional world music superstars.
- **Bastille Day in Harvard Square** • Mid July • Free admission to block party and concert/DJs, paid food spearheaded by Sandrine's Bistro."
- **Puerto Rican Festival** • Late July • Franklin Park goes loco for 5 days with amusement rides, food, and general fun in the name of Puerto Rico. Lots of live music.
- **Feast of St. Agrippina** • Early Aug • Featuring a procession, block party, and a giant tug-of-war.
- **August Moon Festival** • Mid Aug • At the Chinatown Gateway arch on Harrison Ave, celebrating Chinese culture and marked by tasty flaky pastries with an interesting history,
- **Feast of the Madonna del Soccorso** • Mid Aug • www.fishermansfeast.com • Boston's longest-running Italian festival.
- **St. Anthony's Feast** • Late Aug • www.saintanthonysfeast.com • With Italian-American festivals in the North End every weekend throughout late July and August, this is the one to get off your coolie for. True combination of kitsch and classic.
- **Summer Restaurant Week** • August • www.bostonusa.com • Discounted *prix-fixe* meals at scores of area restaurants—a terrific bargain.
- **Boston Carnival** • Late Aug • www.bostoncarnival.com • Celebration of Caribbean culture in Dorchester.
- **Boston Film Festival** • Mid/Late Sep • www.bostonfilmfestival.org • Plenty to please the most finicky cinephile.
- **Boston Freedom Rally** • Mid/Late Sep • www.masscann.org • That ain't freedom they're smoking.
- **Phantom Gourmet Food Festival** • Late Sep • www.phantomgourmetfoodfestival.com • $40 for the Landsdowne St Grand Bouffe that's unlike any other in Boston, featuring booths hand picked by the Phantom himself.
- **Boston Tattoo Convention** • Labor Day Weekend • www.bostontattooconvention.com • Celebrating the newly legal (in Mass) art form.
- **Opening Night at the Symphony** • Sept 22 • www.bso.org • Kicks off another season of BSO goodness.
- **Harvard Square Oktoberfest** • Early Oct • www.harvardsquare.com • Don't expect liters of free beer.
- **Head of the Charles** • Oct 23–24 • www.hocr.org • The world's largest two-day rowing event.
- **Belgian Beer Fest** • Late Oct • www.beeradvocate.com/fests • *Sluit je aan bij de Bierrevolutie!*
- **Boston Jewish Film Festival** • Nov • www.bjff.org • Now in its 17th season.
- **Boston International Antiquarian Book Fair** • Mid Nov • www.bostonbookfair.com • The country's longest running antiquarian book fair features autographs, photographs, maps, and more.
- **Black Nativity** • Weekends in Dec • www.blacknativity.org • One part Harlem Renaissance, one part folk music, dance, and verse celebration of the birth of Jesus Christ. Held at the Tremont Temple.
- **Prudential Center Christmas Tree Lighting** • Early Dec • www.prudentialcenter.com • Each year Nova Scotia thanks Boston for helping Halifax recover from a 1917 disaster by sending down a huge tree.
- **Boston Tea Party Reenactment** • Mid Dec • www.oldsouthmeetinghouse.org • A fine excuse to don your tri-cornered hat.
- **Boston Common Menorah Lighting** • Late Dec • www.cityofboston.gov/arts • Celebrating the first night of Hanukkah.

Television

2	WGBH	(PBS)	www.wgbh.org
4	WBZ	(CBS)	www.wbz4.com
5	WCVB	(ABC)	www.thebostonchannel.com
7	WHDH	(NBC)	www1.whdh.com
25	WFXT	(FOX)	www.fox25.com
27	WUNI	(Univision)	www.wunitv.com
38	WSBK	(UPN)	www.upn38.com
44	WGBH	(PBS)	www.wgbh.org
56	WLVI	(WB)	www.wb56.trb.com
66	WUTF	(Telefutura)	www.univision.com
68	WBPX	(PAX)	www.paxboston.tv

AM Radio

590	WEZE	Christian radio	www.wezeradio.com
680	WRKO	Talk	www.wrko.com
740	WJIB	Instrumental Pop/Light Oldies	
850	WEEI	Sports	www.weei.com
950	WROL	Religious	
1030	WBZ	News/Talk/Sports	www.wbz.com
1060	WBIX	Business Talk	
1090	WILD	Urban	
1120	WBNW	Financial Talk	www.moneymattersradio.net
1150	WJTK	Religious	
1260	WMKI	Radio Disney	www.radio.disney.go.com/mystation/Boston/
1510	WWZN	Sports	www.1510thezone.com
1600	WUNR	Leased-time/ethnic	
1670	Allston-Brighton Free Radio		www.abfreeradio.org

FM Radio

88.1	WMBR	MIT	wmbr.mit.edu
88.9	WERS	Emerson College	www.wers.org
89.7	WGBH	NPR News/Classical	www.wgbh.com
90.3	WZBC	Boston College	www.wzbc.org
90.9	WBUR	NPR/BU	www.wbur.org
91.5	WMFO	Tufts University	www.wmfo.org
91.9	WUMB	Folk/Jazz	www.wumb.org
92.5	The River	Rock/Pop Modern	www.wxrv.com
92.9	WBOS	Modern AC	www.wbos.com
93.7	WEEI	Sports Talk Radio	www.weei.com
94.5	WJMN	Hip-Hop/R&B	www.jamn.com
95.3	WHRB	Harvard University	www.whrb.org
96.9	WTKK	Talk	www.wtkk.com
98.5	Sports Hub	Sports Talk Radio	http://boston.cbslocal.com/category/sports/
99.5	WCRB	Classical	www.wcrb.com
100.1	WBRS	Brandeis University	www.wbrs.org
100.7	WZLX	Classic Rock	www.wzlx.com
101.7	WFNX	Modern Rock	www.wfnx.com
102.5	WKLB	Country	www.wklb.com
102.9	WCFM	Caribbean Music	www.choice1029.com
103.3	WODS	Oldies	www.oldies1033.com
104.1	Mix FM	Pop	http://mix1041.radio.com/
104.9	WBOQ	Soft Rock	www.northshore1049.com
105.7	WROR	Classic Rock	www.wror.com
106.7	WMJX	Soft Rock	www.magic1067.com
107.3	WAAF	Active Rock	www.waaf.com
107.9	WXKS	Pop	www.kissfm.com

Print Media

Bay Windows	www.baywindows.com	617-266-6670	LGBT newsweekly.
Beacon Hill Times	www.beaconhilltimes.com	617-523-9490	Newsweekly serving Beacon Hill.
Boston Business Journal	www.bizjournals.com/boston	617-330-1000	Business weekly.
Boston Globe	www.boston.com	617-929-2000	Daily broadsheet.
Boston Haitian Reporter	www.bostonhaitian.com	617-436-1222	Free monthly for Haitian-American community.
Boston Herald	www.bostonherald.com	617-426-3000	Daily tabloid.
Boston Irish Reporter	www.bostonirish.com	617-436-1222	News from and about the Irish in Boston.
Boston Metro	www.metropoint.com	617-338-7985	Weekday tabloid aimed at commuters.
Boston Magazine	www.bostonmagazine.com	617-262-9700	Glossy monthly.
Boston Review	www.bostonreview.net	617-258-0805	Leftish politics and culture magazine.
Boston Russian Bulletin	www.russianmass.com	617-277-5398	Russian community news, in Russian.
Brookline TAB	www.townonline.com/brookline	617-566-3585	Brookline newsweekly.
Cambridge Chronicle	www.townonline.com/cambridge	617-577-7149	Cambridge newsweekly.
Cambridge TAB	www.townonline.com/cambridge	617-497-1241	Cambridge newsweekly.
Charlestown Patriot-Bridge	www.charlestownbridge.com	617-241-8500	Charlestown newsweekly.
Dorchester Reporter	www.dotnews.com	617-436-1222	Dorchester news.
Improper Bostonian	www.improper.com	617-859-1400	Free entertainment and lifestyle magazine.
In Newsweekly	www.innewsweekly.com	617-426-8246	LGBT news and entertainment.
Jamaica Plain Gazette	www.jamaicaplaingazette.com	617-524-2626	JP news.
The Jewish Advocate	www.thejewishadvocate.com	617-367-9100	News about Boston's Jewish community.
Mass High Tech	www.masshightech.com	617-242-1224	Technology news.
Mattapan Reporter	www.bostonneighborhoodnews.com	617-436-1222	Mattapan neighborhood news.
Patriot Ledger	www.patriotledger.com	617-786-7000	Daily south shore news.
Pilot	www. thebostonpilot.com	617-746-5889	Catholic newsweekly.
Sampan	www.sampan.org	617-426-9492	Chinese/English bimonthly.
Somerville Journal	www.townonline.com/somerville	617-625-6300	Weekly Somerville news.
South Boston Tribune	www.southbostoninfo.com	617-268-3440	Weekly South Boston news.
Stuff	www.stuffboston.com	617-859-3333	Entertainment listings and "what's hot."
Weekly Dig	www.weeklydig.com	617-426-8942	Humor, news and nightlife.

Hungry?

Seafood

Boston is a seafood lover's paradise: steamers, oysters, lobster rolls, clam chowder, and every kind of fish imaginable are presented on plates all over the city. Historic **Union Oyster House (Map 2)** is Boston's oldest restaurant, and it has retained the antiquated décor; **Neptune Oyster (Map 2)** has a more contemporary vibe. For pomp and old school elegance, try **Anthony's Pier 4 (Map 10)** overlooking the harbor. The best lobster roll is at **Jasper White's Summer Shack (Map 5, 22)**, and JP's **Galway House (Map 14)** makes a mean clam chowder. Inman Square's **East Coast Grill & Raw Bar (Map 28)** is a lively local spot with a well-stocked raw bar and glorious barbeque for those who prefer land over sea. If you want something different than the standard New England-style preparations, **Peach Farm (Map 4)** specializes in shrimp and scallops with a Chinese flair. Make the obligatory trip to **Legal Sea Foods (Map 3, 6, 10, 20, 26)** first because it's a Boston institution, and second for the sinfully good fried platters. Just be prepared to drop some dough.

Italian

The scent of garlic permeates the air in the North End, Boston's charming Italian quarter. While almost any restaurant on Hanover Street is bound to be authentic and delicious, there are a few standouts, like **Maurizio's (Map 2)**, **Lucca (Map 2)**, and **Bricco (Map 2)**. **Mamma Maria (Map 2)** is a cozy spot ideal for romancing a significant other. Try **Prezza (Map 2)** for fancier fare. Outside of the North End, modern Italian restaurants like **Sportello (Map 10)** and **Via Matta (Map 3)** give the more traditional spots a run for their money. **Anchovies (Map 6)** is a Back Bay staple, while Brookliners frequent **Pomodoro (Map 17)** and **La Morra (Map 17)**. **L'Impasto (Map 22)** holds down the fort for Cambridge.

Pizza

There's a lot of diversity in Boston's pizza offerings for something that's basically made of three ingredients. **Pizzeria Regina (Map 2)** and the **Upper Crust (Map 7, 19, 29)** serve traditional sloppy, cheesy pies, and are the top two for most locals. **Penguin Pizza (Map 15)** draws in the college scene with a long beer list. Kendall Square favorite **Emma's (Map 28)** puts an upscale spin on pizza with gourmet toppings, and Cambridge's **Stone Hearth (Map 23)** caters to locavores with organic ingredients. While Bostonians tend to avoid anything hailing from NYC, **New York Pizza (Map 3)** is actually quite good. The uncommonly friendly staff at **Leone's (Map 24)** and **Captain Nemo's (Map 14)** make it worth a visit for a neighborly chat along with your slice.

East Asian

Chinatown is to Chinese what the North End is to Italian. If you're looking for full-on dim-sum craziness, try **China Pearl (Map 4)** or **Hei La Moon (Map 4)** for weekend brunch. If you want more sedate surroundings in Chinatown, try **King Fung Garden (Map 4)**, **Hong Kong Eatery (Map 4)**, or **Peach Farm (Map 4)**. It's a tie for best Thai between **Wonder Spice (Map 14)** and **Dok Bua (Map 17)**. Check out **BonChon (Map 19, 20)** for Korean fried chicken. Sushi joints abound in Brookline; **Fugakyu (Map 17)** and **Genki Ya (Map 17)** are a cut above. Try **Elephant Walk (Map 16, 22)** for Cambodian, and **Pho Viet (Map 19)** or **Xinh Xinh (Map 4)** for Vietnamese. When in doubt, Asian fusion restaurants like **Myers + Chang (Map 7)** and **Thelonious Monkfish (Map 27)** offer a little bit of everything.

South Asian

Indian restaurants can be found in almost every corner of the city, although many of the best are clustered in Cambridge, like **Punjabi Dhaba (Map 28)**, **Diva Indian Bistro (Map 22)**, **Tamarind Bay (Map 20)**, and **India Pavilion (Map 17)**. **Helmand (Map 26)** is a mainstay for Afghan. Back across the river, JP residents get their curry fix at **Bukhara (Map 14)**. **Mela (Map 7)** in the South End is one of the more affordable options in the area, and even has a lunch buffet. The Back Bay has **Kashmir (Map 5)**, a classy lunch spot with a patio prime for people watching, and Kenmore has **India Quality Restaurant (Map 16)**, a small hole in the wall with astoundingly solid food.

Bars

Sometimes a bothersome urge to eat gets in the way of downing beers, and in these situations it's worthwhile to know that some bars serve a higher grade of grub than others. **Blarney Stone (Map 32)**, **Harry's (Map 19)**, and the **Galway House (Map 14)** dish up unpretentious dinner entrees on the cheap. Be warned that the barbecue chips at **Trina's Starlite Lounge (Map 28)** are dangerously addictive; same deal with the crab guacamole at **Lolita (Map 6)**. **Stats (Map 10)**, **Miracle of Science (Map 27)**, and **Silvertone Bar & Grill (Map 3)** have lighter options, but to really fortify your stomach for some serious drinking (read: fried anything), try the **Pour House (Map 5)**, **The Lower Depths (Map 16)**, or **Flash's (Map 6)**.

Grease

Bostonians are keener on upscale brunches than down home diners, but there are still a few places to get eggs and pancakes in the morning in all their greasy glory. Head to **Mul's Diner (Map 10)**, **South Street Diner (Map 4)**, or the **Allston Diner (Map 19)** for a low-key no-frills start to the day. **Sound Bites (Map 23)** is a half-step up from the average diner without being overly prissy—heck, they serve hash. For out and out gluttony, try the funky '50s-esque **Friendly Toast (Map 28)** if you don't mind waiting in line with scores of hipsters. Allston's **Tavern in the Square (Map 19)** has an all-you-can-eat brunch buffet where college students congregate to nurse hangovers.

Top-End

Looking to impress a date? Try **Ten Tables (Map 14)**, **Hungry I (Map 1)**, **Meritage (Map 4)**, or **Hamersley's Bistro (Map 7)**. Foodies that are interested in innovative cuisine will delight in the complex creations at **O Ya (Map 32)**, **Journeyman (Map 24)**, and **Bondir (Map 28)**. Head to **Hungry Mother (Map 28)** or the **South End Buttery (Map 7)** for upscale comfort food. **L'Espalier (Map 7)**, **No. 9 Park (Map 3)**, and **Mistral (Map 6)** are seasoned establishments that have only gotten better with age. **Craigie on Main (Map 27)** and **Henrietta's Table (Map 20)** are both geared towards seasonal and local fare. The classic elegance of **Eastern Standard (Map 16)** is the restaurant equivalent of the little black dress.

It's not quite the city that never sleeps, but Boston's nightlife is vast and varied, catering not only to teeming masses of college students but eager yuppies and disaffected hipsters alike. Since this is a city founded by people that were so uptight the British annoyed them (Pot paging kettle...), we are still stuck with the blue-law mentality that anything that might be fun has to be completely controlled at all times. Thus, all of our bars shutter for the evening at 1 or 2 a.m. This would be fine for most people if the MBTA, you know, the way the majority of people get around in a city with little parking, didn't manage to close BY TWELVE F*@KING THIRTY. After-hours joints do exist, but are for members only, so when those lights come up and you are doing your best Last Call Shuffle to get a number—keep in mind cabs are as easy to get after closing time as Red Sox-Yankee ticks are on opening day. Despite these best efforts, though, the variety of bars, dance clubs, and live music venues keep growing, so you'll be able to find just the right spot to be seen, be picked up, dance, throw some Red Sox-Yankee darts, or sit and share a pint with a friend while you catch a live band. Remember that clubs are always in flux, so it makes sense to call ahead and confirm what's up before rounding up your crew and hitting the town.

Beer

A wave of craft beer fanaticism has swept Boston, and while you can still get a Sam or a Harpoon just about anywhere, many bars now stock more unusual stuff. **Meadhall (Map 26)** is the holy grail for beer lovers, with over 100 beers on tap—none of them Coors, Miller, or Bud products. Nearby, **Lord Hobo (Map 28)** caters to the budding hipster beer snob. Allston's rowdy student hangout **Sunset Grill & Tap (Map 19)** serves yards of beers, while more refined Allstonians head to **Deep Ellum (Map 19)**. Two solid options in the Back Bay are **Bukowski Tavern (Map 5)** and the **Pour House (Map 5)**—the selection isn't the best at the latter but no one's complaining about the dirt cheap 22 oz. drafts. **Brendan Behan Pub (Map 14)** pours the smoothest Guinness in the city, but if you insist drinking your pint among Irish accents, head to the **Blackthorn Pub (Map 10)** in Southie. Gastropubs **Canary Square (Map 14)**, the **Squealing Pig (Map 15)**, and the **Publick House (Map 17)** all have extensive beer lists. Fenway's **Tasty Burger (Map 15, 20)** pays homage to the art of the canned beer. If you're curious to investigate the brewing process, take a tour at either the **Sam Adams (Map 14)** or **Harpoon (Map 11)** breweries. Hop on the trolley after the Sam tour to be shuttled to **Doyle's (Map 14)**, the first bar in America to serve Sam Adams. Want to get really adventurous? Buy a spin on the beer wheel at **Redbones (Map 22)**, and cross your fingers that you'll like your pick.

Sports

Almost every bar in Boston becomes a sports bar when the Red Sox, Celtics, Bruins, or Patriots are playing—just try to find a bar where the game isn't on. The best Sox bars are **Jerry Remy's (Map 15)**, **Cask 'n' Flagon (Map 16)**, **Game On! (Map 16)**, **Bleacher Bar (Map 16)**, and **The Baseball Tavern (Map 15)**. Head to **The Four's (Map 1)** or the **Greatest Bar (Map 1)** for hockey and basketball. Football fans should check out **Stadium (Map 10)**, **McGreevey's (Map 5)**, **Tavern in the Square (Map 19)**, or **Stats (Map 10)**. **Coolidge Corner Clubhouse (Map 19)** is Brookline's resident sports bar, and **Orleans (Map 22)** is Somerville's. Brighton's **Cityside (Map 18)** is a relaxed, anything goes spot with a killer patio, while **Champions (Map 6)** is a sports bar for the preppy set.

Elegant and Nice

If you feel like getting gussied up and playing socialite for a night, **Clink (Map 1)**, **Bond (Map 4)**, **Towne (Map 5)**, and **City Bar (Map 6)** are some of the trendiest spots in the city. **Sonsie (Map 5)** has the sophistication of a Parisian café, while **Eastern Standard (Map 16)** pours expertly mixed drinks in a lavishly elegant room. Sip a calm glass of wine at **Parker's Bar (Map 3)** or **Upstairs on the Square (Map 20)**, or if a craft cocktail is more your speed, stop by **Local 149 (Map 11)**. Relive the roaring twenties at **Cuchi Cuchi (Map 27)**. **Franklin Southie (Map 12)** proves that Southie isn't all rough edges. While a bit pricey, **Top of the Hub (Map 5)** offers a birds-eye view of the city skyline from the top floor of the Prudential Center. **Saloon (Map 22)** is a modern day speakeasy with an exhaustive whiskey list.

Dive

There are two types of dives in Boston: fun and quirky holes in the wall where college students ironically chug PBRs, and seriously run down places full of lotto scratching regulars. **Punter's Pub (Map 15)**, the **Silhouette Lounge (Map 19)**, and the **Midway Café (Map 14)** all fall in the first camp. Those who'd like to leave the safety net of the college crowd can pull up a bar stool at the **Beacon Hill Pub (Map 1)**, **J.J. Foley's Fireside Tavern (Map 30)**, or the **Galway House (Map 14)**. **An Tain (Map 4)** and the **Sligo Pub (Map 22)** attract a good mix of the young and old.

Live Music

Boston has a thriving live music scene, its local community of musicians nurturing each other and able to get lots of exposure in a wide array of venues. The Cars, The Pixies, Jonathan Richman, J. Geils, Passion Pit, Mission of Burma, and Aerosmith are just a few decent names to come out of this town. The homegrown bands get as much attention as the national acts mostly due to the sheer number them kicking around artist boroughs Allston, Somerville, and JP. Whether you're in the mood for rock, blues, roots, punk, folk, rockabilly, jazz, or yes, even bluegrass, somebody in Boston is playing it. If you're looking for country music—Rhode Island is south of here. Go find it.

While huge national acts play at the Garden and Comcast Center, many also opt for smaller venues like the 2,800-seat Orpheum Theater for its great acoustics. Berklee College has graduated the likes of Branford Marsalis, Quincy Jones, and Diana Krall, and at its Berklee Performance Center (**www.berklee.edu/BPC**, 617-747-2261) you can catch performances by big names and famous alumni or cheap concerts by teachers and students. Who knows? You may be watching the next John Mayer. Another place to catch national acts in a club atmosphere is the incredibly awesome **House of Blues (Map 16)** that has eaten the club corpses of Axis and Avalon. If it's summer, the best venue in all of Beantown is the **Bank of America Pavilion (Map 11)** right on the waterfront, and Bostonians come out in droves to see the Pops' famous Fourth of July Concert at the **Hatch Shell (Map 6)**.

For jazz, you can grab dinner and a show at the classy **Regattabar (Map 20)** or **Scullers (Map 19)**. Both in Cambridge, they host world-class performers. If you're on a budget, check out smaller venues like **Ryles (Map 28)** in Inman Square, **Good Life (Map 4)** in Downtown Crossing, and **Wally's (Map 5)** in the South End, a tiny neighborhood bar where you'll sometimes find Berklee students sitting in with the evening's combo. Get some scat along with your eggs at **The Beehive's (Map 7)** jazz brunches.

Rock 'n rollers head to **Paradise Rock Club (Map 19)**. If the downstairs is packed, go upstairs for a bird's-eye view of the band. If you get tired of moshing, the adjoining lounge features smaller bands and food in a more relaxed setting. In Central Square, lines form out the door for **T.T. the Bear's Place (Map 27)**. At next door's **Middle East (Map 27)**, one of the coolest clubs on the planet, you can grab some grape leaves before heading to one of its three rooms of music. **Brighton Music Hall (Map 19)**, the former Harper's Ferry, has continued its predecessor's legacy of rock, blues, and New Orleans funk. Punk and garage bands frequent JP's **Midway Café (Map 14)**.

If you're pining for some old school blues and rock, head to the **Cantab (Map 27)** on the weekend for the still standing Little Joe Cook and the Thrillers. Smaller bars to catch a good groove include **O'Brien's (Map 19)**, **P.A.'s Lounge (Map 24)**, and **Church (Map 15)**. Great Scott (Map 19) has epic DJ dance nights in addition to underground bands. **Johnny D's (Map 22)** in Somerville reigns supreme for the older blues crowd.

Folkies and singer-songwriters worship at the altar that is **Club Passim (Map 20)**, a 40-plus-year-old landmark dedicated to promoting independent musicians. Joan Baez, Bob Dylan, and Muddy Waters have all graced its stage. Craft beer and wine is now available for purchase along with a wide array of vegetarian snacks. And if you're dying to dust off that old banjo of yours, return to the **Cantab (Map 27)** on Tuesday nights for its bluegrass pickin' party.

You can find reggae, hip-hop, and Afrobeat at **Western Front (Map 27)**. Latin music and salsa dancing heat up **Green Street Grill (Map 27)**, **Mojitos Lounge (Map 3)**, and **Bella Luna (Map 14)**, which has a dedicated lesbian following.

Can't decide what mood you're in? The **Lizard Lounge (Map 20)**, a laid-back neighborhood hang in Cambridge, hosts an eclectic mix of music and performances seven nights a week, ranging from punk to acoustic, rock and roll, experimental, and poetry slams. Dueling piano bar **Howl at the Moon (Map 4)** is a novelty in Boston, and bachelorettes slinging cocktail "buckets" abound. Pianists play requests exclusively, so you'll hear "Piano Man" to the Backstreet Boys and everything in between.

Many pubs and bars feature local bands or musicians, often for free or a minimal cover charge. It's a great way to get to know the scene. Check weekly listings for schedules. Some worth paying a visit to are **The Plough & Stars (Map 27)**, the **Green Briar (Map 18)**, **The Asgard (Map 27)**, and **Atwood's Tavern (Map 28)**. Probably the best of these is **Toad (Map 23)**. The room is small, and you usually have to sneak past the bass player to get to the bathroom, but the wide variety and high quality of bands make this a popular gathering place.

Clubs

Whether you're into breaking a serious sweat or just delicately nodding your head to the beat, there's a club in Boston where you can get your preferred level of groove on. Fist pumping bros flock to **Joshua Tree (Map 19)**. Don heels and a slinky dress to fit in at **District (Map 4)**, **Venu (Map 3)**, or **Rise (Map 6)**. Kick it old school at **Storyville (Map 6)**. **Tommy Doyle's (Map 20)** and **Good Life (Map 28)** have a jolly middle school dance vibe, and the varied DJ nights at **Phoenix Landing (Map 27)** draw in a different crowd every night. Hipsters who deign to dance do it at **Middlesex Lounge (Map 27)**. A booming LGBT scene can be found at **dbar (Map 32)**, **Club Café (Map 6)**, and **Machine (Map 15)**.

Karaoke

You get enough booze into even the shyest person, and suddenly repressed desires for superstardom bubble up. Grab a mic and quell those urges at the popular karaoke nights at **Tommy Doyle's (Map 20)**, **The Purple Shamrock (Map 2)**, **The Asgard (Map 27)**, **King's (Map 5)**, or **The Hong Kong (Map 2)**. The gay and lesbian crowd heads to JP for Queeraoke at the **Midway Café (Map 14)**. Belt your heart out at the **Jeanie Johnston Pub (Map 14)** or **Flann O'Brien's (Map 15)**, and you're sure to get some cheers no matter how off-key you are. For hardcore karaoke junkies, **Limelight Stage and Studio (Map 3)** applies pitch correction technology so you can finally nail that high note from "Don't Stop Believin'" in front of a large crowd or in a private studio. **Do Re Mi (Map 19)** rents private rooms for those who aren't up to performing in front of strangers. While they technically have a no alcohol policy, the owners tend to look the other way as long as you're not ostentatiously ripping shots.

It's difficult to typecast Boston shoppers, due in part to the diversity of its people, from the Burberry-sporting, Beacon Hill elite to Cambridge funksters in paint-splattered Chuck Taylors. The city's climate (11 months of winter and four weeks of spring, summer, and fall) compels most Bostonians to spend their weekends popping into climate-controlled shops that range from uncomfortably exclusive to quietly quaint to downright weird. In addition to the extreme consumerist lifestyle of many of its dwellers, the city also has its fair share of psychotic, year-round outdoor athletes, for whom purveyors of gear appear throughout the city. The fleet of moving trucks clogging this college town on the first of every month from March through October keeps the furniture and houseware hawkers in business. Despite the few malls that have weaseled their way onto the scene, the dependable disparity and constant movement of the city results in a throbbing, colorful, and sometimes shocking mass of consumers.

Clothing: New, Used & Vintage

For the label checking, what-do-you-drive-yuppies in our midst, the Boston shopping scene certainly delivers. Start in the Back Bay on Berkeley Street at **Louis Boston (Map 6)**, then head to **Brooks Brothers (Map 6)** around the corner on Newbury Street. More reasonably priced but still plenty preppy is **Eddie Bauer (Map 3)** downtown. On the other side of the coin, Boston has a ton to offer those seeking funkier duds—you just need to know where to look. **The Garment District (Map 28)** in Cambridge is a gargantuan thrift/vintage store with everything from '60s sweaters to contemporary second-hand treasures, as well as new offerings from local designers. Just a few blocks over, **Poor Little Rich Girl (Map 28)** also has a great selection of vintage duds. Even upscale Newbury Street has its share of vintage chic—the **Army Barracks (Map 5)** is an old fave. And Boston is really a walking city (you know, when it's not hailing), so outfit your feet with shoes from **Berk's (Map 20)** in Harvard Square, **The Tannery (Map 6, 20)** in Back Bay and Harvard Square, or **Cambridge Clogs (Map 23)** in Porter Square.

For the Home/Apartment/Dorm

Though driving through Brookline and Beacon Hill on September 2—after most apartments have been vacated, their perfectly usable furniture left on the curb—is a fabulous way to outfit your own digs, you may wish to take a gander at the furniture 'n' stuff offered throughout a city that's constantly turning over. If nothing else, you won't have to worry about that greenish blue stain on the free chair from the corner. Despite the terrific selection and prices offered by the obvious **Crate & Barrel (Map 6, 27)**, beware the slalom of newly-engaged couples registering for gifts. **Sunshine Lucy's (Map 22)** in Davis Square and **Circle Furniture (Map 21)** in West Cambridge are locally owned joints offering a wide variety of furniture and appliances. **Economy Hardware (Map 5, 16, 27)** is a reliable bet for furniture, gadgets, even paint (oh, and hardware), but often comes with a complimentary headache. Check out counter-intuitive spots like **Urban Outfitters (Map 5, 19, 20)**, **Anthropologie (Map 6, 20)**, and **Boutique Fabulous (Map 28)** for finishing touches like pretty pillows, cool lamps, and funky artwork. Antique hunters will be kept happy at **Cambridge Antique Market's (Map 26)** five floors of yesteryear.

Sports

As the city most associated with a certain 26.2 mile race, Boston is well equipped to provide you with whatever you need to get your heart rate pumping. **Marathon Sports (Map 6, 17, 20)** lets you test drive their sneakers on the sidewalk to make sure you leave with exactly the right pair. Whatever the season, you can find what you're looking for at **City Sports (Map 3, 6, 19, 20, 23)**. Boston's also a biker city (think pedals, not crotchrockets). Riders can get tune-ups, gear, and honest advice at **International Bicycle Center (Map 19)**. **REI (Map 16)** and **Eastern Mountain Sports (Map 5, 19, 20)** are also good for bikes along with anything you might need for a cliff-hangin' good time.

Computing Machines

Thanks to its many universities, hospitals, and research facilities, Boston is awash with computer-loving dweebs. **Micro Center (Map 27)** is swarmed on the weekends. Three centrally located **Best Buys (Map 16, 26)** feature their usual merchandise and crowds. The PC-user-repellant **Apple Store (Map 26)** in the Cambridgeside Galleria is one stylin' geek boutique only matched by the three-story **Apple Store (Map 6)** that sits like a see-through shrine to Geekdom on Boylston Street.

Music Maniacs

The rise of the iPod has given Bostonians yet another excuse to avoid interaction with other humanoids who dare cross their path. But plenty of options still exist for those in search of discs, vinyl, and other types of tangible tunes. **Newbury Comics (Map 2, 5, 20)** delivers on their offer of "a wicked good time" with not only music, but movies, novelties, and general craziness. For those in search of vinyl, vintage, and generally hard-to-find tunes, stroll along Mass Ave in Cambridge to find **Cheapo**

Records (Map 27) and **Stereo Jack's (Map 20)**, as well as **Somerville Grooves (Map 24)** in the always hip Union Square. Comm Ave near BU and Harvard Square are also places to troll for rare stuff with stores like **In Your Ear (Map 19)**, **Nuggets (Map 16)**, and **Planet Records (Map 20)**. If you're one of the real out-there cats looking for the most random of discs, try **Weirdo Records (Map 27)** in Central Square for 100% truth in advertising.

Foodie Fanatics

You literally cannot go wrong in the North End. **Mike's Pastry (Map 2)**, **Modern Pastry (Map 2)**, and the 24/7 **Bova's Bakery (Map 2)** are three of about 1,000 places to try for sweet goodies. For savory Italian treats try **Salumeria Italiana (Map 2)**. Equally tempting treats can be found at **Athan's Bakery (Map 17)** in Brookline or **Cardullo's (Map 20)** in Harvard Square. For ice cream, **Christina's Homemade (Map 28)** in Inman Square is a favorite, as well as **J.P. Licks (Map 14, 19, 20)**, **Toscanini's (Map 27)**, **Lizzy's (Map 20)**, and **Emack & Bolio's (Maps 5, 9, 17)**, all with lines out the door in warmer months. Fans of more solid sweets will fare just as well at **Sweet (Map 3, 5, 6, 20)** and **KickAss Cupcakes (Map 22)**. **Dave's Fresh Pasta (Map 22)**, **City Feed & Supply (Map 14)**, and **Pemberton Farms (Map 22)** carry a mix of local, organic specialty and standard items, sandwiches, prepared foods, and fresh bread. For the gourmet addicts, there's nothing like the cheese counters at **South End Formaggio (Map 7)** or **Formaggio Kitchen (Map 21)** to give you the artisan deliciousness you've been craving. Drool, drool.

Malls and 'hoods

Boston has seemingly avoided the typical suburban oasis of a mall more than other cities, but it does it one better by providing several neighborhood locations where you can store-hop, grab a bite, and people watch simultaneously, with real food, not food court swill. Downtown Crossing is a high-energy center of rabid consumerism, very convenient to the T, and boasting the gigantic department store **Macy's (Map 3)** (which has recently gobbled up the beloved Filene's), discount stores (**Marshall's (Map 3, 6, 12, 26)** and **TJ Maxx (Map 3, 19)**), and other joints like **H&M (Map 3, 6, 26)**. Clothes aren't the only things for sale around here—there are jewelers, shoe stores, street vendors, and performers. It's also within walking distance of Faneuil Hall Market Place, another splendid mallternative. Likewise, one could easily spend a solid afternoon wandering around Harvard Square. **Newbury Comics (Map 2, 5, 20)**, **Black Ink (Map 20)**, **Joie De Vivre (Map 23)** and **Leavitt & Peirce (Map 20)** are great for gift shopping (for yourself or anyone else), and **Urban Outfitters (Map 20)** always has the latest in hipster apparel and home decor (check out their bargain basement with savings that will melt your face off). Stop for a snack at **Cardullo's (Map 20)** or recharge at **Tealuxe (Map 20)**, and flip through a book at the **Co-op (Map 20)** or **Harvard Bookstore (Map 20)**. Walk the length of Newbury Street and you'll find everything from bookstores (**Trident Booksellers & Café (Map 5)** to foodie paraphernalia (**O & Co. (Map 5)** to art (**International Poster Gallery (Map 6)**, plus clothes and clothes and clothes. Though most of what's found on Newbury is decidedly pricey, things do get more reasonable as you get closer to Mass Ave. Boylston Street runs parallel to Newbury with offerings like **Anthropologie (Map 6)** and **City Sports (Maps 3, 6, 19, 20, 23)**. And yes, as much as we hate to admit it, Boston does have a few genuine malls—though they are well camouflaged and the word "mall" does not actually appear in their titles. The Shops at Prudential Center include **Sephora (Map 5)**, **Lord & Taylor (Map 6)**, and several others. It cuts through to the even higher-end Copley Place, where those of you that have the cash can drop quite a load of it at **Barneys New York (Map 6)**. The Cambridge Side Galleria is a multi-level Mecca where MIT kids, biotech execs, and European tourists flock to the **Apple Store (Map 26)** to satisfy their Mac addictions. **Peirce (Map 20)** are great for gift shopping (for yourself or anyone else), and **Urban Outfitters (Map 20)** always has the latest in hipster apparel and home decor (check out their bargain basement with savings that will melt your face off). Stop for a snack at **Cardullo's (Map 20)** or recharge at **Tealuxe (Map 20)**, and flip through a book at the **Co-op (Map 20)** or **Harvard Bookstore (Map 20)**. Walk the length of Newbury Street and you'll find everything from bookstores (**Trident Booksellers & Café (Map 5)**) to foodie paraphernalia (**O & Co. (Map 5)**) to art (**International Poster Gallery (Map 6)**, plus clothes and clothes and clothes. Though most of what's found on Newbury is decidedly pricey, things do get more reasonable as you get closer to Mass Ave. Boylston Street runs parallel to Newbury with offerings like **Anthropologie (Map 6)** and **City Sports (Maps 3, 6, 19, 20, 23)**. And yes, as much as we hate to admit it, Boston does have a few genuine malls—though they are well camouflaged and the word "mall" does not actually appear in their titles. The Shops at Prudential Center include **Sephora (Map 5)**, **Lord & Taylor (Map 6)**, and several others. It cuts through to the even higher-end Copley Place, where those of you that have the cash can drop quite a load of it at **Barneys New York (Map 6)**. The Cambridge Side Galleria is a multi-level Mecca where MIT kids, biotech execs, and European tourists flock to the **Apple Store (Map 26)** to satisfy their Mac addictions.

With all the students and schools that Boston manages to cram into it's small borders, we suffer from a distinct lack of places to catch a film. Currently we're down to two locations—the **AMC Loews Boston Common (Map 3)** and **Regal Fenway 13 (Map 16)**. Be forewarned as these joints are the only players in the game, the ticket and food prices reflect the lack of competition. Also, for those of you that actually want to WATCH the movie, these locations draw a large number of teenagers who can't shut off their cell phones for 90 minutes. Still, if it's a new release that's a must see, they both deliver. If you can wait until the movie of your desire is a bit older, **The Somerville Theater (Map 22)** does a good chunk of second run business, and it also has hooch.

To watch a movie with 90% less teenager text message ringtone, then you'll have to venture to **Landmark Kendall Square Cinema (Map 26)**, the **Brattle Theatre (Map 20)**, the **Harvard Film Archive (Map 20)**, the **Museum of Fine Arts (Map 15)**, or the best damn joint to see a flick in greater Boston—the **Coolidge Corner Theatre (Map 17)**.

From the end of June through the end of August, check out Free Friday Flicks at the **Hatch Shell (Map 6)** on the Esplanade. Movies start at sundown, but arrive early to get your spot on the grass. And for heaven's sake, don't forget to bring some wine and cheese.

Huge-screen freaks should hit the **Mugar Omni Theater (Map 1)** at the Museum of Science and the **Simons IMAX Theatre (Map 2)** at the New England Aquarium. If you just have to shop for furniture before seeing a movie in IMAX or 3-D, you owe yourself a trip to **Jordan's Furniture** (1-866-8JORDANS) in either Natick (ext. 2860) or Reading (ext. 6800). It might be worth the trip alone if the Red Sox are doing well in the standings, and you feel like taking them up on whatever World Series promo they have running.

Movie Theater	*Address*	*Phone*		*Map*
Mugar Omni Theatre	1 Science Park	617-723-2500	Don't move your head, you'll puke.	1
Simons IMAX Theatre	1 Central Wharf	617-973-5206	MOMMY! DOLLLLPHINS!!!!	2
AMC Loews Boston Common 19	175 Tremont St	617-423-5801	Blockbusters.	3
Institute of Contemporary Art	100 Northern Ave	617-478-3100	It's contemporary art, so prepare for weirdness.	10
Museum of Fine Arts	465 Huntington Ave	617-369-3770	Ever changing array, filmmaker Q&A.	15
Regal Fenway Stadium 13	201 Brookline Ave	617-424-6111	On-site parking. Video games in the lobby.	16
Coolidge Corner Theatre	290 Harvard St	617-734-2500	Theme nights and film festivals.	17
Brattle Theatre	40 Brattle St	617-876-6837	*Casablanca*. Every year.	20
Harvard Film Archive	24 Quincy St	617-495-4700	Films you won't see at Boston Common.	20
Apple Cinema	168 Alewife Brook Pkwy	617-661-2900	A bit sticky.	22
Somerville Theatre	55 Davis Sq	617-625-5700	Now serving beer and wine.	22
Landmark Kendall Square Cinema	One Kendall Sq	617-499-1996	Movies for smart grown-ups.	26

Newbury Street has Boston's largest and densest concentration of art galleries. You've probably passed by the several dozen galleries on Newbury Street many times without taking a look at what's inside, but popping into just a few of them will give you some idea of the broad scope of what's on offer (even if your budget means you're more likely to be striking deals at the MFA's gift shop). Commercial art fans should check out **International Poster Gallery**'s **(Map 6)** expansive collection of Italian, travel, and Soviet-era posters. The gallery of the **Copley Society of Boston (Map 6)**, also on Newbury Street, hosts several competitions over the course of the year, including showcases of student work.

While Newbury Street galleries may have the city's most established spots, the interesting developments are happening in the South End, where a number of galleries have opened or relocated. The center of the action is the converted warehouse at 450 Harrison Avenue between Thayer Street and Randolph Street. (Take the Silver Line to East Berkeley Street, walk one block to Harrison Avenue, and hang a right.) Big names at the "SoWa Building" include **Carroll and Sons (Map 7)** and the **Kingston Gallery (Map 7).** If you're interested in what's emerging in Boston's contemporary art scene, head to SoWa on the first Friday of the month to see the new exhibits. (At the very least, it's an excuse to get dressed up and consume some free wine.) Elsewhere in Boston, consider seeing what's on display at **Boston Cyberarts Gallery (Map 14)** in Jamaica Plain's Green Street T Station, the **Fort Point Arts Community Gallery (Map 10)**, Roxbury's **Hamill Gallery of African Art (Map 13)**, and Kenmore Square's **Panopticon Gallery of Photography (Map 15)**. Cheaper rents continue to attract artists to East Boston, where the newly reopened **Atlantic Works Gallery (Map 9)** holds regular exhibitions and potluck get-togethers.

In addition to standard galleries, many of the city's neighborhoods put on "open studio" events where you can satisfy your nosy streak by poking around the studios of artists willing to open them up to the public. Go to www.cityofboston.gov/arts.

For art too bad to be ignored, hit up MOBA (www.museumofbadart.org), with rotating locations in Brookline, Somerville, and Dedham. No joke, this place is real!

Outside of a dog, a book is man's best friend. Inside of a dog it's too dark to read. —Groucho Marx

Big

As in so many cities, **Barnes & Noble (Map 5 & 16)** is the big dog on the Boston bookstore scene. If you're shopping for a book, but not also for a low-fat latte or a high-fat chocolate croissant, get familiar with the large independents **Brookline Booksmith (Map 19)** and the 75-year-old **Harvard Book Store (Map 20)** (unaffiliated with the university). Both focus on new titles but have cellars that handle used books.

Used

Davis Square's **McIntyre & Moore Books (Map 22)** sells an array of used books, with a bent toward school textbooks. When in Roslindale, stop by **Pazzo Books** (4268 Washington St, 617-323-2919, Map 30) for used and rare books and a round of skee-ball on the old machine in the basement. Some people think **Raven Used Books (Map 20)** in Harvard Square delivers the best bang for your buck. A good place to find used guidebooks and fiction is **Rodney's Bookstore (Map 17, 27)**, with locations in both Central Square and Brookline. Downtown Crossing's **Brattle Book Shop (Map 3)** is a well-known used book specialist—check out the outdoor book racks on dry days. Also in Central Boston, and worth checking out for antiquarian books, are **Lame Duck Books (Map 20)** and **Commonwealth Books (Map 3, 16)**. There's also the **Boston Book Annex (Map 16)**, sloppy but well stocked, a fun place for cat lovers and long-term browsing.

Specialty

Quantum Books (Map 26) is the best computer bookstore in the city. The **MIT Press Bookstore (Map 26)** is the best for social sciences, philosophy, economics, and sciences—pretty much everything MIT is best for. For little kids, take a look at Brookline's **Children's Book Shop (Map 17)**. Slightly older kids who dig gaming will enjoy **Pandemonium (Map 27).** **Ars Libri (Map 7)** has an exemplary collection of rare and out-of-print fine art books. The only remaining LGBT bookstore in Boston is **Calamus (Map 4)**, near South Station. A big tip of the chapeau is due to **Schoenhof's Foreign Books (Map 20)** for its broad selection. **James & Devon Grey Booksellers (Map 20)** specializes in books printed before 1700. **Lucy Parsons Center (Map 6),** in the South End, stocks many progressive titles. **Trident Booksellers & Café (Map 5)** stocks books and a good variety of mainstream and alternative magazine titles, in addition to serving a mean breakfast.

Cambridge

Several years ago there were more than 25 bookstores in Harvard Square, the greatest concentration of bookstores in the city (and perhaps the country). No longer. Blame high rents, online retail, large chains dominating the market, or a general waning interest in the printed arts, but the sad fact is that many fine shops have packed it in. That being said, there are still a lot of friggin' bookstores and they range from the nuanced to the Coop. **Grolier Poetry Book Shop (Map 20)**, a national poetry landmark, is nothing less than a beacon of art in its tiny space on Plympton Street. Another Harvard Square stalwart is **Revolution Books (Map 20)**, a bookstore particularly conducive to raging against the machine. **The Harvard Coop (Map 20)** is managed by Barnes & Noble and unaffiliated with the school. The previously mentioned Raven, Schoenhof's, James & Devon Grey's, and probably three or four others round out a full day of page flipping. If the clogged walkways and impossible parking makes Harvard Square more trouble than it's worth, there's always **Porter Square Books (Map 23)** and Inman Square's **Lorem Ipsum (Map 28),** the latter being one of the best resources for used fiction and literature in the area. Now get going, you bookworm.

Map 1 • Beacon Hill / West End

Suffolk University Bookstore	148 Cambridge St	617-227-4085	Schoolbooks and campus merchandise.

Map 2 • North End / Faneuil Hall

Newbury Comics	Faneuil Hall	617-248-9992	Comics.

Map 3 • Downtown Crossing / Park Square / Bay Village

Brattle Book Shop	9 West St	617-542-0210	Used; outdoor racks when warm.
Commonwealth Books	134 Bolyston St	617-338-6328	Scholarly, used, antiquarian.
Emerson College Bookstore	114 Bolyston St	617-824-8696	Schoolbooks and campus merchandise.
Peter L Stern & Co	15 Court Square	617-542-2376	Antiquarian, especially first editions.
Suffolk Law School Book Store	110 Tremont St	617-227-8874	Schoolbooks and campus merchandise.

Map 4 • Financial District / Chinatown

Barbara's Bestsellers	2 S Station	617-443-0060	In South Station.
Calamus Bookstore	92 South St	617-338-1931	Gay & lesbian.
Central China Book Co	44 Kneeland St	617-426-0888	Chinese.
FA Bernett	144 Lincoln St	617-350-7778	Rare and scholarly art and architecture.
Tufts Health Sciences & New England School of Law Bookstore	116 Harrison Ave	617-636-6628	Schoolbooks and campus merchandise.
World Journal	216 Lincoln St	617-542-1230	Chinese.

Map 5 • Back Bay (West) / Fenway (East)

Barnes & Noble	800 Boylston St	617-247-6959	General.
Berklee College of Music Bookstore	1090 Boylston St	617-747-2402	Schoolbooks and campus merchandise.
Newbury Comics	332 Newbury St	617-236-4930	Now featuring a large DVD section.
Trident Booksellers & Café	338 Newbury St	617-267-8688	Independent; eclectic.

Map 6 • Back Bay (East) / South End (Upper)

Bromer Booksellers	607 Boylston St	617-247-2818	Fine, rare, and unusual.
Buddenbrooks Rare Books & Manuscripts	31 Newbury St	617-536-4433	Fine, rare.
Lucy Parsons Center	549 Columbus Ave	617-267-6272	Progressive.

Map 7 • South End (Lower)

Ars Libri	500 Harrison Ave	617-357-5212	Rare and out-of-print books on art.

Map 13 • Roxbury

Roxbury Community College Bookstore	1234 Columbus Ave	617-442-8150	Schoolbooks and campus merchandise.

Map 14 • Jamaica Plain

Boston Book Co	705 Centre St	617-522-2100	Antiquarian.
Commonwealth Books	9 Spring Park Ave	617-338-6328	Scholarly, used, antiquarian.
Tres Gatos	470 Centre St	617-477-4851	Record store, tapas bar and bookstore ingeniously fused.

Map 15 • Fenway (West) / Mission Hill

Emmanuel College Bookstore	400 The Fenway	617-739-2232	Schoolbooks and campus merchandise.
Mass College of Pharmacy & Art Bookstore	625 Huntington Ave	617-739-4772	Textbooks.
Medical Center Coop	333 Longwood Ave	617-499-3300	Schoolbooks and campus merchandise.
Northeastern University Bookstore	360 Huntington Ave	617-373-2286	Schoolbooks and campus merchandise.
Simmons College Book Store	300 The Fenway	617-521-2054	Schoolbooks and campus merchandise.
Wentworth Book Store	103 Ward St	617-445-8814	Textbooks.

Map 16 • Kenmore Square / Brookline (East)

Barnes & Noble at Boston University	660 Beacon St	617-267-8484	General/schoolbooks and campus merchandise.
Comicopia	464 Commonwealth Ave	617-266-4266	Comics.

Map 17 • Coolidge Corner / Brookline Hills

Book World	77 Harvard St	617-739-5768	Russian.
Children's Book Shop	237 Washington St	617-734-7323	Children's.
Horai-san	242 Washington St	617-277-4321	New age/spiritual.
New England Comics	316 Harvard St	617-566-0115	Comics.
Petropol	1428 Beacon St	617-232-8820	Russian.

Map 19 • Allston (South) / Brookline (North)

Brookline Booksmith	279 Harvard St	617-566-6660	Independent; used book cellar.
Cheetah Trading	214 Lincoln St	617-451-1309	Chinese.
Harvard Business School Co-op	117 Western Ave	617-499-3245	Business.
Israel Book Shop	410 Harvard St	617-566-7113	Judaica.
The Kabbalah Center	14 Green St	617-566-0808	Religious
Kolbo Fine Judaica	437 Harvard St	617-731-8743	Judaica.

Map 20 • Harvard Square / Allston (North)

Globe Corner Book Stores	90 Mt Auburn St	617-497-6277	Travel.
Grolier Poetry Book Shop	6 Plympton St	617-547-4648	Poetry books.
Harvard Book Store	1256 Massachusetts Ave	617-661-1515	Independent, with an academic bent.
Harvard Coop	1400 Massachusetts Ave	617-499-2000	General/schoolbooks and campus merchandise.
James & Devon Gray Booksellers	12 Arrow St	617-868-0752	Pre-18th-century.
Million Year Picnic	99 Mt Auburn St	617-492-6763	Comics.
New England Comics	14A Eliot St	617-354-5352	Comics.
Raven Used Books	52-B JFK St	617-441-6999	Scholarly used.
Revolution Books	1158 Massachusetts Ave	617-492-5443	Revolution.
Robin Bledsoe Books	1640 Massachusetts Ave	617-576-3634	Out-of-print books on horses and art.
Schoenhof's Foreign Books	76A Mt Auburn St	617-547-8855	Foreign languages.

Map 21 • West Cambridge

Bryn Mawr Book Store	373 Huron Ave	617-661-1770	Used and rare, stocked by donations.

Map 23 • Central Somerville / Porter Square

Barefoot Books	1771 Massachusetts Ave	617-349-1610	Picture books for the wee.
Barefoot Books	2067 Massachusetts Ave	617-576-0660	Picture books for the wee.
Comicazi	407 Highland Ave	617-666-2664	Comics.
McIntyre & Moore Booksellers	1971 Massachusetts Ave	617-229-5641	Scholarly used.
Porter Square Books	25 White St	617-491-2220	Fiercely independent!

Map 24 • Winter Hill / Union Square

CPAD Bookstore	100 Washington St	617-625-1234	Brazilian.

Map 25 • East Somerville / Sullivan Square

Bunker Hill Community College Book Store	250 Rutherford Ave	617-241-5161	Textbooks.

Map 26 • East Cambridge / Kendall Square / MIT

MIT Coop	3 Cambridge Ctr	617-499-3200	Schoolbooks and campus merchandise.
MIT Press Bookstore	292 Main St	617-253-5249	MIT Press authors and quality trade.

Map 27 • Central Square / Cambridgeport

MIT Coop at Stratton	84 Massachusetts Ave	617-499-3240	Schoolbooks and campus
Pandemonium	4 Pleasant St	617-547-3721	Sci-fi, fantasy, and gaming.
Rodney's Bookstore	698 Massachusetts Ave	617-876-6467	Used, out-of-print, remainders.
Seven Stars	731 Massachusetts Ave	617-547-1317	New Age.

Map 28 • Inman Square

Lorem Ipsum	1299 Cambridge St	617-497-7669	Used.

Map 29 • West Roxbury

Pazzo Books	1898 Centre St	617-323-2919	Used, General Interest.

If you're familiar with every painting at the **Gardner (Map 15)**, every print in the **MFA (Map 15)**, every fish in the **Aquarium (Map 2)**, and every cobblestone on the **Freedom Trail** (pg 121), then it's time to take it to the next level by ferreting out some of the city's hidden treasures and discovering something new about some old favorites.

The new facility of the **Institute of Contemporary Art (Map 10)**, whose design evokes a laptop, opened in the winter of 2006. If you're looking for a reason to make your way over to Fan Pier, here it is.

Release your inner child on a Friday night at the **Boston Children's Museum (Map 4)**—from 5 pm to 9 pm, admission is just $1. Or, engage your inner adult at the **Museum of Science (Map 1)** with a cocktail (yes, a real cocktail), a movie in the Mugar Omni Theater, or free stargazing at the Gilliland Observatory.

If you want to take in some art during a drive out of town, check out the **DeCordova Museum and Sculpture Park** in Lincoln (not far from Route 2 and Route 128). The DeCordova's 35 acres of woodlands is the largest sculpture garden in New England. The contemporary American outdoor sculpture park changes its exhibitions on a regular basis. Admission to the sculpture park is $14 for adults, $10 for students, and $12 for seniors (65+). Children 12 and under, as well as active duty military personnel, are admitted free. For more information, visit www.decordova.org.

And if all of those museums are just too good to be true, check out the **Museum of Bad Art (MOBA)** way out in Dedham (580 High St, 781-444-6757). Contemplate art so bad, it can't be ignored.

Museum	*Address*	*Phone*	*Map*
Ancient and Honorable Artillery Company	Faneuil Hall	617-227-1638	2
Arthur M Sackler Museum	485 Broadway	617-495-9400	20
Boston Athenaeum	10 Beacon St	617-227-0270	1
Boston Children's Museum	308 Congress St	617-426-6500	10
Boston Tea Party Ship & Museum	306 Congress St	617-338-1773	10
Brighton-Allston Heritage Museum	20 Chestnut Hill Ave	617-635-1436	18
Busch-Reisinger Museum	32 Quincy St	617-495-9400	20
Carpenter Center for Visual Arts	24 Quincy St	617-495-3251	20
Commonwealth Museum	220 Morrissey Blvd	617-727-9268	32
Fogg Art Museum	32 Quincy St	617-495-9400	20
Gibson House Museum	137 Beacon St	617-267-6338	6
Harvard Mineralogical & Geological Museum	24 Oxford St	617-495-3045	20
Harvard Museum of Comparative Zoology	26 Oxford St	617-495-2460	20
Harvard Museum of Natural History	26 Oxford St	617-495-3045	20
Institute of Contemporary Art	100 Northern Ave	617-478-3100	10
JFK National Historic Site	83 Beals St	617-566-7937	19
John F Kennedy Presidential Library and Museum	Morrissey Blvd & Columbia Pt	617-514-1600	32
Larz Anderson Auto Museum	15 Newton St	617-522-6547	n/a
The Loring-Greenough House	12 South St	617-524-3158	14
Mapparium/Mary Baker Eddy Library	200 Massachusetts Ave	617-450-7000	5
MIT List Visual Arts Center	20 Ames St	617-253-4680	26
Museum of African American History	46 Joy St	617-725-0022	1
Museum of Bad Art	580 High St	781-444-6757	n/a
Museum of Fine Arts	465 Huntington Ave	617-267-9300	15
Museum of Science	Science Park	617-723-2500	1
National Center for Afro-American Artists	300 Walnut Ave	617-442-8614	13
New England Aquarium	Central Wharf	617-973-5200	2
Nichols House Museum	55 Mt Vernon St	617-227-6993	1
Old South Meeting House	310 Washington St	617-482-6439	3
Old State House	206 Washington St	617-720-1713	3
Otis House	141 Cambridge St	617-994-5920	1
Paul Revere House	19 N Sq	617-523-2338	2
Paul S. Russell, MD Museum of Medical History and Innovation	2 North Grove St	617-724-8009	1
Peabody Museum of Archaeology and Ethnology	11 Divinity Ave	617-496-1027	20
Pierre Menard Gallery	10 Arrow St	617-868-2033	20
The Semitic Museum at Harvard University	6 Divinity Ave	617-495-4631	20
Somerville Museum	1 Westwood Rd	617-666-9810	23
The Sports Museum	150 Causeway St	617-624-1234	1
USS Constitution Museum	Charlestown Navy Yard	617-426-1812	8
Vilna Shul	18 Phillips St	617-523-2324	1
Warren Anatomical Museum	10 Shattuck St	617-432-6196	15

General Information

NFT Map: 10
Address: 100 Northern Ave
Phone: 617-478-3100
Website: www.icaboston.org
Hours: Tues, Wed, Sat, Sun: 10 am–5 pm; Thurs, Fri 10 am–9 pm; closed Mon, except on Martin Luther King, Jr. Day, Presidents' Day, Memorial Day, Labor Day, Columbus Day, and Veterans' Day. Closed Thanksgiving, Christmas, New Year's Day, and July 4.
Admission: $15 for Adults, $10 for students, $13 for seniors. Free for Members and children under 17. Free from 5 to 9 pm every Thursday night.

Overview

In 2006, the city's stodgy art scene got a royal kick in the rear when the Institute of Contemporary Art unveiled its new digs on South Boston's waterfront. The building's architecture by itself—an awe-inspiring modern masterpiece that offers a spectacular view of the harbor, an outdoor grandstand, and open gallery spaces—is well worth the museum's pricey $15 cover charge. Founded in 1936 as The Boston Museum of Modern Art, the original space was a cramped laboratory where artists were encouraged to create works that both inspired and provoked. Renamed in 1948, the ICA continued to push the envelope with a cavalcade of media, ranging from visual arts, film, video, performance, and literature. While many viewed video and digital media as the art scene's bastard stepchild in the '90s, the ICA embraced the marriage of visual design and technology.

The ICA is still Boston's newest and most dynamic museum, bringing in huge shows like Shepard Fairey's Obey exhibit, and even hosting indie rock concerts. It's a museum that's cooler than the hipsters it's attracting!

The MoMA-ized new space continues the site-specific tradition with its Art Wall, located along the eastern interior of the museum's glass-enclosed lobby. In 2006, exhibitor Chiho Aoshima unleashed her digitally manipulated monster mural, "The Divine Gas," on the wall. Illustrated on a Macintosh G4 and printed on adhesive vinyl, the installation was a brazen statement with a Gothic sensibility. With Aoshima's mixed-media piece, it was almost like the ICA was shooting a metaphorical middle finger at those who doubted the impact digital media would eventually have on our cultural landscape.

What to See

A quick stroll from South Station or directly on the Silver Line, the ICA sits right in the middle of the newly constructed Fan Pier at the top of South Boston. You'll want to take them up on their offer of an audio tour narrated by the exhibiting artists and ICA curators that you can download to your MP3 player, or you can borrow an iPod at front desk. They also offer a phone number for people to dial into the audio tours as well, but you might get some dirty looks from the art purists strolling with you. It's interesting to be able to listen to the inspiration behind something as vexing as Misaki Kawai's "Momentum 7," a free-floating home of the future inhabited by puppets juxtaposed with the voices from the ICA's permanent collection, with luminaries like Nan Goldin, Cornelia Parker, Thomas Hirschhorn, and Paul Chan.

Nestled beneath the museum's larger-than-life cantilever is the Poss Family Mediatheque where you have access to one of the museum's 18 computer stations. Here's where you can download clips with the art and artists featured at the ICA and check out the museum's footage-archive collection which offers a glimpse of exhibitions from the museum's past. Also, the Mediatheque is where you can experience the dramatic, horizonless view of the Boston Harbor.

Amenities

The museum is handicapped accessible. All bags (including your laptop) will be checked and stored in the lobby. The ICA has limited space to hang coats and it does not have its own parking garage. However, there's a paid lot immediately adjacent to the museum. Both the men's and women's restrooms are located on the first floor.

As far as food, Wolfgang Puck's Water Café offers another stellar view—not to mention some great French-bistro cuisine—where you can open the restaurant's glass doors for outdoor dining. For those who want to skip the art and head straight for the yummy pastries, museum admission is not required to dine.

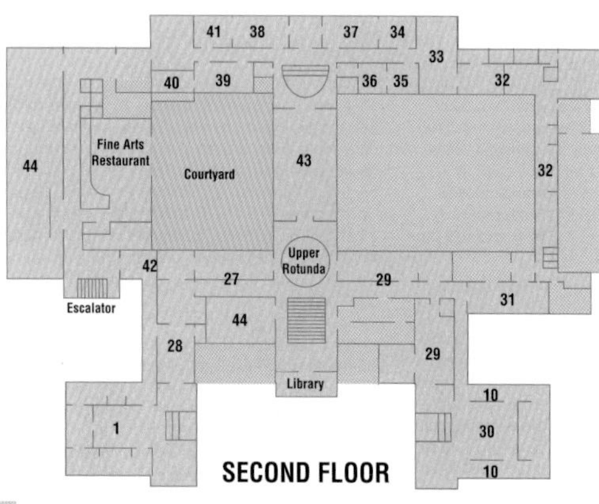

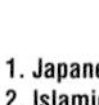

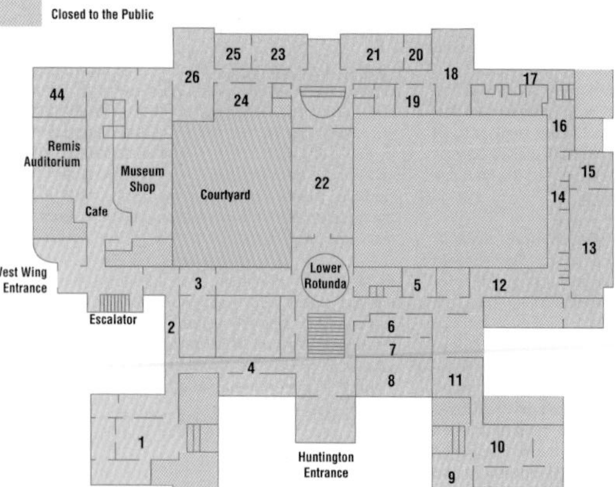

1. Japanese Art
2. Islamic Art
3. Brown Gallery
4. Indian Art
5. Egyptian Mummies
6. Graphics
7. Musical Instruments
8. Nubian Art
9. Etruscan Art
10. Greek Art
11. Near-Eastern Art
12. 18th-Century American Furniture
13. 18th-Century French Art
14. 18th-Century Boston
15. English-Silver
16. 19th-Century American
17. American Federal
18. Copley & Contemporary
19. American Neoclassical & Romantic
20. American Folk Painting
21. 19th-Century Landscape
22. American Modern
23. American Masters
24. Early 20th-Century Ameri & European
25. Chinese Art
26. Egyptian Art
27. Roman Art
28. Medieval Art
29. Euro Decorative Arts
30. Impresses
31. 19th-Century French & English
32. Post-Impressionism
33. Coolidge Collection
34. 18th-Century Italian
35. Dutch & Flemish Art
36. Renaissance
37. Spanish Chapel
38. Baroque Art
39. Himalayan Art
40. Tapestries
41. Special Exhibitions

General Information

NFT Map: 15
Address: 465 Huntington Ave
Boston, MA 02115
Phone: 617-267-9300
Website: www.mfa.org

Overview

The Museum of Fine Arts is Boston's largest and most famous art institution. The extensive permanent collection of paintings and sculpture, as well as the various lectures, films, concerts, and special traveling exhibitions, offer something for one-time sightseers and regular visitors alike. While you're there soaking up a little sophistication, enjoy a meal at one of the museum's four restaurants, and buy an artifact from the gift shop or some of their little postcards with the pretty paintings on them. Why? Because the museum needs the money. Though it's one of the largest art museums in the country, it receives little public funding. This, in part, accounts for the high admission fee. But don't worry: You get what you pay for.

In 2010, the MFA completed a ma.m.moth project that increased the size of the museum by 28%. To replace the old east wing of the museum, the MFA built a new, 60,000-square-foot four floor addition featuring the massive Art of the Americas collection. The new wing focuses heavily on the museum's peerless colonial art of New England collection, and features a gallery devoted entirely to John Singer Sargeant.

Hours

The museum is open Mon, Tues, Sat, and Sun 10 am–4:45 pm, and Wed–Fri 10 am–9:45 pm. Special exhibitions close 15 minutes before the museum closes. The gift shop is open during regular hours.

Admission Fees

Admission to the MFA costs $25 for adults, $23 for seniors (65+) and students (18+), $10 for youths 7–17 on weekdays before 3 p.m. (free at all other times), and children 6 and under are admitted for free. School group visits are discounted but must be scheduled in advanced.

Paid admission entitles visitors to one free visit within ten days of ticket purchase. On Wednesday evenings 4 pm–9:45 pm, admission is by voluntary contribution.

Tickets for entry can be purchased at the museum. Tickets for concerts, films, lectures, or special exhibitions can be purchased at the museum or online at www.mfa.org.

How to Get There—Driving

From the north, take I-93 S to Exit 26 (Storrow Drive). From Storrow Drive, take the Fenway/Kenmore exit. From the exit, take a left at the first traffic light, heading toward Boylston Street inbound. At the second traffic light, bear right onto The Fenway and proceed to the next set of lights. After passing through two stone gates, take the first right onto Hemenway Street and proceed to the end of the street. Take a left onto Forsythe Way and then a right onto Huntington Avenue. The museum is located a few lights down and on your right. Go past the museum and turn right onto Museum Road to reach the museum's parking lots.

From the south, take I-93 N to Exit 18 and follow the signs for Massachusetts Avenue. Turn right on Massachusetts Avenue, go past Columbus Avenue, and then turn left onto St. Botolph Street. Drive one block and turn right onto Gainsborough Street. Drive one block and turn left onto Huntington Avenue. The museum will be a couple of blocks down on your right. Go past the museum and turn right onto Museum Road to reach the museum's parking lots.

From the west, take the Mass Pike (I-90) E. Upon approaching the Boston city limits, look for Exit 22 (Prudential Center/Copley Square), the first exit after the Cambridge/Brighton toll plaza. You will enter a tunnel and Exit 22 will be on your right. Once on the exit ramp, get into the left lane (Prudential Center) and follow the exit to Huntington Avenue. Follow Huntington Avenue past the Christian Science Center (go through the underpass) and Northeastern University. The museum is located a few lights down on the right. Drive past the museum and turn right onto Museum Road to reach the museum's parking lots.

Parking

There is limited parking available at the museum, including two parking lots on Museum Road. Museum members pay $4 for each half-hour, $15 maximum. Non-members pay $6 for each half-hour with a $29 maximum for the day. A far cheaper option is public transportation.

How to Get There—Mass Transit

The museum is close to the Green Line's Museum stop (E train only) or the Orange Line's Ruggles stop. You can also take the 39 bus to the Museum stop or the 8 bus, 47 bus, or CT2 bus to the Ruggles stop.

Children's Museum of Boston

General Information

Address: 300 Congress Street
Boston, MA 02210

Phone: 617-426-6500

Website: www.bostonchildrensmuseum.org

Hours: Daily 10 am–5 pm; Fridays 10 am–9 pm.
Closed Thanksgiving and Christmas

Admission: General Admission $14, Seniors $14,
Children (Aged 1–15) $14,
Children (0–12 months) Free;
Members are free.
Friday nights 5 pm–9 pm, $1 for everybody.

Overview

A word of advice to adults visiting the Boston Children's Museum: Bring earplugs. The sound of children delighting in scientific wonder can be deafening, and this interactive hands-on museum tends to be very crowded, even on weekdays. The exhibits are fun even for adults, who most likely have forgotten everything they learned in middle school science classes, but if you've ever driven the mean streets of Boston you'll appreciate how difficult it is to fight for space at many of the activities.

Created by a group of teachers in Jamaica Plain in 1913, the Boston Children's Museum moved to its current location near Fort Point Channel on the waterfront in 1979. The goal of the original museum was to teach kids about nature, cultural diversity, and science through hands-on experiences. In the 1960s, the museum expanded and became an innovator in the concept of interactive exhibits, and today there are over 16 permanent learning areas.

Now occupying a former wool factory on the prized Boston waterfront, the small and crowded Children's Museum went through a much needed renovation and expansion in 2007. A new glass-paneled addition borders the newly expanded Harborwalk, with open spaces for additional outdoor exhibits, summer concerts, and special events. More space means more exhibits, including a 3-story climbing maze (New Balance Climb), a health and fitness area with bikes, basketballs, and interactive dance activities in Kid Power, and a brand new 160-seat theater at the Kid Stage. Popular areas include the Science Playground, where kids can engage in scientific exploration, the Japanese silk merchant's house, which is an actual house transported to the museum, the Arthur exhibit, where kids can become a part of the famous children's book and TV series, and the PlaySpace for kids under three.

The outdoor area is still being developed, but there is a Nature trail, boulders to climb on, and a waterfront park to eat lunch, escape the kids, or just sit by the water with a view of the Boston skyline. Disconcertingly, a museum promoting kids' education and healthy development once housed a McDonald's, but since the renovation, it has been replaced by the somewhat healthier Au Bon Pain. The museum is a nonprofit institution which also offers workshops, seminars, and classroom kits for teachers in their Teacher Leadership Center. Check its Website or call about special events and concerts during the summer.

How to Get There—Driving

From the north: Take I-93 South to Exit 23 "Purchase Street." At the first set of lights, take a left onto Seaport Boulevard. At the next light, take a right onto Sleeper Street. The museum is on your right.

From the south: Take I-93 North to Exit 20 "South Station/I-90." Follow signs for I-90 East, and once in the tunnel, take the first exit, labeled "South Boston." At the end of the ramp, go straight onto East Service Road. At the next intersection, turn left onto Seaport Boulevard. At the first set of lights, turn left onto Sleeper Street. The museum is on the right.

From the east: Take I-90 West to Exit 25 "South Boston." At the end of the ramp, go straight onto B Street. At the next light, take a left onto Seaport Boulevard. At the third set of lights, turn left onto Sleeper Street. The museum is on your right.

From the west: Take I-90 East towards Logan Airport. Once in the tunnel, take Exit 25 "South Boston." At the top of the ramp, bear left towards "Seaport Boulevard." At the next set of lights, stay straight onto East Service Road all the way to the end. At the next light, turn left onto Seaport Boulevard. At the second set of lights, turn left onto Sleeper Street. The museum is on your right.

Parking

The museum doesn't have its own lot or garage, but there are discounted prices for nearby lots. Both the Farnsworth Street Garage (two blocks away) and the Stillings Street Garage (four blocks away) are $16 on weekdays and $12 on weekends with museum validation. Farther away is the Moakley Courthouse Parking Lot. Street parking is hard to find and not recommended.

How to Get There—Mass Transit

Commuter rail and the MBTA Red Line and Silver Line drop you off at South Station, which is about a five minute walk away. The MBTA Silver Line stop at Courthouse Station is only a block away. Bus #4, 6, 7, and #11 all stop at South Station.

Boston may not have the Great White Way, but the theater scene—including musical venues—is alive and vibrant; you just might have to look a little harder for it. Where to start looking? Well, the most enthused patron of theatre in the region is Larry Stark of www.theatermirror.com. If there's a production taking place anywhere within 100 miles, Larry and his cast of writers are all over it. DigBoston will also point you to good productions.

Broadway in Boston runs popular mainstream shows (e.g. *Wicked, Swan Lake, Les Miserables*) at Boston's flagship theaters such as the **Wang Theatre (Map 3)**, neighboring **Shubert Theater (Map 3)**, and the **Opera House (Map 3)**. These theaters also produce readings, dance, and a wide variety of performances. Also of note in the Theater District is **Emerson's Cutler Majestic Theatre (Map 3)** and the **Charles Playhouse (Map 3)**, with long-running favorites *Blue Man Group* and *Shear Madness*.

Away from the clamor of the Theater District down Tremont Street, you'll find the **Boston Center for the Arts (Map 7)**, containing four performance spaces that accommodate fare ranging from *Forbidden Broadway* to one-man shows. **The Lyric Stage Company (Map 6)** nearby on Clarendon Street showcases wide-ranging seasons. The **Huntington Theatre (Map 5)** attracts top-name actors in local productions, while the **American Repertory Theater (ART) (Map 20)** in Cambridge features renowned innovative stagings.

For something a little different, check out the **Puppet Showplace Theater (Map 17)** in Brookline. For laughs, try Inman Square's **ImprovBoston (Map 28)** or the North End's **ImprovAsylum (Map 2)** (both, despite the names, do more than just improv). A smaller theater worth a look is **Boston Playwrights' Theatre (Map 19).**

If you're more of a choir and orchestra person, keep your eye on what's playing at the **Sanders Theatre (Map 20)**, which also hosts the occasional jazz, folk, or roots concert. Located in Harvard's Memorial Hall, Sanders Theatre offers terrific acoustics in a classic interior. Built to offer a 180-degree perspective for the audience, the theater was inspired by a Christopher Wren design. And of course, the Boston Symphony Orchestra at **Symphony Hall (Map 5)** has a thing or two to offer as far as classical music goes. The acoustics just can't be beat.

You can pick up half-price, same-day tickets at the BosTix booth in Copley Square or at Faneuil Hall Marketplace. You can find out performances for which tickets are available at www.bostix.org.

Theater	*Address*	*Phone*	*Map*
BCA Plaza Black Box	539 Tremont St	617-426-5000	7
Berklee Performance Center	136 Massachusetts Ave	617-747-2261	5
Blackman Auditorium/Studio Theatre	360 Huntington Ave	617-373-2247	15
Boston Center for the Arts	527 Tremont St	617-426-5000	7
Boston Children's Theater	316 Huntington Ave	617-424-6634	6
Boston Opera House	539 Washington St	617-259-3400	3
Boston Playwrights' Theatre	949 Commonwealth Ave	617-353-5443	5
Charles Playhouse	74 Warrenton St	617-426-6912	3
Colonial Theatre	106 Boylston St	617-426-9366	3
Devanaughn Theatre at The Piano Factory	791 Tremont St	617-247-9777	13
Footlight Club	7A Eliot St	617-524-3200	14
Huntington Theatre Company	264 Huntington Ave	617-266-0800	5
ImprovAsylum	216 Hanover St	617-263-6887	2
ImprovBoston	40 Prospect St	617-576-1253	27
Jorge Hernandez Cultural Center	85 W Newton St	866-811-4111	7
Kresge Little Theatre	48 Massachusetts Ave	617-253-6294	27
Loeb Drama Center	64 Brattle St	617-547-8300	20
Lyric Stage Company	140 Clarendon St	617-437-7172	6
McCormack Theatre	100 Morrissey Blvd		32
Nancy and Edward Roberts Studio Theater	539 Tremont St	617-426-5000	7
Orpheum Theatre	1 Hamilton Pl	617-679-0810	3
The Publick Theatre	1400 Soldiers Field Rd	617-782-5425	19
Puppet Showplace Theatre	32 Station St	617-731-6400	17
Remis Auditorium	465 Huntington Ave	617-369-3770	15
Sanders Theatre	45 Quincy St	617-496-2222	13
Semel Theatre at Emerson College	10 Boylston Pl	617-824-8364	3
Shubert Theatre	265 Tremont St	617-482-9393	3
Stuart Street Playhouse	200 Stuart St	617-426-4499	3
Symphony Hall	301 Massachusetts Ave	617-266-1492	5
Theatre Cooperative	277 Broadway	n/a	24
Tower Auditorium	621 Huntington Ave	617-879-7000	15
Tribe Theater	67 Stuart St	617-510-4447	6
Virginia Wimberley Theatre	539 Tremont St	617-266-0800	7
Wang Center for Performing Arts	265 Tremont St	617-482-9393	3
Wang Theatre	270 Tremont St	617-482-9393	3
Wheelock Family Theatre	180 The Riverway	617-879-2000	16
Wilbur Theatre	246 Tremont St	617-248-9700	3
Willoughby and Baltic	195 Elm St	617-501-0197	23
Zero Arrow Theater	0 Arrow St	617-547-8300	20

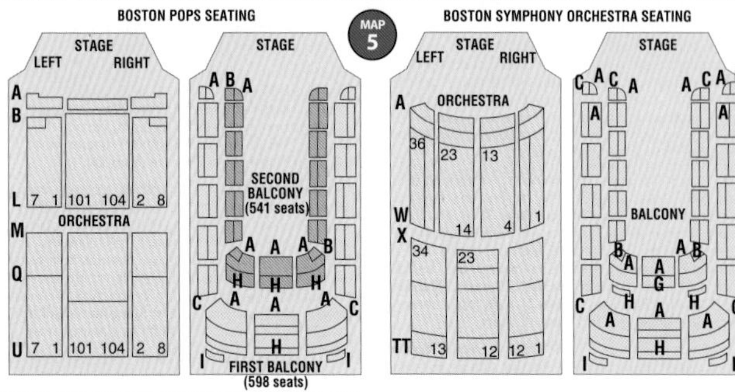

General Information

NFT Map:	5
Address:	301 Massachusetts Ave, Boston, MA 02115
Website:	www.bso.org
Phone:	617-266-1492
Tickets:	617-266-1200; www.bso.org

Overview

Boston Symphony Hall, home of the Boston Symphony Orchestra and Boston Pops, is regarded as one of the finest concert halls in the world. Modeled after the German Leipzig Gewandhaus and the old Boston Music Hall, Symphony Hall was the first American hall designed to maximize acoustics, thanks to Harvard physics professor Wallace Clement Sabine (and to think you slept through your physics class!). Classical music connoisseurs recognize the hall as a space that produces a near-perfect sound experience, thanks to the sloping walls and floor of the stage and the alignment of the recessed Greek and Roman statues. The Hall, designed by New York architects McKim, Mead, & White, opened in 1900, replacing the Boston Music Hall, which was in the way of the burgeoning subway system. The hall seats 2,625 people in the Boston Symphony Orchestra (BSO) season and 2,371 in the Boston Pops Orchestra season (in the original leather seats from 1900). Don't leave without checking out the Aeolian-Skinner organ with 67 stops and 5,130 pipes. Free tours offer an insight into the history and features of Symphony Hall.

Symphony Hall contains dozens of museum-like items documenting notable events in its history. You can learn just what was so revolutionary about the acoustics and famous composers. Excitement and pride leaps from a reprinted *Boston Globe* article documenting the first performance. A 2006 renovation of the concert floor rebuilt it using the original processes, equipment manufacturers, and the exact same materials, in order to retain its premium acoustic properties.

In the past the Hall has hosted auto shows, mayoral inaugurations, meetings of the Communist Party, and a performance by Harry Houdini. You can also celebrate New Year's in style here as the orchestra performs in the background. (Bring your tux.) The tradition of hosting non-traditional events looks set to continue. In recent years, the US Open Squash Tournament has been held at Symphony Hall, using portable glass courts placed just below the stage.

If you're looking to throw your own Diddy-like party, function rooms and hall spaces can be rented for your own private shindig. But unless you're making Manny Ramirez-style money, you probably can't afford it. Renting out Symphony Hall for a night costs between $5,400 and $6,800. Five different function spaces are available for rent and cost between $1,200 and $3,900 per night.

How to Get Tickets

You can purchase tickets to any of the Symphony Hall performances online at www.bso.org, in person at the Symphony Hall box office, or by phone on 617-266-1200 or 617-638-9283 (TDD/TTY).

How to Get There—Driving

From the north, take I-93 to Storrow Drive (Exit 26). Once you're on Storrow Drive, bear left towards Copley Square/Back Bay. Turn right onto Beacon Street. Turn left onto Clarendon Street. Turn right onto St. James Avenue. Bear left onto Huntington Avenue. Symphony Hall is on the corner of Huntington Avenue and Massachusetts Avenue.

From the south, take I-93 to Exit 18 and follow signs toward Massachusetts Avenue. Turn right onto Massachusetts Avenue.

From the west, take the Mass Pike (I-90) to the Prudential Center/Copley Square (Exit 27) and merge onto Huntington Avenue. Symphony Hall is on the corner of Huntington Avenue and Massachusetts Avenue.

Parking

There are two pay parking garages on Westland Avenue, another parking garage on Gainsborough Street next to Jordan Hall at the New England Conservatory, and very limited street parking. The Prudential Center Garage offers discount parking with the presentation of a performance ticket stub from the same day if you enter the garage after 5 pm.

How to Get There—Mass Transit

The Green Line's E train stops at Symphony Hall. Other Green Line trains that stop at the Hynes Convention Center will get you close. Another option is to take the Orange Line to the Massachusetts Avenue stop.

The #1 bus, which runs down Massachusetts Avenue from Harvard Square to Dudley Square, stops mere feet from Symphony Hall.

MAP 3

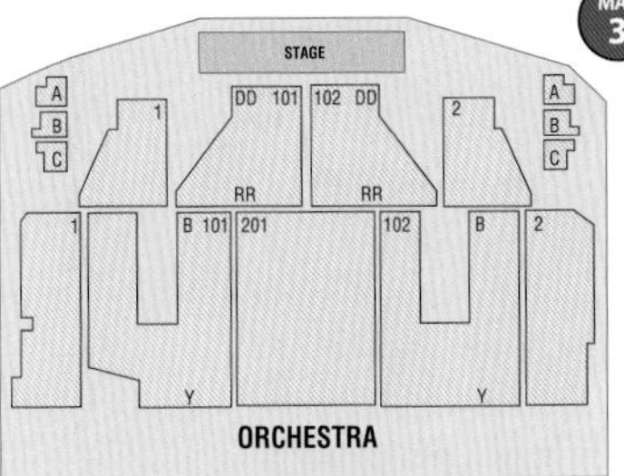

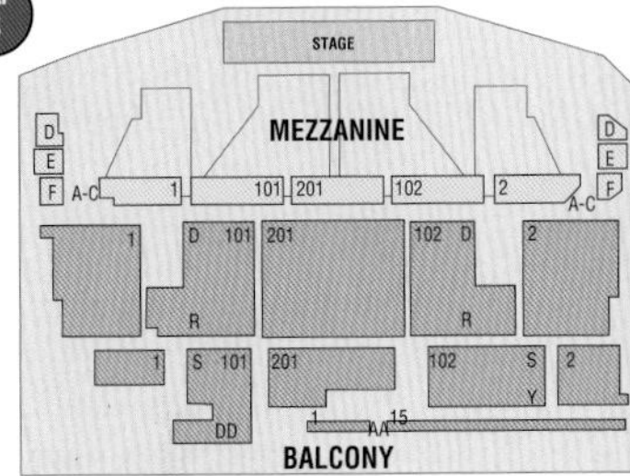

General Information

NFT Map: 3
Address: One Hamilton Pl, Boston, MA 02108
Website: www.ticketmaster.com/venue/8318
Phone: 617-679-0810
Ticketmaster: www.ticketmaster.com

Overview

The Orpheum has been around since 1852, and despite renovations, it can still feel like its age, which many consider part of the charm. (Apparently, they have not heard of this thing called The Internet either...) The Orpheum originally had an eye on high-brow stuff: Tchaikovsky along with the Boston Symphony Orchestra made debuts there. Now, it packs in close to 3,000 people to witness an eclectic lineup of acts ranging from Larry the Cable Guy to Norah Jones to Nine Inch Nails, and tickets often sell out quickly. Bands love the Orpheum for its premium acoustics (several live albums have been recorded here), and view-wise there isn't a bad seat in the house, though leg room is notably sparse.

How to Get Tickets

Tickets can be purchased from the Orpheum Theatre Box Office Mon–Sat, 10 am–5 pm. Tickets can also be purchased online at www.ticketmaster.com or by calling 617-679-0810.

How to Get There—Driving

From the north, take I-93 S to Exit 24A (Government Center). At the bottom of the ramp, bear right onto New Chardon Street. At the second set of lights, take a left onto Cambridge Street. Stay on the right-hand side of Cambridge Street, which will become Tremont Street as soon as you pass City Hall Plaza (on your left). Drive two blocks farther on Tremont Street. The Orpheum will be on your left on Hamilton Place.

From the south, take I-93 N to Exit 23 (Government Center). At the end of the ramp, follow signs for Government Center/Faneuil Hall. At the set of lights, make a left onto North Street. Drive a quarter-mile to the end of North Street, then make a left onto Congress Street. Take your first right onto State Street, which turns into Court Street after a few feet. Follow Court Street to the end, then make a left at the fork onto Tremont Street. Drive two blocks farther on Tremont Street. The Orpheum will be on your left on Hamilton Place.

From the west, take the Mass Pike (I-90) E to Exit 24B, which will dump you onto I-93 N. From there follow the directions above for driving from the south.

Parking

Street parking will be scarce, especially during event hours. The closest parking lots are on Tremont Street, under Boston Common, and on Washington Street.

How to Get There—Mass Transit

Take the Red or Green Line to the Park Street stop or the Orange Line to Downtown Crossing. The theater is just a short walk from both stops. It's directly across from the Park Street Church.

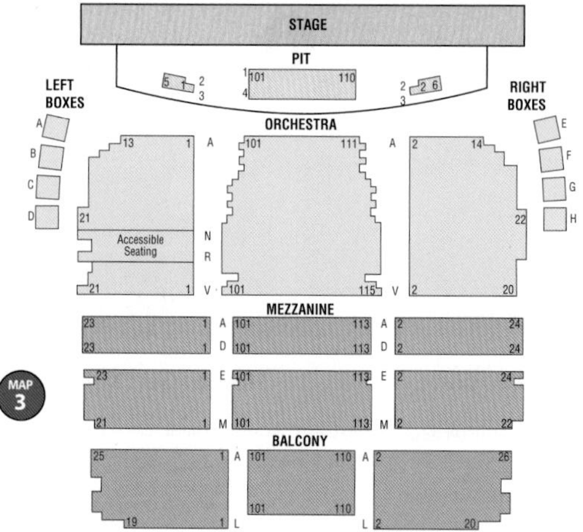

General Information

NFT Map: 3
Address: 270 Tremont St, Boston, MA 02116
Website: www.citicenter.org/theatres/shubert
Phone: 617-482-9393
Tele-charge: www.telecharge.com, 800-447-7400

Overview

The Shubert Theatre is the "Little Princess" to the Wang Theatre's "Grand Dame." The 1,600-seat venue opened in 1910 and has since undergone two major renovations. The theater's elaborate entranceway was destroyed during the widening of Tremont Street in 1925, and in 1996, $6 million was spent restoring and improving the theater's original ornate French Renaissance architecture. The intimacy within the Shubert remained intact, and the theater is now the home of the Boston Lyric Opera, many Boston arts organizations, as well as several touring companies. Broadway shows, including such classics as The King and I and South Pacific, debuted at the Shubert before making their way to New York. Once part of the not-for-profit Wang Center for the Performing Arts, both theaters have sadly had to sell off naming rights in an attempt to stay solvent. The Wang and Shubert are now owned by the Citigroup umbrella and carry the Citi moniker in front of their traditional names.

How to Get Tickets

You can purchase tickets for the Shubert Theatre online at www.citicenter.org/events or by calling Tele-charge at 800-447-7400. You can also buy tickets for Shubert shows (without the nasty service charges) at the Wang Theatre Box Office, which is open Tuesday through Saturday from 12 p.m. until 6 p.m.

How to Get There—Driving

From the north, take I-93 S to Exit 23 (South Station), which dumps you onto Purchase Street. Immediately after the Chinatown Gate (on your right), take a right onto Kneeland Street. Go straight for several blocks and then turn left onto Tremont Street. The Shubert Theatre is on your right.

From the south, take I-93 N to Exit 20 (South Station) and immediately get into the left-hand lane. The sign overhead will read "Detour South Station via Frontage Road." Take this left exit off the ramp and follow Frontage Road north to South Station. Turn left onto Kneeland Street. Go straight for several blocks, and then turn left onto Tremont Street. The Shubert Theatre is on your right.

From the west, take the Mass Pike (I-90) E to Exit 24A. Turn left onto Kneeland Street. Go straight for several blocks and then turn left onto Tremont Street. The Shubert Theatre is on your right.

Parking

Your best bets are the parking lot on the corner of Tremont and Stuart Streets, the lot at the Radisson Hotel on Stuart Street, the Kinney Motor Mart on Stuart Street, or the Fitz-Inn lot on Kneeland Street.

How to Get There—Mass Transit

The Orange Line's New England Medical Center stop and the Green Line's Boylston Street stop are both one block away from the theater. The Red Line's Park Street stop on Tremont Street is three or so blocks from the theater.

MAP 3

General Information

NFT Map:	3
Address:	270 Tremont St, Boston, MA 02116
Website:	www.citicenter.org/theatres/wang
Phone:	617-482-9393
Tele-charge:	www.telecharge.com, 800-447-7400

Overview

Surviving several name changes and heavy renovation over the years, the Wang Theatre has remained a prominent feature of the Boston theater scene. With 3,600 seats, it is the larger of the two performance spaces once operated by the Wang Center for the Performing Arts and now owned by Citigroup (the other is the famous Shubert Theatre) across the street). Though the Wang and Shubert keep their names, the complex is now known as the Citi Performing Arts Center.

Opened in the "Roaring Twenties" (1925) as the Metropolitan Theatre, the venue was considered to be a "magnificent movie cathedral" with its ornate interior resembling something from Louis XIV's palace. Renamed the Music Hall in 1962, the theater became home to the then-fledgling Boston Ballet. As the years passed, the shiny gem began to lose some of its luster and relevance. Some minor renovations were made, but it wasn't until 1983, when Dr. An Wang stepped in to resuscitate the theater, that things took a turn for the better. Since the restoration, the theater has played host to such classics as *Les Miserables*, *The Phantom of the Opera* , and *Spamalot*, and still houses one of New England's largest movie screens. Still home to the Boston Ballet, the Wang has expanded its repertoire to include pop concerts and comedians. The *Nutcracker at the Wang* (snicker...) holiday tradition is no more (it moved to The Opera House), replaced by the very un-Boston "Radio City Christmas Spectacular" featuring high-kicking Rockettes wearing reindeer antlers.

How to Get Tickets

You can purchase tickets for the Wang Theatre online at www.citicenter.org/events or by calling Tele-charge at 800-447-7400. The Wang Theatre Box Office, open Tuesday through Saturday from 12 p.m. until 6 p.m., sells tickets without the nasty service charges levied by external vendors.

How to Get There—Driving

From the north, take I-93 S to Exit 20A (South Station), which dumps you onto Purchase Street. Immediately after the Chinatown Gate (on your right) take a right onto Kneeland Street. Go straight for several blocks and then turn left onto Tremont Street. The Wang Theatre is on your left.

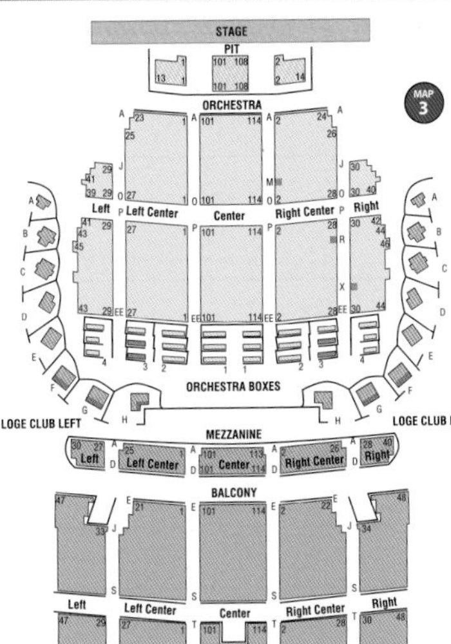

From the south, take I-93 N to Exit 20 (South Station) and immediately get into the left-hand lane. Follow signs for South Station and take the left exit for South Station/Chinatown. At the second light, turn left onto Kneeland Street. Go straight for several blocks, turn left onto Tremont Street. The Wang Theatre is on your left.

From the west, take the Mass Pike (I-90) E to Exit 24A. Turn left onto Kneeland Street. Go straight for several blocks and then turn left onto Tremont Street. The Wang Theatre is on your left.

Parking

Your best bets are the parking lot on the corner of Tremont and Stuart Streets, the lot at the Radisson Hotel on Stuart Street, the Kinney Motor Mart on Stuart Street, or the Fitz-Inn lot on Kneeland Street.

How to Get There—Mass Transit

The Orange Line's New England Medical Center stop and the Green Line's Boylston Street stop are both one block away from the theater. The Red Line's Park Street stop on Tremont Street is about three blocks from the theater.

Key to Boston neighborhoods

AL ..... Allston
BR ..... Brighton
DO ..... Dorchester
EB ..... East Boston
HP ..... Hyde Park
JP ..... Jamaica Plain
MT ..... Mattapan
RS ..... Roslindale
RX ..... Roxbury
SB ..... South Boston
WR ..... West Roxbury

Boston

Street Index

Street Index

Street Index

Street Index

Street Index

Street Index

Street Index

Brookline

Street Index

Cambridge

Street Index

Charlestown

Somerville

Street Index